JAMES

Sacra Pagina Series

Volume 14

James

Patrick J. Hartin

Daniel J. Harrington, S.J.
Editor

A Michael Glazier Book

LITURGICAL PRESS
Collegeville, Minnesota

www.litpress.org

A Michael Glazier Book published by Liturgical Press

Cover design by Ann Blattner. Illustration reproduced with the permission of the Universitätsbibliothek Graz, Austria, Cod. 143, fol. 501b (13th c. Breviarium Benedictinum), from a microfilm in the Hill Monastic Manuscript Library, Collegeville, Minnesota.

ISBN: 978-0-8146-5975-5

1	2	3	4	5	6	7	8	9

Library of Congress Cataloging-in-Publication Data

Hartin, P. J. (Patrick J.)
    James / Patrick J. Hartin ; Daniel J. Harrington, editor.
        p.   cm. — (Sacra pagina series ; v. 14)
    "A Michael Glazier book."
    Includes bibliographical references and indexes.
    ISBN 0-8146-5816-4 (alk. paper)
        1. Bible. N.T. James—Commentaries.   I. Harrington, Daniel J.   II. Title.
    III. Sacra pagina series ; 14.

    BS2785.53 .H37 2003
    227'.91077—dc21

                                                                    2003009441

CONTENTS

Translation, Notes, Interpretation

Indexes

EDITOR'S PREFACE

Sacra Pagina is a multi-volume commentary on the books of the New Testament. The expression *Sacra Pagina* ("Sacred Page") originally referred to the text of Scripture. In the Middle Ages it also described the study of Scripture to which the interpreter brought the tools of grammar, rhetoric, dialectic, and philosophy. Thus *Sacra Pagina* encompasses both the text to be studied and the activity of interpretation.

This series presents fresh translations and modern expositions of all the books of the New Testament. Written by an international team of biblical scholars, it is intended for biblical professionals, graduate students, theologians, clergy, and religious educators. The volumes present basic introductory information and close exposition. They self-consciously adopt specific methodological perspectives, but maintain a focus on the issues raised by the New Testament compositions themselves. The goal of *Sacra Pagina* is to provide sound critical analysis without any loss of sensitivity to religious meaning. This series is therefore catholic in two senses of the word: inclusive in its methods and perspectives, and shaped by the context of the Catholic tradition.

The Second Vatican Council described the study of the "sacred page" as the "very soul of sacred theology" (*Dei Verbum* 24). The volumes in this series illustrate how biblical scholars contribute to the council's call to provide access to Sacred Scripture for all the Christian faithful. Rather than pretending to say the final word on any text, these volumes seek to open up the riches of the New Testament and to invite as many people as possible to study seriously the "sacred page."

DANIEL J. HARRINGTON, S.J.

AUTHOR'S PREFACE

This commentary is the culmination of more than twenty years of research and reflection on the letter of James. My focus on this writing dates back to my early years of teaching when I conducted a regular undergraduate course on the letter of James. The stimulating discussions generated by the students provoked an investigation of many issues that still continue to intrigue me. I am indebted to them for guiding my research in this direction.

The letter of James still remains the stepchild of New Testament scholarship. Originally it struggled to gain admittance into the New Testament canon. Once it was accepted, its importance was proclaimed by its placement at the head of the third major section of New Testament writings, the so called "General Epistles." At the time of the Reformation this letter fell into disrepute among Protestant scholars because of its perceived challenge to the Pauline teaching on the doctrine of justification by faith. Among Roman Catholics it has not fared much better. Despite providing a scriptural basis for two sacraments (penance and anointing of the sick), the letter of James is seldom used in the liturgical worship of the community.

This commentary calls for a reassessment of the value and importance of the letter of James. It endeavors to situate James within the context of the thought world of Judaism and early Christianity. In particular the Notes will attempt, among other things, to show how James's thought and language are rooted within the traditions of the house of Israel, especially the heritage of Wisdom.

While the commentary rests on the foundations of the historical-critical method, I have endeavored to broaden the methodological approaches by taking cognizance of two exciting new approaches to interpretation that have generated much interest within New Testament scholarship in more recent times. In the first instance, attention is given to the approach of rhetorical criticism by examining the letter from the perspective of ancient rhetoric. In particular, attention is given to the structure of a perfect argument that is evident in many writings within the framework of the first-century C.E. Mediterranean. This commentary will demonstrate James's use of this structure of a perfect argument to communicate his message. Attention will also be given to a social-scientific analysis of the letter. An examination of the cultural scripts behind the letter of James will show that concepts such as patron-client, friendship, and the social status of the poor all help to shed light upon this text and to situate it squarely within the context of the first-century C.E. Mediterranean.

Among the characteristics that emerge in the course of the analysis of this letter, the following are ones to which I should like to draw attention: (1) James is clearly a writing that emerges from the context of those followers of Jesus who still remain firmly rooted within the traditions and thought world of the house of Israel. As such, the letter of James is a wonderful mirror onto that world, where it is in effect a crossing-over point between the Jewish world of the first century C.E. and emerging early Christianity. (2) James shows an awareness and use of the Jesus traditions. This commentary will endeavor to demonstrate how the voice of James is not only in harmony with the voice of Jesus, but of all the traditions within the New Testament writings the letter of James emerges as the true heir to the message and spirit of Jesus' teaching. (3) A closer examination of the letter of James demonstrates that this letter gives us insight into another major tradition within early Christianity. (4) The letter of James is not written in opposition to the letters and thought of Paul. To view James only from the perspective of Paul limits its value and insights. The position of this commentary is that while the relationship between James and Paul is a significant question, it must nevertheless be viewed within the wider understanding that both writers are giving testimony to their own world and context within the emergence of first-century Christianity. The consequence of this perspective is that the letter of James must be read through its own eyes rather than through Paul's eyes.

Following the format of the Sacra Pagina Series, this commentary provides its own translation of the Greek text into English. In making the translation I have endeavored to remain as close as possible to the Greek text by providing what is in effect a literal translation. At the same time I have also endeavored to be attentive to the use of inclusive language. This was a particular challenge because the Greek text of the letter of James often uses the singular masculine form of the pronoun. Where possible I have translated the singular into the plural to avoid too many masculine references, particularly in instances where clearly all the people are being referred to and not just one group based upon gender.

In the sections of Notes I have endeavored to explain the meaning of the words and phrases against the background of the world of the Israelite traditions as well as the Greek world of the first-century Mediterranean. All issues necessary for a clearer understanding of these phrases and words are discussed in the context of these Notes. In the sections on Interpretation I have endeavored to provide a reading that seeks to find meaning through an understanding of its context within the whole of the passage. Within the framework of the Interpretation I have endeavored to use the insights gained from the methodologies of rhetorical criticism and social-scientific analysis.

By means of excursuses I deal with issues that go beyond the wider treatment of the passage under consideration. These excursuses are important for gaining a deeper appreciation of the context of the letter of James. Among the issues addressed are: (1) James's relationship to the Jesus tradition and in particular to the traditions of the Sayings Source Q and the Sermon on the Mount, (2) James's relationship to the world of the Israelite traditions and the world of Judaism, and (3) the application of a social-scientific analysis to the text by examining those cultural scripts (especially patron-client relationships within Mediterranean society) fundamental for attaining an understanding of the dynamics of interactions within James's community and world.

Another feature I have endeavored to implement within this commentary is the selective incorporation of references to the works of significant ancient authors. Rather than simply list every occurrence where a certain word appears, be it in the rest of the New Testament or in the world of ancient Greek writers, I have endeavored to let these sources speak for themselves by selecting one or two examples that illustrate the usage of the word or thought. Consequently, I have deliberately chosen to quote the text in full to illustrate the connections that James forges through his use of language, style, and vocabulary.

My intent within this commentary has been to interact as well with more recent commentaries on the letter of James in order to illustrate how a consensus might appear or where I differ from their perspectives. As can be seen in the interaction, I am indebted especially to the work of scholars such as Joseph B. Mayor, James Hardy Ropes, Martin Dibelius, Peter H. Davids, Franz Mussner, Luke Timothy Johnson, and Robert W. Wall, among others.

All biblical quotations are taken from the New Revised Standard Version of the Bible except for those instances where I note that I have translated the text myself. Naturally, the letter of James is quoted according to the translation I have provided.

I should like to acknowledge my appreciation for the assistance given me in the production of this manuscript. In particular I am indebted to Gonzaga University for providing me with the opportunity for a sabbatical, during which time I was able to work on and complete this manuscript. I am especially grateful to Father Ken Krall, s.j. for his painstaking reading and correction of the transliterated Greek text and references. My enormous thanks also go to Kevin Eiler for his meticulous assistance with bibliographical material and his laborious checking of the manuscript in its various stages of development. Finally, I should like to thank all the editors of the Liturgical Press for their assistance in bringing this project to fruition: Daniel Harrington, S.J., Linda Maloney, Colleen Stiller, and Mark Twomey.

I dedicate this volume to the memory of two very close friends: Bishop Reginald Orsmond of Johannesburg, South Africa, and Monsignor Martin Killoran. Their encouragement and support over many years have made this work possible.

Patrick J. Hartin

ABBREVIATIONS

Biblical Books and Apocrypha

Gen	Nah	1–2–3–4 Kgdms	John
Exod	Hab	Add Esth	Acts
Lev	Zeph	Bar	Rom
Num	Hag	Bel	1–2 Cor
Deut	Zech	1–2 Esdr	Gal
Josh	Mal	4 Ezra	Eph
Judg	Ps (*pl.*: Pss)	Jdt	Phil
1–2 Sam	Job	Ep Jer	Col
1–2 Kgs	Prov	1–2–3–4 Macc	1–2 Thess
Isa	Ruth	Pr Azar	1–2 Tim
Jer	Cant	Pr Man	Titus
Ezek	Eccl (*or* Qoh)	Sir	Phlm
Hos	Lam	Sus	Heb
Joel	Esth	Tob	Jas
Amos	Dan	Wis	1–2 Pet
Obad	Ezra	Matt	1–2–3 John
Jonah	Neh	Mark	Jude
Mic	1–2 Chr	Luke	Rev

Other Ancient Texts

Abr.	Philo, *De Abrahamo* (On the Life of Abraham)
Ad Her.	*Rhetorica Ad Herennium*
Adul. Amic.	Plutarch, *Quomodo adulator ab amico internoscatur* (How To Tell a Flatterer from a Friend)
Adv. Haer.	Irenaeus, *Adversus Haereses* (Against All Heresies)
Aen.	Virgil, *Aeneid*
A.J.	Josephus, *Antiquitates judaicae* (Jewish Antiquities)
Alc.	Plato, *Alcibiades I*
Amic.	Cicero, *De amicitia* (On Friendship)
Ant.	Sophocles, *Antigone*
Ant. Rom.	Dionysius of Halicarnassus, *Antiquitates romanae*

Apoc. Mos.	*Apocalypse of Moses*
Apol.	Plato, *Apologia* (Apology of Socrates)
1 Apol.	Justin, *Apologia 1* (First Apology)
2 Apol.	Justin, *Apologia 2* (Second Apology)
Ascen. Isa.	*Ascension of Isaiah*
Autol.	Theophilus, *Ad Autolycum* (To Autolycus)
Bacch.	Euripides, *Bacchae*
2 Bar.	*2 Baruch* (Syriac Apocalypse)
3 Bar.	*3 Baruch* (Greek Apocalypse)
Barn.	*Barnabas*
B.J.	Josephus, *Bellum judaicum* (The Jewish War)
Ben.	Seneca, *De beneficiis* (On Benefits)
C. Ap.	Josephus, *Contra Apionem* (Against Apion)
Cels.	Origen, *Contra Celsum*
CD	Damascus Document
Clement.	Seneca, *De clementia*
1–2 Clem.	*1–2 Clement*
Comm. Rom.	Origen, *Commentarii in Romanos*
[Cons. Apoll.]	Plutarch, *Consolatio ad Apollonium* (Letter to Apollonius)
Contempl.	Philo, *De vita contemplativa* (On the Contemplative Life)
Cyr.	Xenophon, *Cyropaedia*
Decal.	Philo, *De decalogo* (On the Decalogue)
Deus	Philo, *Quod Deus sit immutablilis* (That God is Unchangeable)
Dial.	Justin Martyr, *Dialogo cum Tryphone* (Dialogue with Trypho)
Dial. Mort.	Lucian, *Dialogi mortuorum* (Dialogues of the Dead)
Diatr.	Epictetus, *Diatribai* (Dissertationes)
Did.	*Didache*
Diogn.	*Diognetus*
Doctr. chr.	Augustine, *De doctrina christiana* (Christian Instruction)
Ebr.	Philo, *De ebrietate* (On Drunkenness)
1 En.	*1Enoch* (Ethiopic Apocalypse)
2 En.	*2 Enoch* (Slavonic Apocalypse)
3 En.	*3 Enoch* (Hebrew Apocalypse)
Ench.	Epictetus, *Encheiridion* (Manual)
Ep.	Seneca, *Epistolae morales* (Moral Letters)
Eth. Nic.	Aristotle, *Ethica nichomachea* (Nichomachean Ethics)
Eum.	Aeschylus, *Eumenides*
Fin.	Cicero, *De finibus bonorum et malorum* (Concerning the Ends of Good and Evil)
Garr.	Plutarch, *De garrulitate* (Concerning Talkativeness)
Georg.	Menander, *Georgos*
Gos. Thom.	*Gospel of Thomas*
Grat.	Augustine, *De gratia et libero arbitrio* (Grace and Free Will)
Her.	Philo, *Quis rerum divinarum heres sit* (Who is the Heir?)
Herm. *Mand.*	Shepherd of Hermas, *Mandate*
Herm. *Sim.*	Shepherd of Hermas, *Similitude*
Herm. *Vis.*	Shepherd of Hermas, *Vision*

Hermot.	Lucian, *Hermotimus* or *De sectis* (Hermotimus, or Sects)
Hist.	Herodotus, *Historiae* (Histories)
Hist. eccl.	Eusebius, *Historia ecclesiastica* (Ecclesiastical History)
Hom. Exod.	Origen, *Homiliae in Exodum*
Hom. Jes. Nav.	Origen, *In Jesu Nativitate Homiliae xxvi*
Hom. Lev.	Origen, *Homiliae in Leviticum*
Ign. *Eph.*	Ignatius, *Letter to the Ephesians*
Ign. *Magn.*	Ignatius, *Letter to the Magnesians*
Ign. *Phld.*	Ignatius, *Letter to the Philadelphians*
Ign. *Pol.*	Ignatius, *Letter to Polycarp*
Ign. *Smyrn.*	Ignatius, *Letter to the Smyrnaeans*
Ign. *Trall.*	Ignatius, *Letter to the Trallians*
In Arist. de cael.	Simplicius, *In Aristotelis de caelo commentaria* (A commentary on Aristotle's "Heavens")
Il.	Homer, *Ilias* (Iliad)
Ira	Seneca, *De ira* (On Anger)
Jub.	*Jubilees*
Legat.	Philo, *Legatio ad Gaium* (On the Embassy to Gaius)
Leges	Plato, *Leges* (Laws)
Leg. 1, 2, 3	Philo, *Legum allegoriae I. II. III* (Allegorical Interpretation 1, 2, 3)
LXX	Septuagint
Mart. Pol.	*Martyrdom of Polycarp*
Med.	Marcus Aurelius Antoninus, *Meditationes* (Meditations)
Mem.	Xenophon, *Memorabilia*
Migr.	Philo, *De migratione Abrahami* (On the Migration of Abraham)
Mor.	Plutarch, *Moralia*
MT	Masoretic Text
Nat.	Pliny the Elder, *Naturalis historia* (Natural History)
Nat. d.	Cicero, *De natura deorum* (On the Nature of the Gods)
NT	New Testament
Od.	Homer, *Odyssea* (Odyssey)
Odes Sol.	*Odes of Solomon*
Opif.	Philo, *De opificia mundi* (On the Creation of the World)
Orest.	Euripides, *Orestes*
OT	Old Testament
Parad.	Cicero, *Paradoxa Stoicorum*
Phaed.	Plato, *Phaedo*
Phaedr.	Plato, *Phaedrus*
Pol.	Aristotle, *Politica* (Politics)
Pol. Phil.	Polycarp, *Letter to the Philippians*
Post.	Philo, *De posteritate Caini* (On the Posterity of Cain)
Praed.	Augustine, *De praedestinatione sanctorum* (The Predestination of the Saints)
Praem.	Philo, *De praemiis et poenis* (On Rewards and Punishments)
Prob.	Philo, *Quod omnis probus liber sit* (That Every Good Person is Free)
Prot.	Plato, *Protagoras*
Pss. Sol.	*Psalms of Solomon*

1QH	*Thanksgiving Hymns*
1QM	*The War Scroll*
1QS	*The Rule of the Community*
Resp.	Plato, *Respublica* (The Republic)
Rhet.	Aristotle, *Rhetorica* (Rhetoric)
Somn.	Philo, *De somniis* (On Dreams)
Spec.	Philo, *De specialibus legibus* (On the Special Laws)
Strom.	Clement of Alexandria, *Stromata* (Miscellanies)
Symb.	Rufinus, *Commentarius in symbolum apostolorum*
Symp.	Plato, *Symposium*
T. Ash.	Testament of Asher
T. Benj.	Testament of Benjamin
T. Dan	Testament of Dan
T. Gad	Testament of Gad
T. Iss.	Testament of Issachar
T. Job	Testament of Job
T. Jud.	Testament of Judah
T. Levi	Testament of Levi
T. Naph.	Testament of Naphtali
T. Reu.	Testament of Reuben
T. Sim.	Testament of Simeon
Tranq.	Plutarch, *De tranquillitate animae* (On the Tranquility of the Mind)
Tyr.	Lucian, *Tyrannicida* (The Tyrannicide)
Vict. salubr.	Hippocrates, *De ratione victus salubris* (Regimen in Health)
Virt. Mor.	Plutarch, *De virtute moralia* (On Moral Virtue)
Vila	Josephus, *Vita* (The Life)
Vit. Apoll.	Philostratus, *Vita Apollonii*
Vit. beat.	Seneca, *De vita beata*

Periodicals, Reference Works, and Serials

AB	Anchor Bible
ABD	*Anchor Bible Dictionary.* Edited by David Noel Freedman. 6 vols. New York: Doubleday, 1992.
ACNT	Augsburg Commentaries on the New Testament
ACW	Ancient Christian Writers
ANT	The Ante-Nicene Fathers
ANRW	*Aufstieg und Niedergang der römischen Welt: Geschichte und Kultur Roms im Spiegel der neueren Forschung.* Edited by Wolfgang Haase and Hildegard Temporini. Berlin and New York: Walter De Gruyter, 1972–
ANTC	Abingdon New Testament Commentaries
APNTG	Max Zerwick, s.j., *Analysis Philologica Novi Testamenti Graeci.* 3d ed. Rome: Pontifical Biblical Institute, 1966.
AThR	*Anglican Theological Review*

BA	*Biblical Archaeologist*
BAR	Biblical Archaeology Review
BDAG	Walter Bauer. *A Greek-English Lexicon of the New Testament and Other Early Christian Literature*. 3d ed., revised and edited by Frederick William Danker, based on Walter Bauer's *Griechisch-deutsches Wörterbuch zu den Schriften des Neuen Testaments und der frühchristlichen Literatur,* 6th ed., edited by Kurt Aland and Barbara Aland with Viktor Reichmann and on the previous English editions by W. F. Arndt, F. W. Gingrich, and F. W. Danker. Chicago and London: The University of Chicago Press, 2000.
BDF	Friedrich Blass, Alfred Debrunner, and Robert W. Funk. *A Greek Grammar of the New Testament and Other Early Christian Literature.* A Translation and Revision of the ninth–tenth German editions incorporating Supplementary Notes of Alfred Debrunner by Robert W. Funk. Chicago: University of Chicago Press, 1961.
Bib	*Biblica*
BJRL	*Bulletin of the John Rylands University Library of Manchester*
BN	*Biblische Notizen*
BNTC	Black's New Testament Commentaries
BSac	*Bibliotheca sacra*
BTB	*Biblical Theology Bulletin*
BZ	*Biblische Zeitschrift*
BZNW	Beihefte zur Zeitschrift für die neutestamentliche Wissenschaft und die Kunde der älteren Kirche
CBC	Cambridge Bible Commentary
CBQ	*Catholic Biblical Quarterly*
CNT	Commentaire du Nouveau Testament
CurTM	*Currents in Theology and Mission*
DNTB	*Dictionary of New Testament Background.* Edited by Craig A. Evans and Stanley E. Porter. Downers Grove, Ill.: InterVarsity Press, 2000.
EBib	*Etudes bibliques*
EvT	*Evangelische Theologie*
ExpTim	*Expository Times*
FB	Forschung zur Bibel
FRLANT	Forschungen zur Religion und Literatur des Alten und Neuen Testaments
GNT	*The Greek New Testament.* Fourth revised edition. Edited by Kurt Aland and others. Stuttgart: Deutsche Bibelgesellschaft/ United Bible Societies, 1994.
HNT	Handbuch zum Neuen Testament
HR	*History of Religions*
HTKNT	Herders theologischer Kommentar zum Neuen Testament
HTR	*Harvard Theological Review*
HvTSt	*Hervormde teologiese studies*
IBS	*Irish Biblical Studies*
ICC	International Critical Commentary

Int	*Interpretation*
JAAR	*Journal of the American Academy of Religion*
JB	*Jerusalem Bible*
JBC	*Jerome Biblical Commentary*. Edited by Raymond E. Brown, s.s., Joseph A. Fitzmyer, s.j., and Roland E. Murphy, o.carm. Englewood Cliffs, N.J.: Prentice-Hall, 1968.
JBL	*Journal of Biblical Literature*
JETS	*Journal of the Evangelical Theological Society*
JPT	*Journal of Pentecostal Theology*
JR	*Journal of Religion*
JRT	*Journal of Religious Thought*
JSNT	*Journal for the Study of the New Testament*
JSNTSup	Journal for the Study of the New Testament: Supplement Series
JSPSup	Journal for the Study of the Pseudepigrapha: Supplement Series
JTS	*Journal of Theological Studies*
JTSA	*Journal of Theology for Southern Africa*
KD	*Kerygma und Dogma*
LB	*Linguistica Biblica*
LCL	Loeb Classical Library
L&N	*Greek-English Lexicon of the New Testament: Based on Semantic Domains*. 2 vols. Edited by Johannes P. Louw and Eugene A. Nida. New York: United Bible Societies, 1988.
MNTC	Moffatt New Testament Commentary
MPG	*Patrologia graeca* [= *Patrologiae cursus completus: Series graeca*]. Edited by J.-P. Migne. 162 vols. Paris, 1857–86.
MPL	*Patrologia latina* [= *Patrologiae cursus completus: Series latina*]. Edited by J.-P. Migne. 217 vols. Paris, 1844–64.
NAB	*New American Bible*
NCBC	New Century Bible Commentary
NCE	*New Catholic Encyclopedia*. Edited by W. J. McDonald et al. 15 vols. Washington, D.C.: Catholic University of America, 1967.
NICNT	New International Commentary on the New Testament
NIGTC	New International Greek Testament Commentary
NovT	*Novum Testamentum*
NovTSup	Supplements to Novum Testamentum
NRSV	*New Revised Standard Version*
NTD	Das Neue Testament Deutsch
NTM	New Testament Message
NTS	*New Testament Studies*
ÖTK	Ökumenischer Taschenbuch-Kommentar zum Neuen Testament
OTP	*The Old Testament Pseudepigrapha*. 2 vols. Edited by James H. Charlesworth. Garden City, N.Y.: Doubleday, 1983; London: Darton, Longman and Todd, 1985.
RB	*Revue biblique*
ResQ	*Restoration Quarterly*
RevExp	*Review and Expositor*
RHPR	*Revue d'histoire et de philosophie religieuses*

RHR	*Revue de l'histoire des religions*
RivB	*Rivista biblica italiana*
RQ	*Römische Quartalschrift für christliche Altertumskunde und Kirchengeschichte*
SB	Sources bibliques
SBL	Society of Biblical Literature
SBLDS	Society of Biblical Literature Dissertation Series
SBLSP	Society of Biblical Literature Seminar Papers
SBS	Stuttgarter Bibelstudien
SE	*Studia evangelica*
SJT	*Scottish Journal of Theology*
SNT	Studien zum Neuen Testament
SNTSMS	Society for New Testament Studies Monograph Series
SNTSU	Studien zum Neuen Testament und seiner Umwelt
SP	Sacra Pagina
ST	*Studia theologica*
TBC	Torch Bible Commentaries
TDNT	*Theological Dictionary of the New Testament.* Edited by Gerhard Kittel and Gerhard Friedrich. Translated by Geoffrey W. Bromiley. 10 vols. Grand Rapids: Eerdmans, 1964–76.
TLZ	*Theologische Literaturzeitung*
TNTC	Tyndale New Testament Commentaries
TU	Texte und Untersuchungen
TZ	*Theologische Zeitschrift*
WBC	Word Biblical Commentary
WMANT	Wissenschaftliche Monographien zum Alten und Neuen Testament
WTJ	*Westminster Theological Journal*
WUNT	Wissenschaftliche Untersuchungen zum Neuen Testament
ZNW	*Zeitschrift für die neutestamentliche Wissenschaft und die Kunde der älteren Kirche*
ZTK	*Zeitschrift für Theologie und Kirche*
ZWT	*Zeitschrift für wissenschaftliche Theologie*

INTRODUCTION

1. *Approaches to the Letter of James*

The letter of James is one of the most enigmatic writings of the New Testament, posing some tantalizing questions. On the one hand it shows deep and abiding roots within the heritage of Judaism, yet on the other hand from the perspective of language and style it is among the most Hellenistic of New Testament books. It opens in the form of a letter, only to disregard the traditional epistolary format evident in the writings of Paul. It demonstrates close connections with the wisdom tradition, yet in form and content it differs remarkably from traditional Jewish wisdom writings such as Proverbs, Sirach, Wisdom, etc.

Its connections with early Christianity are also tantalizing. The letter mentions the name of Jesus Christ directly only twice (1:1; 2:1), yet there are numerous echoes of Jesus' teaching and sayings. This commentary will endeavor to illustrate the letter's roots in the heritage of Jesus. Of all New Testament writings the letter of James appears to lie closest to Jesus' spirit and message.

From the outset the interpretation of the letter of James has been uniquely influenced by a number of important thinkers and scholars. Through the authority and influence of scholars such as Origen, Rufinus, Jerome, and Augustine this letter ultimately gained universal recognition and acceptance as part of the Christian canon. Martin Luther's rejection of the letter on the grounds that it contradicted Paul's doctrine of justification by faith alone prevailed among Protestant scholars for centuries; his views have influenced interpretations of the letter of James from the sixteenth century to the present. In particular the question of the relationship between James and Paul has dominated scholarship, with the consequence that the letter of James continues to be read in connection with or even in opposition to Paul.

A number of insightful studies on the letter of James emerged in the course of the last century. Probably most significant of all was Martin Dibelius's commentary, *Der Brief des Jakobus* (11th rev. ed. Göttingen:

Vandenhoeck & Ruprecht, 1964), which influenced scholarship for many decades. First published in Germany in 1921 as part of Meyer's Kritisch-Exegetischer Kommentar über das Neue Testament, it was later revised after Dibelius's death by Heinrich Greeven in 1964 and translated into English in 1976 as part of the Hermeneia series. Dibelius approached the letter of James using the historical-critical method and applied the principles of form criticism to the letter in a consistent and extremely penetrating way. His abiding contribution was to take the letter of James seriously. This sounded the death knell to those dominant approaches of the past that had read James solely through the eyes, thought, and interests of Paul. In his own way Dibelius was to exercise an unconscious hegemony over future scholarship through a characterization of the letter as *paraenesis*, meaning that the letter of James was composed of a series of unconnected sayings with no relationship to any historical context (3). These sayings were derived from the Jewish and Greco-Roman worlds; their purpose was to give the hearer/reader ethical or moral direction for life. The major interest of the letter of James as well as the heritage it handed on to future generations was this ethical instruction. Since these instructions were not connected to any historical context, scholarship on this letter was relegated to the sphere of ethics. Todd C. Penner has summarized Dibelius's legacy extremely well:

> At the same time, he (Dibelius) effectively relegated inquiry into James to the level of ethics. However, when scholars came along who were not interested in the ethical world of early Christianity but concerned with historical and theological development, there was little in James of relevance: Dibelius had taken the history and theology out of the text. . . . This is perhaps Dibelius's most significant legacy. If one accepts his premise—not just that James is paraenesis, but especially that it is paraenesis *as understood by Dibelius*—then there is little incentive for further critical inquiry ([1999] 265).

Until the 1970s the dominant set of tools for interpreting New Testament writings was the historical-critical method; it focused largely on form- and source-critical issues related to the text and to its origin and growth. Over the past few decades *new methods* have emerged to supplement the historical-critical set, and these have also had an impact on the study of the letter of James. As a result, in recent years this largely neglected writing has been read with new interest and excitement. Two new approaches are especially worth noting in this regard.

1. *The social-scientific approach* developed models on the basis of other disciplines such as anthropology and sociology that are invaluable for understanding the New Testament writings. Those scholars who have done groundbreaking work in this area have been Bruce Malina (*Christian*

Origins and Cultural Anthropology: Practical Models for Biblical Interpretation [Atlanta: John Knox, 1986] and *The New Testament World: Insights from Cultural Anthropology* [rev. ed. Louisville: Westminster John Knox, 1993]); John H. Elliott (*A Home for the Homeless: A Social-Scientific Criticism of 1 Peter, Its Situation and Strategy* [Minneapolis: Fortress, 1990] and *1 Peter: A New Translation with Introduction and Commentary.* AB 37B [New York: Doubleday, 2000]); Jerome H. Neyrey (*Honor and Shame in the Gospel of Matthew* [Louisville: Westminster John Knox, 1998]); and from another very different perspective Gerd Theissen ("Die soziologische Auswertung religiöser Überlieferungen: Ihre methodologischen Probleme am Beispiel des Urchristentums," *Kairos* 17 [1975] 284–99, and "Theoretische Probleme religionssociologischer Forschung und die Analyse des Urchristentums," *Neue Zeitschrift für Systematische Theologie und Religionsphilosophie* 16 [1974] 35–56). Some attempts have been made to apply this social-scientific methodology to the letter of James: e.g., Pedrito U. Maynard-Reid, *Poverty and Wealth in James* (Maryknoll, N.Y.: Orbis, 1987); Elsa Tamez, *The Scandalous Message of James: Faith without Works is Dead* (New York: Crossroad, 1992); John H. Elliott, "The Epistle of James in Rhetorical and Social Scientific Perspective: Holiness-Wholeness and Patterns of Replication," *BTB* 23 (1993) 71–81; David Rhoads "The Letter of James: Friend of God," *CurTM* 25 (1998) 473–86; and David Hutchinson Edgar, *Has not God Chosen the Poor? The Social Setting of the Epistle of James* (Sheffield: Sheffield Academic Press, 2001).

2. *Rhetorical criticism* is another important methodology that has developed and been applied both to the New Testament writings in general and to the letter of James in particular. Vernon K. Robbins and Burton L. Mack have made great contributions from their studies of ancient rhetoricians (e.g., *Patterns of Persuasion in the Gospels* [Sonoma, CA: Polebridge Press] 1989). Robbins has argued very strongly that more biblical scholarship should be devoted to Hellenistic rhetoric so that these insights might be applied to the New Testament writings, especially the synoptic gospels (see, in the above volume, his "Chreia and Pronouncement Story in Synoptic Studies," 1–29, and Mack, "Elaboration of the Chreia in the Hellenistic School," 31–67). The first attempt to apply rhetorical criticism to the letter of James was in the groundbreaking study of Wilhelm H. Wuellner ("Der Jakobusbrief im Licht der Rhetorik und Textpragmatik," *LB* 43 [1978] 5–66). He gave special emphasis to rhetoric as the art of persuasion and examined how the letter of James consistently performed this persuasive function. Another very recent and insightful study of James from a rhetorical perspective has been the work of Wesley Hiram Wachob, *The Voice of Jesus in the Social Rhetoric of James* (Cambridge: Cambridge University Press, 2000).

Most commentaries on James, as I have indicated, have examined and interpreted this writing from a historical-critical perspective. The approach here will be to build upon this historical-critical method by embracing perspectives arising from the more recent methodologies just described (see, e.g., Chapters 2 and 3). Attention is also given to the most significant commentaries of the past, but with emphasis on the most recent.

This commentary also attempts to uphold *the importance of the letter of James in its own right*. An important consequence is the light the letter throws on the beautiful diversity that was early Christianity. Hopefully this will mean that the voice of James will be read independently of the hegemony of the Pauline letters, thought, and style that have dominated approaches to the letter of James in the past. Luke Timothy Johnson has argued strongly in support of this approach: "The most important gain from breaking the Pauline fixation is that it liberates James to be read in terms of 108 verses rather than 12 verses, in terms of its own voice rather than in terms of its supposed muting of Paul's voice" (*The Letter of James* [New York: Doubleday, 1995] 114). The letter of James hands on the message of Jesus in its own distinctive way in relation to other traditions of early Christianity. My intention in the course of this commentary will be to allow James's unique voice to emerge, bearing witness to another tradition within early Christianity: "In our present postmodern world where diversity is treasured for the wealth that different cultures, perspectives, beliefs, etc., bring, the letter of James with its distinctiveness and difference resonates with this postmodern consciousness" (Patrick J. Hartin, *A Spirituality of Perfection: Faith in Action in the Letter of James* [Collegeville: The Liturgical Press, 1999] 3).

The community dimension of the letter of James is another aspect that has become more evident in recent times. Most often James's ethical advice and admonitions are read as though the letter is addressed to an individual. This is surely a consequence of the modern world's individualistic nature, which tends automatically and uncritically to impose an individualistic perspective on the biblical writings. James's message is directed undoubtedly first and foremost to a community, a group, "the twelve tribes in the Dispersion" (1:1). James consistently introduces a new topic with the phrase "My brothers (and sisters)" (1:2, 16, 19; 2:1, 14; 3:1; 4:11; 5:7, 12, 19). The individual is addressed only insofar as he or she is part of the community. James's instructions are intended to build up the community and to socialize the individual into the community of believers. Consequently, James's morality differs greatly from the individualistic ethic of the twenty-first century. This community ethic challenges believers to be aware of their identity as the "first fruits of (God's) creatures" (1:18). They are also challenged to show concern for one another. The final verses of the letter capture this concern very well: all members of the community have a responsibility for bringing back a brother or sister who has wandered away.

The distinctiveness of the letter of James is evident from its strong theological rather than christological approach. As Johnson expresses it: "James' grounding of its exhortations in *theological* rather than *Christological* principles, for example, provides a genuine bridge between Christians and others (such as Jews and Muslims) who share belief in one God who is creator and lawgiver and judge, but who do not share the specific gift given in Jesus" (*Letter of James* 164). On the negative side, the letter of James has consistently been criticized for a lack of reference to the person of Jesus Christ and a failure to refer to Jesus' death and resurrection. On the positive side, the focus in the letter of James is on the relationship between the community and God. The community is both "the twelve tribes in the Dispersion" (1:1) and "the first fruits of (God's) creatures" (1:18). This short letter presents a very rich image and clear understanding of God as the Creator, the Father of Lights, the source of all wisdom, the Lawgiver, the one who bestows all good gifts (see Hartin, *A Spirituality of Perfection* 7). This theocentric vision demonstrates James's roots in the world of Judaism. There is nothing in the thought and vision of this short letter that is not at home in that world. Of all the writings of the New Testament the letter of James provides the closest link to Judaism and is an eternal reminder to Christians of their origins and roots within that heritage. This letter is a remarkable testimony to what Christians and Jews hold in common.

James's letter also provides a bridge to the world of Islam. Everything in this letter resonates with Islam's religious worldview and beliefs. Its focus on God as the one from whom all good comes and on whom all rely is central to Islam's monotheistic vision.

Finally, the letter of James provides a message that *remains a challenge to everyone who reads it:* the challenge to put faith into action. The focus on social issues transcends time and place. Although it was written to communities in the second half of the first century C.E., many of the issues this letter raises are as relevant today as they were then. The concern to *avoid every form of discrimination* clearly resonates with us in the twenty-first century. The letter's *concern for the poor* and the obligation for the Christian community to champion their cause is one that faces Christians today in a world where divisions between rich and poor nations are becoming increasingly more acute. James gives a voice to the poor and challenges every Christian community to reevaluate its approach to those in need. The letter's stress on *the community dimension of Christianity* is badly needed today as a corrective to an ever-increasing individualism within society as well as in many Christian churches. The letter of James calls believers to see themselves as members of both the Christian and human communities with responsibilities toward both. It is a call to remember one's roots and to accept responsibility for one another.

2. *Text and Canonicity*

This commentary is based on the established Greek text of the 27th revised edition of Nestle-Aland's *Novum Testamentum Graece* (1994) and the 4th revised edition of the United Bible Societies' *The Greek New Testament*, which uses the same Nestle-Aland text. A recent publication of the *Editio Critica Maior of the Greek New Testament* for the letter of James, edited by Barbara Aland, Kurt Aland, Gerd Mink, and Klaus Wachtel (1997) provides a valuable resource for ascertaining the manuscript evidence for the established text.

This Greek text is not based on any one manuscript or even a family of manuscripts, but instead on what Bruce Metzger calls "a judicious eclecticism" (*The Text of the New Testament: Its Transmission, Corruption, and Restoration* [2nd ed. Oxford: Clarendon Press, 1968] 178). This approach involves a critical textual evaluation of every variation among the ancient texts to establish the more original reading.

The earliest and best witnesses to the complete text of James are the Greek uncials from the fourth century, Codex Vaticanus (B) and Codex Sinaiticus ($\aleph$), and from the fifth century the Codex Alexandrinus (A). In addition there are a number of fragmentary papyri manuscripts: from third-century Egypt there are $\mathfrak{P}^{23}$ (containing 1:10-12, 15-18) and $\mathfrak{P}^{20}$ (containing 2:19–3:2, 4-9); and from the sixth to seventh centuries there is $\mathfrak{P}^{74}$, which contains almost all of the letter of James (1:1-6, 8-19, 21-23, 25; 1:27–2:15, 18-22; 2:25–3:1, 5-6, 10-12, 14; 3:17–4:8, 11-14; 5:1-3, 7-9, 12-14, 19-20). There are also a number of Greek manuscripts witnessing to the text from the fifth through the ninth centuries. Added to these are also a number of important versions of the text of James in Old Latin, the Vulgate, Coptic (Sahidic and Bohairic), Armenian, Ethiopic, and Syriac (Peshitta, Philoxenian, Harclean, and Palestinian).

No Western text like that extant for the Acts of the Apostles appears among these witnesses to the text of James. Consequently, the text of James is relatively uniform. Only a very few variations occur in the readings, and the only real difficulties that arise are in 1:3, 12, 17, 19, 27; 2:3, 19, 20; 3:3, 9, 12; 4:4, 5, 14; 5:4, 7, 16, 20 (see Bruce M. Metzger, *A Textual Commentary on the Greek New Testament* [New York: United Bible Societies, 1975] 679–86). Attention will be given to these different readings in the course of the commentary.

A study of the acceptance of James as part of the canon is intriguing and raises many questions that defy answers. Two writings outside the New Testament point to a probable early knowledge of James in the Church of Rome. First Clement, written from Rome around 95 C.E., appears to quote James very freely. There are a number of verbal allusions as well as themes that are strikingly similar. A comparison of *1 Clem.* 29:1–30:5 with

Jas 4:1-10 reveals some thirteen similarities either verbal or thematic (see Johnson, *Letter of James* 72–75 for a detailed examination of the correspondences between James and 1 Clement). The use of the figure of Abraham in both writings is also striking. Like James, 1 Clement identifies Abraham as "a friend of God" (*1 Clem.* 10:1; Jas 2:23). Both James and 1 Clement quote Gen 15:6: "Abraham believed God, and it was reckoned to him as righteousness" (see Jas 2:23 and *1 Clem.* 10:6).

The Shepherd of Hermas, written in Rome around the middle of the second century C.E., also shows some parallels with the letter of James. The Shepherd of Hermas uses the term *dipsychos* (1:8; 4:8) as well as different variations of the word (e.g., Herm. *Vis.* 3:2, 2; 3:3, 4; 3:4, 3; Herm. *Mand.* 9:1, 5, 7, 9, 11; Herm. *Sim.* 1:3; 6:2; 8:11, 3). This is remarkable, since this word does not occur in the rest of the New Testament or other Greek literature. Further, the letter of James and the Shepherd of Hermas both reflect on the nature of speech. For James the tongue is a "restless evil, full of death-dealing poison" (Jas 3:8) that is "set on fire by Gehenna" (3:6). Hermas describes speech in a similar vein: "Evil-speaking is wicked; it is a restless devil, never making peace, but always living in strife. Refrain from it then, and you shall have well-being at all times with all men" (Herm. *Mand.* 2:3 [Lake, LCL]). For both James and Hermas wicked speech is also symbolic of double-mindedness (Herm. *Sim.* 8:7, 2 and Jas 3:9-10). For a full examination of the correspondences between James and Hermas see Johnson (*Letter of James* 75–79). He summarizes this detailed examination of the connections by saying (p. 79): "Hermas meets all the criteria for deciding in favor of a literary dependence. Within a document of manifestly different literary character and purpose, there is an extended sharing in outlook, theme, and language with James. The similarities are found throughout Hermas, although they dominate in the *Mandates*. And they are derived from every part of James."

Despite this knowledge and probable use of the letter of James in the Church in Rome, it took a long time for it to be accepted there as part of the canon. One of the oldest canons containing a list of New Testament books, the Muratorian Fragment, coming from Rome toward the end of the second century C.E., did not mention it in its list (see Bruce M. Metzger, *The Canon of the New Testament: Its Origin, Development, and Significance* [Oxford: Clarendon Press, 1987] 191–201; Harry Y. Gamble, *The New Testament Canon: Its Making and Meaning* [Philadelphia: Fortress, 1985]). The traditionally accepted view of the early dating of the Muratorian Canon has been challenged by Albert Carl Sundberg ("Canon Muratori: A Fourth Century List," *HTR* 66 [1973] 1–41). However, Everett Ferguson has refuted these arguments of Sundberg ("Canon Muratori: Date and Provenance," *Studia Patristica* 18 [1982] 677–83). The omission of James from the Muratorian Canon is surprising, given the fact that it does mention Jude and two letters of John. It appears that in the Western Church James was not considered canonical before the fourth century C.E.

It was in the Eastern Church that James first gained status as a canonical writing. There was a slow development beginning with Origen, the successor of Clement of Alexandria as head of the catechetical school of Alexandria, at the beginning of the third century C.E. He included James in his canon of New Testament writings (*Hom. Jes. Nav.* 7:1) and quoted from it more than thirty times in the course of his writings. He refers to the letter as "scripture" when he quotes from Jas 5:20 (*Hom. Lev.* 2:3), identifies it as having been written by "James the Apostle" when he quotes Jas 4:7 (*Hom. Exod.* 3:3), and refers to James as the "brother of the Lord" when quoting Jas 4:4 (*Comm. Rom.* 4:8). Origen's support for the letter of James shows that it must have been known and accepted either in his home city of Alexandria or in Palestine (where Origen had also been active).

Origen's influence prevailed in the church of Alexandria, where the letter of James continued to be used. The earliest commentary on James that we possess comes from Didymus the Blind (313–398 C.E.), who also headed Alexandria's catechetical school. In 367 C.E. Bishop Athanasius of Alexandria (296–373 C.E.), who had been educated at the catechetical school of Alexandria, wrote an Easter Letter in which he listed the canonical books of the New Testament. James was named alongside the other New Testament writings. For the first time the canon of the New Testament was defined as comprising only twenty-seven books. Athanasius hereby gives evidence for the canonical status of James in the churches of the East.

In the West there is evidence of some use of James, as can be seen from the *Old Latin Versions.* However, it was largely Origen's influence on three scholars that would encourage the general acceptance of James as canonical as well as its use in the West. Rufinus (345–410 C.E.) was a translator of Origen's work and in 401 he included the letter of James ("brother of the Lord and Apostle") in his list of canonical books (*Symb.* 37). Jerome (331–420 C.E.), who was greatly influenced by Origen, included it in his Vulgate translation that would become the standard text of James until the time of Erasmus. Jerome also quoted frequently from the letter of James. Finally, the influence of Augustine (354–430 C.E.) was responsible for the firm acceptance of James in the West. He included it among the canonical writings, and at the Third Synod of Carthage (in 397 C.E.) the letter of James was listed among the canonical writings. Augustine also produced a commentary on James that has subsequently been lost.

From this survey it appears that James gained acceptance into the canon very slowly. However, from the end of the fourth century onward there was no dispute about its position until the time of the Reformation. We do not know why James took so long to gain acceptance. The shortness of the writing would have had something to do with it, although the letter of Jude (which is even shorter than James) gained acceptance earlier. Its final reception was ultimately due to a slowly growing consciousness of its use, spurred on by the authority of a number of scholars, among whom Origen and Augustine were the most influential.

Doubts about James's place in the canon surfaced again in the sixteenth century. Erasmus supported its inclusion in the canon, but he did question its apostolic authorship. Martin Luther (1483–1546) also doubted its apostolic authorship, but his criticism went far deeper. He saw James as contradicting the teaching of Paul on which he based his belief in justification by faith alone. For this reason, in the Preface to his 1522 translation of the New Testament (*Luther's Works: Word and Sacrament I*, vol. 35, ed. E. T. Backmann [Philadelphia: Fortress, 1960] 362), Luther writes:

> In a word St. John's Gospel and his first epistle, St. Paul's epistles, especially Romans, Galatians, and Ephesians, and St. Peter's first epistle are the books that show you Christ and teach you all that is necessary and salvatory for you to know, even if you were never to see or hear any other book or doctrine. Therefore St. James' epistle is really an epistle of straw, compared to these others, for it has nothing of the nature of the gospel about it.

A further argument against James in Luther's mind came from the lack of any reference to central Christian beliefs such as the suffering, death, and resurrection of Jesus. In printing the Bible Luther placed the letter of James, together with Hebrews, Jude, and Revelation at the end, considering them less significant writings:

> In a word, he [James] wanted to guard against those who relied on faith without works, but was unequal to the task. He tries to accomplish by harping on the law what the apostles accomplish by stimulating people to love. Therefore I cannot include him among the chief books, though I would not prevent anyone from including or extolling him as he pleases, for there are otherwise many good sayings in him (397).

John Calvin (1509–1564), on the other hand, adopted a positive attitude to the letter of James. He focused on the letter's practical teaching, which he judged had value for everyday Christian life, and concluded that he could find no reason for excluding the epistle from the canon (see John Calvin, *Commentaries on the Epistle of James* (1551), translated and edited by John Owen [Grand Rapids: Eerdmans, 1959] 276).

Philip Melanchthon also attempted to reconcile the apparent contradictions between James and Paul. Nevertheless, despite the views of Calvin and Melanchthon, Luther's position on James won the day and continued to influence the Protestant assessment on James down to the present.

In the Roman Catholic Church a contrary reaction developed. The Council of Trent (1546) defended the canonicity of James as well as its apostolic authorship (see Henrici Denzinger, *Enchiridion Symbolorum Definitionum et Declarationum de Rebus Fidei et Morum* [German ed. by Peter Hünermann with Helmut Hoping, *Kompendium der Glaubensbekenntnisse und kirchlichen Lehrentscheidungen* (37th ed. Freiburg: Herder, 1991)] 1503). Trent used James to defend the biblical basis for the anointing in the sacrament of the sick (see Denzinger, *Enchiridion* 1699; see also the Notes and Interpretation on Jas 5:14).

In more recent times in particular, James's concern for integrity and a way of life that conforms to one's faith speaks to a Christianity that is intimately concerned with the social issues of our times. Both Jesus' and James's concern for the poor and for the outcasts of society reflect the rediscovery of the Christian church's understanding of the social gospel and of God's fundamental option for the poor.

3. *Genre and Purpose*

The literary genre of the letter of James has been much discussed over the course of the centuries. Without doubt this writing belongs to the general category of Wisdom literature so widespread throughout Israel and the Near East in the two centuries leading up to the first millennium and beyond. Wisdom literature communicates advice and instructions by one in authority (king, teacher, parent) based upon his or her experience of how to lead life successfully and live according to wisdom. In the Israelite Wisdom tradition further reflection also took place on the nature of wisdom itself. Both these aspects of the Wisdom tradition are found within the letter of James (see *Excursus 3: The Wisdom of James*).

Martin Dibelius's commentary had important consequences for understanding the Wisdom dimension of James. As we saw above, he viewed James as a *paraenesis*, a "book of popular slogans," individual passages that were simply strung together by means of catchwords (*James: A Commentary on the Epistle of James* xii, 6). Scholars tended to embrace this view almost uncritically. Since the late 1980s, however, this approach has been seriously challenged. Many scholars have attempted to identify various themes that give the writing a unity. For example, as John H. Elliott has noted, a number of investigations have pointed to wholeness or perfection as an important theme within the letter of James (Elliott [1993] 71–81; see also Oscar J. F. Seitz, "Two Spirits in Man: An Essay in Biblical Exegesis," *NTS* 6 [1959/60] 82–95; Hubert Frankemölle, "Gespalten oder ganz; Zur Pragmatik der theologischen Anthropologie des Jakobusbriefes," in Hans-Ulrich von Brachel and Norbert Mette, eds., *Kommunikation und Solidarität* [Fribourg: Exodus, 1985] 160–78; Wiard Popkes, *Adressaten, Situation und Form des Jakobusbriefes* [Stuttgart: Katholisches Bibelwerk, 1986]; Richard J. Bauckham, *James: Wisdom of James, Disciple of Jesus the Sage* [London and New York: Routledge, 1999] 177–85; Hartin [1999]; and Scot McKnight, "A Parting within the Way: Jesus and James on Israel and Purity," in Bruce Chilton and Craig A. Evans, eds., *James the Just and Christian Origins* [Leiden: Brill, 1999] 83–129). What is even more noteworthy is that this identification has been reached largely independently.

Dibelius' classification of James as *paraenesis* is clearly in need of clarification and refinement. John Gammie's studies on paraenetic literature have brought clarity and direction to the discussion ("Paraenetic Literature: Toward the Morphology of a Secondary Genre," *Semeia* 50 [1990] 41–77). He has demonstrated that paraenetic literature was a secondary form of the primary literary genre, namely Wisdom literature. Paraenetic literature sets forth moral exhortation, either encouraging the community to continue its way of life or directing the community to a specific way of action. Paraenetic literature embraces a number of subgenres, two of which are important for the study of the letter of James, namely *paraenesis* and protreptic discourse (ibid. 51–57). The major difference between the two lies in their way of expression. "*Paraenesis* is a form of address which not only commends, but actually enumerates precepts or maxims which pertain to moral aspiration and the regulation of human conduct" (ibid. 51). On the other hand, protreptic discourse contains a sustained argument that seeks to develop the theme more fully through a "demonstration which is stylistically expressed in a clear, logical, and syllogistic manner" (Hartin [1999] 47).

The distinction between *paraenesis* and protreptic discourse can best be seen by looking at two writings, the book of Wisdom and the *Letter of Aristeas*. The book of Wisdom was probably written in Greek during the course of the first century B.C.E. in Alexandria with the intention of strengthening the faith, life, and traditions of Jews living outside their homeland. It achieved its purpose through more developed and sustained arguments and demonstrations, which define it more closely as belonging to the genre of protreptic discourse. The *Letter of Aristeas*, on the other hand, was written some time between the third century B.C.E. and the first century C.E. and records the translation of the Mosaic Law from Hebrew to Greek in Alexandria (see "Letter of Aristeas" [*OTP* 2:7–34]). The *Letter of Aristeas* presents a series of sayings (rather than sustained arguments) aimed at converting those sympathetic to the religion of Israel. This conforms more closely to what is termed *paraenesis*.

Gammie has presented three critieria for distinguishing between *paraenesis* and protreptic discourse: "(1) presence or absence of precepts and purpose for which they are adduced; (2) extent of sustained demonstration and organization with a view to persuade; and (3) breadth of topics covered and/or sharpness of focus" (Gammie [1990] 54–55). An examination of the letter of James shows how these criteria support the designation of James as protreptic discourse (see Hartin [1999] 48–49).

- While *precepts* are an essential element of *paraenesis*, they may occur in but are not essential for protreptic discourse. Precepts do occur in the letter of James, but they are not at the heart of the letter's teaching. They function more to introduce the main argument: e.g., "Let not many of you become teachers, my brothers (and sisters) . . ." (Jas 3:1). Here the command not to become teachers introduces James's argument on the need to watch one's speech. Characteristic of whatever precepts occur in James is the way they are used to serve the argument.

- The *role of argumentation* is central to the letter of James. Protreptic discourse aims at persuading hearers/readers to adopt a particular way of action. An examination of the letter of James shows that a sustained argument is carefully developed in a number of pericopes: the condemnation of partiality shown for the rich against the poor in the community (2:1-7), the relationship between faith and works (2:14-26), and evils of the tongue (3:1-12). In the commentary it will be shown that the structure of argumentation James uses is that of the perfect argument as found in the *Rhetorica ad Herennium*. The structure of the perfect argument outlined by *Ad Her.* 2:18, 28 is at the heart of every argumentation, and it helps to shed light on James's argument.

- The *Greek Diatribe* is a further stylistic feature that the letter of James adopts in order to communicate its argument. It is not a literary genre, but rather a written style that encompasses a way of exhorting the hearers/readers. As Abraham J. Malherbe defines it, "a diatribe is essentially a popular philosophical treatment of an ethical topic and has the practical aim of moving people to action rather than reflection" (*Moral Exhortation. A Greco-Roman Sourcebook* [Philadelphia: Westminster, 1986] 129; see also 129–34, as well as Stanley K. Stowers, *The Diatribe and Paul's Letter to the Romans* [Chico: Scholars, 1981] chapters 2 and 3, and "Diatribe," *ABD* 2:190–93). Above all the diatribe introduces an imaginary "sparring partner" whose objections the author introduces and then proceeds to answer. The origin of the diatribe emerges clearly from the context of the Greek and

Roman classroom. The style of the diatribe appears especially in ch. 2, where James introduces an imaginary adversary: "But someone will say . . . *(all' erei tis)*" (2:18). Having introduced the objection, James proceeds to answer it. Through this imaginary opponent James achieves his aim of persuading his hearers/readers about the importance of faith expressed in action. The style of the diatribe continues throughout this chapter. In 2:2-7 James presents a hypothetical situation of discrimination in favor of the rich. This is an indictment against the community, as it demonstrates a betrayal of their faith in Jesus, the Christ (2:1). Then vv. 9, 14, and 18 all present imaginary objections that James proceeds to refute in order to carry his argument forward. Other stylistic features of the diatribe also emerge: the presentation of rhetorical questions (2:5-7, 14-15, 20-21) and the use of examples to illustrate the argument (2:21-25).

• The *vision of protreptic discourse remains highly focused.* While *paraenesis* encompasses within its embrace almost every aspect of human life and action, this is not the case with protreptic discourse. The letter of James focuses primarily on the call to maintain "friendship with God" as opposed to "friendship with the world" (4:4). This is what separates it from other Wisdom writings such as the book of Proverbs, which embraces every aspect of life and culture. Themes such as the discipline of the young and faithfulness to one's married spouse so dominant in the Wisdom literature of the Hebrew writings are totally absent from the letter of James, for they do not form part of its concern.

Both protreptic discourse and *paraenesis* aim at "social formation" (Leo G. Perdue, "The Social Character of Paraenesis and Paraenetic Literature," *Semeia* 50 [1990] 23–27). This means that individuals are socialized in such a way that they accept the values and ethos of the society to which they belong, or which they have most recently joined. Peter L. Berger and Thomas Luckmann define this as "socialization": "the comprehensive and consistent induction of an individual into the objective world of a society or a sector of it" (*The Social Construction of Reality: A Treatise in the Sociology of Knowledge* [Garden City, N.Y.: Doubleday, 1966] 120). This is exactly what the letter of James sets out to achieve. The author draws the attention of his hearers/readers to the ethos and values that are necessary for them to be part of "the Twelve Tribes in the Dispersion" (1:1). The rhetorical function of the letter of James is to socialize its hearers/readers as the twelve-tribe kingdom by reminding them of those values that give them identity and separate them from the wider society. James does not intend that the community to whom he writes should separate from society as the Qumran people did, but he does want them to realize that their identity is distinct from the society in which they live. This is what he means when he calls them to "keep [themselves] un-stained from the world" (1:27). James's admonitions aim at training the addressees to lead lives in friendship with God as opposed to friendship with the world (4:4).

A key characteristic of life within this new society is the equality that all experience. This is graphically depicted in James's parable about the way the rich and poor are received into the community. The faith of "our glorious Lord Jesus Christ" (2:1) requires that they both be welcomed into the community in the same manner: no distinction is made between rich and poor, or by implication between any groups. Equality within the com-munity is also experienced in the way it is structured. The only people who exercise leadership positions within it are teachers (3:1) and elders (5:14). James reminds them that they exist to help and serve the commu-nity. Such is their responsibility that they are held accountable for what they say and teach and they "will receive a more severe judgment" (3:1).

James's choice of the genre of protreptic discourse serves his rhetorical purpose admirably. He has a vision that focuses upon the nature of the community as the twelve-tribe kingdom who are called to lead their lives in friendship with God. This led James to develop sustained arguments highlighting the values that give identity and direction to those who be-long to this community.

To disseminate this protreptic discourse to the hearers/readers, James sends it out in the form of a letter. The opening of the writing conforms strictly to the format of a Hellenistic letter with the identification of its au-thor and those to whom it is addressed, and the short greeting *(chairein)*. The further dimensions of a letter, familiar from those of Paul (namely a thanksgiving section that precedes the body of the letter and a conclusion with final greetings), are lacking in James's writing. This has raised the question: "Can the letter of James be called a letter?"

Research into the form of the letter has come a long way since Adolf Deissmann's studies drew a clear distinction between a letter and an epistle (*Light from the Ancient East,* translated by L. R. M. Strachan [4th ed. Grand Rapids: Baker Book House, 1910] 218–46) and identified Paul's writings as true letters (233–42). Examination of rhetorical handbooks has shown that the world of letter writing was far more complicated than originally thought and that the letter genre could be expressed in a number of different forms (see, e.g., Malherbe [1986] 79–82, and Klaus Berger, "Hellenistische Gat-tungen im Neuen Testament," *ANRW* II. 25.2 [1984] 1031–432). Some New Testament letters can be categorized with more precision as either letters of commendation (Romans 16; Philemon) or circular letters (Ephesians; 1 Peter; 1 John). To reject the epistolary nature of James solely on the basis of its nonconformity to the formal elements of a letter as known from Paul's writing would be unfair (see, e.g., the discussion in Francis [1970] 110–26; and Hartin [1991] 23–34).

Some characteristic features of a letter are also missing. There are no personal references to the hearers/readers and their situations. The writer does not provide any information about himself except for identifying himself as "James, a slave of God and of the Lord Jesus Christ" (1:1). On the other hand there are some clearly identifiable epistolary features in his writing. James adopts the direct style of address: he frequently addresses his hearers/readers as *adelphoi* ("brothers [and sisters]") (1:2; 2:1, 14; 3:1; 4:11; 5:7, 12, 19). The whole presentation addresses an audience in the second person as though speaking directly to the hearers/readers, which is the very nature of a letter.

A careful examination of the actual addressees helps to define the characteristics of this writing more clearly. By addressing the letter to "the twelve tribes in the Dispersion" the writer places his writing within the framework of a "Diaspora letter." As such it is written to Jewish communities living outside the homeland of Israel/Palestine. Karl-Wilhelm Niebuhr has recently demonstrated ([1998] 420–43) that the letter of James is very similar to other known Jewish letters to the Diaspora such as 2 Maccabees 1; the Letter of Jeremiah (or Bar 6:1-73); and Baruch's letter in 2 (Syrian Apocalypse of) Baruch (2 Bar 78:1–87:1). Peter Davids in a chapter on "Palestinian Traditions in the Epistle of James" comments on the significance of James as belonging to the category of "Diaspora letters," making some insightful remarks that are worth quoting in full:

> This letter-to-the-Diaspora form, even when purely literary, was modeled on the actual letters of the period, particularly those from leading Jewish authorities in Palestine to Diaspora communities. Thus, while this evidence can not determine whether James is only the implied author or the actual author of our letter, it does place the Epistle of James into a particular literary world. In other words, the genre of James fits the Palestinian milieu. Furthermore, it fits the need of the early Christian movement centered in Jerusalem to extend its instruction to Diaspora Christian communities ([1999] 41).

This would certainly account for the lack of personal details and references to concrete situations of the hearers/readers. Nevertheless, as Luke Timothy Johnson has observed, irrespective of what the original understanding was, the moment James was read aloud it was "experienced as a letter from James" ([1995] 24).

In light of the above I conclude that James should be categorized as a protreptic discourse whose intention was to further the socialization process of its hearers/readers. The author sent this protreptic discourse in the form of a letter to Diaspora communities of followers of Jesus who had originated from the world of Israel.

4. *Author and Date*

The author identifies himself as "James, a slave of God and of the Lord Jesus Christ to the twelve tribes in the Dispersion" (1:1). The name "James" (*Iakōbos* in Greek) recalls the Hebrew for Jacob *(ya^căqōb)*, father of the "twelve tribes of Israel." The author presents himself in the role of Jacob in the Hebrew Scriptures as he addresses a letter to the new twelve-tribe people on how they are to live.

The New Testament itself refers to a number of people who bear the name *Iakōbos:* the son of Zebedee, an apostle and brother of John (Mark 1:19); the son of Alphaeus, also an apostle (Mark 3:18); the "brother" of Jesus (Mark 6:3; Gal 1:19); James the younger (Mark 15:40); and James the father of Jude (Luke 6:16). From the way the author identifies himself as "a slave of the Lord" with no further elaboration, he presumes the hearers/readers know who he is. Of all those called James in the New Testament only two emerge as possible candidates for the authorship of this letter because of the important role they exercised in the early Christian communities: James the son of Zebedee, and James "the brother of the Lord." James the son of Zebedee was put to death by Herod Agrippa I around 44 C.E. (Acts 12:2), which is far too early for the appearance of this letter. Further, the author identifies himself as "a slave" rather than "apostle," a title Paul always used. This leaves James the "brother of the Lord" as the most likely candidate.

Evidence in the New Testament

The meaning of the term "brother of the Lord" has generated a lot of discussion and emotion. Two basic ways of understanding this term are adopted by scholars. Some understand it in the literal sense it has in the Anglo-Saxon world as referring to a physical brother of Jesus. Other scholars interpret it in a broader sense, arguing that kinship degrees in the ancient world were more loosely defined than they are in modern languages. Two aspects tend to make a decision difficult. On the one hand theological considerations tend to influence the historical determination. On the other hand, the exact reference of the terms "brother and sister" in Western civilization distorts the imprecision of other cultures. Unconsciously scholars betray their theological as well as their cultural background and bias in this discussion.

An analogy drawn from societies in Africa can provide a direction toward a solution. In Africa the extended family is the major social network and members of this wider family are designated by the familial terms "brother and sister." The important thing is not physical generation, but rather being part of a family network. It is clearly a problem or issue that belongs to the world of Western culture and thought. It would not arise in the context of societies in Africa and even less in the world of Mediterranean first-century culture. The issue here in referring to James as "the brother of the Lord" is not to identify physical generation, but rather to show that he belongs to the same family network as Jesus. For these reasons one should respect the wider context of society of that time and see the term as referring to someone who belongs to a wider family network.

What do we know about this James "the brother of the Lord" from the rest of the New Testament? Since references to him emerge in almost all New Testament traditions, he obviously exercised an important role within the early church.

The Gospels: James does not feature much in the gospels. He is identified as a member of Jesus' family: "Is not this the carpenter, the son of Mary and the brother of James and Joses and Judas and Simon, and are not his sisters here with us? And they took offense at him" (Mark 6:3; cf. Matt 13:55). Who are those who took offense at Jesus? At first sight it appears that it is the family of Jesus, but a careful examination of the context of the account shows that those who posed the question are the ones who take offense at him. The quotation of the saying "Prophets are not without honor, except in their hometown, and among their own kin, and in their own house" (Mark 6:4) reinforces this perspective. The presence of Jesus' family is perhaps an indication that they were part of his circle of followers (see Painter [1999] 31–33).

A further significant reference to the family of Jesus is found in the Gospel of John: "So his brothers said to him, 'Leave here and go to Judea so that your disciples also may see the works you are doing; for no one who wants to be widely known acts in secret. If you do these things, show yourself to the world.' (For not even his brothers believed in him.)" (John 7:3-5). This passage has been largely responsible for the view that "the brothers of Jesus" were unbelievers during the course of his ministry. However, this evaluation is based on a lack of understanding of the main theme of John's Gospel. Throughout the course of his narrative John illustrates different aspects of belief in Jesus. The narrator's evaluation is a statement that says that during the course of the public ministry the "brothers" of Jesus did not have true or "authentic" faith (as Painter {[1999] 16} expresses it). Only later the power of the risen Christ brought them to this true belief. That is not to say that during the ministry of Jesus they did not have some level of faith, although it was not the fullness of true discipleship. If Jesus questions the disciples at this point, we should hesitate before concluding that the narrator's comment in 7:5 indicates that the brothers were total unbelievers. As was the case with the disciples themselves, the faith of "the brothers of Jesus" was an inadequate faith, but that still presupposes they had some measure of faith. They were, as in Mark's Gospel, present with Jesus in Galilee. Only the encounter with the risen Christ would transform their faith. Contrary to the view that "the brothers of Jesus" were unbelievers during his ministry, a careful assessment of the sparse references to them in the gospels reveals that this assumes too much. Like the disciples they were struggling to make sense of the person and ministry of Jesus. They did not reject Jesus, but continued to follow him.

The Acts of the Apostles: James appears on three significant occasions in the course of this narrative. The beginning of the narrative notes that "Mary, the mother of Jesus, as well as his brothers" (Acts 1:14) were among those who had gathered in prayer awaiting the gift of the Spirit. James is first introduced by name into the narrative only after the death of another James, the son of Zebedee (Acts 12:2), and Peter's escape from prison (12:6-17). Before leaving Jerusalem, Peter instructs the believers: "Tell this to James and to the brothers" (12:17). From this point on James assumes the leadership of the Jerusalem community. At the Council of Jerusalem James's voice was decisive for accepting the Gentile mission and laying out the basic freedom of Gentile believers from the stipulations of the Jewish Law (Acts 15:13-21). James initiates the sending out of a letter to believers throughout the world explaining this decision and the four requirements that Gentile believers were to uphold (15:20). At the end of the narrative James appears again in relationship to Paul's final appearance in Jerusalem (21:17-26). Paul meets with James and the elders, who all glorify God for God's actions among the Gentiles (21:20). Luke's picture is one of harmony between Paul and the Jerusalem leadership. They advise Paul to undertake a ritual purification in the Temple in order to allay the concerns, not of the Jerusalem leadership, but of many of the believers from the house of Israel about Paul's allegiance to the traditions of his people. James is clearly the leading figure in the Jerusalem Church; hence the designation "James of Jerusalem" is clearly an appropriate way to distinguish this James from others who bear the same name.

The Letters of Paul: The first reference to James in Paul's correspondence occurs in the letter to the Galatians, where James is mentioned on three occasions. Paul says that he first went up to Jerusalem three years after his conversion, and the only apostle he saw was "James the Lord's brother" (Gal 1:19). Here Paul includes James among the leaders of the Jerusalem Church, and he further identifies him as an apostle. In Gal 2:1

Paul notes that he went up to Jerusalem again fourteen years after his call and he identifies James, Cephas, and John as the pillars of the church (2:9). He also draws attention to the "right hand of fellowship" they offered him (2:9) by accepting his Gentile mission. No further demands were made on Paul's mission or message (2:6) beyond showing concern for the poor, something Paul was eager to do (2:10). Paul openly acknowledges their leadership in Jerusalem and in no way criticizes it. Finally, in Gal 2:11-14 Paul narrates a dispute he had with Peter in Antioch over table fellowship. Scholarship has used this passage to support an intense conflict between Paul and James, but a careful examination of the passage fails to support such an interpretation. Peter had openly eaten with Gentile believers, but after "certain people came from James" (2:12) Peter changed and would only eat with Christian Jews. Paul's criticism is of Peter's behavior, not of James's. It is difficult to see what role James actually played in this controversy. The most one can deduce about James's involvement is that his disciples objected to believers from the Gentile and Jewish worlds sharing a common table fellowship. Further, Paul does not associate James or the leadership in Jerusalem with the difficulties and opposition he encountered in Galatia and elsewhere over circumcision. In his first letter to the Corinthians, written a few years after the letter to the Galatians, Paul refers to James by naming him among the witnesses to the Risen Christ: "Then he appeared to James, then to all the apostles" (1 Cor 15:7). He implies that James is to be considered an apostle (in the same way as he, Paul, is an apostle: someone who has seen the risen Christ and been sent on a mission [1 Cor 9:1]). Paul concludes his consideration by acknowledging a unified harmony that exists between his message and those of the other apostles (including James): "Whether then it was I or they, so we proclaim and so you have come to believe" (1 Cor 15:11). This letter gives no indication of any tension between Paul and James or the Jerusalem leadership. Quite the reverse is the case: Paul and James continue to hand on a unified message. The conclusion to be drawn from this brief examination of Paul's presentation of James in his letters is one of harmony that upholds James's role and leadership. Nowhere does Paul identify James as the source of the opposition he encountered in his mission.

Summary: While it is difficult to harmonize the specific historical details in the Acts of the Apostles with the letters of Paul, particularly the letter to the Galatians, it is important to acknowledge the different rhetorical functions and theological visions the specific writings embrace and wish to communicate. While remaining conscious of this rhetoric, it nevertheless appears, as indicated from the above analysis, that Paul and James (together with the Jerusalem leadership) were more in harmony and in agreement with each other than in opposition (see Johnson [1995] 98).

Paul's focus was on the mission to the Gentiles while James's concern rested on preserving the mission to his own people.

Evidence from Beyond the New Testament Writings

The New Testament picture of James is enhanced in the developing tradition of extra-canonical writings, where his *persona* continued to exercise an important role. The following are among the more important writings in which the figure of James appears:

Josephus (37/38–101 C.E.) contains probably the most significant of the references in that he, a Jewish historian, narrates an account of James's death. Of interest in this account is his portrayal of James, which supports the basic historicity of the New Testament picture. He designates James as "the brother of Jesus" and leader of the Jerusalem Church, and says that he was stoned to death (*A. J.* 20:200). The high priest, Ananias the Younger, put a number of people to death for disregarding the Law during a period in between Roman procurators. This would be around 62 C.E.

Eusebius: The first historian of the Christian Church, Eusebius (ca 260–339 C.E.) provides a more developed account of James's death (*Hist. eccl.* 2:23, 4-18). Eusebius handed on a tradition he had received from Hegesippus (an early church writer [died ca. 180 C.E.]). James is presented as a truly righteous person. He is given the title "James the Just," a designation that was used throughout the early Christian world (excluding the New Testament). James 5:6 ("the righteous one") could possibly be the origin for this title. In this account, because of his intense prayers on behalf of his people his knees became calloused like those of a camel. Eusebius further says that James was thrown from the pinnacle of the Temple on the feast of Passover for his refusal to deny Jesus, and that the future Roman emperor, Vespasian, began his siege of Jerusalem following James's death. There are obviously numerous legendary details in this account, but it does demonstrate the continued importance and authority that the figure of James exercised within the Christian Church.

The Gnostic Writings: The importance of the figure of James emerges in a number of Gnostic writings. Particularly in the Nag Hammadi Library discovered in Egypt in 1945, the figure of James plays a significant role. In the *Gospel of Thomas* the authority of James is acknowledged very strongly: "The disciples said to Jesus, 'We know that you will depart from us. Who (then) is to be our leader?' Jesus said to them, 'Wherever you are, you are to go to James the Just, for whose sake heaven and earth came into being'" (Logion 12*). In another writing known as the *Letter* (or *Apocryphon*) *of James* the author identifies himself as James and says that he is sending out a "secret book" (*apocryphon*) that had been revealed to himself and Peter. In this writing James is the leader of Jesus' followers in Jerusalem.

Entrusted with a secret knowledge, he now communicates it to them. Other writings from the Nag Hammadi collection include the *First* and *Second Apocalypses of James*. These are writings in which James receives a special revelation in the course of dialogues with the risen Jesus. In the *First Apocalypse* James is referred to as "the brother of the Lord" as well as "the Just." The *Second Apocalypse* records another account of James's death together with a discourse that contains a revelation received from the risen Jesus. These writings span a period stretching from the beginning of the second to the end of the third century and show the important authority the figure of James exercised in the ongoing development of the early Christian Church.

The Gospel of the Hebrews, the Protevangelium of James, and the Pseudo-Clementine Literature: These writings give further witness to the importance of the figure of James in early Christianity. The information they contain does not add much to the portrait of James. What they do show is how the developing tradition is being shaped by certain ideological concerns. James is identified as "the Just" and is above all the recipient of a special revelation. This literature shows that certain centers within the developing Christian tradition continued to appropriate the figure of James for themselves to give support to their tradition.

Evidence from the Letter of James

From the letter the following information can be deduced about the implied author:

The writer presumes the hearers/readers know his identity: The author did not find it necessary to identify himself beyond stating that he was "a slave of God and of the Lord Jesus Christ" (1:1). This implies that he is well known to his hearers/readers despite the fact that many people bore the name James in the early Christian communities. He is also someone who holds a position of leadership. He advises and admonishes his hearers/readers and thereby presumes that they respect his views and accept his leadership. He does not exercise his role with domination, but speaks in a way that stresses the bonds that exist between them. "My brothers (and sisters)" is a familiar refrain that identifies almost every new section he introduces. He also identifies himself as a teacher and notes the heavy responsibilities placed upon every teacher of the word (3:1).

He was at home in the world of the traditions of Israel: The letter of James continues to reflect upon and use the thoughts and traditions of Israel. The author is heir above all to the Hebrew wisdom tradition and his letter reflects the concrete thought and expression so characteristic of the Hebrew Scriptures rather than the more abstract thought patterns of the Hellenistic world. Concepts such as the Law, wisdom, and perfection all have their roots in the world of Israel. See especially *Excursus 2: James and the Heritage of Israel* for a perspective that shows James's debt to the world of Judaism.

The author is also at home within the world of nascent Christianity: As will be shown in *Excursus 4: James and the Heritage of Jesus,* James is undoubtedly the real heir to the message and vision of Jesus. He shows how close he is to both Jesus' thought and vision. He remains especially true to Jesus' central vision in his concern for the poor. At the same time he uses the Jesus sayings traditions as a means to communicate his own advice. The author shows the closest affinity to the Matthean Sermon on the Mount.

The relationship with Paul: The supposed animosity between Paul and James is a false ideological imposition on Paul's letters. Further examination of what James says on the relationship between faith and works (see *Excursus 7: Faith and Works in James and Paul*) demonstrates that he is not writing against Paul's thought. In fact, he addresses a different aspect of the issue. It is the understanding of this commentary that James's treatment of the topic of faith and works must be interpreted within the framework of his own argument and the thought development of the letter. Those scholars who see it as an attack on Paul's understanding of "justification through faith alone" are influenced by an ideological perception that wishes to see everything in the New Testament as related to Paul and his thought.

The language of the letter: According to the general judgment of scholars the letter of James is written in excellent Greek (e.g., Ropes 24–27; Mayor ccvi–cclix; Mussner [1981] 26–33). This quality can be immediately seen in a close examination of the opening verses (1:2-4): Sentences develop through the use of subordinate clauses introduced by conjunctions *(hotan, hina)* and participial constructions *(ginōskontes, leipomenoi).* The author intentionally uses alliteration throughout the letter and shows a desire to achieve a type of rhythm through the separation of adjectives from the nouns they qualify *(peirasmois perimesēte poikilois).* His thought develops toward a climax: *testing, endurance, perfection.* The use of catch-phrases to connect the different pericopes is a key feature of this letter and is observable here in Jas 1:2-4: *chairein* (1:1) and *charan* (1:2).

The vocabulary of James consists of some 570 words, of which about 73 do not occur in the rest of the New Testament (see Ropes 25). James knew and used the LXX throughout (e.g., 1:10-11 is based on Isa 40:6-8 LXX). The style of the LXX permeates the letter, giving it what Ropes calls "a distinct Biblical flavour" (26).

These features make it virtually certain that the letter of James was not an Aramaic original later translated into Greek, as some scholars had argued (see the detailed discussion in Mayor cclx–cclxviii). Instead, it was composed in Greek by someone with an excellent proficiency in that language.

Some scholars have been convinced that the quality of the Greek is such that someone born in Palestine, as James was, could not have composed it (e.g., see Dibelius: "Nor does the language of our text point to an author who spent his life as a Jew in Palestine" [17], and Ropes 50). However, recent research has demonstrated the great extent to which Hellenistic culture and especially the use of the Greek language had influenced Palestine over a long period beginning with the conquests of Alexander the Great. Galilee showed a wider use of Greek and greater influence of Greek culture than the rest of Palestine. Archaeological studies of cities such as Sepphoris have demonstrated how much Greek had influenced the Israelite way of life (see Eric Meyers et al., "Sepphoris, 'Ornament of all Galilee,'" *BA* 49 [1986] 4–19).

An interesting work by Jan Nicolaas Sevenster *(Do You Know Greek? How Much Greek Could the First Jewish Christians Have Known?)* has helped to clarify this issue (3-21). He examined specifically the letter of James and came to the conclusion that the knowledge and usage of Greek that the letter of James demonstrates is such that it would certainly have been at home in first-century Palestine. As he says: "Even though absolute certainty cannot be attained on this point, in view of all the data made available in the past decades the possibility can no longer be precluded that a Palestinian Jewish Christian of the first century A.D. wrote an epistle in good Greek" (191). Joseph B. Mayor has also noted that a number of important Greek philosophers and rhetoricians emanated from Galilee shortly before the letter of James was written. The comments of Mayor are worth quoting:

> Not many years before, four of the most accomplished literary men of the time were natives of Gadara, Philodemus the Epicurean, a friend of Cicero and one of the poets of the Anthology, whose writings fill the larger part of the Herculanean scrolls; Theodorus the instructor of Tiberius in Rhetoric; Meleager, the famous writer of Epigrams and collector of the first Greek Anthology; and Menippus the Cynic, whose dialogues were imitated by Varro and Lucian . . . but these considerations may perhaps lead us to the conclusion that it was not more impossible for a peasant of Galilee to learn to write good Greek, than for one who had been brought up as a Welsh peasant to learn to write good English, or for a Breton to write good French . . . (lx–lxi).

A further point to bear in mind is that the early Christian community in Jerusalem shows evidence of having a strong Greek-speaking presence from the beginning. The Acts of the Apostles shows one of the initial controversies within that community revolving around concern for the equal treatment of Hebrew-speaking and Greek-speaking followers of Jesus (Acts 6:1-7). Also, the community in Jerusalem was concerned about maintaining close ties and connections with the believers who had migrated to Antioch (Acts 11:19-26). Again Greek would be the necessary bond that would maintain those connections.

Conclusion: James of Jerusalem as Author

The above examination points the way toward a solution regarding the authorship of this letter. Arguments that tried to see the letter as originally a work emanating from the world of Judaism are to be excluded on the basis of the strong connection this letter shows to the Jesus traditions. Further, this letter was not originally a translation from an Aramaic source; it was composed in Greek by someone whose fluency in Greek was excellent.

The major argument against James of Jerusalem as the author of this document has been that the letter is reacting to Paul's thought. This stems from the notion that everything in the New Testament derives its significance from Paul's position and thought, not from any evidence within the text. Further arguments against James of Jerusalem's authorship have emanated from the preconceived idea that his knowledge of Greek would not have been sufficient (see Brown [1997] 741).

An early date for this writing is required from the evidence noted above, namely (1) the way the author refers to himself, expecting his hearers/readers to know his identity; (2) the closeness of the author to the heritage of Israel (he still sees himself as belonging to that world); (3) the use made of the Jesus traditions (prior to the appearance of the canonical gospels); (4) the closeness to the spirit and vision of Jesus; (5) the total lack of reference to the Gentiles in any form; and (6) the omission of any reference to the destruction of the Temple at Jerusalem.

Taking all this into consideration, James of Jerusalem, "the brother of the Lord," remains the most reasonable candidate for the authorship of this writing. All the evidence converges to support what did become the tradition of the Christian Church over the course of the centuries. The question still remains: "How exactly do we understand James's authorship?" There are two ways to understand this evidence: in the first instance, just as Paul acknowledges the help of scribes in the writing or composition of his letters (see 1 Cor 16:21; Gal 6:11), so it is also most likely that James had the assistance of a scribe in the composition of his work. Such a view would also resolve the concerns of those who feel that James of Jerusalem would not have had the education necessary to be able to compose the quality of Greek that this letter demonstrates. This would still uphold the authority and voice of James of Jerusalem behind the letter.

In the second instance one could see the composition of the letter as having taken place shortly after the death of James at Jerusalem. A close associate of James with an excellent ability in Greek writes in his name to those Christian-Jewish communities in the Diaspora who recognized James's leadership and authority. Using the teaching of James and his message, the writer reminds his hearers/readers of James's teaching and vision so that they may remain true to the values and way of life that James handed on in fidelity to Jesus' teaching and so withstand the attractions of the world ("friendship with the world" [4:4]) to which they are being drawn. To my mind this solution gives the best account of all the available evidence. It will be in this sense that I refer to James as the author throughout the commentary.

In summary, the best reading of the evidence points to James of Jerusalem as the authority behind this circular or encyclical letter to believers from the world of Israel ("the twelve tribes in the Dispersion") found scattered throughout the Roman world. This letter is sent in the name of James shortly after his death in order to remind communities in the Diaspora of his teachings and the relevance they hold for building themselves up as "the first fruits of his (God's) creatures" (1:18). This would date the letter somewhere in the late sixties of the first century C.E.

5. *Addressees and Context of the Letter*

Martin Dibelius had argued that one could not deduce anything about the hearers/readers of this letter from the contents because of its nature as *paraenesis* (46). However, the examination of the genre of the letter has shown that, as a protreptic discourse, it aims at social formation. Its rhetorical purpose is to encourage hearers/readers to embrace a vision and values necessary for them to lead lives as members of the "twelve tribes in the Dispersion." The moral exhortation concerns issues that are important to give the hearers/readers identity and direction.

It is true that specific controversies and problems cannot be deduced from the letter of James as can be done with Paul's letters (such as the Corinthian correspondence). This does not mean that nothing can be said about the situation and context of the hearers/readers of this letter. The issues to which James draws attention are ones that were undoubtedly relevant to the communities that received the letter. From them we can derive a certain insight into their life and concerns.

Of first importance is the address to the "twelve tribes in the Dispersion" (see *Excursus 1: To The Twelve Tribes in the Dispersion*). This phrase refers in the literal sense to believers from the world of Judaism who are scattered outside Palestine throughout the Roman empire. In almost every city of the empire one would find ghettoes or communities of Jewish people among whom were some who had become believers in "the Lord Jesus Christ."

Josephus quotes the geographer Strabo as saying: "There were four classes in the state of Cyrene; the first consisted of citizens, the second of farmers, the third of resident aliens (metics), and the fourth of Jews. This people has already made its way into every city, and it is not easy to find any place in the habitable world which has not received this nation and in which it has not made its power felt" (*A. J.* 14:115 [Marcus, LCL]). Members of the house of Israel living in the Diaspora maintained their bonds with the land of Palestine by sending a yearly Temple tax to Jerusalem and by going to Jerusalem once in their lifetime to offer sacrifice in the Temple. The Acts of the Apostles illustrates this well when it lists those present in Jerusalem at the feast of Pentecost: "Parthians, Medes, Elamites, and residents of Mesopotamia, Judea and Cappadocia, Pontus and Asia, Phrygia and Pamphylia, Egypt and the parts of Libya belonging to Cyrene, and visitors from Rome, both Jews and proselytes, Cretans and Arabs . . ." (Acts 2:9-11).

Philo also showed how Jews were spread throughout the Roman world and identified the following places where Jewish people dwelt:

> Egypt, Phoenicia, Syria in general, and especially that part of it which is called Coelo-Syria, and also with those more distant regions of Pamphylia, Cilicia, the greater part of Asia Minor as far as Bithynia, and the furthermost corners of Pontus. And in the same manner into Europe, into Thessaly, and Boeotia, and Macedonia, and Aetolia, and Attica, and Argos, and Corinth and all the most fertile and wealthiest districts of Peloponnesus. And not only are the continents full of Jewish colonies, but also all the most celebrated islands are so too; such as Euboea, and Cyprus, and Crete (*Legat.* 281-282).

Just as people from the world of Judaism would look to Jerusalem as their spiritual home and feel a spiritual bond with their homeland, so also Christians from the world of Judaism would continue to look toward Jerusalem and Palestine as their spiritual homeland. James, as the leader of the Christian community in Jerusalem, would feel a certain bond with and responsibility for these believers living outside Palestine. This emerges from the picture presented by the Acts of the Apostles. At the Council of Jerusalem James directed a letter be sent throughout the Diaspora to communicate the decisions of the Council of Jerusalem (Acts 15:22-30). At the same time Paul notes that James asked him to take up a collection for the poor in Jerusalem (Gal 2:10). As with the Temple tax, this collection for the poor was a symbolic way of demonstrating a bond with Jerusalem.

What does the letter itself reveal about the hearers/readers? They are first of all people from the world of Judaism who have come to believe in Jesus as Lord and as Messiah/Christ (Jas 2:1). They uphold the Torah as the perfect law of liberty (1:25; 2:12). Abraham is referred to as "our father" (2:21) in a very straightforward way. The readers are well versed in the history and thought of Israel: references are made to the story of Job (5:11), the prophets (5:10), Elijah (5:17), and Rahab the prostitute (2:25). God is referred to by the title "Lord of hosts (Sabaoth)" (5:4). The place where they assemble is called the synagogue (2:2) and their approach to the taking of oaths is discussed (5:12). All this strengthens the view that the hearers/readers are from the world of Judaism.

While concrete situations cannot be deduced from this letter, nevertheless certain impressions do emerge. It appears that the communities who receive this letter are poor, and suffering at the hands of the rich. The letter refers to this theme on three occasions (2:1-7; 4:13-17; 5:1-6). Those addressed are communities of the poor, at the mercy of their rich neighbors. If the hearers/readers of this letter are Christian Jews living in Jewish ghettoes, it is quite possible that the rich oppressors are themselves Jewish.

This letter makes no mention at all of the Gentiles. Nothing is said about experiencing difficulties from them, or the need to evangelize them, or what to do in order to receive them into the community. The issues with which Paul grappled are not a concern to this writer. Neither are the concerns of 1 Peter felt here. For 1 Peter the Gentiles were indeed the ones who had laid false charges against Christians. That letter is deeply concerned that Christians be seen as valuable members of society: "Conduct yourselves honorably among the Gentiles, so that, though they malign you as evildoers, they may see your honorable deeds and glorify God when he comes to judge" (1 Pet 2:12). This is further support for seeing the letter of James as focusing exclusively within the context of the world of Judaism.

In summary, I see the letter stemming indirectly from James "the brother of the Lord" and written from Jerusalem to believers living in Jewish ghettoes throughout the Roman world. Sent as an encyclical letter, it was meant to speak to all those communities without being confined to just one. Antioch was the community that had the closest bonds with Jerusalem and the Christian leadership, and Antioch would have been one of the recipients of this letter, yet as a Diaspora letter its circulation went beyond just one community. When referring to "the community of James" throughout the commentary I understand it in the sense described above as referring to recipients that comprised in effect many communities spread throughout the Diaspora.

6. *Structure of the Letter*

The letter of James falls into three parts:

Introduction (1:1-27)

Following the epistolary opening, ch. 1 presents a twofold introduction. The two sections (1:2-11 and 1:12-27) begin respectively with: "Consider it nothing but joy . . ." *(charan hēgēsasthe . . .)* and "Blessed . . ." *(makarios)*. The opening lacks the customary thanksgiving section that is found in Paul's letters immediately following the opening address. However, Paul also deviated at times from strict adherence to this structure. For example, in the letter to the Galatians, in which Paul clearly feels an urgent need to address the issue at hand, the characteristic opening (Gal 1:1-5) is followed immediately by the body of the letter (1:6).

Five main themes emerge within the two opening pericopes in James 1: the testing of faith that produces steadfastness (in both passages: 1:2-4, 12-16), the gift of wisdom (1:5-8), rich and poor (1:9-11), control of one's speech (1:26), and being doers of the word (1:22-25). All these themes will be taken up again more than once in the body of the writing.

Body of the Letter (2:1–5:6)

While most scholars offer varying divisions for the structure of James, there are also some close agreements (see, e.g., Bauckham [1999] 61–69; Elliott [1993] 72–73). I follow here the structure I identified previously (Hartin [1991] 29–33) with some modifications. The major divisions of these chapters are easily discernible from markers James has built into the text. On many occasions he indicates that he is beginning a new section by addressing his hearers/readers directly as *adelphoi* ("brothers [and sisters]": see 2:1, 14; 3:1; 4:11; 5:7, 12). Twice he uses the prophetic address to warn his hearers/readers: *Age nun . . .* ("Come now . . .": see 4:13; 5:1). Attention to these markers allows us to divide the body of the letter of James into the following sections:

2:1-13	Do not Show Favoritism
2:14-26	Doers of the Word/Faith and Works
3:1-12	The Tongue and Speech
3:13–4:10	Call to Friendship with God
4:11-12	Speaking Evil against Another
4:13–5:6	Judgment on the Rich because of Friendship with the World

Conclusion to the Letter (5:7-20)

The letter concludes with a call to patient endurance as the hearers/readers wait for the Lord's coming (5:7-11), a further appeal to avoid the taking of oaths (5:12), and finally an admonition to pray for the needs of others (5:13-18). The theme of prayer acts as an inclusion with the opening of the letter (1:5-8), which introduced the theme of praying with full confidence of being heard. James concludes (5:19-20) with the theme of praying and working so that sinners may turn from their evil ways. Both 1 John 5:14-21 and Jude 17-25 conclude their letters with a similar theme of working and praying for the conversion of sinners.

7. Theological Vision

In Dibelius's view of the letter of James as a loose collection of sayings, "the admonitions . . . do not apply to a single audience and a single set of circumstances; *it is not possible to construct a single frame into which they will all fit*" (Dibelius [1976] 11). The consequence was to deny any possibility of discovering a comprehensive theological vision in the letter (ibid. 47–48). This view was to influence scholars for many decades. In recent times, with approaches that see the letter as more deliberately structured, there is increased interest in discovering the theological vision that inspires this writing. Especially from James's ethical admonitions and advice one is able to uncover an ethical belief system giving direction to that advice. To put it another way, this ethical advice is founded on a consistent and cohesive vision or belief. Sophie Laws offers an important insight into the foundation and direction for James's ethical advice: "What I have suggested so far is that the ways in which James speaks of God and of human conduct are so similar as to be likely to be connected, and that the connection would most easily be understood in terms of human conduct being ideally the imitation of God" (Laws [1982] 304).

James's rhetoric did not aim at presenting a well-developed theoretical understanding of faith. This author is more concerned with the way faith is expressed. As Lenski observed: "This entire epistle deals with *Christian faith*, and shows how this faith should be genuine, true, active, living, fruitful" (Lenski 538). James's concern is with how faith is lived, not how faith is intellectualized. "His purpose is practical rather than doctrinal" (Hiebert [1979] 223). From such a short writing, mainly concerned with practical ethical admonitions, it is, of course, not possible to discover a systematically worked out theology such as we find in Paul's writings or in any of the gospels. We can, however, derive some insights that contribute to understanding James's distinctive theological perspective. The intention here is not to try to give a comprehensive overview of the letter's theology. This theology will emerge in the course of the commentary, where attention will be drawn, particularly in the excursuses, to James's thoughts on theological aspects and themes such as suffering, perfection, wisdom, the Law, grace, friendship, the rich and the poor, faith and works. In this Introduction attention will be devoted to six aspects that lie at the foundation of James's theological vision, namely faith, God, Christ, eschatology, prayer, and social concern.

Faith

The letter's belief system emerges only indirectly. The rhetorical purpose of the letter is to offer a way of being in the world and to show believers how to lead their lives as members of the twelve-tribe kingdom (Hartin [1999] 96). This is evident from the way the concept of faith operates within the letter.

The noun *pistis* ("faith") occurs sixteen times in James (1:3, 6; 2:1, 5, 14[2x], 17, 18[3x], 20, 22[2x], 24, 26; 5:15), while the verb *pisteuein* occurs three times (2:19[2x], 23). Just as faith is central to the writings of Paul, so it is for the letter of James. We also note that the first theme to be introduced in this writing is that of the testing of one's faith (1:3) that leads through endurance to perfection (1:3-4). In a sense, as Hiebert suggests, "'The testing of your faith' (1:3) seems to be the key which James left hanging at the front door, intended to unlock the contents of the book" (Hiebert [1979] 224).

When referring to the testing of faith James intends the faith of the community rather than simply individual faith. From the opening of the letter James shows that his concern rests primarily with the community rather than with the individual. This sets the parameters for the interpretation of the exhortations and moral advice James communicates. They are placed within a community context, showing the values and way of life that members of the twelve-tribe kingdom are to embrace.

For the letter of James faith means a total and complete trust in God that enables believers to withstand every form of testing and ultimately to survive the final eschatological test. This emerges clearly in 2:5 in the description of the faith of the poor: "Has not God chosen the poor in the world to be rich in faith and heirs of the kingdom that he has promised to those who love him?" The faith of the poor, their total trust and confidence in God, enables them to pass through trials and testing and become fellow members of God's twelve-tribe kingdom, which will attain fulfillment in the future. This complete trust in God emerges in 1:6 in reference to prayer: "But let him ask in faith, never doubting. . . ." The person who prays does so with the firm trust and confidence that God will hear the prayer. The same is true in 5:15 where "the prayer of faith will save the hopelessly sick person, and the Lord will raise him up." In the context of suffering and illness a person's true faith emerges: "the prayer of faith" is addressed to God with the firm conviction and trust that God will respond to the prayer for healing.

The faith of Jesus Christ is also held up for emulation: "My brothers (and sisters), do not hold the faith of our glorious Lord Jesus Christ while showing acts of favoritism" (2:1). As the *Notes* and *Interpretation* to this verse will show, the phrase "the faith of our glorious Lord Jesus Christ" is to be understood as a subjective genitive, referring to the faith that Jesus Christ holds in his Father. It is a faith that demonstrates a total trust and confidence in the Father. For James, Jesus' whole life was an example of faithfulness that the believer is to emulate. His life and teaching bore witness to a commitment to the poor and marginalized within society and demonstrated an obedience to the Torah as exemplified above all in Leviticus 19 with its call to show a love of neighbor within the context of the injunction to avoid showing partiality to poor or rich (Lev 19:15-18).

Above all, faithfulness and trust in God must be illustrated in actions. One's deeds and total way of life demonstrate trust in and commitment to God: "My brothers (and sisters), what good does it do if someone claims to have faith but does not have works?" (2:14). For James "the works" are works of faith that illustrate the quality of a faith that emulates the faith of Jesus Christ. Total trust and confidence in God lead to a concern for others, particularly the poor in society. See *Excursus 7: Faith and Works in James and Paul* for a more detailed examination of how James understands the relationship between faith and works and how this differs from Paul's understanding.

God

The starting point for any theology is its understanding of God. While the letter of James does not present a systematic treatment of God, it does presume much in common with its audience. There is what social-scientific methodology terms "a high context compression" in that so much is shared with the hearers/readers that there is no necessity to actually spell out their common views: they presume a common understanding. Without doubt the letter of James has an understanding of God that fits into the world and belief of first-century C.E. Judaism. The entire theology is *theocentric* rather than *Christocentric* (Johnson [1995] 164). While the name of Jesus occurs only twice (1:1; 2:1), the references to God are far more frequent: e.g., *(ho) theos* ("God") occurs sixteen times (1:1, 5, 13[2x], 20, 27; 2:5, 19, 23[2x]; 3:9; 4:4[2x], 6, 7, 8); *kyrios* ("Lord") occurs eleven times, referring to God on six occasions (1:7; 4:10, 15; 5:4, 10, 11) and to Jesus on five (1:1; 2:1; 5:7, 14, 15), while *patēr* ("Father") occurs three times (1:17, 27; 3:9). The title of *nomothetēs kai kritēs* ("lawgiver and judge") is also given to God (4:12).

The Jewish profession of faith in God as one *(Shema Israel)* is presumed. The world of evil is subordinated to God and even demons acknowledge the oneness of God: "You believe that God is one. You do well! Even the demons believe—and shudder!" (2:19). This leads James to stress the theme of submission to God throughout the letter. A clear choice is presented before the reader between friendship with God and friendship with the world (4:4). One is called to submit to God and shun the forces of evil: "Therefore submit to God. But resist the devil and he will flee from you. Draw near to God and he will draw near to you. Cleanse your hands, you sinners, and purify your hearts, you double-minded!" (4:6-8).

God is compassionate and merciful (5:11). The goodness of God emerges as a fundamental tenet of James's faith. This leads James to distance God clearly from evil either in the sense that God causes evil or that God tempts people to perform evil. "Let no one say when tested, 'I am being tempted by God.' For God is not tempted by evil, and he himself tempts no one" (1:13). Laws comments insightfully on this passage: "What must be understood is that temptation is an impulse to sin, and since God is not susceptible to any such desire for evil he cannot be seen as desiring that it be brought about in man" ([1980] 71). For James, God is the giver of all good gifts, especially the gift of wisdom: "But if any of you is lacking in wisdom, let him ask God who gives to everyone without hesitation and without reproach, and it will be given him" (1:5).

As the Father of Lights God is understood as creator of the world: "Every good act of giving and every perfect gift is from above, coming down from the Father of lights with whom there is no variation or shadow of change" (1:17). God's nature is such that God's generosity never wavers. It belongs to the very nature of God, the creator of the world, to be always generous. This contrasts with the world. While God is always steadfast and unchangeable, the creation on the contrary is always fickle and changeable. "The affirmation is that to send good gifts belongs to God's unvarying nature. In this he is unlike the sun, which sends now the full light of noon, now the dimness of twilight, and which at night sends no light at all. God's light ever shines; from him proceeds no turning shadow" (Ropes 161).

God is also creator of the human person, who is created in God's own image: ". . . human beings made in God's likeness" (3:9). The consequences are enormous for humanity. Every person is made in God's image. This means that everyone strives to act like God. Since the basic tenet of the letter is that of putting faith into action, believers endeavor to imitate God in their every action. This imitation occurs in two fundamental ways: in the first instance God is described as giving "to everyone without hesitation and without reproach" (1:5). God is unchangeable and single-minded in what God does for humanity. This is contrasted with the human being who is "double-minded, vacillating in all his ways" (1:8). The believer must also be single-minded in all that she or he does.

In the second instance God is portrayed as the champion of the poor. For James, as for the prophets, God is the God of social justice (Mussner [1981] 98). In defining religion James says: "Religion that is pure and undefiled before God (who is) also Father is this: to care for orphans and widows in their affliction, and to keep oneself unstained from the world" (1:27). Just as the prophets called their hearers to a religion that embraced social justice, so James does likewise. The motivating vision behind his conception of religion is the way God acts toward us. God is the champion of the poor, and those who imitate God act in like manner. This way of life must embrace a concern for the poor (5:1-6), the avoidance of every form of discrimination (2:1-7), concern for those who are ill (5:13-18), and the bringing back of a brother or sister who wanders from the truth (5:19-20).

Christ

In comparison to what James had to say about God the Father, the letter says very little directly about Jesus Christ. Jesus is present in this writing in three ways:

(1) James mentions Jesus twice *directly*, in 1:1 and 2:1, proclaiming that Jesus is the "glorious Lord" (2:1). He is the Messiah whose message has been authenticated when the Father raised him to glory. This is an indirect reference to the resurrection of Jesus. Jesus is alive now and his message continues to resonate through the lives of his followers. There is no reference to the death of Jesus in the letter. This shows that unlike the theology of Paul, James's theology is not based on Jesus' death but rather on his teaching, which bears witness to God's action in the lives of those who faithfully follow that teaching. Just as the Father raised Jesus to life, so God will bestow life on those who put their faith into action.

(2) James refers to Jesus on a number of occasions *indirectly*. While most often the title "Lord" is used to refer to God, on three occasions Jesus is referred to as Lord: twice in the context of the anointing of the sick ("Is anyone of you sick? Let that person call on the elders of the assembly and let them pray over him, anointing him with oil *in the name of the Lord*. And the prayer of faith will save the hopelessly sick person, and *the Lord will raise him up*" [5:14-15]). "In the name of the Lord" undoubtedly refers to Jesus, as it does in 2:7 ("the excellent name that was invoked over you"). The further reference ("the Lord will raise him up") echoes the language

of the gospels and Acts, where this phrase occurs frequently in the context of Jesus' miracles: Jesus "raises up" *(egerei)* the sick and grants both physical and spiritual healing. It also refers to the future, when the Lord Jesus raises the person to fullness of life in the future resurrection (5:20) (see the Notes on Jas 5:14-15). Finally, in reference to "the coming of the Lord" (5:7-8) the implication is the return of Jesus at the end of time. Certainly this phrase can be understood either as a reference to the Father or to Jesus; however, in this particular context it appears to refer to the coming of Jesus (see the Notes on 5:7-8).

(3) Jesus is referred to *indirectly through the words and sayings* James draws upon to hand on his instruction. As will be argued (see *Excursus 4: James and the Heritage of Jesus*), James's thought and teaching are founded on Jesus' sayings, which he hands on in his own inimitable way. Jesus' fulfillment of the Law (as the Sermon on the Mount presents Jesus' role) is also reflected here in James's teaching. James instructs his hearers/readers to carry out the Law of freedom, the perfect Law, the royal Law. Through their obedience to the Torah they show their identity as members of the twelve-tribe kingdom that God has started to reconstitute. The believers are the first fruits of this new kingdom, which the Messiah Jesus has inaugurated through his life and teaching. This new kingdom will reach a culmination at the end of time. The Torah sets the boundary lines for the members of this new kingdom by highlighting the values its members are to carry out—values that set them apart from the world.

Eschatology

In the letter of James the prophetic, wisdom, and eschatological traditions all converge. This commentary will endeavor to draw attention to all three. While the genre of the writing has been identified as protreptic discourse that uses traditional wisdom material to communicate its vision, the eschatological dimension should not be ignored. The writing opens with a clear eschatological vision. The writer shows he belongs to the Jewish tradition that hopes for the restoration of God's people as the twelve-tribe kingdom. His hearers/readers belong to that new kingdom for which the people of Israel had been hoping for centuries. God's new creative activity begins with these Christian Jews as "the first fruits of his (God's) creatures" (1:18). This is the beginning of a process that will culminate in the future eschatological age at the end of time. This creative activity is meant to embrace all humanity.

Toward the conclusion of the letter (5:7-11) James turns to a vision of the end-time as he urges his hearers/readers to be patient while they wait for the coming of the Lord that is near (5:8). In this sense the letter situates itself within an eschatological framework where God's creative activity is already operative in bringing to birth the eschatological age that will burst more fully into reality in the not-too-distant future.

As Peter H. Davids says: ". . . eschatology is not the burden of the book; it is the context of the book. James shares a thought-world with his hearers/readers, so there is no need to give detailed instruction" (Davids [1982] 39). By opening and closing the writing with a conscious reference to the eschatological age James provides the horizon for communicating all the ethical wisdom instruction. The present acts as a preparation for this end-time. In 5:1-6 the writer condemns the rich for the way they have acted: they "stored up treasure in the last days" (5:3). The "coming of the Lord" (5:7) will bring salvation and judgment: judgment against those who have failed to put their faith into action and salvation for those whose lives follow the Law of the kingdom. The themes of judgment and salvation run throughout the letter. The rich are the ones who are the object of God's judgment: they fade away like a flower of the field (1:11). By contrast the poor are the heirs of God's kingdom (2:5). Even the sick are promised the eschatological gift of the forgiveness of sins (5:15). The life of every believer is oriented toward a future eschatological end of judgment or salvation.

In expressing his instruction within this eschatological horizon James is very restrained in his use of the apocalyptic imagination and language. He does not develop any of those elements so characteristic of apocalyptic thought. In another context I have proposed two reasons to explain why James deliberately distances himself from the use of apocalyptic language:

> First of all, the usual apocalyptic signs of the end are missing. James is convinced that the eschatological age is upon them with the "Judge standing at the doors!" (5:9); however, those elements that belong to a truly apocalyptic era are absent. This leads James to a reinterpretation of the apocalyptic signs. The ordinary sufferings of the present are reinterpreted as signs of the end. . . .
>
> Secondly, despite the view that the coming age does bring with it judgment, the ethos of the whole epistle is that this coming age is to be approached not with fear and trepidation, but with joy and happiness as the letter itself opens: "Count it all joy" . . . (Hartin [1996b] 495).

Without doubt James shares with his contemporaries a common apocalyptic worldview. These thought patterns do not distract from his primary goal of providing moral instruction for his hearers/readers on how they are to put their faith into action in the present. The coming of the Lord provides the motivation for James's advice on how to conduct life in the present and gives the ethical advice meaning and direction.

Prayer

James often gives attention to the theme of prayer throughout this short letter and shows a very specific approach to it. He appears to have Jesus' teaching in mind when he speaks about prayer: "Ask, and it will be given you; search, and you will find; knock, and the door will be opened for you" (Matt 7:7; Luke 11:9). From experience James knows that not all prayers are answered. He gives two reasons to explain this. His solution is not to deny the promise of Jesus, but rather to draw attention to certain implied conditions that are necessary for granting this promise.

Prayer must first of all be made by someone who has a wholehearted commitment to God. True prayer is offered to God "in faith, never doubting" (1:6), and God will give "to everyone without hesitation and without reproach . . ." (1:5). On the other hand, there is the double-minded person who does not receive what he asks because he is "vacillating in all his ways" (1:8). This shows that prayer demands an absolute confidence and trust in God.

A second condition for the fulfillment of Jesus' promise emerges in Jas 4:3: "You ask and you do not receive because you ask wickedly in order to spend it on your desires." For James the true object of prayer is the gift of wisdom: "If any of you is lacking in wisdom, let him ask God . . ." (1:5). The double-minded, on the other hand, are only concerned about themselves and their own desires. Their concern is not with the will of God, but with the pleasures that come from the world. Once again the contrast between friendship with God and friendship with the world is evident. Only friends of God will have their requests answered. As true friends they wish God's will to be done, not their own. The importance of carrying out God's will is exemplified in the instructions given to the merchants who carry on business operations without reference to God: "Instead of this you ought to say, 'If the Lord wishes, we will both live and do this or that'" (4:15). In all prayer God's sovereign will must be paramount.

Finally, 5:13-18 reflects the important role of prayer within James's community. These final verses show great confidence in the power of prayer to heal individuals and the community spiritually and physically. Prayer is to be made in faith by those who are sick as well as by the community on their behalf (5:13-14). Communal prayer and the ritual of anointing will bring the sick person healing. Prayer is made not only for physical healing but also for spiritual healing, for the forgiveness of sins (5:16). The concluding verses draw attention to further qualities of prayer: it should be fervent, constant, and persistent (5:17-18).

Prayer becomes another social marker that identifies the members of James's community and separates them from the wider society. The members of this community pray in this way and through prayer experience their identity in relationship with God and with one another.

A Theology of Social Concern

James's hearers/readers are faced with a fundamental choice between friendship with the world and friendship with God (4:4). This choice expresses itself in the values that give identity to those who live in friendship with God. Their values stem ultimately from God, and are expressed concretely in the Torah (the Law), the manifestation of God's will for humanity. Chief among the values one is to emulate is God's concern for the poor as is demonstrated in the context of Leviticus 19, which is a central inspiration behind the ethical admonitions of James (see Johnson [1982]). The royal Law "You shall love your neighbor as yourself" (Jas 2:8, quoting Lev 19:18) occurs in the context of Leviticus 19 where the Mosaic tradition calls for a concern for the poor. Partiality or discrimination against the poor is an issue that James specifically attends to in 2:1-7, and it is one the prophets constantly addressed in their oracles and admonitions. God's concern for the poor is a belief common to the writings of the Hebrew and Christian Scriptures and provides the model for how believers are to act. Concern for the poor is a concrete way of imitating God.

Just as the prophets did in the past, James speaks out against the social evils of his day (see his criticism of the merchants [4:13-16] and the rich [5:1-6]). In particular James identifies a number of issues of social injustice, such as the withholding of the daily wages due to the laborers (5:4) and murdering the righteous one (5:6). While these passages are harsh in condemnation, the letter of James is by and large a letter of consolation. James encourages his hearers/readers to turn to God, who is on the side of the oppressed and the poor. James teaches the poor to turn to God for redress in situations of suffering and discrimination. If God is on their side, God will ultimately come through for them. "The wages of the laborers who mowed your fields—which you held back by fraud—are crying out. And the cries of the harvesters have reached the ears of the Lord of hosts" (5:4). James's theology encourages believers to trust themselves to God's care. They are not to take matters into their own hands, but rather to allow God to be the one to respond to the situation.

James's definition of religion sums up succinctly his whole theological perspective: "Religion that is pure and undefiled before God (who is) also Father is this: to care for orphans and widows in their affliction . . ." (1:27). Believers must show a concern for the powerless in society ("orphans and widows" [see Deut 24:17]). Throughout the letter James illustrates how religion reaches out with a social concern (see especially 2:1-7). Here James closely resembles Jesus' teaching and spirit. Matthew 25:31-46 is a perfect example that emphasizes the social responsibility of one's relationship with Jesus. At the eschatological judgment Jesus shows that the separation between people will be based on their concern and response to the needs of others: "Truly I tell you, just as you did it to one of the least of these who are members of my family, you did it to me" (Matt 25:40).

The prominence given to this theme in such a short letter (1:9-11, 27; 2:1-7, 14-17; 5:1-6) is noteworthy. True piety and true religion embrace care for the poor and needy. James's teaching stresses a reversal of roles within the kingdom (1:9-10; 4:9-10; 5:1-6). The community experiences God's eschatological kingdom when it treats the poor with equality and with a love that reflects God's basic "option for the poor" (Maynard-Reid 98). Following the teaching of Jesus, James embraced an option for the poor and challenged his hearers/readers to make that choice their own. "The poor" probably reflects the background of James's community among the economically poor. It is a self-definition for his community: "Listen, my beloved brothers (and sisters). Has not God chosen the poor in the world to be rich in faith and heirs of the kingdom that he has promised to those who love him?" (2:5). The members of James's community are distinguished by two important social markers: their concern for the poor and the equality they all experience within the community whereby every form of discrimination is avoided.

8. *Outline of the Letter of James*

Introduction (1:1-27)

1. 1:1   Greetings
2. 1:2-11   Testing, Wisdom, and the Lowly
3. 1:12-27   Testing, Hearers and Doers of the Word

Body (2:1–5:6)

4. 2:1-13   Do Not Show Favoritism
5. 2:14-26   Doers of the Word/Faith and Works
6. 3:1-12   The Tongue and Speech
7. 3:13–4:10   Call to Friendship with God
8. 4:11-12   Speaking Evil against Another
9. 4:13–5:6   Judgment on the Rich because of Friendship with the World

Conclusion (5:7-20)

10. 5:7-11   Call to Patient Endurance
11. 5:12   Call to Avoid Taking Oaths
12. 5:13-18   Prayer
13. 5:19-20   The Great Commission

9. General Bibliography

More specialized references are included in the bibliographies that follow each section of the commentary. Books listed below and in the section bibliographies are referred to in the Introduction and throughout the commentary in an abbreviated form as follows: where reference is made to only one work of an author, the name and the page number alone are noted; where more than one work is listed, the date is also included.

I. Commentaries on James

Adamson, James B. *The Epistle of James.* NICNT. Grand Rapids: Eerdmans, 1976.

Barclay, William. *The Letters of James and Peter.* The Daily Study Bible. 2nd ed. Philadelphia: Westminster, 1960.

Blackman, Edwin C. *The Epistle of James.* TBC. London: SCM, 1957.

Calvin, John. *Commentaries on the Catholic Epistles.* Translated and edited by John Owen. Grand Rapids: Eerdmans, 1959.

Cantinat, Jean. *Les Épîtres de Saint Jacques et de Saint Jude.* SB. Paris: J. Gabalda, 1973.

Casciaro, José María and others, eds. *The Catholic Epistles: The Navarre Bible.* Dublin: Four Courts Press, 1992.

Chaine, Joseph. *L'Épître de Saint Jacques.* EBib. Paris: J. Gabalda, 1927.

Davids, Peter H. *The Epistle of James: A Commentary on the Greek Text.* NIGTC. Grand Rapids: Eerdmans, 1982.

Dibelius, Martin. *James: A Commentary on the Epistle of James.* Hermeneia. Translated by Michael A. Williams and edited by Helmut Koester. Philadelphia: Fortress, 1976; English translation of *Der Brief des Jakobus.* 11th ed. revised by Heinrich Greeven. Göttingen: Vandenhoeck & Ruprecht, 1964.

Frankemölle, Hubert. *Der Brief des Jakobus.* 2 vols. ÖTK 17,1 2. Gütersloh: Gütersloher Verlagshaus; Würzburg: Echter, 1994.

Hiebert, D. Edmond. *The Epistle of James: Tests of a Living Faith.* Chicago: Moody, 1979.

Hodges, Zane C. *The Epistle of James.* Irving, Texas: Grace Evangelical Society, 1994.

Hort, Fenton John Anthony. *The Epistle of St. James: The Greek Text with Introduction, Commentary as far as Chapter IV, Verse 7, and Additional Notes.* London: Macmillan, 1909.

Hubbard, David A. *The Book of James: Wisdom that Works.* Waco, Texas: Word Books, 1980.

Johnson, Luke Timothy. *The Letter of James.* AB 37A. New York: Doubleday, 1995.

Kistemaker, Simon J. *The New Testament Commentary: Exposition of the Epistle of James and the Epistles of John.* Grand Rapids: Baker Book House, 1986.

Kugelman, Richard. *James and Jude.* NTM 19. Wilmington: Michael Glazier, 1980.

Laws, Sophie. *A Commentary on the Epistle of James.* BNTC. London: Adam & Charles Black, 1980.

Martin, Ralph P. *James.* WBC 48. Waco, Texas: Word Books, 1988.

Marty, Jacques. *L'Épître de Jacques.* Paris: F. Alcan, 1935.

Mayor, Joseph B. *The Epistle of St. James. The Greek Text with Introduction, Notes and Comments, and Further Studies in the Epistle of St. James.* 2nd ed. London: Macmillan, 1897; reprint Grand Rapids: Zondervan, [1913], 1954.

Mitton, C. Leslie. *The Epistle of James.* Grand Rapids: Eerdmans; London: Marshall, Morgan & Scott, 1966.

Moffatt, James. *The General Epistles.* MNTC. London: Hodder & Stoughton, 1928.

Moo, Douglas J. *The Letter of James: An Introduction and Commentary.* TNTC. Grand Rapids: Eerdmans, 1985.

Mussner, Franz. *Der Jakobusbrief.* HTKNT 13/1. 4th ed. Freiburg: Herder, 1981.

The Navarre Bible. *The Catholic Epistles in the Revised Standard Version and New Vulgate with a Commentary by Members of the Faculty of Theology of the University of Navarre.* Dublin: Four Courts Press, 1992.

Perkins, Pheme. *First and Second Peter, James, and Jude.* Interpretation: A Bible Commentary for Teaching and Preaching. Louisville: John Knox, 1995.

Plummer, Alfred. *The General Epistles of St. James and St. Jude.* New York: A. C. Armstrong, 1903.

Reicke, Bo Ivar. *The Epistles of James, Peter, and Jude.* AB 37. Ed. William Foxwell Albright and David Noel Freedman. Garden City, N.Y.: Doubleday, 1964.

Ropes, James Hardy. *A Critical and Exegetical Commentary on the Epistle of St. James.* ICC 41. Ed. Charles A. Briggs, Samuel R. Driver, and Alfred Plummer. Edinburgh: T & T Clark, [1916] 1978.

Ross, Alexander. *The Epistles of James and John.* NICNT. Grand Rapids: Eerdmans, 1954.

Schlatter, Adolf. *Der Brief des Jakobus.* 2nd ed. Stuttgart: Calwer, 1956.

Schrage, Wolfgang, and Horst Robert Balz. *Die katholischen Briefe.* NTD 10. Göttingen: Vandenhoeck & Ruprecht, 1973.

Sidebottom, E. M. *James, Jude, 2 Peter.* NCBC. Grand Rapids: Eerdmans; London: Marshall, Morgan & Scott, 1967.

Stevenson, Herbert F. *James Speaks for Today.* London: Marshall, Morgan & Scott, 1966.

Stulac, George M. *James.* Downers Grove, Ill.: InterVarsity Press, 1993.

Tasker, R.V.G. *The General Epistle of James.* TNTC. 1st ed. Grand Rapids: Eerdmans; London: Tyndale Press, 1957.

Vouga, François. *L'Épître de Saint Jacques.* CNT 13A. Genève: Labor et Fides, 1984.

Wall, Robert W. *Community of the Wise: The Letter of James.* The New Testament in Context. Valley Forge, Pa.: Trinity Press International, 1997.

Williams, R. R. *The Letters of John and James.* CBC. Cambridge: Cambridge University Press, 1965.

Windisch, Hans. *Die katholischen Briefe.* Ed. Herbert Preisker. HNT 15. Tübingen: J.C.B. Mohr, 1951.

II. Studies on James

Abegg, Martin G. "Paul, 'Works of the Law,' and the MMT," *BAR* 20 (1994) 52–55.

Adamson, James B. *James: The Man and His Message.* Grand Rapids: Eerdmans, 1989.

Aland, Kurt. "Der Herrenbruder Jakobus und der Jakobusbrief," *TLZ* 69 (1944) 97–104.

Alonso-Schökel, Luis. "Literary Genres, Biblical." *NCE*. Ed. William J. McDonald. New York: McGraw-Hill, 1967, 8:803–809.

Bauckham, Richard J. *James: Wisdom of James, Disciple of Jesus the Sage*. London and New York: Routledge, 1999.

_____. "Review of P. J. Hartin, James and the Q Sayings of Jesus," *JTS* 44 (1993) 298–301.

_____. "The Study of Gospel Traditions outside the Canonical Gospels: Problems and Prospects," in David Wenham, ed., *Gospel Perspectives: The Jesus Tradition outside the Gospels*. Sheffield: JSOT Press, 1985, 5:369–403.

Brown, Raymond E. "The Epistle (Letter) of James," in idem, *An Introduction to the New Testament*. Anchor Bible Reference Library. New York: Doubleday, 1997, 724–47.

Bruce, Frederick F. *Peter, Stephen, James, and John: Studies in early Non-Pauline Christianity*. Grand Rapids: Eerdmans, 1979.

Buchanan, George W. "The Role of Purity in the Structure of the Essene Sect," *RQ* 4 (1963) 397–406.

Burchard, Christoph. "Zu Jakobus 2,14-26," *ZNW* 71 (1980) 27–45.

Cargal, Timothy B. *Restoring the Diaspora: Discursive Structure and Purpose in the Epistle of James*. SBLDS 144. Atlanta: Scholars, 1993.

Charue, André Marie. "Quelques Avis aux Riches et aux Pauvres dans l'Épître de St. Jacques," *Collationes Namurences* 30 (1936) 177–87.

Chester, Andrew, and Ralph P. Martin. *The Theology of the Letters of James, Peter, and Jude*. New Testament Theology. Cambridge: Cambridge University Press, 1994.

Chilton, Bruce, and Craig A. Evans, eds. *James the Just and Christian Origins*. NovTSup 98. Leiden: Brill, 1999.

Cranfield, Charles E. B. "The Message of James," *SJT* 18 (1965) 182–93, 338–45.

Crouzel, Henri. "L'Imitation et la 'Suite' de Dieu et du Christ dans les Premières Siècles Chrétiens, ainsi que Leurs Sources Gréco-Romaines et Hébraïques," *Jahrbuch für Antike und Christentum*. Münster, Westfalen: Aschendorffsche Verlagsbuchhandlung, 1978, 21:7–41.

Davids, Peter H. "James and Jesus," in David Wenham, ed., *Gospel Perspectives: The Jesus Tradition outside the Gospels*. Sheffield: JSOT Press, 1985, 5:63–84.

_____. "Palestinian Traditions in the Epistle of James," in Bruce Chilton and Craig A. Evans, eds., *James the Just and Christian Origins*. NovTSup 98. Leiden: Brill, 1999, 33–57.

Davies, William D., and Dale C. Allison. *A Critical and Exegetical Commentary on the Gospel according to Saint Matthew*. 3 vols. ICC 1–3. Edinburgh: T & T Clark, 1988–97.

Deppe, Dean B. *The Sayings of Jesus in the Epistle of James*. Dissertation, Free University of Amsterdam, 1989. Privately published: Chelsea, Mich.: Bookcrafters, 1989.

DuPlessis, Paul J. *TELEIOS: The Idea of Perfection in the New Testament*. Kampen: J. H. Kok, 1959.

Dyrness, William A. "Mercy Triumphs over Justice: James 2:13 and the Theology of Faith and Works," _Themelios_ 6 (1981) 11–16.

Edgar, David Hutchinson. _Has not God Chosen the Poor? The Social Setting of the Epistle of James._ Sheffield: Sheffield University Press, 2001.

Elliott, John H. "The Epistle of James in Rhetorical and Social Scientific Perspective: Holiness-Wholeness and Patterns of Replication," _BTB_ 23 (1993) 71–81.

Felder, Cain Hope. "Partiality and God's Law: An Exegesis of James 2:1-13," _JRT_ 39 (1982/3) 51–69.

Francis, Fred O. "The Form and Function of the Opening and Closing Paragraphs of James and 1 John," _ZNW_ 61 (1970) 110–26.

Frankemölle, Hubert. "Gespalten oder ganz: Zur Pragmatik der theologischen Anthropologie des Jakobusbriefes," in Hans-Ulrich von Brachel and Norbert Mette, eds., _Kommunikation und Solidarität._ Fribourg: Exodus, 1985, 160–78.

_____. "Zum Thema des Jakobusbriefes im Kontext der Rezeption von Sir 2,1-18 und 15,11-20," _BN_ 48 (1989) 21–49.

Fuller, Reginald H. "The Decalogue in the New Testament," _Int_ 43 (1989) 243–55.

Gammie, John G. "Paraenetic Literature: Toward the Morphology of a Secondary Genre," _Semeia_ 50 (1990) 41–77.

Geyser, Albert S. "The Letter of James and the Social Condition of his Addressees," _Neotestamentica_ 9 (1975) 25–33.

Hadidian, Dikran Y. "Palestinian Pictures in the Epistle of James," _ExpTim_ 63 (1952) 227–28.

Halson, B. R. "The Epistle of James: 'Christian Wisdom?'" _SE_ 4. Papers presented to the Third International Congress on New Testament Studies held at Christ Church, Oxford, 1965. Part I: The New Testament Scriptures, ed. F. L. Cross. Berlin: Akademie-Verlag, 1968, 308–14.

Harrington, Daniel J. _The Gospel of Matthew._ SP 1. Collegeville: The Liturgical Press, 1991.

Hartin, Patrick J. "James: A New Testament Wisdom Writing and its Relationship to Q." D.Th. Dissertation, University of South Africa: Pretoria, 1988.

_____. "James and the Sermon on the Mount/Plain," _SBLSP_ 28. Ed. David J. Lull. Atlanta: Scholars, 1989, 440–57.

_____. _James and the Q Sayings of Jesus._ JSNTSup 47. Sheffield: JSOT Press, 1991.

_____. "'Come Now, You Rich, Weep and Wail . . .' (James 5:1-6)," _JTSA_ 84 (1993) 57–63.

_____. "Call to be Perfect through Suffering (James 1,2-4): The Concept of Perfection in the Epistle of James and the Sermon on the Mount," _Bib_ 77 (1996a) 477–92.

_____. "The Poor in the Epistle of James and the Gospel of Thomas," _HvTSt_ 53 (1997) 146–62.

_____. _A Spirituality of Perfection: Faith in Action in the Letter of James._ Collegeville: The Liturgical Press, 1999.

Held, Heinz Joachim. "Glauben ohne 'Ansehen der Person': Zu Jakobus 2,1-13. Zugleich ein biblischer Beitrag zum Thema Diskriminierung," in Günther Metzger, ed., _Zukunft aus dem Wort._ Stuttgart: Calwer, 1978, 209–25.

Hengel, Martin. "Der Jakobusbrief als antipaulinische Polemik," in Gerald F. Hawthorne and Otto Betz, eds., _Tradition and Interpretation in the New Testament._ Grand Rapids: Eerdmans, 1987, 248–78.

Hoppe, Rudolf. *Der theologische Hintergrund des Jakobusbriefes.* FB 28. Würzburg: Echter, 1977.

Johnson, Luke Timothy. "The Use of Leviticus 19 in the Letter of James," *JBL* 101 (1982) 391–401.

_____. "The Social World of James: Literary Analysis and Historical Reconstruction," in L. Michael White and O. Larry Yarbrough, eds., *The Social World of the First Christians: Essays in Honor of Wayne A. Meeks.* Minneapolis: Fortress, 1995, 178–97.

Kee, Howard C. *Who are the People of God?* New Haven: Yale University Press, 1995.

Kirk, J. A. "The Meaning of Wisdom in James: Examination of a Hypothesis," *NTS* 16 (1969/70) 24–38.

Kittel, Gerhard. "Der geschichtliche Ort des Jakobusbriefes," *ZNW* 41 (1942) 71–105.

_____. "Der Jakobusbrief und die apostolischen Väter," *ZNW* 43 (1950) 54–112.

Klein, Martin. *"Ein vollkommenes Werk": Vollkommenheit, Gesetz und Gericht als theologische Themen des Jakobusbriefes.* Stuttgart: Kohlhammer, 1995.

Knox, Wilfred L. "The Epistle of St James," *JTS* 46 (1945) 10–17.

Lautenschlager, Marcus. "Der Gegenstand des Glaubens im Jakobusbrief," *ZTK* 87 (1990) 163–84.

Laws, Sophie. "The Doctrinal Basis for the Ethics of James," *SE* 7. Papers Presented to the Fifth International Congress on Biblical Studies Held at Oxford, 1973. Berlin: Akademie-Verlag, 1982, 299–305.

Limberis, Vasiliki. "The Provenance of the Caliphate Church: James 2.17-26 and Galatians 3 Reconsidered," in Craig A. Evans and James A. Sanders, eds., *Early Christian Interpretations of the Scriptures of Israel. Investigations and Proposals.* JSNTSup 148. Sheffield: Sheffield Academic Press, 1997, 397–420.

Lodge, John G. "James and Paul at Cross-Purposes? James 2,22," *Bib* 62 (1981) 195–213.

Longman, Tremper. "Form Criticism, Recent Developments in Genre Theory, and the Evangelical," *WTJ* 47 (1985) 46–67.

Lorenzen, Thorwald. "Faith without Works Does Not Count before God: James 2:14-26," *ExpTim* 89 (1978) 231–35.

Massebieau, Louis. "L'Épitre de Jacques, est-elle l'Oeuvre d'un Chrétien?" *RHR* 32 (1895) 249–83.

Maynard-Reid, Pedrito U. *Poverty and Wealth in James.* Maryknoll, N.Y.: Orbis, 1987.

Meyer, Arnold. *Das Rätsel des Jakobusbriefes.* BZNW 10. Giessen: Töpelmann, 1930.

Miller, Patrick D. "The Place of the Decalogue in the Old Testament and Its Law," *Int* 43 (1989) 229–42.

Mussner, Franz. "Die Idee der Apokatastasis in der Apostelgeschichte," in Heinrich Gross and Franz Mussner, eds., *Lex Tua Veritas. Festschrift für Hubert Junker zur Vollendung des siebzigsten Lebensjahres am 8. August 1961.* Trier: Paulinus-Verlag, 1961, 293–306.

_____. "Das Toraleben im jüdischen Verständnis," in Karl Kertelge, ed., *Das Gesetz im Neuen Testament.* QD 108. Freiburg: Herder, 1986.

_____. "Die ethische Motivation im Jakobusbrief," in Helmut Merklein, ed., *Neues Testament und Ethik.* Freiburg: Herder, 1989, 416–23.

Niebuhr, Karl-Wilhelm. *Gesetz und Paränese: Katechismusartige Weisungsreihen in der frühjüdischen Literatur.* Tübingen: J.C.B. Mohr [Paul Siebeck], 1987.

_____. "Weisheit als Thema biblischer Theologie," *KD* 44 (1998) 40–60.

Overman, J. Andrew. "The Diaspora in the Modern Study of Ancient Judaism," in idem and Robert S. MacLennan, eds., *Diaspora Jews and Judaism: Essays in honor of, and in dialogue with, A. Thomas Kraabel*. STSHJ 41. Atlanta: Scholars, 1992, 63–78.

Painter, John. *Just James: The Brother of Jesus in History and Tradition*. Minneapolis: Fortress, 1999.

Peck, George. "James 5:1-6," *Int* 42 (1988) 291–96.

Penner, Todd C. *The Epistle of James and Eschatology: Re-reading an Ancient Christian Letter*. JSNTSup 121. Sheffield: Sheffield Academic Press, 1996.

_____. "The Epistle of James in Current Research," *Currents in Research: Biblical Studies* 7 (1999) 257–308.

Perdue, Leo G. "Paraenesis and the Epistle of James," *ZNW* 72 (1981) 241–56.

_____. "The Wisdom Sayings of Jesus," *Forum* 2 (1986) 3–35.

_____. "The Social Character of Paraenesis and Paraenetic Literature," *Semeia* 50 (1990) 5–39.

Popkes, Wiard. *Adressaten, Situation und Form des Jakobusbriefes*. SBS 125/126. Stuttgart: Katholisches Bibelwerk, 1986.

_____. "The Composition of James and Intertextuality: an Exercise in Methodology," *ST* 51 (1997) 91–112.

_____. "James and Scripture: An Exercise in Intertextuality," *NTS* 45 (1999) 213–29.

Porter, Stanley W. "Is *dipsychos* (James 1:8; 4:8) a 'Christian' Word?" *Bib* 71 (1990a) 469–98.

_____. "Mt 6:13 and Lk 11:4: 'Lead us not into Temptation,'" *ExpTim* 101 (1990) 359–62.

Rhoads, David. "The Letter of James: Friend of God," *CurTM* 25 (1998) 473–86.

Seitz, Oscar J. F. "James and the Law," *SE* 2. Papers Presented to the International Congress on "The Four Gospels in 1957." Berlin: Akademie Verlag, 1964, 472–86.

Sevenster, Jan Nicolaas. *Do You Know Greek? How Much Greek Could the First Jewish Christians have Known?* NovTSup 19. Leiden: Brill, 1968.

Shepherd, Massey H. "The Epistle of James and the Gospel of Matthew," *JBL* 75 (1956) 40–51.

Spitta, Friedrich. "Der Brief des Jakobus," in idem, *Zur Geschichte und Litteratur des Urchristentums*. 3 vols. in 4. Göttingen: Vandenhoeck & Ruprecht, 1893–1907, 2 (1896):1–239.

Stagg, Frank. "Exegetical Themes in James 1 and 2," *RevExp* 66 (1969) 391–402.

Tamez, Elsa. *The Scandalous Message of James: Faith without Works is Dead*. New York: Crossroad, 1992.

Thomas, John Christopher. "The Devil, Disease, and Deliverance: James 5:14-16," *JPT* 2 (1993) 25–50.

Thyen, Hartwig. *Der Stil der jüdisch-hellenistischen Homilie*. FRLANT n.s. 47. Göttingen: Vandenhoeck & Ruprecht, 1955.

Tsuji, Manabu. *Glaube zwischen Vollkommenheit und Verweltlichung: Eine Untersuchung zur literarischen Gestalt und zur inhaltlichen Kohärenz des Jakobusbriefes*. WUNT 2nd ser. 93. Tübingen: J.C.B. Mohr [Paul Siebeck], 1997.

Van Voorst, Robert E. *The Ascents of James: History and Theology of a Jewish-Christian Community.* SBLDS 112. Atlanta: Scholars, 1989.

Verseput, Donald. "James 1:17 and the Jewish Morning Prayers," *NovT* 39 (1997) 177–91.

_____. "Reworking the Puzzle of Faith and Deeds in James 2:14-26," *NTS* 43 (1997) 97–115.

_____. "Genre and Story: The Community Setting of the Epistle of James," *CBQ* 62 (2000) 96–110.

Via, Dan Otto. "The Right Strawy Epistle Reconsidered: A Study in Biblical Ethics and Hermeneutics," *JR* 49 (1969) 253–67.

Vokes, Frederick E. "The Ten Commandments in the New Testament and in First Century Judaism," *SE* 5. Papers Presented to the International Congress on "The Four Gospels in 1957." Berlin: Akademie Verlag, 1968, 146–54.

Waanders, F.M.J. *The History of TELOS and TELEO in Ancient Greek.* Amsterdam: Grüner, 1983.

Wachob, Wesley Hiram. *The Voice of Jesus in the Social Rhetoric of James.* SNTSMS 106. Cambridge: Cambridge University Press, 2000.

Wall, Robert W. "James as Apocalyptic Paraenesis," *ResQ* 32 (1990) 11–22.

Wuellner, Wilhelm H. "Der Jakobusbrief im Licht der Rhetorik und Textpragmatik," *LB* 43 (1978) 5–66.

III. Texts

Ad C. Herennium: De Ratione Dicendi (Rhetorica ad Herennium). Translated by Harry Caplan. LCL. Cambridge, Mass.: Harvard University Press, 1954.

Aland, Barbara, and others. *Nestle-Aland: Novum Testamentum Graece.* 27th rev. ed., 2nd printing. *Apparatum criticum novis curis elaboraverunt Barbara et Kurt Aland una cum Instituto Studiorum Textus Novi Testamenti Monasterii Westphaliae.* Stuttgart: Deutsche Bibelgesellschaft, 1994.

_____. *The Greek New Testament.* 4th rev. ed. In cooperation with the Institute for New Testament Textual Research, Münster, Westphalia. Stuttgart: Deutsche Bibelgesellschaft/United Bible Societies, 1994.

_____. *Novum Testamentum Graecum. Editio Critica Maior. IV. Catholic Letters. Part 1 Text and Part 2 Supplementary Material. Installment 1: James.* Edited by the Institute for New Testament Textual Research. Stuttgart: Deutsche Bibelgesellschaft, 1997.

Apostolic Fathers. Vol. I. I Clement, II Clement, Ignatius, Polycarp, The Didache, Barnabas. Translated by Kirsopp Lake. LCL. Cambridge, Mass.: Harvard University Press, 1965.

Apostolic Fathers. Vol. II. The Shepherd of Hermas, The Martyrdom of Polycarp, The Epistle To Diognetus. Translated by Kirsopp Lake. LCL. Cambridge, Mass.: Harvard University Press, 1970.

Aristotle. *The 'Art' of Rhetoric.* Translated by John Henry Freese. LCL. Cambridge, Mass.: Harvard University Press, 1939.

Aristotle. *The Nicomachean Ethics.* Translated by R. W. Browne. London: Henry G. Bohn, 1950.

Aristotle in Twenty-Three Volumes. Vol. 17. The Metaphysics, Books 1–9. Translated by Hugh Tredennick. LCL. Cambridge, Mass.: Harvard University Press, 1989.

Augustine. *Grace and Free Will (De gratia et libero arbitrio). The Fathers of the Church.* Vol. 59. Translated by Robert Russell. Washington: The Catholic University of America Press, 1968.

Augustine. *The Writings of Saint Augustine. Letters. Vol. IV (165–203). The Fathers of the Church.* Vol. 12. Translated by Sister Wilfrid Parsons. New York: Fathers of the Church, Inc., 1955.

Charles, Robert H., ed. *The Apocrypha and Pseudepigrapha of the Old Testament in English with Introduction and Critical and Explanatory Notes to the Several Books.* Oxford: Clarendon Press, 1913.

Charlesworth, James H., ed. *The Old Testament Pseudepigrapha. Vol. 1. Apocalyptic Literature and Testaments.* Garden City, N. Y.: Doubleday, 1983.

Charlesworth, James H., ed. *The Old Testament Pseudepigrapha. Vol. 2. Expansions of the "Old Testament" and Legends, Wisdom and Philosophical Literature, Prayers, Psalms, and Odes, Fragments of Lost Judeo-Hellenistic Works.* London: Darton, Longman and Todd, 1985.

Cicero. *On Old Age and On Friendship.* Translated by Frank O. Copley. Ann Arbor: University of Michigan Press, 1967.

Denzinger, Henrici. *Enchiridion Symbolorum Definitionum et Declarationum de Rebus Fidei et Morum. Kompendium der Glaubensbekenntnisse und kirchlichen Lehrentscheidungen. 37. Auflage verbessert, erweitert, ins Deutsche übertragen von Peter Hünermann unter Mitarbeit von Helmut Hoping; herausgegeben von Peter Hünermann.* Freiburg: Herder, 1991.

Diogenes Laertius. Lives of Eminent Philosophers. Vol 2. Translated by R. D. Hicks. Cambridge, Mass.: Harvard University Press, 1958.

Epicurus. The Extant Remains with Short Critical Apparatus, Translation and Notes. Translated by Cyril Bailey. Oxford: Clarendon Press, 1926.

Epictetus. The Discourses as Reported by Arrian, The Manual, and Fragments. Vols. 1 and 2. Translated by W. A. Oldfather. Cambridge, Mass.: Harvard University Press, 1956–69.

Euripides. Vol. 2. Translated by Arthur S. Way. LCL. Cambridge, Mass.: Harvard University Press, 1939.

García Martínez, Florentino, ed. *The Dead Sea Scrolls Translated: The Qumran Texts in English.* Translated by Wilfred G. E. Watson. Leiden: Brill, 1994.

Herodotus. *Histories (Historiae).* Translated by A. D. Godley. LCL. Cambridge, Mass.: Harvard University Press, 1950.

Hippocrates. *Regimen in Health.* Vol. 4. Translated by W.H.S. Jones. LCL. Cambridge, Mass.: Harvard University Press, 1959.

Homer. *Iliad.* Vols. 1 and 2. Translated by A. T. Murray, revised by William F. Wyatt. LCL. Cambridge, Mass.: Harvard University Press, 1999.

Josephus. *Jewish Antiquities.* 9 vols. Translated by Ralph Marcus et al. LCL. Cambridge, Mass.: Harvard University Press, 1926-65.

Layton, Bentley. *The Gnostic Scriptures. A New Translation with Annotations and Introductions.* Garden City, N.Y.: Doubleday, 1987.

Liddell, Henry George, and Robert Scott. *An Intermediate Greek-English Lexicon.* 7th ed. Oxford: Clarendon Press, 1968.

Louw, Johannes P., and Eugene A. Nida. *Greek-English Lexicon of the New Testament Based on Semantic Domains.* Vol. 1. New York: United Bible Societies, 1988.

Lucian. *The Works of Lucian.* 8 vols. Translated by A. M. Harmon, K. Kilburn, M.D. Macleod, and others. LCL. Cambridge, Mass.: Harvard University Press, 1955–61.

Luther, Martin. *Luther's Works: Word and Sacrament I.* Vol. 35. Ed. T. Backmann. Philadelphia: Fortress, 1960.

Metzger, Bruce M. *A Textual Commentary on the Greek New Testament.* New York: United Bible Societies, 1975.

Moule, Charles F. D. *An Idiom-Book of New Testament Greek.* 2nd ed. Cambridge: Cambridge University Press, 1971.

New Revised Standard Version of the Bible: Catholic Edition. Nashville: Thomas Nelson, Catholic Bible Press, 1989.

Philo. *The Works of Philo.* Translated by Charles D. Yonge. Peabody, Mass.: Hendrickson, 1993.

Philostratus. *The Life of Apollonius of Tyana.* Translated by F. C. Conybeare. LCL. Cambridge, Mass.: Harvard University Press, 1960.

Plato. *The Dialogues of Plato. Vol. 1. The Apology and Other Dialogues.* Translated by Benjamin Jowett. London: Sphere Books, 1970.

Plato. Phaedrus. Translated with Introduction and Notes by Alexander Nehamas and Paul Woodruff. Indianapolis and Cambridge: Hackett Publishing Company, 1995.

Plato in Twelve Volumes. Vol. 1. Euthyphro, Apology, Crito, Phaedo, Phraedrus. LCL. Translated by Harold N. Fowler. Cambridge, Mass.: Harvard University Press, 1977.

Plato in Twelve Volumes. Vol. 6. The Republic. Translated by Paul Shorey. LCL. Cambridge, Mass.: Harvard University Press, 1980.

Plutarch. *Moralia.* 15 vols. Translated by Frank Cole Babbitt and others. LCL. Cambridge, Mass.: Harvard University Press, 1960–62.

Seneca Moral Essays. Vol. 1–3. Translated by John W. Basore. LCL. Cambridge, Mass.: Harvard University Press, 1958.

Sentences of Sextus. Translated by Richard A. Edwards and Robert A. Wild. Chico: Scholars, 1981.

Xenophon. Memorabilia and Oeconomicus. Translated by E. C. Marchant. LCL. Cambridge, Mass.: Harvard University Press, 1938.

Xenophon. Cyropaedia. Vol. 1. Translated by Walter Miller. LCL. New York: Macmillan, 1954.

Xenophon. Anabasis, Books 4–7; Symposium and Apology. Translated by O. J. Todd. Cambridge, Mass.: Harvard University Press, 1932.

Zerwick, Max. *Analysis Philologica Novi Testamenti Graeci.* 3rd ed. Rome: Pontifical Biblical Institute, 1966.

TRANSLATION, NOTES, INTERPRETATION

1. *Greetings* (1:1)

1. James, a slave of God and of the Lord Jesus Christ,
To the twelve tribes in the Dispersion:
Greetings.

NOTES

1. *James:* Many in the early Christian world were known as James. Only "James, the brother of the Lord" could identify himself with such simple authority (see the Introduction for a detailed discussion on authorship). The Greek word *Iakōbos* recalls the Hebrew *Jacob (ya'ăqōb)*, the father of the "twelve tribes of Israel." This gave rise to interpretations that viewed the writer as imitating works such as the *Testaments of the Twelve Patriarchs* (see Meyer [1930]). A major criticism of such views is that no father/son language appears in the letter of James.

slave of God: A thoroughly Hebrew term *('ebed)* expressing the relationship between God and God's people. It captures the concept of God's ownership of God's people and their willingness to carry out God's will. It emphasizes the qualities of obedience, loyalty, and service that mark the relationship. In the LXX the people of Israel are referred to as God's "slaves" *(douloi;* see Deut 32:36). Particularly in the Psalms people refer to themselves in the singular in relationship to God as "your slave" *(doulos sou;* see Ps 119:38 [Ps 118:38 LXX]; 143:12 [142:12 LXX]). The Hebrew Scriptures also designate certain individuals as God's *doulos:* Moses (1 Kgs 8:53, 56; Mal 3:24); David (1 Kgs 8:66); the prophets (Jer 7:25; Amos 3:7). In the New Testament writings the term continues to be used with the same notion of obedience and dedication to God's service. Jesus is referred to as God's *doulos* in Phil 2:7, as are believers in general (1 Pet 2:16), the prophets (Rev 10:7), and the apostles (Acts 4:29). In the opening of some of his letters Paul refers to himself as *doulos* (see Phil 1:1; Titus 1:1; Gal 1:10). In this vein James presents himself to his hearers/readers as one whose whole aim is to carry out God's will. While elsewhere in the New Testament James may be referred to as "the brother of the Lord," this is not the designation he chooses for himself. Instead he selects a term that captures the essence of the relationship between God and the believer.

49

and of the Lord Jesus Christ: Jesus is identified by name on only two occasions in this letter (1:1; 2:1). This led Massebieau (249–83) and Spitta (1–239) to advance the theory that the letter of James was originally a writing stemming from the world of Israel, later Christianized through the insertion of a twofold reference to Jesus (1:1; 2:1). Such a theory fails to take account of this letter's closeness to Jesus' thought and sayings, which permeate the writing. Furthermore, no manuscript evidence can be given to support such a theory. The Greek nouns *theos* and *kyrios* are both without the article. This has led some scholars to see the phrase as referring solely to Jesus: "Jesus Christ, God and Lord" (e.g., Vouga, "Jésus-Christ, Dieu et Seigneur," 35). For Jesus to be described in such an unequivocal way as God would be extremely unusual in the context of the New Testament writings, especially if the letter of James is judged to be a relatively early writing (see the Introduction). Some manuscripts try to remove the ambiguity by identifying God as "Father" *(patēr)*. This is clearly not the original text, but an interpretation. James is a slave both of God (as Father) and Jesus (as Lord), which implies an equality between God (as Father) and Jesus (as Lord), but their exact relationship is not discussed in any depth. In calling Jesus "Lord" James reflects a practice found in very early Christian liturgical texts: "Come, Lord Jesus!" (Rev 22:20) and "Our Lord, come!" (1 Cor 16:22). The LXX used the noun *kyrios* for God. In the New Testament it gradually becomes a title applied to Jesus showing a growing consciousness and confession of Jesus as God. In the letter of James the term *kyrios* is used sometimes in reference to Jesus and other times in reference to God (Father). Only the context can decide. The noun *christos* is the Greek form of the Hebrew word Messiah, meaning Anointed One. This title indicates that the hearers/readers belong to a messianic movement that sees in Jesus the fulfillment of the messianic hopes of the house of Israel.

To the twelve tribes in the Dispersion: In its original sense the phrase "the twelve tribes" *(tais dōdeka phylais)* referred to the totality of the people of Israel as descended from the twelve patriarchs (e.g., "Moses . . . built an altar at the foot of the mountain, and set up twelve pillars, corresponding to *the twelve tribes of Israel*" [Exod 24:4]; see also Exod 28:21; 39:14). Following the division of the nation of Israel after the reign of Solomon into two kingdoms and their subsequent destruction, a messianic hope emerged for the reconstitution of the nation of Israel as the twelve-tribe kingdom. This hope is contained in the *Psalms of Solomon:* "He will gather a holy people whom he will lead in righteousness; and he will judge the tribes of the people that have been made holy by the Lord their God . . ." *(Pss. Sol.* 17:26 [*OTP* 2:667]; see also 1QS 8:1). James sees his hearers/readers as the fulfillment of this hope of a reconstituted Israel (see below, *Excursus 1: To the Twelve Tribes in the Dispersion*). The word *diaspora* ("Dispersion") literally means "scattering." With the article, *hē diaspora* indicates either the *Israelites* scattered outside the land of Israel or the *areas* where they are dispersed (Deut 30:4; Neh 1:9; Jdt 5:19). Some scholars read this phrase in a metaphorical sense as addressed to Christians as the true Israel whose real homeland is heaven, while here on earth they are living in the dispersion (see Dibelius, *James* 66). If the writing were addressed to Christians coming from the pagan world this would be a logical interpretation. However, the hearers/readers are clearly Christians originating from the house of Israel. It is being addressed in the literal sense to the true Israel scattered throughout the Roman world.

Greetings: Infinitive *chairein*, the standard form of greeting that opens Greco-Roman letters (like the Latin *salutem*), as seen in numerous papyrus letters that have been preserved. It also occurs in the LXX in the letters of Alexander, Demetrius, and Jonathan (1 Macc 10:18, 25; 11:30, 32; 12:6), in the writings of Josephus (*Vita* 217; 365), in the New Testament in the letter from the Council of Jerusalem (Acts 15:23) and in the letter of Lysias to the governor Felix (Acts 23:26). This is in contrast to the Jewish greeting of "peace" *(šālôm)* as it occurs in Dan 4:1; Ezra 4:17; 2 Macc 1:1. James's formality and conformity to the Hellenistic format contrast sharply with other New Testament letters that generally commence with a wish for "grace and peace" for their hearers/readers (see the Pauline, Petrine, and Pastoral letters as well as Rev 1:4 in the address to the seven churches). The introductions to the letters of Ignatius (*Magn.*, *Trall.*, *Smyrn.*, *Pol.*) contain the phrase *pleista chairein* ("abundant greetings"). While this is similar to James, the references to the sender and receivers are much further developed. James deliberately employs this brief greeting to create a connection with *charan* (joy) in the following verse. This literary device of catchphrases occurs frequently and develops the flow of the letter. It is a clear illustration of the writer's literary ability.

INTERPRETATION

The writing is identified as coming from "James, servant of the Lord." Since the author does not find it necessary to identify himself further, the reader is led to associate him with the most important James within the early Christian community, the leader in Jerusalem, who bore responsibility for the spread of the Christian message within the house of Israel (see the discussion in the Introduction).

The opening formula identifies the writing as a letter. Those who hear/read this writing will immediately embrace it within that framework. The address to the twelve tribes in the Diaspora characterizes it as an encyclical letter sent to those Christian communities from the house of Israel who are now living outside the land of Palestine. Such hearers/readers would immediately see the writing as addressed to them. It is not necessary to seek to identify the readership more closely because the letter intends for it to be passed on from community to community. Further, the writer identifies the hearers/readers a little later as "the first fruits of his (God's) creatures" (1:18). As such they see in their communities the beginnings of God's reconstitution of God's twelve-tribe kingdom.

With the reference to the "twelve tribes" James has also situated his writing within an eschatological framework. The long-awaited hope of the past is now being realized. The end-times have begun with these Christian communities emerging within the house of Israel. James uses the eschatological perspective as motivation for his wisdom advice. This horizon culminates at the end of the letter with an exhortation to his hearers/readers to patient endurance: "Be patient, then, my brothers (and sisters), until the coming of the Lord" (5:7). As the first fruits of the reconstitution of God's people, his hearers/readers must hold fast to this identity until the end-times have reached fulfillment.

This interpretation of "the Dispersion" distances itself from those interpretations that understand the reference to *diaspora* in a metaphorical or spiritualizing sense, much in the manner in which 1 Pet 1:1 uses the phrase: "Peter . . . to the exiles of the Dispersion in. . . ." In such language Peter sees the true homeland as heaven, while Christians on earth are on pilgrimage to that true homeland. As such they truly are exiles (from heaven) living in the dispersion (on earth). First Peter's readership would include all Christians irrespective of their origins, either from the world of the nations or from the house of Israel.

While such an interpretation is appropriate to the first letter of Peter, it is not a responsible interpretation for the letter of James. The whole tone of this letter is one that shows a knowledge of the world of Israel. James identifies the hearers/readers as those who belong to a messianic sect. The term "twelve tribes" situates them against the background of Israel's hope for God's intervention in the world, reconstituting God's people. James brings his hearers/readers to understand the type of life they must lead in order to conform to their new identity. The way of life, the values stressed in this writing, define the boundaries that separate them as a community from those outside who embrace a different way of life. From the outset this writing sets the contrast between those who belong to the "twelve tribes" and those who do not. This contrast continues throughout the letter, reaching a climax in 4:4 with the antithesis between "friendship with the world" and "friendship with God."

The image of the "twelve tribes" can only be understood against the background of the traditions of Israel and most importantly the Torah that defines the identity of those who belong to God and wish to carry out God's will. James situates his writing within that context and identifies his hearers/readers as heirs to that tradition. The hearers/readers of this text, whether the first hearers/readers at the time of James or even hearers/readers of today, all see themselves belonging to that tradition. Today this writing challenges Christians to see themselves as part of that reconstituted people of God who are true heirs to Israel's traditions. This writing helps hearers/readers of every age to connect back to the roots of the true heritage of Christianity within the world of Israel.

For Reference and Further Study

Lieu, Judith M. "'Grace to You and Peace': The Apostolic Greeting," *BJRL* 68 (1985) 161–78.

Malherbe, Abraham J. "Ancient Epistolary Theorists," *Ohio Journal of Religious Studies* 5, 2 (1977) 1–77.

Stowers, Stanley K. "Social Typification and the Classification of Ancient Letters," in Jacob Neusner et al., eds., *The Social World of Formative Christianity and Judaism*. Philadelphia: Fortress, 1988, 78–90.

Excursus 1:

To the Twelve Tribes in the Dispersion (James 1:1)

Elsewhere I have argued that this expression should be read against the background of Israel's hope in a restored twelve-tribe kingdom (cf. Hartin [1996b] 490–92 and [1999] 70–71). When the nation was first destroyed by the Assyrians in 721 B.C.E. and then later by the Babylonians in 587 B.C.E., the hope emerged that God at some stage in the future would reconstitute the twelve-tribe kingdom (Jackson-McCabe [1996] 504–17). This hope was based on God's fidelity to past promises. Since God had promised Abraham that the land given him and his descendants would last in perpetuity, the hope grew that God would reconstitute this twelve-tribe kingdom. This hope was further strengthened by the prophet Nathan's promise to King David: "Your house and your kingdom shall be made sure forever before me; your throne shall be established forever" (2 Sam 7:16). The prophets in particular gave strength and impetus to this hope: "Thus says the Lord GOD: I will take the people of Israel from the nations among which they have gone, and will gather them from every quarter, and bring them to their own land. I will make them one nation in the land . . ." (Ezek 37:21-22; see the full text of Ezek 37:15-28 and Ezek 47:13-23, as well as chs. 45 and 48; see also Jer 3:18). The events surrounding Rome's occupation of Palestine from 63 B.C.E. onward renewed the people's longing for a restoration of their nation. This appears in a number of writings emanating from this time. The *Psalms of Solomon* (written in the middle of the first century B.C.E.) look forward to the future restoration of the kingdom of Israel in this way:

> See, Lord, and raise up for them their king,
> the son of David, to rule over your servant Israel
> in the time known to you, O God.
> Undergird him with the strength to destroy the unrighteous rulers,
> to purge Jerusalem from gentiles

> who trample her to destruction . . .
> He will gather a holy people
> whom he will lead in righteousness;
> and he will judge the tribes of the people
> that have been made holy by the Lord their God.
> He will not tolerate unrighteousness (even) to pause among them,
> and any person who knows wickedness shall not live with them.
> For he shall know them
> that they are all children of their God.
> He will distribute them upon the land
> according to their tribes;
> the alien and the foreigner will no longer live near them (*OTP* 2:667).

The Qumran community's eschatological expectation was centered around the reconstitution of God's twelve-tribe kingdom. They saw their exile in the desert as analogous to the forty years that Israel spent in the wilderness before they entered to take possession of the land. They saw the future unfolding in parallel to Joshua's entry into the promised land; the land will be redivided once again among the twelve tribes. The Qumran community even imagined the battle order for the upcoming clash that will bring about this restoration of the fortunes of Israel, following the structure of the twelve tribes: "They shall arrange the chiefs of the priests behind the High Priest and of his second (in rank), twelve chiefs to serve in perpetuity before God. And the twenty-six chiefs of the divisions shall serve in their divisions and after them the chiefs of the levites to serve always, twelve, one per tribe" (1QM 2:1-3).

The traditions behind the Gospel of Matthew give expression to this restoration hope and present Jesus as conducting a ministry whose chief aim was to reconstitute this twelve-tribe kingdom. Matthew 10:5-6 is most revealing in this context. In sending out the twelve, Jesus instructs them: "Go nowhere among the Gentiles, and enter no town of the Samaritans, but go rather to the lost sheep of the house of Israel." While the Gospel of Matthew endorses a mission and outreach to the gentiles, the traditions on which it depends show Jesus' own mission confined to the people of Israel (see Brooks 49–50). This mission embraces the restoration of the twelve-tribe kingdom. Jesus' task is envisaged as gathering together the lost tribes of Israel (e.g., "I was sent only to the lost sheep of the house of Israel" [Matt 15:24]). Not only is that Jesus' task, but he extends it to his disciples: they share in the same outreach and vision (Matt 10:5-6).

The fulfillment of this outreach and ingathering is reserved for the end of time. The twelve apostles are given the responsibility of judging the twelve tribes: "and I confer on you, just as my Father has conferred on me, a kingdom, so that you may eat and drink at my table in my kingdom, and you will sit on thrones judging the twelve tribes of Israel" (Luke

22:29-30; Matt 19:28). The ministry of the twelve disciples is seen to continue to the end of time, when they will share in Jesus' role of bringing in those who belong to the twelve-tribe kingdom.

We are to read this address of the letter of James against this background. James stands immersed in Israel's enduring vision that hoped for the restoration of God's twelve-tribe kingdom. In a similar vein to Jesus, who (in the traditions behind Matthew's gospel) saw his ministry as directed to the restoration of God's twelve-tribe kingdom, James addresses his hearers/readers as the fulfillment of this centuries-long hope. As the "first fruits of his (God's) creatures" (1:18) they constitute the beginnings of this twelve-tribe kingdom.

The theological implications of this vision are important. God is at work bringing this restoration to birth (1:18). The community associated with Jesus during his ministry as well as during the time of James is the beginning of that restored twelve-tribe kingdom. In this symbol of the twelve-tribe kingdom James shows his indebtedness and closeness to Jesus' vision. The parting of the ways between the house of Israel and Christianity has not yet taken place. Theologically James's vision still lies at the heart of the world of Israel and sees no incompatibility between being a follower of Jesus and an adherent of Israel's traditions. As McKnight says: ". . . the two presentations of James are a witness to the kind of Christian Judaism that continued the vision of Jesus into the next generation as this form of faith in Jesus led to a parting, yet within the way of Judaism" (129).

For Reference and Further Study

Brooks, Stephenson H. *Matthew's Community: the Evidence of His Special Sayings Material.* JSNTSup 16. Sheffield: Sheffield Academic Press, 1987.

Hartin, Patrick J. "'Who is Wise and Understanding among You?' (James 3:13): An Analysis of Wisdom, Eschatology and Apocalypticism in the Epistle of James," *SBLSP* 35. Atlanta: Scholars, 1996b, 483–503.

Jackson-McCabe, Matt A. "A Letter to the Twelve Tribes in the Diaspora: Wisdom and 'Apocalyptic' Eschatology in the Letter of James," *SBLSP* 35. Atlanta: Scholars, 1996, 504–17.

McKnight, Scot. "A Parting within the Way: Jesus and James on Israel and Purity," in Bruce Chilton and Craig A. Evans, eds., *James the Just and Christian Origins.* Leiden: Brill, 1999, 83–129.

Niebuhr, Karl-Wilhelm. "Der Jakobusbrief im Licht frühjüdischer Diasporabriefe," *NTS* 44 (1998) 420–43.

2. *Testing, Wisdom, and the Lowly* (1:2-11)

2. My brothers (and sisters), consider it nothing but an occasion of joy whenever you encounter various trials, 3. because you know that the testing of your faith produces endurance. 4. And let endurance produce a perfect work so that you may be perfect and complete, lacking in nothing.

5. But, if any of you is lacking in wisdom, let him ask God who gives to everyone without hesitation and without reproach, and it will be given him. 6. But, let him ask in faith, never doubting, for the one who doubts is like a wave of the sea, driven and blown about by the wind. 7. Let not that type of person imagine that he will receive anything from the Lord. 8. He is a double-minded man, vacillating in all his ways.

9. Rather, let the brother (or sister) in humble circumstances boast in exaltation, 10. and the rich in humiliation because (the rich) will pass away like a flower of the field. 11. For the sun rises with its burning heat and parches the field; and its flower falls and the beauty of its appearance perishes. In the same way the rich will waste away in the midst of their activities.

NOTES

2. *My brothers (and sisters), consider it nothing but an occasion of joy:* This form of address, *adelphoi mou* ("my brothers [and sisters]") occurs throughout the letter (1:16, 19; 2:1, 5; 3:1, 10; 5:12, 19). Some of these references reflect a more intimate bond: "my *beloved* brothers (and sisters)" (1:16, 19; 2:5). While Vouga (38) judges this to be a part of James's rhetoric, Mussner ([1981] 63) sees it as a way of drawing conscious attention to the bonds that unite author and readers. The Israelites used the phrase to identify their common bonds as members of the house of Israel (see, e.g., the usage in the LXX: Exod 2:11; Deut 15:3; Jdt 7:30; Tob 2:2; 2 Macc 1:1). This last is particularly interesting in that it opens a letter: "The brothers *(adelphoi)* of the house of Israel in Jerusalem send greetings *(chairein)* to the brothers *(adelphois)* of the house of Israel in Egypt." It also occurs in the writings of Josephus, who identifies the members of the Essene community in this way: ". . . the individual's possessions join the common stock and all, like brothers *(hōsper adelphois)* enjoy a single patrimony" (*B.J.* 2:122). The followers of Jesus continued this usage by calling themselves "fellow members in the new Israel" (Ropes 132). E.g., Paul uses the phrase frequently (Rom 7:4; 1 Cor 1:10; Gal 1:11; Phil 3:1); Matthew identifies the disciples as *adelphoi* ("brothers [and sisters]") (Matt 23:8); and Luke uses the same term for the first followers in Jerusalem (Acts 1:15). This word identifies fellow members of a particular society and embraces them all as equals. James emphasizes this equality through his use of the relative adjective "*my* brothers [and sisters]." He does not address them from the status of authority, but from their own level. This form of address also distinguishes James from the wisdom literature of the Hebrew Writings where the usual form of address was "my son *(huie)*" (see Prov 1:8), where the writer, an elderly man, is handing on

his wisdom to his child. James's focus in his frequent use of this term is to identify fellow members who follow Jesus and see themselves as heirs of the traditions of the house of Israel. Such a term distinguishes them from those outside the community. In using this term it is not his intention to make a distinction between male and female within the community. Hence I translate it as "brothers (and sisters)" in order to stress the focus on the members of the community as opposed to those outside. The Greek word *pasan* (literally "all") is used here as an intensifying adjective to express the concept of "nothing but" (Ropes 129). The predicate accusative *charan* (literally "joy") defines the imperative "consider" *(hēgēsasthe)*. James's use of this catchphrase or play on words *(chairein—charan)* enables him to move immediately into his main topic of interest. This call to rejoice embraces the whole section. The Israelite wisdom tradition often makes a connection between the search for joy and the search for wisdom, e.g., "Wine and music gladden the heart, but the love of wisdom (Hebrew text and NRSV have "friends") is better than either" (Sir 40:20 LXX). The search for wisdom often embraces testing (Sir 4:17). (See Johannes Thomas, "Anfechtung und Vorfreude, ein biblisches Thema nach Jak 1,2-18 im Zusammenhang mit Ps 126, Röm 5,3-5 und 1 Petr 1,5-7," *KD* 14 [1968] 183–206.)

whenever you encounter various trials: James speaks very generally here and refers to every kind of trial *(peirasmos)* or situation of adversity that could befall the believer. Such trials can come from outside the person or from within (see 1:13). Heinrich Seesemann *(TDNT* 6:29) sees that "sufferings for the sake of the faith are implied by *peirasmoi*." These trials are directed against the individual as well as the community. James's advice embraces a community dimension rather than a merely individual one. The use of alliteration is also to be noted here *(peirasmois peripesēte poikilois).*

3. *the testing of your faith:* James is more specific here, identifying the trials encountered in the testing of faith. The people of Israel have a long history of enduring such testing. Abraham persevered through the testing of his faith (Genesis 22), while the people of Israel in their wanderings through the desert constantly turned away from faith in their God (Num 14:20-25). The prophets became the symbol of those who persevered through the testing of their faith (e.g., Jeremiah 38). Jesus in the Q saying in the Sermon on the Mount identifies his followers as sharing in a testing of faith that goes back to the prophets: "Blessed are you when people revile you and persecute you and utter all kinds of evil against you falsely on my account. Rejoice and be glad, for your reward is great in heaven" (Matt 5:11-12; Luke 6:22-23). This saying shows a number of connections with James's thought. The trials and sufferings are all associated with faith. In this sense they are persecutions (social, economic, and physical) as occurred within the early church from the time of Stephen onward. Such sufferings are to be embraced with joy. Most manuscripts read *dokimion* ("a means or instrument of testing"), while an alternative reading, *dokimon* ("that which is approved or genuine"), is found in some witnesses (see Metzger [1975] 679). The reading of the majority of the witnesses *(dokimion)* is to be preferred, as it is the more unusual reading. *Dokimon* appears to be the

work of a scribe correcting the reading. The context also suits the understanding of "means of testing" (Davids [1982] 68). The word *dokimion* occurs on only two occasions in the New Testament, here and in 1 Pet 1:7. However, the meaning in each case is different (*contra* Grundmann, *TDNT* 2:259). James 1:3 uses the neuter noun in the sense of "the means of testing (of one's faith)." In 1 Pet 1:7 it is actually the neuter singular adjective that is used, with the sense "the genuineness of one's faith." The plural in "your faith" indicates that James has in mind not just an individual's faith, but also the faith of the whole community.

produces endurance: The virtues of steadfastness and endurance are the outcome of the situation of having one's faith tested. This Greek word occurs frequently in 4 Maccabees (1:11; 7:22; 9:30) with the meaning of "heroic endurance" (Dibelius, *James* 73). See Nigel Turner (*Christian Words* [Edinburgh: T & T Clark, 1980] 318–19) for a detailed examination of the different nuances of *hypomonē* in the various New Testament contexts. The testing of one's faith is not simply aimed at producing heroism, but also has an educative function. Abraham, Joseph, and Job were examples of how God in the past educated God's own people in their faith. In Jas 5:11 the example of the endurance of Job returns.

4. *Let endurance produce a perfect work:* James moves his thought forward with a number of careful steps: joy is experienced in trials; testing leads to endurance; now endurance also "produce[s] a perfect work." This same sequential progression of thought is evident in Rom 5:3-5: "suffering produces endurance, and endurance produces character, and character produces hope, and hope does not disappoint us . . ." In his commentary on James, Dibelius (74–76) provides an excellent excursus on the relationship between Jas 1:2-4 and Rom 5:3-5. He shows how this "concatenation" is a literary device common to that world (75). However, while both James and Paul show agreement in the usage of similar words (*hypomonē* ["endurance"] and the stem *dokim[-ē, -ion]*), this does not prove dependency (75). Instead, Dibelius's study shows that "one can see how closely the words for affliction, endurance or patience, and confirmation must be linked in Jewish-Christian sentiment. And if one further notices how Judaism repeatedly points to the suffering or trials of its heros *(sic)* . . . then it becomes evident how common must have been the ideas which found expression in our two passages" (76). The term "perfect" *(teleios)* is an important concept throughout this letter (see *Excursus 2: James and the Heritage of Israel*). In this instance it means complete, or conforming to the image God had of the person at the beginning. Through the virtue of endurance one reaches this state of integrity. James reiterates the same thought later in 2:22 in reference to Abraham: "You see that faith was active together with his works, and by the works faith was brought to perfection."

so that you may be perfect and complete: The concatenation of terms continues with the word *teleios* ("perfect work" [4a] and "perfect" [4b]). The perfect work produced by endurance is the perfection of the believer. The believer can become an integral person, as opposed to the divided person in 1:6-8. The completeness embraces conformity to God's ideal for the human person. Matthew 5:48 sees the quest for perfection occurring in the context of an *imitatio Dei* (see William D. Davies, *The Settting of the Sermon on the Mount* [Atlanta: Scholars, {1964} 1989] 212–13).

5. *If any of you is lacking in wisdom*: This passage is linked to the previous one by means of the catchwords *leipomenoi – leipetai (lacking in nothing – lacking in wisdom)*. Wisdom is not the Stoic notion of "science" (Ropes 139), but the Hebrew concept of knowing how to conduct life in conformity with God's Law. Wisdom is practical, not theoretical. Solomon was the great example of the wise ruler. E.g., "God answered Solomon, 'Because this was in your heart, and you have not asked for possessions, wealth, honor, or the life of those who hate you, and have not even asked for long life, but have asked for wisdom and knowledge for yourself that you may rule my people over whom I have made you king, wisdom and knowledge are granted to you" (2 Chr 1:11-12; see also Wis 7:7-14). The conditional clause "If any of you is lacking . . ." implies not so much a condition as a fact (Martin 17).

let him ask God: God is the source of true wisdom for the people of Israel. E.g., "For the LORD gives wisdom; from his mouth come knowledge and understanding" (Prov 2:6); "The fear of the LORD is the beginning of wisdom" (Prov 9:10) (see *Excursus 3: The Wisdom of James*). Since James considers wisdom to be God's most important gift, this writing is firmly rooted in the context of the wisdom tradition. The letter sets forth the wisdom advice needed to lead a life in conformity with God's will. In this section (1:5-8) I preserve the masculine references in the text because James endeavors here to present a single example of a person of faith.

who gives to everyone without hesitation and without reproach: God desires to give to all. God's very nature is that of a giver of gifts to all: "The eyes of all look to you, and you give them their food in due season. You open your hand, satisfying the desire of every living thing" (Ps 145:15-16). See also Philo: "God being very munificent gives his good things to all men, even to those who are not perfect . . ." (*Legat.* 1:34). The adverb *haplōs* ("without hesitation") is found only here in the New Testament, but the noun *haplotēs* is used quite frequently to convey a twofold meaning: (1) simplicity or a lack of reservation that is (2) expressed through an act of generosity. In Rom 12:8 Paul expresses the second aspect well: "the giver, in generosity" *(en haplotēti)* (see also Eph 6:5; Col 3:22). Dibelius, in his excursus on this word, notes that outside the New Testament two meanings for the adverb developed alongside the two meanings for the noun: the idea of "without mental reservations" and that of "graciously, generously" (77–79). Dibelius concludes that "the special sense . . . is to be preferred and the word ought to be translated 'without hesitation'" (79). The Shepherd of Hermas also uses the adverb *haplōs* in the context of giving, with the meaning "without hesitation" (see Herm. *Mand.* 2:4, 6). The following phrase, *mē oneidizontos* ("without reproach") supports this interpretation of *haplōs* as "without hesitation." Proverbs 3:27-28 gives advice on the need to respond unhesitatingly to those in need: "Do not withhold good from those to whom it is due when it is in your power to do it. Do not say to your neighbor, 'Go, and come again, tomorrow I will give it'—when you have it with you."

Using words different from those of James, the *Didache* (4:7) nevertheless combines the two ideas together: "Do not hesitate to give, and do not grumble when you do give" (see also *Barn.* 19:11). In the *Psalms of Solomon* the writer contrasts the generous giving of God with humanity's grudging gifts: "Human kindness (comes) sparingly, and tomorrow, and if (it comes) a second time without complaint, this is remarkable" (*Pss. Sol.* 5:13 [*OTP* 2:657]). Against this traditional advice directed at humanity James paints the example of God, the true giver, who acts "without hesitation and without reproach."

and it will be given him: A divine passive—the passive voice indicates God's action (Joachim Jeremias, *New Testament Theology*, trans. John Bowden [London: SCM, 1971] 9–14). The content is similar to the Jesus saying found in the Sermon on the Mount: "Ask, and it will be given you" (Matt 7:7; Luke 11:9). The passage in the Sermon on the Mount is followed by a contrast between the way human fathers give good things to their children and how much more "your Father in heaven give(s) good things to those who ask him!" (Matt 7:11; Luke 11:13). In Jas 1:17 every generous act of giving comes from the Father of lights. James appears here to reflect this Jesus saying.

6. *Let him ask in faith, never doubting:* James turns from God as giver to the human being as petitioner. Prayer is a favorite topic of James: he returns to it again in 4:1-3 and 5:13-18. Faith implies the trust and certainty the petitioner has that the request will be granted: "Whatever you ask for in prayer with faith, you will receive" (Matt 21:22; Mark 11:24; see also Cooper 268–77). James adds the phrase "never doubting," which again appears to reflect a Jesus saying: "Truly I tell you, if you have faith and do not doubt . . ." (Matt 21:21; Mark 11:23). While James does not specify what the doubt entails, the context implies that it concerns the certainty that God either can or will answer the prayer.

like a wave of the sea: The person who doubts is not compared to the wave itself, but to the tempestuous sea that is blown about by the wind. The imagery of the storm-tossed sea is very popular in ancient Greek sources. This suggests that James is building on a popular image rather than using a specific source. The verbs *anemizein* and *ripizein* ("driven" and "blown about") are synonymous, and the alliteration contributes to the imagery of the ebb and flow of the sea. The verb *anemizein* has not been found in any Greek source earlier than James. Laws conjectures that James could have coined it ([1980] 57). The phrase "by the wind" does not literally appear in the text but is added in the translation because it is implied by both verbs.

7. *Let not that type of person (ho anthrōpos ekeinos) imagine that he [she] will receive anything from the Lord:* Since the word *anēr* ("man") appears specifically in the following verse, the word *anthrōpos* is translated here in the inclusive sense as "person." The relationship of this verse to the following one is difficult to determine. There are a number of ways to translate it: (a) to see the doubting person (vv. 6 and 7) as distinct from the double-minded person (v. 8), (b) to see vv. 7 and 8 as one extended sentence (as the *NRSV* translates it: "for the doubter, being double-minded and unstable in every way, must not expect to receive anything from the Lord"), or (c) to preserve the sentence structure and see two separate statements here: "the double-minded man" refers to the

same person as the doubter, being a further development of what the doubter is like. This translation adopts the last possibility as more in conformity with James's style, which often gives a twofold description (see 1:5: "without hesitation and without reproach"). This Greek verb *oiesthein* ("to imagine") is only found in the New Testament here, in John 21:25, and in Phil 1:17. It is a frequently used verb in Hellenistic literature but only occurs some fourteen times in the LXX. The reference here to "the Lord" is to God. Each usage has to be determined on the basis of the context.

8. *a double-minded man:* The precise background for the adjective *dipsychos* ("double-minded") has been much debated. Some see its origin reflected in the Essene writings (Wolverton 166–75; Mussner [1981] 71; Seitz [1957/58] 327–34). Others see it originating in the Greco-Roman world, where the dichotomy between body and soul was a fundamental understanding and the Platonic view of divisions within the soul was widespread (see Rowe 8–10). However, the adjective *dipsychos* is not found in Greek literature before the letter of James. The noun *dipsychia* and the verb *dipsychein* appear in *1 Clem.* 11:2; *2 Clem.* 11:5; *Did.* 4:4. After James *dipsychos* appears especially in writings that seem to depend on this letter. In fact, *dipsychos* and *dipsychein* appear about forty times in the Shepherd of Hermas: e.g., Herm. *Vis.* 2:2, 7 *(dipsychein)* and Herm. *Mand.* 9:6 *(dipsychos)*. All this points to the possibility that James could be responsible for coining this term (see Porter [1990a] 469–98; Johnson [1995] 181; *contra* Ropes 143). At the very least James should be seen as introducing it into the early Christian writings (see Mayor 42). Literally the word means "double-souled" in the sense that the soul is divided between friendship with the world and friendship with God (4:4). The idea conveyed so succinctly by this word is certainly found before James. In the theology of the Hebrew Bible the foundation of the Law rests on loving God "with one's whole heart and soul" *(ex holēs tēs kardias sou kai ex holēs tēs psychēs sou)* (Deut 6:5 LXX). Contrasted with this undivided loyalty to the Lord is the person who is double-hearted (e.g., "with a double heart they speak" *[en kardią kai en kardią elalēsan]*, Ps 12:2 [11:3 LXX]). The book of Sirach contains a similar concept: "Do not disobey the fear of the Lord; do not approach him with a divided mind" *(en kardią dissē)* (Sir 1:28).

vacillating in all his ways: The adjective *akatastatos* ("vacillating") develops the previous idea of being "double-minded" or fickle (see Dibelius 83). This word is found in the New Testament only here and in 3:8, and only once in the LXX (Isa 54:11). "In all his ways" is a Semitic idiom to express the type of life one leads (see Pss 91:11 [90:11 LXX]; 145:15 [144:17 LXX]). The person's behavior is "unstable or vacillating" (Davids [1982] 75).

9. *Rather, let the brother (or sister) in humble circumstances:* The particle *de* occurs frequently in James (1:5, 9, 19, 22) and is used to continue the flow of the argument. It joins one subsection of the introduction with another (*contra* Dibelius 83–84). The term "brother [sister]" *(adelphos)* shows that the person referred to is a Christian. While "in humble circumstances" *(tapeinos)* embraces every aspect of the state of lowliness, the contrast between the "brother [sister] in humble circumstances" and "the rich" shows that James intends the state of

poverty. God is their champion (see Prov 3:34 [which James quotes in 4:6]: "Toward the scorners he is scornful, but to the humble *[tapeinois]* he shows favor"). It is a frequent image in the Psalms: "He will regard the prayer of the destitute *(tapeinōn)* . . ." (Ps 102:17 [101:18 LXX]; see also Pss 34:18 [33:19 LXX]; 82:3 [81:3 LXX]).

boast in exaltation: This continues the theme of joy announced at the beginning. The boasting *(kauchasthein)* is in what God is doing, not in the human person's accomplishments. Outside the letter of James and Heb 3:6 in the New Testament the concept of boasting is found only in Paul's letters. Paul does not boast in his own efforts, but in what God is doing through him (Rom 5:11). The "exaltation" refers either to the future state of the one who perseveres in adherence to the message of Jesus (see Jas 1:12) or to the present state of those who have accepted the Christian message and are now "rich in faith" in God's kingdom (2:5). They must look beyond the present world, where the rich are the ones who boast, in order to see things from the dimension of the poor person. Their situation is reversed: they are now rich through the exalted status received through baptism as heirs of God's kingdom. The hope of the prophets was for the exaltation of the lowly everywhere (Isa 54:11) as well as the lowly people of Israel (e.g., "For you deliver a humble people, but the haughty eyes you bring down" [Ps 18:27 {17:28 LXX}]). This is reminiscent of the Jesus saying: "All who exalt themselves will be humbled, and all who humble *(tapeinōn)* themselves will be exalted" (Matt 23:12; Luke 14:11; 18:14).

10. *and the rich in humiliation:* The term *plousios* ("rich person") refers to someone who is materially wealthy. The interpretation of the verse, however, is difficult. It hinges on whether the rich person is to be understood as a "brother or sister" (a member of the community) or as someone outside the community.

(1) *The rich person as a member of the Christian community:* most interpreters see it in this way (e.g., Mayor 45–46; Ropes 145–46; Adamson [1976] 61–62; Cantinat 78; Mussner [1981] 74; Johnson [1995] 185–86). This is the most natural way to read the Greek text: a parallel symmetry is established between vv. 9 and 10 since the same verb *(kauchasthein* ["to boast"]) must be supplied to v. 10 as well. The brother in lowly circumstances is called to boast, and the brother who is rich is also called to boast.

(2) *The rich person as someone who is outside the community* (e.g., Davids [1982] 77; Laws (1980) 63–64; Martin 25–26; Wall [1997] 56): the bringing low of the rich person "in humiliation" occurs through the loss either of wealth or of prestige. This could occur through becoming a Christian. The Scriptures often speak of the transitory nature of wealth (Job 24:24; Ps 49:16-20; Wis 5:8; Matt 6:19-21; Luke 12:16-34).

like a flower of the field: This image is dependent on the LXX translation of Isa 40:6: "All people are grass, their constancy is like the flower of the field." The LXX translates the Hebrew ṣiṣ haśādeh ("flower of the field") as *anthos chortou* ("flower of grass") instead of *anthos agrou* ("flower of the field"), and James continues with this translation, *hōs anthos chortou* (literally "flower of the grass"). Psalm 102:15 LXX translates the same Hebrew phrase (Ps 103:15) with the correct Greek, *anthos tou agrou.* The noun *chortos* is understood here as referring not just to grass but to any greenery, just as the flower refers to any flower that grows in the meadow (Ropes 148).

11. *For the sun rises with its burning heat and parches the field:* The tenses of the verbs here are difficult to translate. They are gnomic aorists (as in v. 24), in that the past tense is used to convey a wise saying that is always true: it is to be translated in the present tense. It usually occurs in the New Testament in conjunction with comparisons (see BDF 171:333). This proverb is reminiscent of geographical and climatic conditions in Palestine. The Greek word *kausōn* is rare (found only twice in the New Testament and ten times in the LXX). It can be translated in two ways: (1) "with its burning heat," implying that the sun rises and the burning heat dries up and wilts all the vegetation, or (2) "with the burning wind," referring to "the southeast wind common in Palestine in spring and destructive of young growth by reason of its extreme and withering dryness" (Ropes 148). While this latter translation is an interesting possibility, the logic of the sentence seems to exclude it. This southeast wind (the sirocco) that blows continuously for three to four days (night and day) has little to do with the rising sun (Davids [1982] 78).

its flower falls and the beauty of its appearance perishes: James has Isa 40:7-8 in mind: "The grass withers, the flower fades, when the breath of the LORD blows upon it . . . the grass withers, the flower fades; but the word of our God will stand forever." James does not quote Isaiah directly, but he certainly alludes to the text. In Isaiah the reference is to the transitory nature of all humanity before God. James, however, attributes this state specifically to the rich. By using the words of the prophet Isaiah, James is in effect indicating that what the prophet had foretold now comes to fulfillment in the lives of the rich. First Peter 1:24-25 quotes Isa 40:6-8 directly in order to stress the concept of the enduring nature of the word of God. *The beauty of its appearance* is a Semitic expression (literally "the beauty of its face"). The Greek word *euprepeia* ("beauty") is found only here in the New Testament, though it does occur frequently in the LXX.

the rich will waste away in the midst of their activities: The verb *maranthēsetai* ("will waste away") is found in Wis 2:8 and Job 24:24 in reference to human beings wasting away. Outside the Bible it is generally used to refer to plants and things. In his usage here James has in mind a reference to the wealth of the rich that is lost. He may also be thinking of the future torments awaiting the evil rich at the end of time (see 5:1-6; *contra* Ropes 149). While the Greek text has the masculine singular *autou* (literally "his activities"), the translation renders it as plural in order to preserve the inclusive example James intends. The Greek word *poreia* literally means "a journey, a way, or a passage." As a Semitism it is used figuratively to indicate "a way of life" or "activities" (Martin 27; Davids [1982] 78). It refers to the life experiences of the rich (see, e.g., Prov 4:27b LXX: "he will lead all his activities peacefully" [*tas de poreias sou en eirēnē proaxei*]). To understand it as referring to a literal journey is not supported by the context. One would be reading too much into the text to see it foreshadowing the merchants in Jas 4:13-17 (as do Mayor 47; Moo 70; Mussner [1981] 75).

Interpretation

James opens his letter with a call to rejoice: "Consider it nothing but an occasion of joy" (1:2). This spirit of joy permeates the first section and indirectly embraces an element of thanksgiving. James is asking his hearers/readers to be thankful that they do experience the testing of their faith, because it produces a steadfastness that leads to perfection in the faith.

This certainly is the major thrust of this letter. Wholeness comes through the testing of faith in a variety of ways. The letter itself will illustrate different examples of the testing of the community's faith by advocating that it seek friendship with God as opposed to friendship with the world (4:4). The line of thought unfolds carefully as the author leads it forward through a series of phrases or catchwords (Dibelius 70):

- Joy when you meet *trials* (1:2)

- *Testing* of faith produces *endurance* (1:3)

- *Endurance* leads to wholeness or perfection, *lacking* in nothing (1:4)

- But if you *lack* wisdom, *ask* God (1:5)

- *Ask* in faith, never *doubting* (1:6)

- The person who *doubts* is double-minded (1:7-8)

These catchwords are more than an external device to unite what are in fact different and independent thoughts. The connections serve to lead the thought forward toward a climax. Endurance must be allowed to come to completeness. It is not a matter of attaining more virtues and qualities but of striving to see that, through God's grace, endurance in faith continues despite the change of fortunes that occurs in life. The aim is that "you may be perfect and complete, lacking in nothing" (1:4), that you become a whole and integral person, unlike the divided person of 1:6-8.

This first introductory section (see Introduction: 6. The Structure of the Letter) introduces three important themes evident in the three subsections of this passage. These themes will be taken up later in the course of the letter:

Testing of Faith leads to Perfection (1:2-4)

The Gift of Wisdom (1:5-8)

Humiliation of the Rich and Exaltation of the Poor (1:9-11)

(a) Testing of Faith leads to Perfection (1:2-4)

This passage introduces the first major theme: the endurance of faith in the midst of trials and testings leads to wholeness or perfection.

Announced here, this theme spells out its full implications only later in 1:12-18 and at the end of the letter in 5:7-11. Hiebert uses a graphic image to illustrate the importance of this theme: "'The testing of your faith' (1:3) seems to be the key which James left hanging at the front door, intended to unlock the contents of the book" (224).

Nothing is really said about the nature of the trials that the hearers/readers are enduring. Some idea can be inferred from subsequent passages. Not only are individuals exposed to personal difficulties, but communities are also undergoing trials of their faith. James says that whenever these believers as a group are involved in the ordeal of suffering it ought not to be endured with grumbling, but should be accepted joyfully.

Faith that is tested and brought to perfection is the central issue. In fact, the concept of faith is as important for James as it is for Paul. In this writing the noun faith *(pistis)* occurs some sixteen times (1:3, 6; 2:1, 5, 14[2x], 17, 18[3x], 20, 22[2x], 24, 26; 5:15). James has in mind the faith of the community as well as that of the individual. The "you" referred to here is plural, not singular. Consequently, the morality that James advocates embraces both the community and the individual.

The theme of endurance during the testing of faith runs throughout the Hebrew traditions: e.g., "My child, when you come to serve the Lord, prepare yourself for testing. . . . Accept whatever befalls you, and in times of humiliation be patient. For gold is tested in the fire, and those found acceptable, in the furnace of humiliation" (Sir 2:1-5). Throughout the letter James provides examples of faithful people whose lives demonstrated a dramatic testing of their faith: Abraham (2:21-24), Rahab (2:25), the prophets (5:10), and Job (5:11). They showed that faithfulness under trial brought God's blessing. Whatever trials they endure, James asks his hearers/readers to keep in mind these examples of true faith in action.

James calls his hearers/readers to allow endurance under trials to achieve its purpose, namely their perfection. The word "perfect," *teleios* (used twice in 1:4) embraces the Israelite concept of completeness, wholeness, totality, being without blemish (see *Excursus 2: James and the Heritage of Israel*). As a community and as individuals they are complete persons who conform to the original image God had of them in the beginning. They are "the first fruits of his (God's) creatures" (1:18). Through the harmony of faith and action they show their wholeness and integrity. Later James returns to this same thought of the harmony of faith and works when he offers the example of Abraham: "You see that faith was active together with his works, and by the works faith was brought to perfection" (2:22).

Dibelius noted in this context that James did not say that endurance makes you perfect, but rather was issuing an exhortation to his hearers/readers: "Let what endurance produces be perfected, and thus you will be perfected" (74). As such it is in line with the exhortation Matthew's Jesus addresses in the Sermon on the Mount: "Be perfect, therefore, as your heavenly Father is perfect" (Matt 5:48).

Perfecting faith leads to an undivided allegiance to God. By contrast, the world endeavors to lead one away from this exclusive dedication to God. This explains James's definition of religion: "Religion that is pure and undefiled in the sight of God (who is) also Father is this . . . to keep oneself unstained from the world" (1:27).

(b) The Gift of Wisdom (1:5-8)

This line of thought builds on the previous verses. James 1:4 ended with a call to wholeness. Now the letter considers the possibility that the hearers/readers may indeed be lacking the most important thing of all: wisdom. The Israelite wisdom tradition rested on the understanding that God alone was the truly wise person. All human wisdom was a gift from God. The book of Wisdom (8:21) expresses it in the following way: "But I perceived that I would not possess wisdom unless God gave her to me— and it was a mark of insight to know whose gift she was—so I appealed to the Lord and implored him, and with my whole heart I said. . . ."

Solomon was the epitome of the person to whom God gave the gift of wisdom, in response to his request for a spirit of wisdom to rule God's people (1 Kgs 3:5-15). During his rule Solomon's actions demonstrated the true nature of this wisdom he had received from God. Wisdom embraced the gift of discernment, of knowing how to act when faced with the situations and decisions that are part of human existence (see, e.g., his decision regarding the two women who both laid claim to the same baby [1 Kgs 3:16-28]). Faced with life's challenges, and especially here in the context of James with trials that test one's faith, one receives from God's gift of wisdom the divine illumination that shows one how to act. The Book of Sirach presents an interesting parallel reflection on the connection between God's wisdom, the trials of faith, and God's guidance:

> For at first she [Wisdom] will walk with them on tortuous paths;
>   she will bring fear and dread upon them,
> and will torment them by her discipline
>   until she trusts them,
> and she will test them with her ordinances.
> Then she will come straight back to them again and gladden them,
>   and will reveal her secrets to them (Sir 4:17-18).

Joy is the consequence of the gift of wisdom for both Sir 4:18 and Jas 1:2. The gift of wisdom enables people to act in the midst of trials and suffering in such a way that their actions lead to wholeness (perfection). The result is a joyful spirit. Wisdom indeed is the horizon that gives insight into how to act in a way that reflects their community's identity as God's faithful people. The connection between wisdom and perfection is found also in the book of Wisdom: "For even one who is perfect *(teleios)* among human beings will be regarded as nothing without the wisdom *(sophia)* that comes from you" (Wis 9:6).

This explains why James singled out wisdom as the gift that might be lacking in the life of the believer and of the community. As God's gift, wisdom enables one to endure in the midst of trials. Wisdom is that one gift needed for perfection understood as wholeness, completion, and integrity. Since wisdom comes as a gift from God, the believer is instructed to request it from God with absolute assurance that God will grant it (see *Excursus 3: The Wisdom of James*). This is in line with the same spirit of asking that Jesus expresses in the Sermon on the Mount: "Ask and it will be given you" (Matt 7:7).

James's description of God lies in sharp and deliberate contrast to the picture of the double-minded person. God gives without hesitation and without reproach. God's commitment to good for God's people knows no bounds: it is total and immediate. As Matt 7:11 continues: "If you then, who are evil, know how to give good gifts to your children, how much more will your Father in heaven give good things to those who ask him!"

James turns from addressing the quality of God's generous giving to that of the human person's asking. The letter shows a decided interest in the dimension of prayer. Prayer must be addressed in faith (see 5:15; Matt 21:22; Mark 11:24) without doubting. James tackles the problem of prayers that seem to go unanswered from the petitioner's perspective, not from God's perspective (see 4:3).

The root cause of unanswered prayer is the human person's lack of faith in God. The result is a divided allegiance. This theme of divided loyalty runs throughout the letter and culminates in 4:4 with the dramatic choice between friendship with the world and friendship with God. James graphically illustrates the fickleness of the divided person with the image of the wind-tossed sea, its waves driven backward and forward (1:6). The double-minded ("double-souled," *dipsychos*) (1:18) are so filled with uncertainty and indecision that they are unable to choose between alternatives, namely whether to trust in God or not. This is similar to the Jesus saying in the Sermon on the Mount: "No one can serve two masters; for a slave will either hate the one and love the other, or be devoted to the one and despise the other. You cannot serve God and wealth" (Matt 6:24).

James issues a very harsh denunciation of the double-minded person. Such people must not expect to receive anything from God because they have in effect betrayed their faith in God. True faith entails single-minded devotion and exclusive devotion to the one God, as the *Shema Israel* states: "Hear O Israel, the LORD is our God, the LORD alone . . ." (Deut 6:4). James challenges the hearers/readers to imitate God: just as God's response to Israel was a single-minded devotion and faithfulness, so too believers must respond to God with a similar undivided "yes."

James's call to single-minded devotion to God must not be limited in vision to the individual's relationship to God. As has been indicated, James's ethic is directed both to the community and to the individual as part of that community. In drawing attention to the imitation of God's dealings with Israel, James is focusing on God's relationship to the community. Hence James calls for a reciprocal response from the community to God. James is concerned with the moral worth of the community in its faithfulness to God as the source of their existence. As members of the same community, all persons embrace the same vision, the same ethos, in their relationship to God and to one another. Behind the thought of James lies the concept of purity and purity rules that define the way the members of the community maintain their identity and distinguish themselves from those outside the community. James's concern for the Torah reflects this desire to preserve the purity rules that uphold these relationships (see *Excursus 2: James and the Heritage of Israel*). The whole letter is an appeal to remain true to this exclusive vision: no compromise is possible. The choice lies between loyalty to God and allegiance to the world (1:27; 4:4).

(c) Humiliation of the Rich and Exaltation of the Poor (1:9-11)

This third subsection of the opening introduction continues the spirit of rejoicing. The hearers/readers rejoice when they experience the testing of their faith (1:2-4); this joy continues when they request from God the greatest gift, namely wisdom (1:5-8); finally, this joy culminates in the realization that there is a reversal of fortunes within the Christian community (1:9-11). While no catchphrase connection is made with what has gone before, the overarching refrain of the call to rejoice enables the writer to introduce this third theme, which will be taken up again in the rest of the letter in considering the relationship between rich and poor.

As the Notes have indicated, there is much discussion as to whether the rich person (1:10) is a member of the Christian community or not. How one resolves this question will determine the interpretation of this passage. Elsewhere in the letter of James the rich are clearly not members of the community (2:1-7; 5:1-6). They are outsiders who are responsible for the hardships the community experiences. If this is James's intent in 1:10, then the meaning must be ironic. A reversal of situations occurs in God's future kingdom where those who have (the rich) will lose what they have, while those who have not (the poor) will gain much.

The major difficulty with such an interpretation is that it does not remain true to the sentence structure of the Greek text. Structurally James has created a parallelism between the poor and the rich. The poor person is clearly identified as a "brother [sister]." Since the adjective "rich" *(plousios)* does not have a noun to define it, grammatically one should understand the noun to be supplied by the first noun of the sentence, namely "brother [sister]." If James was thinking of the rich person as outside the community he would have indicated that more clearly within this ambiguous phrase. Further, the same verb "to boast" embraces both the poor and the rich as its subject, contrasting the different situations in which the poor and rich are called to boast.

I prefer to understand the reference to the rich in this particular section (1:9-10) as applying to the rich within the Christian community, based on the logic of the sentence structure. The whole antithesis between rich and poor indicates two different situations for boasting: those who do not have boast in their support from God and the community, while those who do have much boast in the humiliation that has brought them into a relationship with God and the community.

The author focuses on the reversal of fortunes. Within the Christian community each has reason to boast. The poor are given an exalted status as members within the community, where they experience equality with one another and with God. And even though the rich have lost the status they had within the larger society, nevertheless within the Christian community they have discovered their true status, namely their value in God's eyes. As Mayor expresses it: "Let the rich brother glory in his humiliation as a Christian" (45). Within the community the rich realize the transitory nature of riches. True riches are discovered in relationship with God and in sharing God's blessings with others. Sirach 3:18 captures well the thought that James expresses here: "The greater you are, the more you must humble yourself; so you will find favor in the sight of the Lord." The rich must practice self-abasement and turn from self-reliance to dependence on God.

The background to James's concept of boasting lies without doubt in the Old Testament concept of God as the source of all blessings (see Wall [1997] 55–56; Mussner [1981] 73–80). As Psalm 49 expresses it, trust in God overcomes the folly of trusting in riches. Jeremiah 9:23-24 provides one of the most insightful texts as a framework for James's thought:

> Thus says the LORD: Do not let the wise boast in their wisdom, do not let the mighty boast in their might, do not let the wealthy boast in their wealth; but let those who boast boast in this, that they understand and know me, that I am the LORD; I act with steadfast love, justice, and righteousness in the earth, for in these things I delight, says the LORD.

Jeremiah stresses that boasting should not be based on what one has acquired through human action, such as wisdom or strength or wealth. Rather, one should boast about one's relationship with God, who acts "with steadfast love, justice, and righteousness in the earth" (Jer 9:24). Those are the qualities God values, and by implication they are the qualities believers should value as well. Like Jeremiah, James calls his hearers/ readers to the realization that the true object of boasting is exclusive confidence and trust in God. The poor rejoice in their status within the community because they are the object of God's special love and care. The whole biblical tradition has stressed God's special choice of the poor. At the same time the poor hope for the eschatological reversal of fortunes at the end-time. As the "first fruits of his (God's) creatures" (1:18) they experience even now this exaltation in God's community of the twelve-tribe kingdom. The rich likewise place trust and confidence in God by moving away from their own activities and accomplishments to rely on God's love and justice. In the present community to which the rich belong, status is not based on wealth (it is worthless). While the reversal of fortunes culminates in the future age with "the crown of life" (1:12), a reversal of fortunes is already experienced within the community of believers, who already place their confidence in God's steadfast love.

James 1:11 ends the reflection by considering the rich "*qua* rich, with no special reference to the rich brother" (Mayor 47). Since they place their confidence in their own abilities and their own wealth rather than in God, "in the midst of their activities" (1:11) they will waste away. Like the wildflower they will be burned up by the scorching heat of the sun and the wind (1:11). The suddenness of this occurrence seems to imply a reference to the coming of the Lord spoken of in 5:1-6, when the rich will suddenly lose everything on which they relied during their earthly life.

In order to present his argument James alluded to a text from Isa 40:7-8 LXX. Behind this argument one can also discover an allusion to the Jesus saying: "All who exalt themselves will be humbled, and all who humble themselves will be exalted (Matt 23:12; Luke 14:11; 18:14) (see *Excursus 4: James and the Heritage of Jesus*). While both Isaiah and the Jesus saying form the foundation for his instruction, James elaborates them in his own way in order to speak to his community in his own voice.

The reflection on the rich and poor will be developed in more detail throughout the letter. Another contrast emerges here between placing confidence and trust in God or in the world. This theme is dramatically enunciated in 4:4, where James throws down the gauntlet, challenging the readers/hearers to choose between friendship with God and friendship with the world. This is the root metaphor of the whole letter. Friendship with God is incompatible with friendship with the world. James has enunciated here a foundational framework for his whole religious vision.

FOR REFERENCE AND FURTHER STUDY

Berger, Klaus. "Hellenistische Gattungen im Neuen Testament," *ANRW* 2.25.2 (1984) 1031–432.

Braumann, Georg. "Der theologische Hintergrund des Jakobusbriefes," *TZ* 18 (1962) 401–10.

Cooper, Robert M. "Prayer: A Study in Matthew and James," *Encounter* 29 (1968) 268–77.

Frankemölle, Hubert. "Das semantische Netz des Jakobusbriefes: Zur Einheit eines umstrittenen Briefes," *BZ* 34 (1990) 161–97.

Grundmann, Walter. *"dokimos," TDNT* 2:255–60.

Hays, Richard B. *Echoes of Scripture in the Letters of Paul.* New Haven: Yale University Press, 1989.

Hiebert, D. Edmond. "The Unifying Theme of the Epistle of James," *BSac* 135 (1978) 221–31.

Luck, Ulrich. "Weisheit und Leiden: Zum Problem Paulus und Jakobus," *TLZ* 92 (1967) 253–58.

Rowe, C. J., ed. "Platonic Conceptions of the Soul," in *Plato: Phaedo.* Cambridge: Cambridge University Press, 1993, 8–10.

Schlier, Heinrich. *"thlibō, thlipsis." TDNT* 3:139–48.

Seesemann, Heinrich. *"peira ktl." TDNT* 6:23–36.

Seitz, Oscar J. F. "Antecedents and Signification of the Term *DIPSYCHOS*," *JBL* 66 (1947) 211–19.

_____. "Afterthoughts on the Term *'Dipsychos,'" NTS* 4 (1957/8) 327–34.

_____. "Two Spirits in Man: An Essay in Biblical Exegesis," *NTS* 6 (1959/60) 82–95.

Wolverton, Wallace I. "The Double-Minded Man in the Light of Essene Psychology," *AThR* 38 (1956) 166–75.

EXCURSUS 2:

JAMES AND THE HERITAGE OF ISRAEL
(PERFECTION AND PURITY [JAMES 1:2-4])

The letter of James is rooted in the world of Judaism, and James defines himself in relation to that heritage. Thoughts and concepts such as Law, wisdom, perfection, etc., all have their foundation in a Jewish background. This may be illustrated by focusing on one aspect that bears this out in a striking way, namely the theme of wholeness or perfection. I choose this aspect deliberately because, as Elliott has noted ([1993] 71), a number of scholars have pointed to perfection as the central theme of James.

The Greek word *teleios* and its cognates occur some seven times throughout this short writing. The adjective *teleios* appears four times in ch. 1 (1:4[2x], 17, 25) and again at 3:2. The verb *teleioō* ("to make perfect or complete") appears at 2:22, while the verb *teleō* ("to fulfill, to accomplish")

occurs at 2:8. This clearly shows that it is a concept that is of importance
for this short letter. Its use is proportionately higher than in any other
New Testament writing. In the LXX *teleios* was used to translate the
Hebrew adjective *tāmîm* in the following instances: Gen 6:9 ("Noah was a
righteous man, blameless *[tāmîm]* in his generation"), Exod 12:5 ("Your
lamb shall be without blemish *[tāmîm]*, a year-old male"), Deut 18:13
("You must remain completely loyal *[tāmîm]* to the Lord your God"),
2 Sam 22:26 ("With the loyal you show yourself loyal; with the blameless
[tāmîm] you show yourself blameless"). More frequently (on about fifty
occasions) *tāmîm* is translated by the Greek adjective *amōmos*.

To understand the meaning of *teleios* that emerges from this usage it is
necessary to understand the breadth of meaning the Hebrew word *tāmîm*
embraces throughout the Hebrew Scriptures. The use of this term *tāmîm*
clearly originated in the cult and the sacrificial worship of Israel. In the
context of the cult *tāmîm* referred to an animal suitable for sacrifice. Cultic
laws defined that only "unblemished" *(tāmîm)* animals could be offered in
sacrifice (e.g., "If the offering is a burnt offering from the herd, you shall
offer a male without blemish *[tāmîm]*" [Lev 1:3]). Only what was whole or
complete could be offered to God. Here appears the essence of the concept
of perfection: a being that conforms to its original makeup; its wholeness
or completeness.

The conceptual meaning of *tāmîm* as it emerged from the different
contexts in the Hebrew Scriptures gives expression to three essential
dimensions:

(1) The first dimension is the idea of wholeness or completeness,
whereby a being remains true to its original constitution.

(2) The second aspect is the giving of oneself to God wholeheartedly
and unconditionally, which includes a relationship between God
and God's people. Above all it rejects idolatry or the worship of
other gods. It is akin to the adjective *ṣaddîq*. If the person was
grounded in this relationship she or he would be seen as whole,
perfect. Perfection includes a community relationship, not just an
individual dimension.

(3) Third is the wholehearted dedication to the Lord that is demonstrated above all in obedience to God's will. This in turn includes a
life led in obedience to the Torah, the laws of the Lord. The Hebrew
phrase "walking with God" (Gen 5:22, 24; 6:9; Mic 6:8; Mal 2:6)
calls for moral obedience in which faith and works are intrinsically
united (Hartin [1999] 26).

This threefold understanding of the conceptual meanings of *tāmîm*
helps us understand the use James makes of *teleios* throughout this letter.

All three dimensions are evident in James's thought and usage. For him the concept of *teleios* embraces a search for *wholeness* as an individual and as a community *in relationship to the one God* who *guides them through the Torah* (see Hartin [1999] 57–92). The cultic origin of *teleios* remains essential to this understanding of perfection. In expressing his understanding of *teleios* James relies heavily on the fundamental notions of purity and holiness within his own society, notions he owes to his Jewish heritage. The social-scientific study of Christian origins has given us increased understanding and awareness, particularly in recent times, of the role that cultic, moral, and social purity rules played in Second Temple Judaism and the world of early Christianity. See the groundbreaking studies that have been undertaken on the concept of purity over the past four decades: Mary T. Douglas, *Purity and Danger, An Analysis of Concepts of Pollution and Taboo* (New York: Praeger, 1966); George W. Buchanan, "The Role of Purity in the Structure of the Essene Sect," *RQ* 4 (1963) 397–406; John H. Elliott, *The Elect and the Holy. NovTSup* 12 (Leiden: Brill, 1966); Jacob Neusner, *The Idea of Purity in Ancient Judaism* (Leiden: Brill, 1973); idem, "History and Purity in First-Century Judaism," *HR* 18 (1978) 1–17; Malina ([1993] 149–83).

These purity rules provided a framework to structure life (whether personal or communal) in order to promote right relationships between the individual, the community, and God. Malina defines purity rules succinctly when he writes:

> If purity rules are to facilitate access to God, and if the God to whom one wants access has human welfare as the main priority in the divine will for the chosen people, it follows that proper interpretation of purity rules must derive from giving primary consideration to relationships with one's fellows. This is what righteousness is about. For righteousness means proper interpersonal relationships with all those in one's society, between God and covenanted human beings and between human beings and their fellow beings ([1993] 174).

Purity rules are designed to indicate how to have and maintain access to God. They set the individual and the community off from the wider society. In effect they identify those who have access to God, who act in a particular way, as the holy ones—those who belong to the sphere of the sacred. Those who do not act in this way are the outsiders, who belong to the world of the profane. The purity laws function as part of a socialization process, defining the boundaries within which those who belong to the people of Israel live. These purity laws become social markers defining the identity of all who belong to the same community.

James describes the Torah as the "perfect law" (1:25). Here the concepts of purity and perfection come together—"holiness and wholeness," as Elliott expresses it ([1993] 71–81). The law defines the boundaries the believing community is to observe in order to maintain access to God and to keep its wholeness. "To be holy, according to James, is to be whole—with respect to personal integrity, communal solidarity, and religious commitment" (Elliott [1993] 78).

James builds his advice around the contrasts of two ways of life: one led in friendship with God, the other in friendship with the world (4:4). These two ways of life are further demarcated through the contrast between a way of life that is informed by the values of wholeness, purity, and harmony as opposed to a way of life that is incomplete, divided, and polluted. This contrast emerges most clearly in the distinction James paints between the two types of wisdom: from above and from below (3:13-18). The very first quality that James identifies regarding the wisdom from above is that it is "pure" (3:17). This pure wisdom is such that it has come down from above (3:17) as opposed to the wisdom from the earth, which is "demonic" (3:15). This provides the backdrop to the search for wholeness and purity: it comes from having access to God, from being in a wholehearted relationship with God. When one is separated from this source of wholeness and holiness one is divided, like a wave of the sea that is tossed about in the wind (1:6).

Fidelity to the way of life that remains true to the whole Law embraces a bond on three levels: the personal, the communal, and God. Wholeness and holiness on all levels are experienced when the individual is in right relation with the community and with God. As James calls out: "Draw near to God, and he will draw near to you. Cleanse your hands, you sinners, and purify your hearts, you double-minded" (4:8). James's definition of religion in 1:27 captures very beautifully the essence of the purity laws. Keeping oneself undefiled from the world implies showing that one has kept oneself away from the alien values of society, while at the same time remaining true to the values that belong to the community of "the twelve tribes of the Dispersion." These values are captured above all in a concern for the poor as exemplified in the widows and orphans.

This examination has shown how the letter of James remains rooted in the traditions and heritage of the world of Israel. Its whole way of thought is at home in these traditions. It will be evident throughout this commentary how vital an understanding of the world of Judaism is for understanding this letter. Clearly the followers of Jesus have not yet separated themselves from the world of Israel. James continues to define himself in relation to the heritage of which he is still a part.

FOR REFERENCE AND FURTHER STUDY

Baasland, Ernst. "Literarische Form, Thematik und geschichtliche Einordnung des Jakobusbriefes," *ANRW* 2.25.5 (1988) 3646–84.

Barkman, Paul F. *Der heile Mensch. Die Psychologie des Jakobusbriefes.* Kassel: Oncken, 1968.

Bauckham, Richard. "James and the Jerusalem Church," in *The Book of Acts in Its Palestinian Setting.* The Book of Acts in its First Century Setting 4. Grand Rapids: Eerdmans, 1995, 415–80.

_____. "James and the Gentiles (Acts 15.13-21)," in Ben Witherington III, ed., *History, Literature, and Society in the Book of Acts.* Cambridge: Cambridge University Press, 1996, 154–84.

Chilton, Bruce D., and Jacob Neusner. *Judaism in the New Testament: Practice and Beliefs.* London: Routledge, 1995.

Malina, Bruce J. *The New Testament World: Insights from Cultural Anthropology.* Rev. ed. Louisville: Westminster John Knox, 1993.

Neyrey, Jerome H. "The Idea of Purity in Mark," in John H. Elliott, ed., *Social Scientific Criticism of the New Testament and Its Social World. Semeia* 35 (1986) 91–128.

Wehnert, Jürgen. *Die Reinheit des 'christlichen Gottesvolkes' aus Juden und Heiden.* FRLANT 173. Göttingen: Vandenboeck & Ruprecht, 1997.

Zmijewski, Josef. "'Christliche Vollkommenheit.' Erwägungen zur Theologie des Jakobusbriefes," in Albert Fuchs, ed., *Studien zum Neuen Testament und seiner Umwelt.* Series A, 5. Linz: SNTU, 1980, 50–78.

EXCURSUS 3:

THE WISDOM OF JAMES (THE GIFT OF WISDOM [JAMES 1:5-8])

It was argued in the Introduction that the genre of the letter of James was to be understood as protreptic discourse whereby the writer communicates a vision of friendship with God by using practical wisdom advice. Throughout this writing the concept and role of wisdom are highly significant (1:5-8, 17; 3:13-18) (see Baasland [1982] 119–39; Bauckham [1999] 74–111). Without doubt, for James wisdom is the horizon within which the community and the believer attain perfection in the eschatological age (Hartin [1999] 65–78).

James's understanding of wisdom needs to be situated against the background of the rich Israelite wisdom tradition. The concept of wisdom is one found in almost all the nations around Israel, and without doubt Israel was indebted to these traditions for much of its wisdom.

Central to Israel's concept of wisdom is that it is founded and rooted in God's wisdom. God alone is the one truly wise. Human wisdom derives from God as its source. This wisdom comes to humanity through God's revelation or by means of God's spirit. One of the clearest associations between the gift of God's spirit and the gift of wisdom occurs in the story of Joseph: "Pharaoh said to his servants, 'Can we find anyone else like this—one in whom is the spirit of God?' So Pharaoh said to Joseph,

'Since God has shown you all this, there is no one so discerning and wise as you'" (Gen 41:38-39). In the prophet Isaiah (11:2) God communicates the gift of "the spirit of wisdom and understanding" to a future descendant of David. God's spirit also gives the Israelites wisdom to construct their tabernacle and all that was necessary for their worship (Exod 31:3). This wisdom is above all practical: God grants skills and abilities to humans. God's real skill and artistry are discovered especially in the creation of the world (Prov 3:19; 8:22-31).

Hebrew poetry used personification to portray the concept of God's wisdom and to provide a deeper reflection on its nature. Proverbs, Sirach, and the book of Wisdom offer a rich reflection on the nature of wisdom. In Proverbs 8 and 9 Wisdom is personified as present with God at the beginning of creation (see Prov 8:22-36), the first of God's creations. Instead of hiding her, God has made her readily accessible to humanity. "For whoever finds me finds life and obtains favor from the LORD" (Prov 8:35). This vision is extremely important, for it provides the horizon for all human action. Wisdom is a gift God communicates to those who seek God.

Sirach 24 continues the reflection begun by Proverbs on Wisdom's personification. Wisdom is presented as an intermediary assisting God in the work of creation; moreover, she exercises her role not only at creation, but throughout the course of salvation history. Particularly to the people of Israel, Wisdom extends her invitation to share in the gift she alone can offer. Wisdom flows "like a canal from a river" (Sir 24:30) and finds expression in the Torah (Sir 24:32). The promise is made that she "will again pour out teaching like prophecy, and leave it to all future generations" (Sir 24:33). The promise of the consolation Wisdom affords finds its fulfillment in the word of Jesus: "Come to me, you who desire me, and eat your fill of my fruits. For the memory of me is sweeter than honey, and the possession of me sweeter than the honeycomb" (Sir 24:19-20; see Matt 11:28; cf. also Sir 24:21; Matt 5:6).

The book of Wisdom contains a much deeper reflection on the nature of Wisdom and her role in the world, particularly in relationship to God's people:

> For she is a breath of the power of God,
> and a pure emanation of the glory of the Almighty . . .
> in every generation she passes into holy souls
> and makes them friends of God, and prophets;
> for God loves nothing so much
> as the person who lives with wisdom (Wis 7:25-28).

Besides reflection upon the nature of divine wisdom, Israelite wisdom literature provided humanity with a clear direction. The gift of wisdom that comes down from God produces a truly practical wisdom for the lives of those who have received it. The clearest illustration of this is in the life of Solomon, who requested this gift so that he could rule his nation wisely (1 Kgs 3:1-14, 16-28). The intention of Israel's wisdom literature was to outline instruction for leading life in order to live happily under God's rule (Hartin [1991] 35–43). The books of Proverbs, Ecclesiastes, and Sirach all have this same aim in mind: to provide ethical wisdom teaching showing how the people of Israel should lead their lives. According to Prov 2:2 ("making your ear attentive to wisdom and inclining your heart to understanding"), a person is attentive to wisdom when he or she follows the instructions of the Torah. The Torah is undoubtedly the source of wisdom for a good ethical life:

> Oh, how I love your law!
>   It is my meditation all day long.
> Your commandment makes me wiser than my enemies
>   for it is always with me (Ps 119:97-98).

The letter of James is clearly at home within this background of Israelite wisdom. The forms so commonly associated with Israelite wisdom literature are easily observable in the letter of James. Among the more important wisdom forms are the following:

- *Wisdom sayings and admonitions* form the heart of this writing. James opens his letter with a positive admonition: "My brothers (and sisters), consider it nothing but an occasion of joy whenever you encounter various trials" (1:2). A very common form of wisdom saying in both the Hebrew Scriptures and the New Testament commences with the phrase "whoever . . ." (e.g., "For whoever keeps the whole Law but fails in one point has become accountable for all [of it]" [2:10]; "Therefore whoever wishes to be a friend of the world becomes an enemy of God" [4:4]). A wise saying often concludes the admonitions: "For judgment is merciless to the one who has not shown mercy. Mercy triumphs over judgment" (2:13); "So also faith by itself, if it has no works, is dead" (2:17).

- *Wisdom forms of comparison* are frequent throughout the letter. Explicit comparisons embrace the use of similes and metaphors: e.g., "for the one who doubts is like a wave of the sea, driven and blown about by the wind" (1:6); "for you are a mist that appears for a little while and then vanishes (4:14). James goes beyond the simple simile or metaphor to construct a brief parable like those so characteristic of Jesus' teaching: "Because, if one is a hearer of the word and not a doer, this person is like those who look at their natural faces in a mirror" (1:23); "(the rich) will pass away like a flower of the field. For the sun rises with its burning heat and parches the field, and its flower falls, and the beauty of its appearance perishes. In the same way the rich will waste away in the midst of their activities" (1:10b-11); "for if a man with gold rings and in fine clothes comes into your assembly, and if a poor person in squalid clothes also comes in . . ." (2:2).

- *Beatitudes:* While the beatitude is a characteristic feature of wisdom literature, it also appears frequently in the psalms (see, e.g., Pss 1:1; 32:1 [31:1 LXX]; 33:12 [32:12 LXX]; 40:4 [39:5 LXX] and in apocalyptic literature (see, e.g., Dan 12:12; *1 En.* 58:2; 81:4; 82:4). One of the distinguishing features of the beatitude in the New Testament as opposed to the Hebrew Scriptures is the time for the fulfillment of the promise attached to the beatitude. In the New Testament the fulfillment is seen to occur in the future, while in the Hebrew Scriptures it takes place in the present. The beatitude appears on two occasions in the letter of James and on both occasions the fulfillment is reserved for the eschatological future: "Blessed is the person who endures testing, because such a person, having stood the test, will receive the crown of life that (God) has promised to those who love him" (1:12); "But those who have looked intently into the perfect law of liberty and have persevered have become not hearers who forget but doers of the deed. They will be blessed in what they do" (1:25). In both instances the blessing is fulfilled in the future as a consequence of one's present way of life. The eschatological becomes the context for the blessing's fulfillment.

- *Woes:* Characteristic features of the prophetic address are condemnations against nations and individuals for not obeying God's will. While this is characteristic of the prophetic tradition, woes also occur in the wisdom tradition. In the letter of James two very graphic passages capture the prophetic mode of address: (1) "Come now, you who say . . ." (4:13-17). James addresses the merchants as a foil much as the prophets did, in order to challenge the community to change its way of life. While James does not envisage the merchants changing their behavior (or even hearing the message), he does count on his hearers/readers hearing the challenge and responding to it. (2) "Come now, you rich . . ." (5:1-6). The eschatological perspective provides the motivation for the community to persevere. James has incorporated aspects from other literary forms (prophetic, eschatological, apocalyptic) into the wisdom genre to strengthen his argument.

- *Models or examples:* The adoption of models for imitation from Israel's history is a further feature of wisdom literature (see, e.g., Tob 4:12; Sir 16:5-11; 1 Macc 2:51-61). James introduces a number of examples taken from the Hebrew Scriptures: Abraham and Rahab are examples of those who put faith into action (2:21-25); Job and the prophets are examples of patient endurance (5:10-11); Elijah, "a man with the same nature as ours" (5:17), becomes an example of a person of prayer.

- *Wisdom themes:* Many of the characteristic themes that occupy the Hebrew wisdom tradition also occur in the letter of James (e.g., concern for the poor [Jas 1:27; Prov 19:17; 31:9], the testing of one's faith [Jas 1:2; Prov 27:21; Job 1 and 2], and the control of one's tongue [Jas 1:26; Sir 5:13]).

A comparison of the letter of James with the sayings of Jesus in the synoptic tradition shows a striking formal feature: almost all the wisdom forms embraced by James are to be found in Jesus' sayings as well (Bauckham [1999] 56). Jesus most commonly communicates his message in a narrative parable incorporating a well-developed story. James also uses the narrative parable, but differs from Jesus in that his use is limited to a few examples (1:10-11, 23-24; 2:2-4, 15-17) that are characteristically brief. See Bauckham ([1999] 35–57); Hartin ([1991] 59–80; [1996] 483–88) for a fuller treatment of wisdom forms contained in the letter of James.

Two dimensions of Israelite wisdom are evident in this letter. First of all, wisdom is a gift that comes down from God above (1:17; 3:17). The way to attain this gift of wisdom is through prayer (1:5). Second, as a consequence of the gift of wisdom the believer receives certain virtues that are essential for leading a life according to God's will. James lists these: "But the wisdom from above is first pure, then it is peaceable, gentle, obedient, full of mercy and good fruits, without a trace of partiality or hypocrisy. But the fruit that is righteousness is sown in peace by those who make peace" (3:17-18). This list is reminiscent of the list of virtues described by the beatitudes in Matt 5:1-12 and Paul's list of the fruits of the Spirit in Gal 5:22-23.

James does not reflect on the nature of wisdom in an abstract way. Instead he wishes to show the significance this gift of wisdom from above has for the community and individual believers. The first consequence is the believer's rebirth "so that we might be a kind of first fruits of his (God's) creatures" (1:18). The rebirth happens through "the implanted word that is able to save your souls" (1:21). This is one of the significant developments of James beyond the Israelite concept of wisdom. As the implanted word, wisdom brings about regeneration and rebirth: it is not just a gift that provides practical moral direction for a way of life; it also accomplishes a transformation within the believer. As Timothy B. Cargal notes, James's system of convictions differs remarkably from that derived from the way wisdom functions in the Hebrew Scriptures: "The solution is indeed 'wisdom,' but this wisdom is not gained by 'enduring' and learning from God's 'reprimands.' Wisdom is 'generously' given by God to those who ask with 'faith.' It is a 'good and perfect gift,' 'implanted' within them and 'able to save [their] souls' from death" (90). This trans-formation also occurs in the community dimension, where they are re-born as God's twelve-tribe kingdom. This is the perfect gift James spoke about in 1:17. They are the beginning of the reconstitution of God's people, called to live in friendship with God.

This gift of wisdom is indeed the perfect gift, for it renders the believer whole and complete, lacking in nothing (1:5). Moreover, this perfection shines through in the call to friendship with God (4:4). All who experience God's gift of wisdom lead a life that encompasses an exclusive relation-ship with God.

Not only does James show himself to be heir to the traditions of Israel-ite wisdom, he is also heir to the way in which Jesus appropriated the Israelite wisdom traditions. Like Jesus, James shows a decided concern for and identification with the poor. Witherington identifies James as a "sage from below" (165). Just as Jesus preached countercultural values, so too does James: God has chosen the poor in the world (2:5); his hearers/readers are called to be peacemakers (3:18; cf. Matt 5:9) who place total trust in and dependence on God (4:7). Above all, the wisdom of James aims at the reconstitution of God's twelve-tribe kingdom, which is the whole focus of Jesus' choice of the twelve disciples: the renewal of God's own people. Bauckham expresses in an insightful way this closeness of James to Jesus' appropriation of wisdom: "His (James') wisdom is the Jewish wisdom of a faithful disciple of Jesus the Jewish sage. He is the dis-ciple of whom Jesus said: 'The disciple is not above his master, but every one when he is fully taught (or more literally: 'made complete') will be like his master' (Luke 6:40)" ([1999] 108).

For Reference and Further Study

Baasland, Ernst. "Der Jakobusbrief als Neutestamentliche Weisheitsschrift," *ST* 36 (1982) 119–39.

Beardslee, William A. "The Wisdom Tradition and the Synoptic Gospels," *JAAR* 35 (1967) 231–40.

Cargal, Timothy B. *Restoring the Diaspora: Discursive Structure and Purpose in the Epistle of James.* Atlanta: Scholars, 1993.

Fohrer, Georg. *"sophia," TDNT* 7:476–96.
Schnabel, Eckhard J. *Law and Wisdom from Ben Sira to Paul.* WUNT 2nd ser. 16. Tübingen: J.C.B. Mohr (Paul Siebeck), 1985.
Von Lips, Hermann. *Weisheitliche Traditionen im Neuen Testament.* WMANT 64. Munich: Neukirchener Verlag, 1990.
Wilckens, Ulrich. *"sophia," TDNT* 7:496–526.
Witherington, Ben III. *Jesus the Sage: The Pilgrimage of Wisdom.* Minneapolis: Fortress, 1994.

EXCURSUS 4:

JAMES AND THE HERITAGE OF JESUS
(JAMES'S USE OF THE JESUS TRADITIONS [JAMES 1:9-11])

A detailed examination of the letter of James reveals how close it stands to the central vision and message of Jesus as well as those traditions that handed on Jesus' teaching. Studies on James have come a long way since the arguments of Louis Massebieau ([1895] 249–83) and Friedrich Spitta ([1896] 1–239), who viewed James as a Jewish *Grundschrift* to which had been added Christian interpolations, namely, of the name of Jesus Christ at 1:1 and 2:1. For example, in the phrase in 1:1, *Iakōbos theou kai kyriou Iēsou Christou doulos* ("James, a slave of God and of the Lord Jesus Christ"), Massebieau bracketed off the words *Iēsou Christou*, while Spitta bracketed off the whole expression *kai kyriou Iēsou Christou*, leaving the simple phrase *Iakōbos theou doulos* ("James, a slave of God"), which is found in Titus 1:1 (*Paulos doulos theou* ["Paul, a slave of God"]). No textual evidence exists for such emendations. Further, it would be strange that such interpolations would be limited to only two brief phrases. The strongest argument against such a view comes from the pulsating spirit of the entire document, which breathes the very spirit of Jesus and contains numerous echoes throughout of the very sayings of Jesus.

The Letter of James and the Jesus Traditions

Some scholars (such as Sophie Laws [1980] 14; Todd C. Penner [1996] 254) have argued that the letter of James reflects the general ethical teaching within the Christian community. Other studies have tried to be more precise by arguing for some form of connection between the letter of James and the sayings traditions of Jesus that lie behind the gospels. I have endeavored elsewhere to make the argument that James is familiar with the Sayings Source Q that lies behind the gospels of Matthew and Luke (see Hartin [1991] 141–72). Different scholars have presented different lists of correspondences between James and the Jesus traditions (e.g.,

Kittel 84–94; Mayor lxxxv–lxxxviii; W. D. Davies, *The Setting of the Sermon on the Mount* [Cambridge: Cambridge University Press, 1964] 402–403; Mussner [1981] 48–50; Davids [1982] 47–48; [1985] 66–67; Painter [1999] 261–62).

An important similarity between the letter of James and the Sayings Source Q lies in the very nature of the two documents. Both the letter of James and the Sayings Source Q are wisdom documents presented within the framework of an eschatological dimension of judgment. A close examination of James's allusions to Jesus material shows that the connections tend to occur chiefly in material found in Matthew's Sermon on the Mount, e.g., the closest correspondence between James and the Jesus tradition occurs with the saying on the taking of oaths in Jas 5:12 and Matt 5:34-37 (see Brooks [60], who identifies it as belonging to Matthew's special tradition). A comparison with the Q version of the Sermon as found in the Gospel of Luke shows that Matthew's Sermon on the Mount had developed through the addition of material coming chiefly from within Matthew's community (M).

A clear understanding of what is meant by an allusion to a Jesus saying is important. James's allusions are not verbatim quotations of Jesus sayings. I endorse the perspective of Peter H. Davids, who defined an allusion as "a paraphrastic use of phrases or ideas from a logion, with the probable intent of reminding the reader of it" ([1985] 68). This means that in his argument James offers a paraphrase of a saying or words of Jesus from the tradition, and that would have reminded his hearer/reader of the saying. Robert Alter argues clearly that the concept of a "literary allusion . . . involves the evocation—through a wide spectrum of formal means—in one text of an antecedent literary text" (112).

The Use of the Jesus Tradition in the Letter of James

A way forward in understanding James's use of the Jesus tradition is to view it analogously to his usage of the Hebrew Scriptures. James does quote the Scriptures directly on a few occasions (e.g., "For the one who said, 'Do not commit adultery' also said, 'Do not kill'" [2:11]; "And the Scripture was fulfilled that says, 'And Abraham believed God, and it was reckoned to him as righteousness'" [2:23]; "Rather, he gives a greater grace; therefore it says: 'God resists the proud, but he gives grace to the humble'" [4:6]). More often the letter simply alludes to scriptural phrases and sayings (as will be illustrated throughout the commentary) by adapting them to its own world and argument.

An examination of these allusions between James and the synoptic tradition shows that they occur throughout the letter and are not confined to

one part. Some years ago Davids gave attention to the use of the Jesus tradition in this letter; he contended that "each major paragraph in the epistle
contains one or more allusion, and further analysis would demonstrate
that in every paragraph the allusion(s) support the main point" ([1985]
70). In order to illustrate James's rhetorical usage of the Jesus tradition in
the course of his argumentation I shall briefly examine one passage,
namely the antithesis between rich and poor (1:9-11), in order to provide
some pointers that could be carried through more fully in another context.

James 1:9-11 centers on a contrast between the lowly and the rich. Each
is given reason to boast: the lowly person rejoices in the conviction of
being raised up while the rich person rejoices in humiliation. The poor are
exhorted to rejoice in a reversal of situations now within the Christian
community where they are raised up to experience equality with others
and a special relationship with God. The rich, on the other hand, rejoice
because in this new community they are no longer honored because of
wealth or status, but simply because they are part of this community.

This contrast in exaltation/humiliation is reminiscent of Jesus' saying
"All who exalt themselves will be humbled, and all who humble themselves will be exalted" (Matt 23:12; Luke 14:11; 18:14). Noteworthy here is
James's rhetorical use of this saying. In these verses (1:9-11) James introduces for the first time what is to become a central focus in his letter,
namely the attitude toward poverty and riches (2:1-7; 5:1-6). James sets
forth his basic premise regarding poverty and riches, namely that a reversal of fortunes of those who embrace Jesus' message occurs within the
community. To accomplish this James reaches back into the Jesus tradition
for a suitable Jesus saying that he now applies to his hearers/readers.
James as it were composes it in his own way. He draws out the contrast
between the lowly and the rich and shows how for each the reversal of
situations within the community can be a reason for rejoicing.

To strengthen his argument James makes rhetorical use of another allusion, this time to the Hebrew Scriptures:

> The grass withers, the flower fades,
>> when the breath of the Lord blows upon it;
>> surely the people are grass.
> The grass withers, the flower fades;
>> but the word of our God will stand forever (Isa 40:7-8).

James does not quote this Isaian text directly here, but the imagery of
grass withering in the heat of the day is surely reminiscent of the images
of Isa 40:7. James's allusion to this Isaian text is instructive. He demonstrates a tremendous freedom in accommodating it to his new context
(Dibelius 85–86). This provides a good illustration for the same freedom

James used, I believe, in applying the sayings of Jesus to a new context and argument.

Studies on the ancient art of rhetoric in application to the New Testament help to shed light on James's method of using both the Hebrew Scriptures and the sayings of Jesus. In a recent monograph Wesley Wachob investigated the *progymnasmata* and the ancient rhetorical handbooks whereby students were taught the art of rhetorical argumentation, and he has attempted to apply this to the letter of James. His analysis argues that "the artful activation of an antecedent text was a common ploy in rendering a given proposal more readily acceptable to an audience" (116). What is significant is that the argument is built upon a previous text that is activated in its own way. The writer does not simply "quote" his previous text, but has the freedom to weave it into his own text in whatever way suits his purpose.

In an important study Vernon K. Robbins has shown that ancient writers, and in particular the synoptic gospels, "continually recast the material by adding to it, subtracting from it, rearranging it, and rewording it" ([1991] 148–49). The rhetorical purpose of the text aimed at getting the hearer/reader to think and to act in a particular way. The aim was not simply to copy the existing text or source; rather, it was to actualize the text or the source in such a way that it became a new performance in the hands of the writer to ensure that it conforms to his new rhetorical function. Robbins expresses this very succinctly when he says:

> In previous research, verbal similarities among written versions of stories and sayings regularly have been discussed in terms of "dependence" on written or oral sources. This terminology emerges from a presupposition that written performance of the material was guided by copying an oral or written antecedent. This language and this perception impose goals and procedures on the writers which are inaccurate, since, even if the writer recently had heard or was looking at a version of the story, the version existed in the eye, ear, and mind of the writer as a "recitation" that should be performed anew rather than a verbal text that should be copied verbatim ([1991] 167).

This entails looking at the relationship between ancient texts in a different way. The approach of source criticism viewed the writer as copying the text/source that lay in front of him. This was not necessarily always the case. An examination of the rhetorical culture out of which the New Testament writings emerged shows that the writers were not intent on simply producing a scribal copy of the text. They saw their goal as performing their source in new ways in order to persuade their hearers/readers to act or think in a particular way. This is what Robbins terms "recitation composition," which he defines thus:

> The dynamics and presuppositions surrounding recitation composition emerged as a teacher recited a traditional fable, anecdote, event, or saying in his own words to one or more students and the students wrote the brief unit in their own words, using as much or as little of the teacher's wording as worked well for them ([1991] 147).

This approach gives insight into what the writer of the letter of James endeavors to do. In this particular context his task is to persuade the hearers/readers about the countercultural reversal of roles within the community of Jesus' followers. He uses the sources to speak to this context, but he recites them in his own way, in his own voice. This is what James did with the Isaian text, and it becomes an illustration for the way in which he deals with the sayings of Jesus.

Wiard Popkes endeavored to explain the freedom James demonstrates with his use of his sources by arguing that James did not have access to the original, but instead was using "second-hand material" ([1999] 227–28). While such an explanation is possible, it fails to appreciate more fully the rhetorical culture of these documents. One needs to make a shift from viewing the world of New Testament documents as part of a *scribal* culture to seeing them as part of a *rhetorical* culture (see Robbins [1991] 145). If we view the New Testament writings as emerging from a scribal culture we see the primary goal as copying their sources. If, however, they emerge from what is termed a rhetorical culture, the concern is different. It does not aim at transmitting the source verbatim, but at performing the source in new ways with a freedom to speak to the new exigencies of the hearers/readers who are addressed.

It is in this way that the letter of James develops. Jesus' sayings as well as quotations from the Hebrew Scriptures form the foundation for James's teaching. James introduces them in his own way, rephrasing them, elaborating on them in order to speak to his community. These allusions to the sayings of Jesus and the way James has used them form an essential part of his argument and show how close James lies to the heritage of Jesus.

In the Spirit of Jesus

James's closeness and fidelity to Jesus' vision are also observable in the following aspects:

The original movement started by Jesus and continued by James was a Jewish restoration movement that did not see itself as separate from the world of Israel's traditions. In both the preaching of Jesus and the letter of James, God is at work reconstituting the people of Israel as the "twelve-tribe kingdom" (see *Excursus 1: To the Twelve Tribes in the Dispersion*). Like Jesus, James's rhetorical concern in his teaching is to uphold the Torah as the expression of God's will for God's people. No attention is given to the ritual aspects of the Torah; the focus rests predominantly on the moral laws that define the relationship of the members of the community with one another and with God.

The earliest picture of Jesus shows someone whose mission extends to his own people. The letter of James reflects a world where the parting of the ways between Christianity and Judaism had not yet taken place. As such it reflects the earliest stage in the development of early Christianity. The letter of James is situated within the context of this earliest paradigm of the Jesus movement. James gives no attention to the issue of the relationship of Gentiles to the Jesus movement. It does not amount to a problem or issue for him; otherwise he would have addressed it. His hearers/readers are identified as the twelve tribes of the Dispersion. While this does not preclude the fact that some Gentile Christians may be members of his community, they would be associated with the movement in a way similar to that expressed by the James of Acts 15. The world of Paul is vastly different from that of the letter of James, for Paul's communities were predominantly Gentile Christian, and this called for the emergence of a new paradigm.

For today's reader the letter of James is a writing that truly bridges the world of Judaism and the world of Christianity. It brings awareness to the common heritage Christians share with Judaism. Above all it shows how the visions of Jesus and James are in conformity with the thought and vision of Judaism and not just different from it (see Johnson [1995] 164).

Fidelity to Jesus' central vision is also expressed in concern for the poor. The message of Jesus is above all countercultural, reaching back into the prophetic message of God's concern for the poor. The economic situation of the poor largely stemmed from their lack of honor, or social status, and hence lack of power. Recent studies using a social-scientific methodology have shown that poverty is something that largely affects one's honor or status (see Malina [1987] 354–67; Hartin [2000] 1070–71). Three groups in the Old Testament world were identified as the poor: the widows, orphans, and strangers (Deut 24:17-18). Their poverty stemmed largely from a lack of social status. Since no one was there to champion their cause, God became their champion (Pss 22:26; 35:10).

In the traditions of Israel the prophets gave voice to the need to extend justice to the poor. They drew attention to the evils of their society, where the rich amassed fortunes at the expense of the poor (e.g., "Ah, you who join house to house, who add field to field, until there is room for no one but you, and you are left to live alone in the midst of the land!" [Isa 5:8]).

As the Hebrew Scriptures did, the letter of James presents God as the vindicator of the poor (5:1-6). He has this tradition in mind when he defines religion as "care for orphans and widows in their affliction" (1:27).

As champion of the poor, James condemns every situation where the poor are unjustly treated (2:6-7). Concern for the poor embraces all those who in any way are rejected or marginalized by society. Since all people are created in "God's likeness" (3:9), all are equal in God's eyes. No one can claim a special status that demands superiority over another. The Christian community's relationship with God requires an equality among all its members. This gives impetus to the countercultural nature of James's community: its values are permeated by the values of equality and concern for the well-being of all. In the ultimate analysis James envisages within his community a reversal of status whereby the rich are brought low and the poor raised up. This achieves equality in faith (1:9-11).

James shows a faithful continuation of the central vision of Jesus' message: an option for the poor and an avoidance of every form of discrimination. The wholeness of the individual and of the community are illustrated through the attention given to achieving this equality in all actions. It is a message that continues to issue a challenge to every believer of every age.

Other aspects of Jesus' wisdom are also continued in the letter of James. Jesus' ministry is characterized as well by actions of healing, forgiveness, outreach to sinners, and a desire to draw all into his kingdom. These features are also characteristic of James's letter. As Rhoads observes: "Other elements of Jesus' teaching that may be reflected in the wisdom of James include: healing, forgiveness, rescuing sinners, prohibiting oaths, a commitment to the poor, the encouragement that those who ask will receive, and the affirmation that God gives good gifts" ([1998] 485). The letter's conclusion (5:13-20) reflects themes that were central to Jesus' ministry. The way James addresses them shows that they are also central to the community to whom he writes. He is not introducing them for the first time, but rather reminds his hearers/readers of the importance of these aspects that form an essential part of their way of life. A continuation of Jesus' own ministry is reflected here.

Conclusion

The letter of James provides a distinct ethic for its hearers/readers to follow: an ethic that is at home both in the world of Judaism and in the vision of Jesus. In its solidarity with the poor, its rejection of all forms of discrimination, and its call for friendship with God as opposed to friendship with the world James advances a vision that is challenging and refreshing. Situated in the context of the rhetorical culture of the world of early Christianity and the people of Israel, the letter of James effectively composes the Jesus tradition in its own way and with its own voice to define the way of life that those who belong to the community to whom this letter is addressed should lead. James shows that he is the true heir to Jesus' message, in fidelity to their common heritage within the house of Israel.

FOR REFERENCE AND FURTHER STUDY

Alter, Robert. *The Pleasures of Reading: In an Ideological Age.* New York: Simon & Schuster, 1989.

Hartin, Patrick J. "Poor," in David Noel Freedman, ed., *Eerdmans Dictionary of the Bible.* Grand Rapids: Eerdmans, 2000, 1070–71.

Kittel, Gerhard. "Der geschichtliche Ort des Jakobusbriefes," *ZNW* 41 (1942) 71–105.

Malina, Bruce J. "Wealth and Poverty in the New Testament and Its World," *Int* 41 (1987) 354–67.

Robbins, Vernon K. "Writing as a Rhetorical Act in Plutarch and the Gospels," in Duane F. Watson, ed., *Persuasive Artistry: Studies in New Testament Rhetoric in Honor of George A. Kennedy.* Sheffield: JSOT Press, 1991, 142–68.

Wachob, Wesley Hiram. *The Voice of Jesus in the Social Rhetoric of James.* SNTSMS 106. Cambridge: Cambridge University Press, 2000.

3. *Testing, Hearers and Doers of the Word* (1:12-27)

12. Blessed is the person who endures testing, because such a person, having stood the test, will receive the crown of life that (God) has promised to those who love him. 13. Let no one say when tested, "I am being tempted by God." For God is not tempted by evil, and he himself tempts no one. 14. But each one is tempted by one's own desire, being lured and enticed by it. 15. Then the desire, having conceived, gives birth to sin; and sin, once it has come to maturity, generates death. 16. Do not be deceived, my beloved brothers (and sisters). 17. Every good act of giving and every perfect gift is from above, coming down from the Father of lights, with whom there is no variation or shadow of change. 18. Because he freely decreed it, he gave us birth by the word of truth, so that we might be a kind of first fruits of his creatures.

19. Know this, my beloved brothers (and sisters): Let every person be quick to hear, slow to speak, slow to anger. 20. For a person's anger does not accomplish God's righteousness. 21. Therefore, put away every sordidness and abundance of wickedness, and welcome with meekness the implanted word that is able to save your souls. 22. But become doers of the word, and not merely hearers who deceive themselves. 23. Because, if one is a hearer of the word and not a doer, this person is like those who

look at their natural faces in a mirror. 24. For they look at themselves and go away and immediately forget what they are like. 25. But those who have looked intently into the perfect law of liberty and have persevered have become not hearers who forget but doers of the deed. They will be blessed in what they do. 26. If any think they are religious, and do not bridle their tongues, but deceive their hearts, their religion is worthless. 27. Religion that is pure and undefiled in the sight of God (who is) also Father is this: to care for orphans and widows in their affliction, and to keep oneself unstained from the world.

Notes

12. *Blessed is the person who endures testing:* The beatitude (macarism, from *makarios*, blessed) is a familiar form of wisdom teaching that is also common to the gospel tradition (particularly the Sayings Source Q), representing a typical mode of Jesus' teaching (see, e.g., Matt 5:3-11; 11:6; 13:16; 16:17; Luke 6:20-22; 7:23; 10:23; 11:27-28). This particular beatitude is very reminiscent of the sayings of Jesus in Matt 5:10-11 and Luke 6:22, where persecutions are said to lead to blessedness. The translation "blessed" is preferred to "happy" since it captures the consequence of leading life in relationship with God. Although the Greek word used here is *anēr* (literally "man" in distinction to *anthrōpos*, "human person," as in 1:8, 20, 23; 2:2; 3:2), James does not intend to make any distinction between men and women. He is using a stock biblical phrase: in the LXX *makarios anēr hos* translates literally the Hebrew *ʾašrê hāʾîš ʾăšer* (see Ps 1:1: *Makarios anēr hos . . .*). The correct Greek would be *makarios hos* without *anēr*. James evokes an example that has universal application. For this reason I translate the text's intent as "person." The phrase "who endures testing" recalls 1:3 and expresses the idea of "standing firmly in the face of something." This concept of *hypomenein* is captured well by Xenophon: "And to which shall we give the habit of not shirking a task, but undertaking it willingly?" *(all'ethelontēn hypomenein)* (*Mem.* 2:1,3 [Marchant, LCL]; see also Herodotus, *Hist.* 6:12). A similar phrase occurs in Dan 12:12 (Theodotion): *makarios ho hypomenōn* ("Blessed is the one who endures").

having stood the test, will receive the crown of life that (God) has promised to those who love him: The adjective *dokimos* indicates the concept of having been examined and approved as a consequence of a test. BDAG defines it as "pertaining to being genuine on the basis of testing, *approved (by test), tried and true, genuine*" (256). In 1:3 it appeared in some manuscripts as a variant for *dokimion:* "a means or instrument of testing." Its appearance here possibly contributed to the variant reading in v. 3. The promise of the reward of a crown reflects the context of the Hellenistic world, where a crown *(stephanos)* was a wreath given to those who had accomplished something great, be it in athletic contests (1 Cor 9:25; 2 Tim 2:5) or public service (Heb 2:7-9) (see Mayor 48 for a detailed examination of the use of the term *stephanos*). It was also a symbol of royal power: e.g., "(David) took the crown of Milcom from his head; the weight of it was a talent of gold" (2 Sam 12:30). For James the "crown of life" is the reward that lies ahead for those who have endured temptation successfully. James has in mind the victor's crown rather than a royal crown. This is a genitive of definition indicating in this context: "the crown that consists in eternal life." The reward is the eschatological life of the age to come. This phrase echoes the call in the Book of Revelation: "Be faithful until death, and I will give you the crown of life" (2:10). It refers to the reward for those who persevere in times of tribulation. The gift of life is also a key theme of the Gospel of John in reference to the present age. James sees this gift of life as related to the future. *(God) has promised:* note that the subject "God" has been supplied in the translation. Many manuscripts whose scribes apparently sensed the need to supply a subject insert "Lord" or "God." The omission in James of the name of God conforms to the careful avoidance of God's name both in Israelite speech and writing. The promise of the reward is made "to those who love God." The *Shema Israel* (Deut 6:4-5) expressed the foundation of Israel's faith in and relationship with God. To love God demonstrates that one is in the covenant relationship and will carry out God's will through obedience to the Torah. "I find delight in your commandments because I love them exceedingly" (Ps 119:17 [118:47 LXX]). James's thought both here and in the previous verses is reflected in a striking way in Ps 5:11b-12 (5:12b-13 LXX): "and all those who love your name will boast in you because you will bless the righteous; O LORD, as with a shield of approval you crowned us." James uses this phrase again in 2:5. There are analogies elsewhere in the New Testament to almost every phrase in 1:12, which shows how steeped James is in the early Christian tradition. First John 5:2 combines the love of God and the carrying out of God's commands: "By this we know that we love the children of God, when we love God and obey his commandments."

13. *Let no one say when tested, "I am being tempted by God":* James brings a certain clarity to the use of *peirasmos* ("test"). His thought has moved in a very specific direction. The noun *peirasmos* refers to external testing or trial, while the verb *peirazesthai* (1:14) refers to internal, subjective temptation. James makes a distinction between the external testing and the internal, psychological temptation. The first occasion where dialogue enters the text is the statement: "I am being tempted by God." James uses the style of the diatribe to introduce an imaginary argument in which he quotes a statement in order to correct it. Such a statement might seem to receive support from the perspective of the Hebrew Scriptures. For example, one could ask: "Did not God tempt Abraham in the command to sacrifice his son, Isaac?" (see Gen 22:1-14). In the wanderings through the desert the Hebrews also experienced the testing of God (see Deut 8:2; 13:3). In later parts of the Old Testament this testing is attributed rather to Satan (see Job 1:12; 2:6). James's concern here is to deny categorically that God has any role in tempting individuals from within so that they would succumb to evil. In such a case God would be seen as the tempter. As Heinrich Seesemann says: "[James] makes a statement about the nature of God which we do not find elsewhere in the Bible, namely, that He cannot be tempted to do evil and that He Himself does not tempt anyone, i.e., lead anyone into sin" (*TDNT* 6:29). James's concern is also supported by the ancient Greek moralists (see,

e.g., Philo, *Legat.* 2:78: "for when the mind sins and departs from virtue, it blames divine things, imputing its own sins to God"). Paul expresses a similar idea, though in different words: "No testing has overtaken you that is not common to everyone. God is faithful, and he will not let you be tested beyond your strength, but with the testing he will also provide the way out so that you may be able to endure it" (1 Cor 10:13).

For God is not tempted by evil, and he himself tempts no one: The adjective *apeirastos* ("not tempted") is not found in the LXX, or elsewhere in the New Testament. However, the phrase became proverbial in later writings (see examples in Mayor 51). It can have many nuances, as Davids indicates: "We may gather them (the translations) for convenience into three groups: (1) 'God cannot be solicited to evil,' (2) 'God is inexperienced in evil,' and (3) 'God ought not to be tested by evil men'" ([1977/78] 387). However, the meaning intended by James is clear: God "has nothing to do with evil" (Johnson [1995] 193). The second reason for denying that the temptation comes from God is that God is not tempted by evil and God tempts no one to evil. James states categorically that God is not directly responsible for temptation (Davids [1982] 83).

14. *But each one is tempted by one's own desire:* "Each one" refers to the individual person. "Desire" *(epithymia)* is singular. The testing comes from the evil impulse within the person, not from without. For James "desire" is not neutral; it is an interior force that drives the person to evil. James thus reflects thoughts popular in both the Hellenistic world and the Jewish intertestamental writings. Popular Hellenistic thought, influenced especially by Stoicism, tended to give "desire" an evil understanding: e.g., "So great and so excessive an evil is covetous desire; or rather, if I am to speak the plain truth concerning it, it is the source of all evils. . . . For most truly may covetous desire be said to be the original passion which is at the bottom of all these mischiefs . . ." (Philo, *Spec.* 4:84-85; see also Epictetus, *Diatr.* 2:18, 8). The book of Wisdom reflects the same idea of the evil nature of desire: "For the fascination of wickedness obscures what is good, and roving desire perverts the innocent mind" (4:12). James reflects here what is evident in later Rabbinic *yēṣer* theology of the two inclinations within the human being that are at war with each other: the inclination to evil *(yēṣer hārāʿ)* and the inclination to good *(yēṣer hāṭôb)* (Cantinat 86–87; Windisch 8–9; Davids [1982] 35–38; 83–84). In fact, the *Testaments of the Twelve Patriarchs* speak about two spirits that dwell within the human person (cf. *T. Jud.* 20:1; see the further discussion on this concept in the Notes and the Interpretation to Jas 4:5). James's main concern is not to stress an interior war between two competing desires, but rather to identify the evil nature of desire within the human person. He uses the emphatic personal pronoun *idios* ("his own") to stress the human origin of temptation.

being lured and enticed by it: Here are two expressions popular in the world of fishing and hunting: "lured" *(exelkomenos)* visualizes the person being drawn by a hook and dragged out of the water, while "enticed" *(deleazomenos)* envisages someone enticed by a trap with bait. This figure of speech is easily applicable to the evil desire. The combination of these images either alone or together with "desire" is found in Greek literature (see examples in Mayor 54).

15. *the desire, having conceived, gives birth to sin:* Desire is personified as a female person who conceives. A logical progression develops in this verse: desire conceives and brings forth sin; sin in turn gives birth to death. The word *tiktein* literally means to give birth. The combination of "conceive and give birth" *(syllabousa . . . tiktei)* is probably a Semitism as it occurs some twenty-four times in the Hebrew Scriptures. Sin (singular, *hamartia*) is itself personified as the child of desire. Later James uses the plural to identify individual transgressions.

    and sin, once it has come to maturity: The personification continues here. Successive generation is indicated: sin in its turn reaches maturity and is able to bring forth its own offspring, namely death. The verb *apokyein* ("to generate") is used metaphorically in accord with the rest of the personification in this image. It occurs again in 1:18 in reference to God. Death as the consequence of sin is common biblical belief (see Gen 3:17-19; Ezek 18:4; Rom 7:7-12). The sequence comes to a conclusion: desire → sin → death, and creates an antithetical parallelism to the previous sequence of testing → endurance → life (1:12).

16. *Do not be deceived, my beloved brothers (and sisters):* The phrase "do not be deceived" is a negative figure of speech that calls attention to an important teaching. It occurs in the diatribes of Epictetus: "Men, be not deceived *(mē planasthe)*, it is well with me" *(Diatr.* 4:6, 23 [Oldfather, LCL]), in the writings of Paul (1 Cor 6:9; 15:33; Gal 6:7) and in Ignatius *(Eph.* 16:1; *Phld.* 3:3). In the active voice the verb *planan* has the meaning of "go astray; wander." James uses it in this sense at the end of the letter (5:19). "My beloved brothers (and sisters)": see v. 2 above for the use of *adelphos.* The adjective "beloved" *(agapētoi)* occurs again in 1:19 and 2:5.

17. *Every good act of giving and every perfect gift is from above:* The structure of the opening part of this sentence represents the metrical verse of a hexameter (see Ropes 159). Some commentators have argued that this is a quotation taken from a Hellenistic poem (Dibelius 99–100; Mayor 57; Amphoux 127–36; Davids [1982] 86). The source of such a quotation is unknown and does not affect the interpretation. The poetical quality of this verse may simply be another indication of James's ability to play with words (Laws [1980] 72). The two phrases *pasa dosis* and *pan dōrēma* are used as synonyms. There is a slight nuance in meaning: *dosis* is a verbal noun and captures the idea of the "act of giving" in contrast to *dōrēma*, which refers to the "gift itself." The word *dosis* occurs in Sirach (e.g., 11:17; 26:14), while *dōrēma* is more poetic and appears in the LXX only in Sir 34:18 (see BDAG 266). The purpose of these synonyms is to stress the goodness and perfection of God's gifts. Perfection *(teleiosis)* is in line with 1:4: God's gifts bring wholeness and completeness. The phrase *anōthen estin* ("is from above") belongs together, hence the translation: "is from above, coming down from . . ." rather than simply "comes down from above" *(contra* Dibelius 100). The concept of gifts from above is considered at 3:13-18, where attention is drawn to God as the source of these gifts. The participle *katabainon* ("coming down") develops the phrase "from above" and explains why the gifts are good and perfect.

from the Father of lights, with whom there is no variation or shadow of change: In the Hebrew writings God as Father had the connotation of God as creator: e.g., "Has the rain a father?" (Job 38:28). This Jewish circumlocution ("Father of lights") refers to God as the creator of the stars, especially the sun and moon (Gen 1:14-18; Ps 136:7; Jer 4:23; 31:35; Sir 43:1-12). God is the source of all light: "For with you is the fountain of life; in your light we see light" (Ps 36:9 [35:10 LXX]). The phrase "Father of lights" is found elsewhere only in *Apoc. Mos.* 36:1-3: "They (the sun and moon) are unable to shine 'before the light of all'" (*OTP* 2:289). Several manuscripts add the phrase "Father of lights" (see Laws [1980] 73). God as creator was thought of as light: "The LORD is my light *(kyrios phōtismos mou)* and my salvation . . ." (PS 27:1 [26:1 LXX]). Philo *(Somn. 1:75)* explains very concisely what is meant when God is referred to as the light:

> And it is easy otherwise by means of argument to perceive this, since God is the first light, 'For the Lord is my light and my Saviour,' is the language of the Psalms; and not only the light, but he is also the archetypal pattern of every other light, or rather he is more ancient and more sublime than even the archetypal model, though he is spoken of as the model; for the real model was his own most perfect word, the light, and he himself is like to no created thing.

While Philo presents an abstract metaphysical speculation on God as light, this is far from James's more concrete presentation. The phrase "there is no variation or shadow of change" contains a number of *hapax legomena.* Consequently scribes tended to emend or correct the text (see Aland [1997] 14 for a survey of the different readings proposed by the different manuscripts). For a discussion and evaluation of the different variations see Ropes 162–65; Dibelius 101–103; Metzger (1975) 679–80; and Johnson (1995) 196–97. I follow the decision of the text of the *Greek New Testament* of the *UBS* fourth revised edition and the *Nestle-Aland* twenty-seventh revised edition *(parallagē ē tropēs aposkiasma),* which Metzger calls "the least unsatisfactory reading" ([1975] 679–80). Despite so many different readings, the actual meaning remains the same: God is unchangeable and consistent, as opposed to the fickleness of creation. This is not an attempt to provide a metaphysical description of God's being, but a reflection of God's moral action: it is always consistent.

18. *Because he freely decreed it, he gave us birth by the word of truth:* This captures God's will and God's firm plan to give salvation. Not only did God firmly decide, but attention is drawn to the content of God's decision. The same verb as in 1:15, *apokouein,* is used here. Whereas in 1:15 the reference was to sin giving birth to death, here God gives birth to life. This is one of the few female images for God within the New Testament. Philo offers a detailed description of God giving birth:

> At all events we speak with justice, if we say that the Creator of the universe is also the father of his creation; and that the mother was the knowledge of the Creator with whom God uniting, not as a man unites, became the father of creation. And this knowledge having received the seed of God, when the

day of her travail arrived, brought forth her only and well-beloved son, perceptible by the external senses, namely the world (*Ebr.* 30).

The phrase *logǭ alētheias* ("by the word of truth") is an instrumental dative. "The word of truth" was the means by which something came to birth. This can be understood in three possible ways: *(1) As a reference to creation:* God created the world and in particular humanity through God's word (Gen 1:26-30). *(2) As a reference to the Torah or Law,* since the Israelite Law is understood as "God's word of truth." Psalm 119 (118 LXX) is a beautiful ode to the glories of God's Torah. It refers to God's Law in phrases that come close to James's "word of truth": "Do not take *the word of truth (logon alētheias)* utterly out of my mouth" (v. 43); "Your righteousness is an everlasting righteousness and *your law is the truth* (*ho nomos sou alētheia*) (v. 142); "Yet you are near, O LORD, and all your commandments are true" (v. 151). *(3) As a reference to God's creation of the Christian community:* the phrase *logos alētheias* occurs a number of times, particularly in Paul's writings with the meaning "the gospel of salvation," e.g., Col 1:5: "You have heard of this hope before in the word of the truth *(en tǭ logǭ tēs alētheias),* the gospel that has come to you." See also Eph 1:13: "In him you also, when you had heard the word of truth *(ton logon tēs alētheias),* the gospel of your salvation . . ." (see as well 2 Cor 6:7; 2 Tim 2:15).

so that we might be a kind of first fruits of his creatures: The construction *eis to* + infinitive is a strong final clause expressing the purpose or goal for God's creation "by the word of truth." The enclitic, indefinite pronoun *tina* "indicates a figurative expression" (Ropes 167) and hence the translation "a kind of." In the LXX *aparchē* ("first fruits") referred to the firstborn of humans or of flocks and the first harvest of the fields: they were sacred to God and were to be offered to God: e.g., "You shall not fail to give the first fruits *(aparchas)* of your threshing floor and your winepresses. The firstborn of your sons you shall give to me. You shall do the same with your firstborn animals and oxen" (Exod 22:28-29). While in the LXX the term is always used in a literal sense, in the New Testament it takes on a metaphorical meaning: "But in fact Christ has been raised from the dead, the first fruits *(aparchē)* of those who have died" (1 Cor 15:20). It refers also to the first believers in certain areas: "You know that members of the household of Stephanas were the first fruits *(aparchē)* of Achaia" (1 Cor 16:15). Greek writers use the term *aparchē* to refer to the first share that will be offered in sacrifice (see Herodotus, *Hist.* 1:92; 4:71). Its more common usage is metaphorical, referring to the first outcome of an undertaking (Plato, *Prot.* 343B). The noun *ktismatōn* ("of his creatures") is derived from the verb *ktizein* "to create" and has the meaning "that which is created by God." It does not occur frequently in the LXX. This is not surprising, given that the concept of creation was not well developed or deeply reflected upon. It does occur in the wisdom literature: Wis 9:2; 13:5; 14:11; Sir 36:20. Its use in the New Testament is also infrequent, occurring only in 1 Tim 4:4 ("For everything created by God is good" *[hoti pan ktisma theou kalon]* and Rev 5:13 ("every creature in heaven . . ." *[kai pan ktisma ho en tǭ ouranǭ]*. In Rev 8:9 it is used in the plural as it is in James: ". . . a third of the living creatures in the sea . . ." *(to triton tōn ktismatōn tōn en tē thalassē . . .).* This plural usage brings

the meaning from a more general reference to creation to a more specific identification of the hearers/readers (us) as God's creatures.

19. *Know this:* Two problems emerge with this verb *iste.* (1) The textual reading is
disputed. The Textus Receptus replaces *iste* ("know") with *hōste* ("and so,
therefore"). However, the Alexandrian and Western manuscripts support the
reading *iste* (see Metzger [1975] 680). The change from *iste* to *hōste* can be explained by a copyist attempting to produce a smoother transition from v. 18 to
v. 19 by drawing out a conclusion. James's style, however, often employs imperatives to begin paragraphs. There is no evidence for his use of the word
hōste. (2) *Iste* can be understood as either an indicative or an imperative of the
verb *oida.* I read it as an imperative (as do Dibelius 108–109; Mussner [1981]
99; Davids [1982] 91; Wall [1997] 69; *contra* Mayor 64–65; Johnson [1995]
198–99). The strongest reason for seeing it as an imperative comes from the
structure, where 1:16-18 parallels 1:19-21: each begins with an imperative followed by a vocative address ("my beloved brothers [and sisters]") that culminates in a reference to the salvific role of the word. In the letter of James the
vocative *adelphoi mou* ("my beloved brothers [and sisters]") occurs some fifteen times, twelve of them in conjunction with an imperative and only once
with a declarative statement (see 3:10). "My brothers (and sisters)" acts as a
marker that indicates the transition to a further point within the main paragraph. In this way James introduces a proverb that contains simple wisdom
about listening carefully, never speaking rashly, and not getting angry.

Let every person be quick to hear, slow to speak, slow to anger: The phrase *pas
anthrōpos* is a Semitism for the more natural Greek *pantes* ("all"). This often
occurs in the New Testament (John 1:9; 2:10; Gal 5:3; Col 1:28). This proverb
applies to all people, not just to those of the house of Israel or to Christians
alone. James's advice comprises a threefold saying whose Greek form is well
balanced: *akousai—lalēsai* ("to hear—to speak") and *tachys—bradys—bradys*
("quick—slow—slow") (see Dibelius 111–12 for an examination of its proverbial character). While the structure of the proverb shows it is being handed
down in Greek, the ideas are at home within the Israelite wisdom tradition.
The three phrases recall many similar references in the wisdom tradition. The
first phrase *"be quick to hear"* is reflected in the book of Sirach, which has a
number of sayings that capture the concept of being ready to hear: e.g., "Be
quick to hear, but deliberate in answering" (Sir 5:11); "If you love to listen you
will gain knowledge, and if you pay attention you will become wise" (Sir
6:33); "Be ready to listen to every godly discourse, and let no wise proverbs
escape you" (Sir 6:35). The second phrase *"slow to speak"* reflects frequent parallels in both Israelite and extra-Israelite wisdom: e.g., "Do you see someone
who is hasty in speech? There is more hope for a fool than for anyone like
that" (Prov 29:20); "Do not be reckless in your speech, or sluggish and remiss
in your deeds" (Sir 4:29). The third phrase *"slow to anger"* recalls the frequent
warnings against anger and its consequences found in ancient wisdom literature: e.g., "Unjust anger cannot be justified, for anger tips the scale to one's
ruin" (Sir 1:22); "Anger destroys the prudent" (Prov 15:1 LXX); "Do not be
irascible, for anger leads to murder" (*Did.* 3:2).

20. *For a person's anger does not accomplish God's righteousness:* The Greek has *anēr* ("man"; see the Notes on 1:12). The intention is to give an example of universal application, as can be seen from the contrast drawn between people's anger and God's righteousness. God is the measure for the way human beings should act. The contrast is between God and human beings, not God and males. This contrast occurs frequently in Homer's *Iliad* and *Odyssey*, where the word *anēr* refers to human beings in contrast to the gods (e.g., "Father Zeus, if ever among the immortals *[athanatoisin]* I aided you by word or deed, fulfill for me this wish: do honor to my son, who is doomed to a speedy death beyond all other men but now has Agamemnon, lord of men *[andrēn]* put dishonor on him . . ." (*Il.* 1:503 [Murray, LCL]; see also 17:446; Mayor 65). The verb *ouk ergazetai* ("does not accomplish") is literally "does not work." This reflects back to *katergazetai* (1:3), where faith produces endurance and endurance effects a "perfect work." It is a connection to James's theme of faith in action. The concept of "God's righteousness" runs throughout the Old and New Testaments. One must remain true to the meaning as it emerges from the relevant biblical witness. This is significant for the discussion on the relationship between Paul and James. In this context James understands it as "the righteousness that God approves" (Ropes 169). "God's righteousness" is *an objective genitive:* it refers to what God demands, the standard God sets for humanity to attain (see J. A. Ziesler, *The Meaning of Righteousness in Paul: A Linguistic and Theological Enquiry.* SNTSMS 20 [Cambridge: Cambridge University Press, 1972] 135; Schrenk, *"dikaioō," TDNT* 2:200–201). It is in line with the use of the concept of righteousness in the Gospel of Matthew, where in the Sermon on the Mount it embraces the understanding of "moral action according to the will of God" (see Luz [1989] 237–38), e.g., "For I tell you, unless your righteousness exceeds that of the scribes and Pharisees, you will never enter the kingdom of heaven" (Matt 5:20); "but strive first for the kingdom of God and his righteousness, and all these things will be given to you as well" (Matt 6:33). A second way of understanding "the righteousness of God" is to see it as a description of how God acts in the course of salvation history. In this sense it is *a genitive of origin:* it is what God gives, God's acts or gifts of salvation to Israel and to the new people of God. This is the meaning the prophets captured and Paul continued, e.g., "they are now justified by his grace as a gift, through the redemption that is in Christ Jesus" (Rom 3:24). Since James considers righteousness within the context of human actions, its meaning must embrace the understanding that human action should live up to the divine standard (the first meaning: an objective genitive) (see Wall [1997] 70–71). The same idea of righteousness continues in 2:21-24, where someone is declared righteous: that person's actions are seen to conform to God's standards with the consequence that such people are measured as "friends of God" (2:23).

21. *Therefore, put away every sordidness and abundance of wickedness:* The emphatic adverb *dio* ("therefore") brings the advice in 1:20-21 to a conclusion (Wall [1997] 71). The participle *apothemenoi* ("put away") functions as an imperative in this context. The verb *apotithēmi* is used for taking off or laying aside one's clothes (see, e.g., 2 Macc 8:35: "took off his splendid uniform . . ." *[tēn doxikēn*

apothemenos esthēta . . .]; see also Josephus, *A.J.* 8:266). In a figurative sense it refers to getting rid of or putting away some vice: e.g., "Let us then lay aside *(apothēmetha)* the works of darkness and put on the armor of light" (Rom 13:12); "but now you must get rid of *(apothesthe)* all such things—anger, wrath, malice, slander, and abusive language from your mouth" (Col 3:8; see also 1 Pet 2:1; *1 Clem.* 13:1). Because of the baptismal ritual of taking off clothes for ritual purification and rebirth to a new life some scholars see the figurative use reflecting a baptismal context (Mussner [1981] 101). This is probably true of the usage in 1 Pet 2:1-3, given the context, but there is no clear evidence to suggest that a baptismal background influenced James. The figure of clothes is continued with the object *ryparia* ("sordidness"), which literally means dirt or filth. Metaphorically it indicates evil habits and inclinations that must be discarded like filthy garments. This is a *hapax legomenon* in the New Testament. James 2:2 uses it again as an adjective *(rypara)* to indicate the poor man's "filthy clothing." The alliteration with *p* in this verse is noteworthy: *apothemenoi / pasan / ryparian / perisseian / prautēti*. A second object is indicated with the phrase *kai perisseian kakias* ("and abundance of wickedness"). The noun *kakias* is a genitive of apposition. The word is generally used for the opposite of virtue *(aretē)* (see Aristotle, *Rhet.* 1383B). It indicates evil action or character rather than an abstract concept of evil (Johnson [1995] 201).

and welcome with meekness the implanted word that is able to save your souls: The positive dimension is now expressed. The verb *dechesthai* literally means to receive, but has a depth of feeling that is captured by the translation *welcome.* The manner in which the welcome is to be extended is *prautēti* ("with meekness"). The Greek noun *praus* ("meekness") is contrasted with *orgē* ("anger") rather than with *kakias* ("wickedness"). In the writings of Aristotle the contrast between these two virtues/vices is expressed clearly (e.g., "and since becoming angry *[orgizesthai]* is the opposite of becoming mild *[praunesthai]*, and anger *[orgē]* of mildness *[praotēti]* . . ." [*Rhet.* 1380A {Freese, LCL}]). Ropes sees this virtue as "the centre of the whole disposition recommended in vv. 19-21" (171). The attitude of meekness captures the central Hebrew concept of the *ᶜānāw* and *ᶜᵃnāwim*, the poor, who abandon themselves to total trust in God. It is reminiscent of Jesus' promise in the beatitude: "Blessed are the meek *(praueis)*, for they will inherit the earth" (Matt 5:5). "Welcome . . . the implanted word" *(emphytos logos):* The meaning of the adjective *emphytos* is much discussed. Two meanings can be given to it: *innate* or *implanted.* (1) The meaning "inate" or "natural" corresponds to the usage found in Wis 12:10: "their inborn wickedness" *(emphytos hē kakia autōn).* While this is the only use in the LXX and the New Testament, it does occur quite frequently in the literature of the Hellenistic world (e.g., Josephus *A.J.* 16:232 ("an inborn hatred" *[kai misos emphyton]*); see also Josephus *B.J.* 1:88; Plato, *Symp.* 191D). This corresponds to the Stoic idea of inborn reason or natural law, as Jackson-McCabe argues: "James's use of the terms 'implanted *logos*' and law as functional equivalents derives from the Stoic identification of human reason as a divinely given natural law. His lavish description of this law as one that is both 'perfect' and 'of freedom' is also best understood in light of the Stoics" ([2001] 154). The difficulty with this

interpretation is the context of its use in James. The idea of receiving something that had already been placed within one from birth is somewhat contradictory. (2) "The *implanted* word" has in mind the word of the gospel, which
they received after their natural birth but which gave them a rebirth. It refers
back to 1:18, where James's hearers are reminded that they are given rebirth
"by the word of truth" and become "the first fruits of his (God's) creatures."
I prefer to understand it in this sense. James's hearers are urged to accept and
to act upon that word of truth, the word of the gospel that had been implanted
within them when they became "the first fruits of God's creatures." The implanted word is able to bring salvation to the *psychē*. This word has a wider
connotation than simply "soul." It is not intended to contrast with the body,
but seeks to capture the whole of a person's being. This is expressed well in
the Gospel of John: "The good shepherd lays down his life *(psychēn)* for the
sheep" (John 10:11; see also Deut 6:5; Job 33:28). The salvation envisaged looks
to the future. For James salvation depends above all on God's gift, to which
the human being responds by acting in a moral way.

22. *But become doers of the word:* The imperative of the verb *ginesthai* is translated
    in the sense of "become," rather than "be" (cf. Ropes 174). This is the way the
    letter of James consistently understands this verb (1:25; 2:4, 10, 11; 3:1). The
    readers/hearers are challenged to put into effect the word they have received,
    which implies a development, a "becoming." The phrase *poiētai logou* ("doers
    of the word") has the meaning "to carry out what is commanded" (Ropes
    175). This is a Semitism, as the Greek *poiētēs* actually means "composer or
    maker" (see, e.g., Plato, *Resp.* 597). The Hebrew Bible spoke of "doing the
    words of the law" (Deut 28:58; 29:29 [29:28 LXX]). The LXX spoke of "doers of
    the law" *(poiētēs tou nomou)* (e.g., 1 Macc 2:67: "doers of the law" *[tous poiētas
    tou nomou]*; see also Sir 19:20). This exact formulation occurs in Jas 4:11.

    and not merely hearers who deceive themselves: The word *akroatai* ("hearers")
    occurs three times in James (1:22, 23, 25). It appears elsewhere in the New Testa-
    ment only once ("For it is not the hearers of the law *[akroatai nomou]* who are
    righteous in God's sight, but the doers of the law who will be justified" [Rom
    2:13]). The similarity between James and Paul here is attributed to their
    common roots within the Jewish moral tradition. "A hearer of the law or of the
    word" implies that the Scriptures are being read in public in the context of a
    liturgical assembly. The participle of the verb *paralogizesthai* ("who deceive
    themselves") goes with the noun "hearers" rather than with the subject ("you")
    of the verb *ginesthe* ("become" *[contra* Dibelius 114]). For James the deception
    comes from hearing and not practicing what one hears. The verb is found in
    the New Testament only here and in Col 2:4 ("I am saying this so that no one
    may deceive you *[paralogizētai]* with plausible arguments").

23. *Because, if one is a hearer of the word and not a doer, this person is like those who:*
    "Because" *(hoti)* introduces a type of argument containing a short parable
    illustrating how one is a hearer and not a doer. The phrase *houtos eoiken andri*
    ("this person is like those") is literally "this person is like the man *(anēr)* . . ."
    (see the Notes on 1:8, 12). Again the example is meant for universal applica-
    tion. For this reason the translation renders it in the plural: "those who. . . ."

In the rest of this paragraph (vv. 23-26) the plural translation of the Greek singular is maintained to prefer the consistency of this understanding of a universal example.

who look at their natural faces in a mirror: While the verb *katanoein* can have the meaning of "to consider, contemplate," in this context it means "to look at," as v. 24 indicates. The person goes away without giving much attention to what has been seen. The same idea of "look at" is found in Gen 3:6 LXX: "it is beautiful to look at *(katanoēsai)*. . . ." The phrase *tēs geneseōs autou* ("their natural faces") means literally "the face of his origin (or birth)." The face that nature gave each person is observed in the mirror with no lasting impression. In like manner people look into the mirror of the law and give little attention to the reflection of their character that the law presents. In James's world people used mirrors made of polished metal such as copper or bronze. Paul also uses the image of a mirror (1 Cor 13:12), but differently from James. Paul contrasts the imperfect knowledge gained from the mirror's reflection to knowledge that comes from seeing reality itself (cf. Plato's image of the cave in *Resp.* 7:514A–517C). The image of a mirror was popular in Hellenistic literature (see references in Mayor 71–72; Johnson [1995] 207–208). Most frequently the emphasis was on the reflection of the actual person, not the ideal person (Ropes 176). Philo, *Contempl.* 78, bears some resemblance to James in that Philo compares the law to a mirror wherein the soul contemplates itself: "The whole of the law . . . in which the rational soul begins most excellently to contemplate what belongs to itself, as in a mirror, beholding in these very words the exceeding beauty of the sentiments."

24. *For they look at themselves and go away and immediately forget:* The use of the tenses of the three verbs is interesting. The first and third verbs "look . . . forget" *(katenoēsen . . . epelatheto)* are gnomic aorists that are used in comparisons to convey universal truths (see 1:11). The gnomic aorist is translated as present. The expression "immediately forget" is borrowed by Herm. *Vis.* 3:13, 2. The second verb, *apelēluthen*, is a perfect tense that conveys a state that lasts, not a momentary action as with the other, aorist, verbs.

what they were like: The form *hopoios* (literally "of what sort") is used in the New Testament as part of an indirect question: see here and in 1 Cor 3:13; Gal 2:6; 1 Thess 1:9 (BDAG 716–17). A question is implied behind the statement: "What were you like?"

25. *But those who have looked intently into the perfect law of liberty:* This verse continues the example or illustration begun in v. 23. For this reason the translation continues using the plural in order to capture the universality of the example. The verb "have looked into" *(parakyptein)* implies peering into the mirror to study the object more closely. Mayor translates it "bending over the mirror in order to examine it more minutely" (72). For excellent charts noting the parallelism between looking into the mirror and into the law of liberty see Martin (50–51) and Mussner ([1981] 106). The first use of the word *nomos* ("law") in the letter occurs here: "into the perfect law of liberty" (see also 2:8, 9, 10, 11, 12; 4:11). The absence of the article before *nomos* is quite common (see 2:8, 12), but

here it is further specified in two ways: "the *perfect* law of *liberty*." *(1) The perfect law:* The use of the word *teleios* must be connected with the same usage in 1:4 and 1:17. "Every perfect gift" (1:17) comes down from God. Without doubt the law is truly the gift from God that brings wholeness and completeness. The law James has in mind is the biblical Torah, the expression of God's will for God's people (see *Excursus 5: The Perfect Law of Liberty*). The Psalms celebrate the Torah as God's great and perfect gift to God's people: "The law of the LORD is perfect, reviving the soul; the decrees of the LORD are sure, making wise the simple" (Ps 19:7 [18:8 LXX]). The LXX uses the word *amōmos* in this context, namely "without blemish or fault." Psalm 119 (118 LXX) celebrates the glories of God's Torah and the psalmist's desire to lead a life directed by the Torah: "Happy are those whose way is blameless, who walk in the law of the LORD" (Ps 119:1 [118:1 LXX]). The importance of the Torah in the letter of James closely resembles the importance that Jesus in Matthew's Gospel gave to his role of fulfilling the law, not abolishing it: "Do not think that I have come to abolish the law or the prophets; I have come not to abolish but to fulfill" (Matt 5:17). *(2) The law of liberty:* this is an objective genitive: the law whose observance renders a person free, or in whose observance a person experiences liberty. What does James understand by this phrase, both here and at 2:12? The Torah is obeyed not because it is externally enforced, but because it is willingly accepted and obeyed from within. The concept of the Torah as the law of liberty is not a new idea introduced by James. He undoubtedly is influenced by the Jewish tradition: e.g., 4 Macc 5:16 speaks of "our own willing obedience to the Law" (*OTP* 2:550). The Stoics had a concept of obedience to the law of nature that renders a person free (see Jackson-McCabe [2001] 136–54). This was a concept that had influenced society widely. It does not mean that James is dependent on the Stoics for its usage here. There are sufficient examples in the traditions of Israel to account for James's usage.

become not hearers who forget but doers of the deed. They will be blessed in what they do: The phrase *akroatēs epilēsmonēs* is a genitive of quality (literally "hearer of forgetfulness"). The following phrase, *poiētēs ergou* (literally "doer of the deed"), is an emphatic way of describing the one who carries out the law. The final phrase of this verse, *houtos makarios* (literally "he will be blessed") introduces a beatitude along the lines of 1:12. It is reminiscent of Jesus' beatitude "Blessed rather are those who hear the word of God and obey it!" (Luke 11:28). *In what they do* refers to the person's total conduct.

26. *If any think they are religious, and do not bridle their tongues:* "To think or consider" *(dokein)* is used in the negative sense of creating a wrong perception. The implication is that those to whom James refers have a wrong opinion of their religious nature. They think they are religious, but in fact they are not. Paul uses the same phrase in a similar way: "If you think *(ei tis dokei)* that you are wise in this age . . ." (1 Cor 3:18; see also 1 Cor 11:16; Gal 6:3). While the adjective "religious" *(thrēskos)* is not found elsewhere in the New Testament, its meaning is clear. It is derived from the noun *thrēskeia* (1:26, 27), meaning "religious worship," which includes rituals as well as pious practices such as almsgiving, prayer, and fasting (Matt 6:1-18). James's hearers/readers would

be aware of numerous religious practices in which they participated. The English translation "religious" or "religion" must be understood in the sense of external observances of worship. While the verb *chalinagōgein* ("to bridle") occurs twice in James (1:26; 3:2), it appears nowhere else in the New Testament or in the LXX (see BDAG 1076). It occurs in Herm. *Mand.* 12:1, 1 in reference to curbing evil desire. Polycarp refers to "the younger men . . . curbing *(chalinagōgountes)* themselves from all evil" *(Phil.* 5:3 [Lake, LCL]). It also occurs in Philo: "their tongue unbridled" *(Somn.* 2:164), as well as Lucian: "curbing his appetite for pleasures"*(tas de tōn hēdonōn orexeis chalinagōgousēs)* *(Tyr.* 4 [Harmon, LCL]). James uses a double metaphor here: *the tongue* stands for speech, while *to bridle* implies control. In a figurative way James argues that his hearers/readers cannot consider themselves religious if they do not control their speech.

but deceive their hearts, their religion is worthless: The Greek phrase *apatōn kardian autou* (literally "deceive his heart") is difficult to translate because of the double antithesis introduced into the protasis: *religious—bridling* and *think—deceive (apatōn):* "If any are *religious* but do not *bridle* their tongues, if any *think* but *deceive* themselves." Uniting the two antitheses gives the translation: "If any think they are religious and do not bridle their tongues, but deceive their hearts." Johnson ([1995] 210–11) fails to see this twofold antithesis by taking "indulging the heart" as in apposition to "bridling the tongue." The consequence is that "their religion is worthless." This adjective *mataios* ("worthless") is often associated in the biblical writings with pagan religions, e.g., "Why have they provoked me to anger with their images, with their foreign idols (literally: worthless things *[en mataiois]*)?" (Jer 8:19); "For the customs of the peoples are false *(mataia)*" (Jer 10:3); "We bring you good news, that you should turn from these worthless things *(apo toutōn tōn mataiōn)* to the living God" (Acts 14:15); "You know that you were ransomed from the futile ways *(mataias)*" (1 Pet 1:18). This adds a further condemnation of their understanding of religion: it is, in effect, idolatrous.

27. *Religion that is pure and undefiled in the sight of God (who is) also Father is this:* The two synonyms *kathara kai amiantos* ("pure and undefiled") present the positive and negative aspects of cultic religion. They are naturally associated with "religion" *(thrēskeia)* because in the ancient world purity rules demanded that both the worshiper and the offering must be ritually pure and without stain. The phrase *para* + dative is a figurative expression indicating "in the sight or judgment of someone" (BDAG 757): e.g., "For it is not the hearers of the law who are righteous *in God's sight*" (Rom 2:13; see also 1 Cor 3:19; Gal 3:11; 1 Pet 2:4, 20). In James's context it means "in the eyes of God; in God's sight/judgment." James further defines God by saying "God (who is) also Father" (literally "God and Father"). Paul often uses the phrase *ho theos kai patēr* or *theos patēr* at the beginning of his letters. The phrases are absent from the gospels and Acts. It is an indication of traditional liturgical language and usage.

to care for orphans and widows in their affliction, and to keep oneself unstained from the world: James's definition of religion embraces social action. The verb *episkeptesthai* carries the meaning of "go to see a person with helpful intent, visit" (BDAG 378). For James the believers are to emulate God's actions by visiting orphans and widows and caring for their needs. Orphans and widows are singled out for special attention because they are bereft of anyone to champion their cause. In the biblical tradition God becomes their champion: "You shall not abuse any widow or orphan. If you do abuse them, when they cry out to me, I will surely heed their cry" (Exod 22:22-23); "Father of orphans and protector of widows is God in his holy habitation" (Ps 85:5 [Ps 67:6 LXX]). God has made a special option for the poor as represented by widows and orphans. Consequently, James places social action at the heart of religious piety. This prepares for the consideration of the poor in the next paragraph (2:1-7). In the New Testament the word *thlipsis* ("affliction") became a standard term for the tribulations preceding the advent of the messianic age (see Matt 24:21, 29; Mark 13:19, 24; Rev 2:10). James understands the sufferings of orphans and widows in terms of the afflictions of the last days. This is the first occurrence of *kosmos* in James (see also 2:5; 3:6; 4:4). "The world" has the ethical connotation of something that is in opposition to God. In the Johannine literature this understanding of "the world" takes on an even harsher note of opposition. The concept was known to James from the worldview and traditions he had inherited from Israel. The final element of James's definition of religion is "to keep oneself unstained from the world." The Greek verb *tērein* means to keep a distance from something (see 2 Cor 11:9; 1 Tim 5:22). "Unstained" *(aspilos)* means literally "without spot." It is used figuratively in a moral sense: to preserve oneself from the evils of the world. See 1 Tim 6:14: "to keep the commandment without spot *(aspilon)* or blame until the manifestation of our Lord Jesus Christ." While this reading comes from the majority of the witnesses to the text, 𝔓⁷⁴ has a textual variant, *hyperaspizein autous* ("to protect themselves") (see Metzger [1975] 680). It does not change the meaning, but simply gives a more intense understanding of how to distance oneself from the world.

INTERPRETATION

James 1:12-27 is the second introductory section of the letter (see Introduction: 6. The Structure of the Letter). It introduces further themes that will be addressed later. Again it functions much in the manner of a table of contents (Johnson [1995] 15). Two subsections are clearly evident:

- Endurance under testing brings the crown of life (1:12-18)

- Religion in word and deed (1:19-27)

Endurance under Testing Brings the Crown of Life (1:12-18)

This subsection returns to the first theme introduced in the letter: endurance in faith in the midst of trials and testings leads to wholeness or perfection (1:2-4). James develops this thought further by bringing a stronger focus and clarity to bear upon it. James now examines the theological background to this testing. More specifically: What in it is attributable to God?

Jas 1:2-4 and 1:12-15 are parallel to each other. In 1:2-4 James shows how endurance under testing comes to perfection, while in 1:12-15 he uses the exact same concepts: endurance in the midst of testing brings the eschatological reward of the crown of life. In a more concrete form James shows how perfection or wholeness embraces an eschatological future vindication for those who love God. Taking these two passages as parallel to each other shows that completeness and fullness of life are ultimately attained in the future, where nothing will be lacking.

This section opens with a beatitude *(makarios)* that connects back to the image of those experiencing trials in general (1:2-4). James deepens the concept of *peirasmos* by narrowing its focus from external testing to internal temptation. James is concerned to bring clarity to the issue of the source and origin of temptations. His fundamental understanding is that God is *not* their origin. This categorical statement may have been prompted by discussions within the early Christian community around certain interpretations of the petition in the Lord's Prayer: "And do not lead us into temptation" (Matt 6:13; Luke 11:4). James wishes to counter the view that God is the source of temptations.

The Notes have demonstrated that in the Hebrew tradition God certainly was seen to test people such as the Israelites in their wanderings through the desert (Deut 13:3: "You must not heed the words of those prophets or those who divine by dreams; for the LORD your God is testing you, to know whether you indeed love the LORD your God with all your heart and soul"). Abraham is a classic example of one who was tried by God: "After these things God tested Abraham" (Gen 22:1). In the later books of the Hebrew Bible a more nuanced or developed understanding of God's relationship to testing emerged. In the classic example of Job, God is not the one who tests, but God allows Satan to test Job (Job 1:11-12).

This illustrates the ever-developing consciousness and understanding of God in the Scriptures. James shows a further development in this understanding. The early biblical texts operate with a concept of a God whose almighty power embraces every dimension, even that of evil, and they have no difficulty in attributing to God actions that a later era would consider to be evil. "But the LORD hardened the heart of Pharaoh, and he would not listen to them, just as the LORD had spoken to Moses" (Exod 9:12).

James portrays an image of God that removes God even further from the world of evil by focusing more specifically on the dimension of temptation. James rejects the notion that "I am being tempted by God" because of his understanding of God. God is defined as one who "is not tempted by evil." However one interprets this unusual Greek word *apeirastos*, the meaning for James remains clear: God is neither drawn toward evil nor does God have any experience in evil (see Davids [1982] 82–83). This is an emphatic way of stating that God is not involved in evil. One must look elsewhere for the source of the temptation.

James continues even more forcefully: "and he (God) himself tempts no one" (1:13). Once again *peirazei* must be understood within the context of the argument. James is considering the concept of temptation to evil, not that of testing in general. God tempts no one to evil for the same reason that God is not involved in evil. In summary, James's thought has developed from a consideration of testing in general to an understanding of temptation in the sense of "incitement to sin" (Casciaro 39). For James, God is not involved in sin and hence incites no one to sin. This is similar to the reflections of Sir 15:11-20: "Do not say: 'It was (God) who led me astray'; for he has no need of the sinful" (15:12). For this very reason no one can accuse God of being responsible for this "inclination to sin" (Casciaro 39).

James develops the argument further. The truth is that a person is tempted by desire (within the human person) that draws and entices to sin. The consequence of desiring is described in terms of the image of giving birth. When desire conceives it gives birth to sin, and when sin is fully mature it in turn gives birth to death. The popular concept of desire *(epithymia)* in James's world sees it as something within the human person that is intrinsically ordered toward evil: it is the seat of all evil. James holds the individual responsible for allowing desire to entice toward sin and ultimately spiritual death. He champions human responsibility for sin and returns to this theme later in 4:1-5, where he illustrates this visibly: "From where do wars and from where do battles among you come? Do they not come from this, namely your desires that are at war within your members?" (4:1; see also 5:1-6).

James's concept of God emerges very clearly from the graphic phrases he uses throughout this passage. God is not the source of evil, but the origin of every good and perfect gift. The gifts that come from God are perfect in that they bring completeness and wholeness. Above all, the gift of wisdom is "from above" (3:15) and is communicated to all who ask (1:5). God is described as the "Father of lights." As creator, God is the Father of the heavenly bodies: God brought them to birth. Light is symbolic of all good things as opposed to darkness, which brings evil. This opposition between light and darkness is clearly evident in the Qumran writings:

> (God) created man to rule the world and placed within him two spirits so that he would walk with them until the moment of his visitation: they are the spirits of truth and of deceit. In the hand of the Prince of Lights is dominion over all the sons of justice; they walk on paths of light. And in the hand of the Angel of Darkness is total dominion over the sons of deceit; they walk on paths of darkness (1QS 3:17-21; see also CD 5:18).

Unlike the heavenly bodies, whose movements change according to times and seasons and result in variations of light, their Creator is unchanging. God is identified with the qualities of stability and consistency rather than instability and fluctuation. Indirectly James contrasts God with the doubter and double-minded person (1:7-8). James's description of God is designed not to give an ontological expression to God's being, but rather to stress God's actions in giving good gifts. God's gifts do not bring forth evil and death, but rather goodness and life (1:18). James uses the generative image to describe God bringing forth God's creatures. While the phrase "he gave us birth by the word of truth" (1:18) can have a number of possible interpretations (see the Notes), from the context it is evident that James is referring to the rebirth of the Christian community. God has brought forth the recipients of this letter as "the first fruits of his (God's) creatures" (1:18). The phrase "first fruits" comes from Israel's cultic world, where the people offered to God the first unblemished produce of flocks and fields. Applying this to his hearers/readers, James in effect is saying that they are the first fruits of a new creation that God is bringing into existence. As such they are unblemished, they are perfect, not through what they do but through what God is doing in re-creating them.

This connects back to the letter's address to "the twelve tribes in the Dispersion" (1:1). "The first fruits of God's creatures" signifies a new beginning with these hearers/readers from the house of Israel. But God's plan does not end there. God's gift of rebirth is meant to embrace all humanity. As "the first fruits" implies, others must follow.

The hearers/readers form part of that reconstituted new twelve-tribe kingdom for which Israel hoped. "The perfect gift" (1:17) to which James alludes in this section is undoubtedly the gift of rebirth as this new, reconstituted people. God has brought into this enduring relationship all those who belong to the reconstituted people.

James urges his readers/hearers that, having received this perfect gift of rebirth as God's people, they should value the generous gifts God bestows on them. God is the source and origin of all good. If this gift is to endure and receive the future "crown of life" (1:12) they have a responsibility to remain true to what they have been given and to lead their lives in ways that rely upon the God of all good gifts. This leads James to turn attention in the next section to the responsibility this gift of new life brings: a responsibility that calls for a specific way of life.

Religion in Word and Deed (1:19-27)

This subsection is still under the influence of the *makarios* statement of v. 12: the one who endures trial is blessed. This long pericope presents examples of areas where testing is experienced. Its wisdom advice shows how to put belief into practice and hence be counted among those who are blessed.

Some commentators divide these verses differently: Johnson ([1995] 191–214) divides them into 1:13-21 and 1:22-27, while Wall ([1997] 68–102) makes the division 1:19-21 and 1:22-27). However, there is a line of thought running throughout 1:19-27 that forges a certain unity. James develops his thought around the "word of truth" (1:18) by focusing on how that influences the way one acts. James 1:19 provides the thesis statement. It is structured in parallel, with three phrases, each containing an adjective, the preposition *eis,* and the infinitive or the noun:

tachys eis to akousai ("quick to hear")

bradys eis lalēsai ("slow to speak")

bradys eis orgēn ("slow to anger")

Each phrase is developed in more detail throughout this unfolding paragraph. James begins, for structural reasons, with the last element of this three-part saying, *bradys eis orgēn* ("slow to anger"). By using it first James forges a closer link with the developing argument. James 1:19 ends with the thought of being "slow to anger," and so he continues with this thought first of all in 1:20-21. Then he turns to the other two elements, *tachys eis to akousai* ("quick to hear") in 1:22-25 and *bradys eis to lalēsai* ("slow to speak") in 1:26-27.

Be Slow to Anger (1:20-21)

Human anger does not conform to God's righteousness, the moral standard set by God. To be slow to anger sets one apart from the world and identifies one closely as a friend of God (4:4). The Shepherd of Hermas understood James in this way: "(T)he working of ill temper, and how evil it is and how it destroys the servants of God by its working, and how it leads them astray from righteousness" (Herm. *Mand.* 5:2, 1 [Lake, LCL]).

In leading their lives according to God's standards in 1:21 the hearers/readers must avoid all filthiness and wickedness. Discarding these ways of acting was compared to the shedding of a dirty garment. In 1:18 James spoke about God's gift of the "word of truth" that brought about a rebirth as God's creatures. By means of a parallel phrase, "the implanted word" (1:21), James gives a deeper understanding of how God's salvation operates. For salvation to be effective this "word of truth" has to be received and put into action. For James, salvation is a reality that is not onesided. As a gift that comes from God it must be welcomed and received in action by human beings. Response is essential.

As the Notes have indicated, the term "implanted word" can be variously interpreted. I understand it as referring to the word of the gospel that was implanted in the hearers at their rebirth as God's creatures. They have to welcome it by putting it into action through the lives they lead.

In these few verses James shows a developing theology. Two aspects are significant: (1) Human action is rooted in the moral standards God sets. (2) By God's action of reconstituting the twelve-tribe kingdom James's hearers/readers have been brought into that community through "the word of truth" and the "implanted word." However, they are called to respond. They work out their response as part of a community that embraces the same standards and values and in this way gives them their identity as "the first fruits of his (God's) creatures" (1:18). God's actions and human actions come together. Salvation depends on their response, the welcome they give to the word of God they have received.

Be Quick to Hear (1:22-25)

"Word" *(logos)* forges a connection with what went before. Here we attend to the first phrase of v. 19: "be quick to hear." To hear the word is now further specified in these verses: the hearers/readers must embrace the life of active followers of the word. This is straightforward wisdom advice on how to lead one's life in conformity to God's will, God's righteousness.

The central verse of this section, "Become doers of the word" (1:22), is in fact a suitable summary of the whole letter. The present imperative "become" reminds James's hearers/readers that their lives involve a constant development and growth. As believers they must put their belief into action. The "word" is God's word as expressed in the biblical Torah (see *Excursus 5: The Perfect Law of Liberty*). The phrase "doer of the law" (4:11) is used synonymously. As the Notes indicate, the concept of "doing the law" was frequent in the Israelite tradition. Philo (*Praem.* 79) shows his concern for both hearing and observing the law: "'If,' says he (Deut 30:10), 'you keep the commandments of God and are obedient to his injunctions, and receive what is said to you, not merely so far as to listen to them, but also to fulfil them by the actions of your lives, you shall have as a first reward victory over your enemies.'" For James it was a natural step to make the transition from "doer of the law" to "doer of the word."

In 1:18 I identified "the word of truth" with the proclamation of the gospel, whose reception made these God's reconstituted people. Johnson rightly notes ([1995] 214) that too sharp a distinction should not be made between the word of the gospel, the message of Jesus, and the biblical Torah. In effect they are different stages of the same reality. They are all bearers of God's word and expressions of God's will. The proclamation of

Jesus and of the gospel continues the proclamation of the biblical Torah by applying God's will to new situations and contexts. Jesus' message aims at reconstituting God's people anew in their adherence to the biblical Torah. This is in line with the spirit of Jesus' proclamation in Matthew's Sermon on the Mount (Matt 5:17-19). Jesus' message encapsulates the biblical Torah in the "royal Law . . . 'You shall love your neighbor as yourself'" (2:8).

To illustrate his point James gives a comparison that is in effect a brief parable. The central point lies in v. 24: if people do not lead their lives in accordance with God's word they are like those who simply glimpse themselves in the mirror and immediately walk away and forget what they look like. As the Notes have shown, the image of a mirror, quite frequent in both Israelite and Hellenistic literature, lends itself to a comparison with moral conduct. Just as the mirror shows how to improve one's appearance, so reflection on the law can lead to moral improvement. This further reinforces James's basic thesis that one must be a doer and not a hearer only.

James 1:25 continues the image of seeing by contrasting "looking at" (or glancing at) the mirror with "looking intently into" the perfect law of liberty. It is the perfect law because it brings wholeness and completion to those who abide by it as "doers of the law." It is the law of liberty because the observance of the Torah brings the experience of liberty. The biblical Torah gives them their identity as God's people and liberates them from the world that is evil. As a community that observes the biblical Torah they are free from the world and free to live in relationship with God and one another.

James concludes his advice with a blessing for those who are doers of the word. There is some ambiguity here: the blessing James pronounces could be a blessing experienced in the present, in the very action of carrying out the law, or it could be an eschatological blessing for the future for those believers who have faithfully carried out God's will. As Laws ([1980] 87–88) notes, probably both interpretations are in play here. This promise of blessing parallels the blessing promised at the beginning of this paragraph (1:12): the crown of life for those who endure the test.

Be Slow to Speak (1:26-27)

Finally, James takes up the third theme of 1:19, namely that of speech. He returns to this theme again later in the body of the letter (3:1-12). A warning is issued for the need to show restraint in speech. At issue here is the inconsistency between the way one speaks and what one claims to be or believe. James returns to this theme of inconsistency in different ways throughout the letter: 2:14-17; 3:9-10; 4:3-4. It corresponds to the image of the double-minded person (1:6) and is a further illustration of the call to be a doer of the word, not a hearer only.

In effect James seems to say that if people think they are religious but lack control of speech they deceive themselves, and their religion is worthless. James's concept of religion shows his heritage within the traditions of Israel in three ways. (1) Religious expression is addressed first and foremost to God as Father. (2) Religion is expressed in terms of action, as a duty to care for the most unfortunate within society, symbolized by the traditional biblical groups of the widows and orphans. They were the objects of God's special care and protection, and to show concern for them was in fact to imitate God. The concept of the imitation of God occurs quite frequently throughout this letter. (3) Religion embraces a way of life that is expressed through remaining faithful to the purity rules that are so essential in defining one's belonging to the community. The community members are concerned with identifying who they are and how they are to lead their lives as the reconstituted people of God's kingdom. The cultic language that pervades these verses (*worthless . . . pure and undefiled . . . unstained from the world*) has the distinct intention of providing those markers whereby the community members can identify themselves as distinct from the world around them. While these terms are readily associated with ritual and cultic practices within Israel's worship, James is not referring to any specific rite of Israelite worship. Rather, he is using the imagery and language of purity in order to capture the essential understanding of separation between those who belong to God and those who belong to the world (see *Excursus 2: James and the Heritage of Israel*).

The community continues to be bound and directed by the biblical Torah as an expression of God's moral will for God's community. James sees this moral will captured not in ritual observances but in an imitation of God's fundamental option for the poor. The community's true relationship with God is demonstrated through concern for the least powerful members. This separates them from society at large. Their community accepts responsibility for those who have no one to champion their cause. Without husband or parent to support them, widows and orphans become the responsibility of the community. This was the teaching throughout the biblical Torah. God is the champion of the weakest members of the community. The community accepts that responsibility to care for the weakest members in imitation of God. It is also a reminder of how God has acted toward them in the past: "You shall not deprive a resident alien or an orphan of justice; you shall not take a widow's garment in pledge. Remember that you were a slave in Egypt and the LORD your God redeemed you from there; therefore I command you to do this" (Deut 24:17-18).

In addition to defining their community by the essential marker of concern for the poor, orphans, and widows, James provides his community with a further identifying characteristic: they are to keep themselves unstained from the world. This challenges the community to preserve themselves in a moral sense from the corrupting influences of the world or the society around them. They do this through the inspiration of the biblical Torah. The community turns for guidance to the Torah's moral direction rather than to the values of the wider world or society. The Torah provides the moral horizon for the life of the community and offers directional pointers on how they are to lead their lives within this moral horizon. The Torah gives them the protection they need from the wider world that is not in conformity with the will of their God and Father, as well as the means to judge what is in conformity with the moral and wise vision and way of life their God calls them to follow. The biblical Torah enables the community ultimately to "keep themselves unstained from the world" (1:27).

These verses are an appropriate conclusion to this introductory section. They give expression to the main themes of the letter and what lies at the heart of James's thought. James writes to a community that shares the heritage of God's dealings with the people of Israel over many centuries. The biblical Torah continues to inspire their way of life. The wisdom instructions James gives provide them with directional pointers for the way they as a community continue to remain in relationship with God and one another. Those who "think they are religious" (1:26) without the corresponding way of life are deceiving themselves and in fact are idolatrous. Faith and action must go hand in hand: faith must express itself in action. True religious expression is found in the treatment of the least fortunate in the community (the orphans and widows). Again religion and social action are not two separate realms: they are one and the same, and each dimension impacts the other. This clearly prepares for the next chapter. Holding on to "the faith of our glorious Lord Jesus Christ" (2:1) demands actions that do not discriminate against the poor.

For Reference and Further Study

Amphoux, Christian-Bernard. "A propos de Jacques 1,17," *RHPR* 50 (1970) 127–36.

Black, Matthew. "Critical and Exegetical Notes on Three New Testament Texts: Heb xi.11; Jude 5; James 1:27," in *Apophoreta: Festschrift für Ernst Haenchen.* Berlin: Töpelmann, 1964, 39–45.

Davids, Peter H. "The Meaning of *apeirastos* in James 1.13," *NTS* 24 (1977/8) 386–92.

Edsman, Carl-Martin. "Schöpferwille und Geburt," *ZNW* 38 (1939) 11–44.

Elliott-Binns, Leonard E. "James 1,18: Creation or Redemption?" *NTS* 3 (1956/7) 148–61.

Greeven, Heinrich. "Jede Gabe ist gut, Jak. 1,17," *TZ* 14 (1958) 1–13.

Hauck, Friedrich. *"makarios,"* TDNT 4:362–70.

Jackson-McCabe, Matt A. *Logos and Law in the Letter of James: The Law of Nature, the Law of Moses, and the Law of Freedom.* NovTSup Vol. C. Leiden: Brill, 2001.

Johnson, Luke Timothy. "The Mirror of Remembrance: James 1:22-25," CBQ 50 (1988) 632–45.

_____. "Taciturnity and True Religion: James 1:26-27," in David L. Balch et al., eds., *Greeks, Romans, and Christians: Essays in Honor of A. J. Malherbe.* Minneapolis: Fortress, 1990, 329–39.

Luz, Ulrich. *Matthew 1–7: A Commentary.* Trans. Wilhelm C. Linss. Minneapolis: Augsburg, 1989.

Manns, Frederic. "Une tradition liturgique Juive sous-jacente à Jacques 1,21b," RSR 62 (1988) 85–89.

Marcus, Joel. "The Evil Inclination in the Epistle of James," CBQ 44 (1982) 606–21.

Roberts, David J. "The Definition of 'Pure Religion' in James 1:27," ExpTim 83 (1971/2) 215–16.

Schrenk, Gottlob. *"dikaios, dikaiosynē,"* TDNT 2:182–225.

EXCURSUS 5:

THE PERFECT LAW OF LIBERTY (JAMES 1:25)

The concept of law in the letter of James again shows his roots within the heritage of Israel (see Hartin [1991] 78–85 for a more detailed treatment of the concept of the law in the letter of James). James refers to the concept of law on three occasions: 1:25; 2:8-12; 4:11-12. Nowhere does he provide a concise explanation of the term. This indicates that it is part of the worldview and language he shares with his hearers/readers. They stand within a common and assumed frame of reference. The social sciences term this "high context compression." Given the fact that James and his hearers/readers come from the world of the house of Israel, the meaning of this term must be seen against that high context.

The best way to express James's understanding of the law is to refer to it as "the law of Israel," which in effect is the biblical Torah. This Torah gives expression to God's moral will for God's people. In his commentary on the letter of James, Robert W. Wall provides a detailed examination on the concept of law in James in his excursus "The Perfect Law of Liberty" ([1997] 83–98). In my use of the term "Torah" to refer to James's law I acknowledge my indebtedness to him for this insight. In speaking of the Torah in this way one endeavors to make explicit what was in effect a high context compression for James and his hearers/readers. The Torah provides God's instruction for Israel, and without doubt the Torah is the main way in which God's people are constituted as a nation separate from the nations and peoples around them. The Torah exercises the same socializing function for the hearers/readers of James's letter: adherence to

God's will gives them their identity as "the twelve tribes in the Dispersion" (1:1), distinct from the world around them. The exact content and understanding of the common insight James and his hearers/readers share on the Torah emerges from a look at James's references to the Torah throughout the letter. The aspect of Torah to which James gives attention is God's moral law for God's people rather than the ritual or ceremonial law. Instead of speaking about ritualistic practices James focuses on the heart of the Torah, the moral guidance provided by the *Shema Israel* and the Ten Commandments, the Decalogue. Throughout the letter James uses a number of phrases that reveal his understanding of the Torah:

The Perfect Torah (1:25)

James owes this concept to the heritage of Israel, e.g., Ps 19:7-8 (Ps 18:8-9 LXX):

> *The law of the* LORD *is perfect,*
> reviving the soul;
> the decrees of the LORD are sure,
> making wise the simple;
> *the precepts of the* LORD *are right,*
> rejoicing the heart,
> the commandment of the LORD is clear,
> enlightening the eyes.

While the LXX uses the Greek word *amōmos* to translate the Hebrew *tamim* ("perfect") instead of *teleios,* the same concept is being expressed, namely that of completeness and wholeness. A further insight into the concept of the Torah emerges through a synonymous parallelism: "the law of the LORD is *perfect* . . . the precepts of the LORD are *right*" (Ps 19:7-8 [Ps 18:8-9 LXX]). The Torah establishes a right relationship with the LORD. This is a dimension that is also characteristic of James's understanding of the Torah.

The use of the term *teleios* ("perfect") in connection with the Torah reminds the reader of its previous usage: "every good act of giving and every perfect gift is from above" (1:17). As such the Torah is also a perfect gift that has come down from above. Given the context of this usage in 1:22-25, James urges the hearers/readers to take seriously this perfect gift of the Torah, not simply by glancing at it, but by obeying it and carrying out its directional pointers. The Torah exercises its role especially on the community level. The Torah is the means to achieve identity as God's people and to distinguish the members from those outside the community.

As indicated in the Notes, the phrase "the law of liberty" (1:25) was known in the world of the Stoics. For them life led according to the law of reason or nature was a life that demonstrated freedom. For example, Seneca says: *In regno nati sumus: deo parere libertas est* "We are born in the kingdom: freedom is to obey God" (*Vit. beat.* 15:7) (see also Cicero, *Parad.* 34). This does not necessarily mean that James was influenced by Stoicism. The term had found its way into the common thought of the Hellenized Roman world, becoming part of its common language. Thus Philo makes use of this concept when he says "those who live in accordance with the law are free" (*Prob.* 45). Fourth Maccabees shows the understanding that the Torah is obeyed freely: "our own willing obedience to the Law" (14:2 [*OTP* 2:550]).

While James may have borrowed language from his surrounding world, he uses it in a very different way from the world of Stoicism. For the Stoics the law of nature was a universalizing concept that embraced all humanity and admitted no boundaries among people: all were recipients of this law by their very human nature. James, on the other hand, has contextualized and identified the Law of Liberty with the Law of Moses, the Law of the Kingdom. James is referring to a Law an in-group accepts and that gives them an identity. It is a Law whose purpose is to define boundaries, as opposed to the Stoic concept, which has no boundaries. James adopts an idiom of his day but expresses it within another context, namely that of the world of Israel.

James bears witness to a very positive understanding of Torah, one that is in line with the thought of Jesus in the Sermon on the Mount (Matt 5:17-20). Jesus presents his task as fulfilling the Torah by stressing its very heart: "You have heard that it was said. . . . But I say to you" (Matt 5:21-22). James is at home in the same thought world. "Both James and the Jesus of the Sermon on the Mount portray the Torah as providing the social fabric of norms that enable those who belong to that new society to remain in relationship with one another and with God. In effect, James is saying to his community: this is who we are and the Torah frees us to maintain this relationship" (Hartin [1999] 82).

The Law of the Kingdom (2:8)

"If you actually fulfill the royal Law according to the Scripture, 'You shall love your neighbor as yourself,' you do well" (2:8). "The law" continues to refer to the Torah, as before. The vocabulary reminds the reader of the reference to the law in 1:25. The verb *telein* means to fulfill in the sense of "to bring to an end, to bring to completion." The same concepts of law and completion operate as in 1:25. The people's actions as a community are praiseworthy if they bring the law to its completion, to wholeness, by abiding by the law of love.

James further identifies the law as "the royal Law" *(nomos basilikos)*. The adjective *basilikos* is related to the noun *basileia* (kingdom), to which James referred in 2:5: "Has not God chosen the poor in the world to be rich in faith and heirs of the kingdom *(basileias)* that he has promised to those who love him?" In both instances the kingdom includes those who love God and neighbor. The concept of kingdom is another of James's high-context statements. The people of Israel are clearly identified as belonging to God's kingdom from the moment of the establishment of the Sinai covenant: "Indeed, the whole earth is mine, but you shall be for me a priestly kingdom and a holy nation" (Exod 19:5-6). By obeying the covenantal laws the people of Israel are constituted as that society, that kingdom, in a relationship with God and one another. This covenantal relationship sets them apart from other peoples: they are God's own nation. The fulfillment of the law is the means by which they maintain their membership in the kingdom.

For James the law of the kingdom finds its fullest expression in the law of love of neighbor taken from Lev 19:18c. In the context of 2:1-13 the law of love gives expression to faith in "our glorious Lord Jesus Christ" (2:1). The faith of Jesus is compromised by those members of the community who show partiality and discriminate against the poor in favor of the rich (2:2-7). Egalitarianism is the hallmark of James's community. Those who make distinctions among people, in this instance based on their wealth or lack thereof, truly compromise membership in this community.

The faith of Jesus (2:1) refers not to an intellectual acceptance of certain facts or doctrines about Jesus but to an imitation of Jesus' faith-response through the way of life Jesus witnessed. Jesus embodied in his life and ministry an outreach to the poor of society. In his ministry he showed a disregard for people's rank and status. Instead he embraced all, especially those whom society rejected. By invoking the faith of Jesus in this context James is expressly drawing attention to the way Jesus interpreted the Torah by illustrating graphically the love of neighbor. Wall expresses this insight well by remaining true to the context when he says: "Again, I do not suppose that James's appeal to Jesus' faith in 2:1 is as authoritative interpreter of wisdom or a new Torah. Rather, the reference to 'the faith of our glorious Lord Jesus Christ' in 2:1 cues up the memory of his ministry among the poor (cf. James 2:2-4 *par.* Luke 14:7-14; James 2:5 *par.* Luke 6:20[-36]) alluded to in the following passage, a ministry that demonstrates his exemplary obedience to the 'royal Torah' of love (2:8)" ([1997] 96).

The law of love of neighbor truly captures the essence of Jesus' moral teaching. For James the law of love of neighbor is also the central focus of the royal Torah. Every New Testament tradition remembers this vision of Jesus and the emphasis he gave to the law of love of neighbor (see, e.g., Matt 19:19; 22:39; Mark 12:31; Luke 10:27; Rom 13:9; Gal 5:14; John 15:12; 1 John 3:11). Just as Jesus raised the law of love of God and neighbor to capture the whole of the Torah (Matt 22:37-40), so James views the love of neighbor as giving fullest expression to the Torah. Above all, in the love that is extended to the poor one sees the finest expression of the Torah. "In like manner, James, following the example offered by Leviticus 19, calls on his hearers/readers to see the Torah as providing the signposts that they as a community must follow in order to function effectively as that new society of the poor living in relationship with one another and with God" (Hartin [1999] 85).

Conclusion

The function of the Torah in the letter of James is one of socialization: it provides the moral and social boundaries within which the members of his community must live. Those who fulfill the Law give expression to their identity as members of God's royal nation in separation from those of other nations. The Law functions both as an identification marker and as a way to separate them from those who are outside. The law of love of neighbor remains at the heart of the Torah. James wishes to socialize his hearers/readers further so that they truly are identifiable as members of God's twelve-tribe kingdom. He wants to unite the community in its understanding of what it means to live in friendship with God (4:4). Conformity to the Torah provides the means by which they preserve their identity. The Torah ultimately accomplishes a fourfold aim in James's overall strategy:

- It creates a collective identity for the twelve-tribe kingdom that distinguishes it from the world.

- It encourages internal solidarity and cohesion among the members of the community.

- It promotes a steadfast commitment to God by showing "friendship with God" as the prime identification marker for the community.

- It requires a choice for God as opposed to the world.

FOR REFERENCE AND FURTHER STUDY

Fabris, Rinaldo. *Legge della Libertà in Giacomo.* Supplementi alla Rivista Biblica 8. Brescia: Paideia Editrice, 1977.

Johanson, Bruce C. "The Definition of 'Pure Religion' in James 1:27 Reconsidered,"
    ExpTim 84 (1972/73) 118–19.
Johnson, Luke Timothy. "The Use of Leviticus 19 in the Letter of James," *JBL* 101
    (1982) 391–401.
Klein, Martin. *"Ein vollkommenes Werk": Vollkommenheit, Gesetz und Gericht als
    theologische Themen des Jakobusbriefes.* Stuttgart: Kohlhammer, 1995.
Marconi, Gilberto. "Una nota sullo specchio di Gc 1,23," *Bib* 70 (1989) 396–402.
Slingerland, H. Dixon. "The Nature of *Nomos* (Law) within the *Testaments of the
    Twelve Patriarchs*," *JBL* 105 (1986) 39–48.

4. *Do Not Show Favoritism* (2:1-13)

1. My brothers (and sisters), do not hold the faith of our glorious Lord
Jesus Christ while showing acts of favoritism. 2. For if a man with gold
rings and in fine clothes comes into your assembly, and if a poor man in
squalid clothes also comes in, 3. and if you take notice of the one wearing
the fine clothes and you say, "Sit here in a good place," while you say to
the poor person, "Stand there" or "Sit at my footstool," 4. have you not
made distinctions among yourselves, and become judges with evil
thoughts? 5. Listen, my beloved brothers (and sisters). Has not God
chosen the poor in the world to be rich in faith and heirs of the kingdom
that he has promised to those who love him? 6. But you have dishonored
the poor person. Is it not the rich who oppress you? Do they not drag you
into court? 7. Have they not blasphemed the excellent name that was
invoked over you?

   8. If you actually fulfill the royal Law according to the Scripture, "You
shall love your neighbor as yourself," you do well. 9. But if you show
favoritism, you commit a sin and are convicted by the Law as transgressors. 10. For whoever keeps the whole Law but fails in one point has become accountable for all (of it). 11. For the one who said, "Do not commit
adultery" also said, "Do not kill." Now if you do not commit adultery
but if you do kill, you have become a transgressor of the Law. 12. So
speak and so act as those who are going to be judged according to the
law of liberty. 13. For judgment is merciless to the one who has not
shown mercy. Mercy triumphs over judgment.

NOTES

1. *Do not hold the faith of our glorious Lord Jesus Christ:* James opens with a negative
   imperative expressing a general prohibition. This conforms to a typical manner
   of expression in the letter: a command followed by an illustration. Three prob-

lems emerge in this text. *(1) The string of genitives:* "the faith of our Lord Jesus Christ of the glory," literally *tēn pistin tou kyriou hēmōn Iēsou Christou tēs doxēs.* This has led some commentators to suggest that the phrase "our Jesus Christ" is a later Christian interpolation into a Jewish work (e.g., Spitta 4–5). However, the addition of titles is characteristic of liturgical language (Davids [1982] 106), which may indicate something about the influences on James. *(2) The meaning of this genitive phrase:* Some interpreters read it as an *objective* genitive: "faith in our Lord Jesus Christ" (see Mayor 79; Ropes 187; Chaine 40). However, the *subjective* genitive is more probable: "the faith of our Lord Jesus Christ." In the letter of James faith is directed toward God, the Father, rather than to Jesus (see 2:19, 23). In this sense (a subjective genitive) the faith to which James refers is Jesus' faithfulness to his Father's will through the obedience of his life. This faithfulness operates as an example for the lives of believers: a faithfulness demonstrated in actions. *(3) The translation of the phrase tēs doxēs ("of glory"):* Some proposed translations are "the Lord Jesus Christ of glory" (Mussner [1981] 114) and "Jesus Christ who is the glory" (Mayor 80–82; Laws [1980] 94–97). More probable is the translation "our glorious Lord Jesus Christ" (Ropes 187; Davids [1982] 106; Johnson [1995] 220–21). This genitive is seen as adding a qualification to an existing title. Stylistically it is similar to the genitive usage "law of liberty" in 1:25. The word glory *(doxa)* is a traditional New Testament way of referencing Jesus' resurrection (see the usage in Luke 24:26; John 17:5; Phil 2:11; 3:21; 1 Pet 1:11).

while showing acts of favoritism (en prosōpolēmpsiais): The two Greek words *prosōpolēmpsia* (the noun in 2:1) and *prosōpolēmptein* (the verb in 2:9) have not been found in secular Greek or in the LXX (BDAG 887). They probably originated in early Christian paraenesis to capture the Hebrew *nāśāʾ panîm* ("to lift up the face" [Lev 19:15]; expressed in the LXX as *prosōpon lambanein*), literally "to show favoritism," especially in the context of judicial courts. God shows no favoritism (Deut 10:17), so neither should human beings. When used in the New Testament this phrase refers expressly to God's righteous judgment in which God shows no favoritism in judging human beings (see Acts 10:34; Rom 2:11; Eph 6:9; Col 3:25; 1 Pet 1:17). James 2:1 and 2:9 use these words exclusively to refer to human ways of treating one another, apparently reflecting Lev 19:15-18. In 2:1 the basis for avoiding favoritism is Jesus' faithfulness, the example of a life that embraced all people.

2. *For if a man with gold rings and in fine clothes comes into your assembly:* This verse begins a question that extends through v. 4 and ultimately expects a positive answer. James presents an example, not an actual occurrence. Dibelius (128–30) argues that no information on the context of the letter can be gained from these examples. While this is an imaginary situation, nevertheless the description does give some understanding of James's cultural context. The wealth of the person is captured in the very description (see Epictetus, *Diatr.* 1.22, 18 for a similar description of a rich person). The gold rings indicate further the wealth he possesses (*chrysodaktylios,* "gold rings" is found only in James, which means it was probably coined by him). While the gold ring was a sign of the equestrian order in the Roman society (see Laws [1980] 98–99), the context

of James does not demand such a specific identification. The wearing of rings was customary in Jewish society (see Luke 15:22). James's intent is to construct a contrast between wealth and poverty. The example goes on to describe the rich man entering the assembly *(synagōgē)*. This is the only usage of the term in the New Testament for a Christian gathering. The usual term is *ekklēsia* (see 5:14). Why then did James use *synagōgē* and not the more normal term *ekklēsia*? Without doubt this indicates James's closeness to the earliest stages of Christianity, when a full separation from its Jewish roots had not yet occurred. But more is indicated by the use of this term. It can designate the place of worship or the community gathering. It is in the latter sense that it is being used here. The community came together for a number of reasons: to worship, to study the Law, to settle community disputes, and to distribute alms to the poor. Given the context of 2:1, which warned against showing favoritism, and the use of the term *(prosōpolēmpsia)*, specifically within judicial contexts, James has in mind a community that has gathered together to exercise a court proceeding. Ward ([1969] 87–97) has presented a decisive and convincing examination and argument for this setting as a judicial court. The two parties who have entered the assembly are participants in a judicial process.

a poor man in squalid clothes: James uses the word *ptōchos* in place of *tapeinos* ("lowly" 1:9). Poverty is contrasted to wealth. This poverty is graphically emphasized through the adjective "squalid" *(rypara)*, which is immediately contrasted to the luxurious *(lampra)* clothes of the wealthy. This contrast is a reminder of the Lukan parable of the rich man and Lazarus (16:19-31).

3. *"Sit here in a good place" . . . "Stand there" or "Sit at my footstool":* This verse, by means of a further contrast, describes actions James rejects. The two people are unfamiliar with this meeting, as they have to be told where to sit. This supports the view that the assembly is a judicial court. The rich person is invited to sit rather than to stand, to be close (here) rather than to be distant (there). The poor person is further insulted by being told to come closer to the speaker and to sit on the floor next to his footrest. The expression *hypo to hypopodion mou* is translated as "at my footstool/rest." The preposition *hypo* does not necessarily mean *under,* but simply *beneath* (Johnson [1995] 223) or *at* (APNTG 526).

4. *have you not made distinctions among yourselves:* The apodosis is framed within a two-part rhetorical question. The word *diekrithēte* comes from the verb *diakrinein* ("to make distinctions") and has a twofold meaning. Literally it refers to being divided within oneself. See Ropes: ". . . practically, by your unsuitable conduct, departed from and denied the faith of v.[1], and thus fallen under the condemnation pronounced in 1[6-8] against the *dipsychos*" (192). This conforms to the dividedness of the person in 1:6 who is compared to the wave of the sea. At the same time it also contains the concept of actively making distinctions among people and discriminating against others.

become judges with evil thoughts: The phrase *dialogismōn ponērōn* is a genitive of quality. James includes a play on words with the two terms *diekrithēte . . . kritai* ("to make distinctions . . . judges"). The judicial context that was begun with *prosōpolēmpsia* (2:1, namely, showing favoritism in a judicial context) and the reference to the *synagōgē* ("assembly" in 2:2 as a judicial court) continues here with the explicit reference to "evil-minded judges" (Davids [1982] 110). Leviticus 19:15 lies close to this verse and possibly accounts for James's usage here (Laws [1980] 102): "You shall not render an unjust judgment; you shall not be partial to the poor or defer to the great: with justice you shall judge your neighbor."

5. *Listen . . . Has not God chosen the poor in the world:* The imperative *akousate* ("listen") is in line with the prophetic call that draws attention to the message (see Isa 1:10; Joel 1:2; Amos 3:1; Mic 6:1). James enunciates an important principle in what follows. The verse begins with a rhetorical question that expects an affirmative answer. The concept of choice or election was the very foundation of the faith of Israel. God had chosen them as God's people (Deut 4:37; 7:7). The followers of Jesus saw themselves as heirs of this choice: "You are a chosen race . . ." (1 Pet 2:9; see also Eph 1:4). "The poor" are counted among God's specially chosen ones. Ropes translates *tous ptōchous tō kosmō* as "poor by the standard of the world" (193). This grammatical construction is a dative of reference or value. By this expression James refers both to the poverty of some people and to the way the world judges them: as inferior. Behind the statement lies James's basic vision: the dualistic opposition between God and the world (4:4). The poor are specially chosen by God while the world regards them as worthless. This contrast is reminiscent of Paul's statement in 1 Cor 1:27-28: "God chose what is foolish in the world to shame the wise; God chose what is weak in the world to shame the strong; God chose what is low and despised in the world, things that are not, to reduce to nothing things that are."

to be rich in faith and heirs of the kingdom: This continues the reference to the poor as the object of God's choice *(exelexato);* they are "rich in the sphere of faith" *(plousious en pistei)* (Mayor 86; Ropes 194). See similar usages of *en* and the dative to indicate "in the sphere of": "you have been enriched in him in every way in the sphere of the word" (1 Cor 1:5); and "to be rich in the sphere of good works" (1 Tim 6:18). A second consequence of their being chosen is that they become "heirs of the kingdom" *(klēronomous tēs basileias).* This is reminiscent of Jesus' beatitude promise, which must provide the source for James's statement: "Blessed are the poor *(ptōchoi)* in spirit, for theirs is the kingdom *(basileia)* of heaven. . . . Blessed are the meek, for they will inherit *(klēronomēsousin)* the earth" (Matt 5:3, 5; see also Luke 6:20; *Gos. Thom.* 54). The expression "to inherit the kingdom" *(klēronomein basileian)* occurs in Matt 25:34; 1 Cor 6:9, 10; 15:50. The heir is the one designated as the recipient of the inheritance. In James this expression occurs only once, while in Paul the concept of the heir is central ("and if children, then heirs, heirs of God and joint heirs with Christ . . ."[Rom 8:17]; ". . . heirs according to the promise" [Gal 3:29]; "this is the pledge of our inheritance . . ." [Eph 1:14]). The word *basileia* ("kingdom") likewise occurs only once in James, which makes it difficult to define exactly what he understands by it. That it is a future blessing can be seen from the following verb *epēngeilato* ("that he has promised"). It would be the equivalent of eternal life or salvation. The irony of this promise is unavoidable: in the assembly the poor person is made to sit at the footrest of the speaker, while God gives that person a place in God's kingdom. The promise further parallels 1:12: "will receive the crown of life that (God) has promised to those who love him." Both 1:12 and 2:5 use the identical phrase *epēngeilato tois agapōsin auton* ("[God] has promised to those who love him"). "Kingdom" parallels "crown of life." This lends further support for understanding the kingdom as equivalent to "eternal life."

6. *you have dishonored the poor person:* James reverses the honor/shame code that is the foundation for the Greco-Roman society of the day. In that world honor was given above all to the patrons, the rich and powerful. Now in God's society it is the poor to whom honor is to be shown (see *Excursus 6: Honor and Shame, Patronage and Grace as Cultural Scripts behind the Letter of James*). By acting according to the values of the Greco-Roman society James's hearers/readers have "dishonored the poor." To shame or dishonor someone is undoubtedly a very serious offense: e.g., "The one who dishonors *(atimazōn)* the needy *(penētas)* sins, but the one who shows mercy to the poor *(ptōchous)* is blessed" (Prov 14:21 LXX); "It is not right to dishonor *(atimasai)* one who is poor *(ptōchon)* but intelligent, and it is not proper to honor one who is sinful" (Sir 10:23). See also the use of the verb *atiman* in Plato, *Phaed.* 107B and Xenophon, *Cyr.* 1:6, 20. Paul presents an equally serious charge against those who fail to honor the poor in the context of the eucharistic celebration (1 Cor 11:22); and 1 Pet 2:17 lays down the charge that Christians are to honor everyone *(pantas timēsate)*.

the rich who oppress you . . . drag you into court: Again James uses rhetorical questions that imply an affirmative answer. Three charges are leveled against the rich, who appear as a group outside the community. The first charge against the rich is for oppressing the poor: "Is it not *they (hoi plousioi)* who oppress *you (hymōn)*?" Such a complaint is found frequently throughout the Hebrew Scriptures. The same verb *katadynasteuein* (oppress) appears frequently in the LXX, especially in the prophets and the wisdom literature (Jer 7:6; 22:3; Ezek 18:7; Amos 4:1; Hab 1:4; Zech 7:10; Mal 3:5; Wis 2:10; 17:2). The verb occurs only twice in the New Testament (here and in Acts 10:38). The second charge against the rich is that they drag members of the community into court (see Luke 12:58). James does not envisage a formal official persecution of believers. It reflects the ordinary social forces at that time whereby the rich harass the poor legally with charges relating to work, debts, wages, rent, etc. James calls attention to the ordinary experiences the poor suffer in their contact with the rich. These experiences have become so common that James's hearers/readers have forgotten that the rich are indeed their true enemies (Dibelius 139).

7. *blasphemed the excellent name . . . invoked over you:* This is the third charge leveled against the rich. The word *blasphēmousin* ("blaspheme") refers to speech that slanders or harms another (see Philo, *Spec.* 4:197). In the religious sense it refers to speaking about God or Christ in an irreverent way. The first biblical reference to the sin of blasphemy occurs in Lev 24:10-16. In 1 Tim 1:13

Paul refers to himself as a blasphemer in that he persecuted Christians. "The excellent name invoked over you" is the name of Jesus. The verb *epikalein* ("to invoke") used in the passive with the word "name" *(onoma)* is a way of indicating ownership: "someone's name is called over someone to designate the latter as the property of the former . . ." (BDAG 373). It is above all a LXX expression indicating God's possession of Israel (see Amos 9:12; Deut 28:10). Christians replaced the name of God with the name of Jesus (Herm. *Sim.* 8:1, 1; 8:6, 4). In light of the context of this verse the name referred to by James must be that of "our glorious Lord Jesus Christ" (2:1). The name of Jesus was called over the believer at baptism (Acts 8:16; 10:48). The blasphemy, then, is the slandering of Jesus' name by the rich, the very name in which believers were baptized.

8. *If you actually fulfill the royal Law:* Verses 8 and 9 contain two contrasting conditional sentences: "if you actually . . . but if you" *(ei mentoi . . . ei de)*. The verb "fulfill" *(teleite)* returns again to the theme of perfection that recurs throughout the letter. The concept implies that the reader carries out the Law fully, wholly, or totally. The Law *(nomos)* to which James refers is the Mosaic Law in its totality as an expression of God's will for God's people. This is supported by the fact that the word *nomos* is used in preference to *entolē*: the Law in its entirety *(nomos)* is meant rather than a single command *(entolē)*. The adjective *basilikos* is a reminder of the noun *basilieia* (kingdom) in 2:5 and so should be interpreted in a similar way. Hence it is the "the Law of the kingdom." James refers here to the Mosaic Law that has been ratified by Jesus. For James the Law refers to the entire will of God as it has been made known in Jesus' teaching. Consequently "the royal Law" is not restricted to Lev 19:18 *(contra* Laws [1980] 108; Mussner [1981] 124), but embraces the entire Law of which the command to love is but a part (Ropes 198). The expression "according to the Scripture" is a reference to Lev 19:18. It could be rendered: "according to the passage of Scripture" (Ropes 199).

"You shall love your neighbor as yourself": This is a quotation from Lev 19:18c (LXX). The following verse (2:9) contains another allusion to Lev 19:15 (see Johnson [1982] for further allusions to Leviticus 19 in James). In Matthew's Sermon on the Mount, Jesus has fulfilled the Law by his coming (Matt 5:17) and taught that to love God and one's neighbor embraces the entirety of the Law and the prophets (Matt 22:34-40).

9. *But if you show favoritism, you commit a sin:* This conditional presents an example of a direct violation of the law of love. Instead of love, one shows favoritism and breaks the law of love. As with 2:1, *prosōpolēmptein* reflects Lev 19:15: "You shall not render an unjust judgment; you shall not be partial to the poor or defer to the great: with justice you shall judge your neighbor." For James the action of showing favoritism was a serious matter. Such action is sin and is contrary to the law of the kingdom.

convicted by the Law as transgressors: The verb *elenchein* expresses the sense of "to convict" (see John 3:20; 8:46). The construction with *hypo* + passive indicates what actually convicts them—in this case the Law. The Law is personified as a judge. See elsewhere for the personification of the Law: "O Law my teacher" (4 Macc 5:34); "I would not have known what it is to covet if the Law had not said, 'You shall not covet'" (Rom 7:7); "the Law was our disciplinarian" (Gal 3:24). The author has deliberately placed the noun *parabatai* ("transgressors") at the end of the sentence in order to stress it. In classical Greek this word (*parabatēs*) seldom occurs in the sense of "transgressor." It usually means "a warrior beside the charioteer, or a certain kind of foot-soldier" (BDAG 759; see Mayor 91 for a discussion of its usage in classical writers). In the LXX the word itself does not occur; more usual is the participle *parabainōn* (see Sir 23:18 "the one who sins . . ."). In the New Testament it is only found in Paul (Rom 2:25, 27; Gal 2:18) as well as in James 2:9, 11 (see *parabatēs*, *TDNT* 5:741–42).

10. *whoever keeps the whole Law but fails in one point:* This is a relative conditional clause (*hostis* + aorist subjunctive) without the participle *an*. James 2:8 had argued that "the royal Law" was to be kept in its entirety. The verb *ptaiein* means "to stumble" and is used metaphorically to indicate failure and sin. James uses it again in 3:2 (see also Deut 7:25; Rom 11:11; 2 Pet 1:10). The phrase *en heni* is understood as neuter ("in one point"). It cannot be read as masculine agreeing with *nomos* (law) because throughout the Bible *nomos* is always used in a collective sense, never in reference to one specific command *(entolē)*.

accountable for all (of it): Enochos has a wide range of meanings (see BDAG 338–39). Here it indicates "liable, answerable, guilty" and denotes that against which the sin has been committed, in this instance "the whole of the Law" (which is the equivalent of "all" [*pantōn*]) (Mayor 92). As Ropes says: "This is a rhetorical way of saying that he is a transgressor of 'the law as a whole' . . . not of all the precepts in it" (200). James's understanding reflects a universal belief within Judaism that since the Law and the commandments came from God and were an expression of God's will they must all be obeyed (see examples in later writings such as Philo, *Legat.* 3:241; 4 Macc 5:20). The Jesus tradition also upholds the idea of obeying the Law in its entirety (see Matt 5:18-19). Augustine discusses Jas 2:10 in a letter to Jerome (*Epistola 167 ad Hieronymum* 4), where he compares James's views to the Stoic doctrine of the solidarity of the virtues and vices. For the Stoics a person was either virtuous or full of vice. The virtuous person always acts without fault, while the one full of vice is incapable of acting rightly. This concept is very different from what James has in mind (see Ropes 200). While Stoic concepts were circulating during the time of James and had influenced Hellenistic Judaism, there really is no need to go beyond the world of Judaism to account for James's idea here: it clearly parallels the Jewish concept of the Law as God's will that is to be obeyed in its entirety.

11. *For the one who said: "Do not commit adultery . . . Do not kill . . .:* The *gar* ("for") is causal, giving the reason for James's basic argument in the preceding verses. He explains why failure to observe one command leads to the breaking of the whole law. *"The one who said" (ho eipōn)* is a circumlocution for God. Both commandments, against adultery and killing, have their origin in the person of God. The unity of the Law stems from the one Lawgiver (4:12) and the expression of the one Will. Sin stems from a disobedience to God's will. This same vision lies behind Jesus' response to the lawyer about the greatest command-

ment in the Law: "You shall love the Lord your God with all your heart, and with all your soul, and with all your mind" (Matt 22:34-40). Love, obedience, and the carrying out of God's will are what lies behind all the commandments. The sequence in which the prohibitions of the Decalogue (Exod 20:13-14; Deut 5:17-18) are quoted here is significant. In the MT and Codex Alexandrinus the sequence of the prohibitions is first killing and then adultery, whereas Codex Vaticanus has the same sequence that is reflected here in James (namely, adultery and then murder). In Christian tradition there appears to be no set order in reciting the commandments: e.g., Rom 13:9 and Luke 18:20 reflect James's sequence while Mark 10:19; Matt 5:21, 27; 19:18 have the MT order. In the Sermon on the Mount, Matthew's Jesus refers to the prohibitions against killing and adultery (in that order) as expressive of all the commandments. As with James, they become illustrations of God's will. Also noteworthy is 4:1-4, where James addresses his concern by calling on his hearers/readers not to kill. He then goes on to address them as "Adulterers!" (see the Interpretation of 4:1-4).

transgressor of the Law: James reinforces his basic point, namely that the Law is violated when only one prescript is broken. As a consequence such a person is a "transgressor" *(parabatēs)* of the Law (see 2:9). As Schneider says: "Because all the commandments come from one author, transgression of one commandment is in God's eyes the same as disregard for all the commandments" (*TDNT* 5:741–42). Some manuscripts (e.g., $\mathfrak{P}^{74}$ and Codex Alexandrinus) read "apostate of the law" *(apostatēs)*. But that reading is influenced by the development within ecclesiastical literature whereby *parabatēs* was interpreted as "renegade or apostate." For example, Eusebius (*Hist. eccl.* 5:18, 9) uses *parabatēs* as the equivalent of *apostatēs* (*TDNT* 5:742).

12. *So speak and so act:* The repetition of *houtōs . . . houtōs* is an emphatic way of stressing the importance of controlling speech and action. This captures what James had in mind in 1:26-27 and 2:1-7. It conforms to James's style (see the repetition of *bradys* ["slow"] in 1:19). Laws ([1980] 116) translates the repetition of *houtōs* as "in every respect" to capture the stress that is placed "not on the observance of a sum total of minutiae, but on the maintenance of a complete integrity of word and deed." This is a solemn way of speaking and may reflect the background of catechetical instruction.

as those who are going to be judged according to the law of liberty: The participle *mellontes* ("going to be") has a future eschatological ring to it. However, James says nothing about the imminence of the judgment (although 5:7-8 implies that it is at hand). What this expression captures is the certainty that judgment will occur (see BDAG 627–28; Davids [1982] 118). God is the one who is the Judge (4:11-12). God's judgment will be carried out "according to *(dia)* the law of liberty." The standard for judgment is the Torah as it has been reinterpreted by the teaching of Jesus and captured in the law of love. $\mathfrak{P}^{74}$ has the expression "word of liberty" *(logou eleutherias)*.

13. *For judgment is merciless to the one who has not shown mercy:* "For" *(gar)* provides the reason why the sin of discrimination will be judged severely. This verse acts as a culmination for the entire paragraph. It was probably an independent

proverb, as appears from the change in number from second person (in 2:12) to third person, indicating the generalization of a wise saying. This saying expresses in negative form what Jesus says positively in the beatitudes: "Blessed are the merciful, for they will receive mercy" (Matt 5:7). The adjective *aneleos* ("merciless") is not found elsewhere either in the LXX or in the New Testament. It is the negative form of the positive *eleos*, a virtue that has a richness and importance throughout the biblical writings. In the LXX *eleos* often translates the Hebrew word *ḥesed*, which refers to "God's acts of loving kindness toward humanity" (see, e.g., Ps 40:11-12 [39:11-12 LXX]). In the book of Sirach the expression "to show mercy" *(poiein eleos)* applies specifically to providing alms for those who are poor in imitation of God's acts of kindness: "Human acts of kindness *(eleos)* are for the neighbor; but the Lord's acts of kindness *(eleos)* are for every living thing" (Sir 18:13).

Mercy triumphs over judgment: The compound verb *katakauchatai* occurs again in Jas 3:14 and in Rom 11:18, while the simple verb *(kauchasthai)* occurs in Jas 1:9. The compound verb embraces the concept of "boasting," together with the prefix *kata*, to give the sense of "boasting over" (Johnson [1995] 234). In this present context it bears the meaning "to triumph over" something (BDAG 517). The basis for this saying is the principle enunciated on many occasions in the Hebrew Scriptures: "For I desire steadfast love and not sacrifice" (Hos 6:6, quoted by Matt 9:13). By the practice of acts of kindness (mercy) a human person "will be laying up a good treasure for yourself against the day of necessity" (Tob 4:9). But it must not be forgotten that acts of kindness stem from God's steadfast love *(ḥesed)*.

INTERPRETATION

Introduction to Chapter 2

James begins the body of the letter with a consideration of the theme of rich and poor that was introduced in the opening section (1:9-11). He returns again to this theme at the end of the letter (5:1-6), thus showing the importance he attributes to it. Up to this point James has presented a wisdom that is expressed through a number of wise sayings, general in application, that offer moral guidance for the community's way of life. In this passage the approach changes, and he offers advice for a concrete life situation. Contrary to the approach of Dibelius (11; 46) that refuses to see paraenesis as having any concrete context, I endorse the view (strongly defended by Wall [1997] 103) that sees the issue referred to here arising from a concrete crisis within the context of the community. The language is so vivid and admonitions so strong that they demand a concrete situation out of which they emerge. James 2:1-3 suggests an actual context whereby the rich and powerful exploit their positions and oppress the powerless.

The structure of James 2: Chapter 2 breaks into two parts, 2:1-13 and 2:14-26, presenting two main arguments (*contra* Johnson [1995] 218–19, who sees one argument sustained throughout). Stylistically these two passages contain many features that were characteristic of the Greek *diatribe:* direct address to the reader (2:1, 5, 14), use of apostrophe (2:20), use of rhetorical questions (2:4, 5, 7, 14, 20) and hypothetical examples (2:2-3, 15-16), as well as examples taken from an authority (in this instance the Hebrew Scriptures) (2:8-11, 21-25) (see Bultmann [1910] 1–64 for a detailed analysis of the stylistic and rhetorical features of the diatribe). Clearly 2:1-13, 14-26 are examples of the use of rhetoric to move the hearers/readers to a change in behavior. However, many commentators (Davids [1982] 58–59; Adamson [1989] 103–104; Wachob 59–61), following the lead of Dibelius (1; 38) have rightly pointed out that while these features may be found in the Greek diatribe it is wrong to classify James as a diatribe. So much of James is comprised of sayings. The two cited passages in ch. 2 show a development of these sayings in what can best be described as the form of a treatise or a theme (Dibelius 1).

Ancient Greek rhetoric helps to illuminate the style and structure of this chapter: Recent studies on ancient rhetoric illuminate James's argument and the way it is structured. Robbins ([1989] 1–29) has made a strong appeal for the use of more detailed studies of Hellenistic rhetoric to give a deeper insight into the art of persuasion in New Testament writings, especially the synoptic gospels: "During the past thirty years interpreters have explored many items observed above using redaction criticism and composition criticism. The question is whether it might be possible, using an approach informed by Hellenistic rhetoric, to explore the inner dynamics and logic of such abbreviation, expansion, and elaboration. The authors of this volume think such a possibility is on the horizon" (Robbins [1989] 22).

Our primary sources for the knowledge of ancient rhetoric are confined to two groups. *The standard textbooks* (or *technai*) were compilations of rhetorical theory designed for those with an advanced knowledge and a good foundation in rhetoric, such as teachers and orators. Among the most important of these textbooks that have come down to us are the *Rhetorica ad Alexandrum* of Anaximenes, the *Rhetorica* of Aristotle, the *Rhetorica ad Herennium,* and some works by Cicero such as *De Inventione, De Optimo Genere Oratorum, Topica, De Oratore, De Partitione Oratoriae,* and *Orator.* Burton Mack comments on their value: "Thus these handbooks presupposed not only an advanced level of proficiency in rhetorical training, but a high level of general education and readership in the canons of literature as well" ([1989b] 33).

A second source of information on ancient rhetoric comes from what are called the *progymnasmata,* which are in fact exercise books aimed at helping the student acquire a basic proficiency in the art of rhetoric: they were aimed at students who had a familiarity with literary studies but were now advancing to studies in rhetoric (Mack [1989b] 33). While the earliest text we possess is Theon's *Progymnasmata* (from the first century C.E.), there is evidence that such exercise books predated this work and had appeared by at least the first century B.C.E. Two other important *Progymnasmata* exist, namely that of *Hermogenes* (from the second century C.E.) and that of *Aphthonius* (from the fourth century C.E.).

An examination of the standard textbook *Ad Herennium* is most revealing for our study of James. It is a treatise on the art of rhetoric written in Latin by an unknown author during the first century B.C.E. and reflecting the Greek rhetorical tradition. In no way do I make an argument that James was aware of this particular treatise, nor that he made use of it. Rather, I see this treatise as providing us with evidence of the fundamentals of the Greek rhetorical art that had become standard throughout the Mediterranean world. Anyone educated in the art of rhetoric would be trained in these same fundamentals. Harry Caplan (in his "Introduction" to the LCL Edition of the *Rhetorica ad Herennium*) captures the spirit and intention of this work when he says:

> Our author, however, gives us a Greek art in Latin dress, combining a Roman spirit with Greek doctrine; it is a technical manual, systematic and formal in arrangement; its exposition is bald, but in greatest part clear and precise. Indeed the writer's specific aims are to achieve clarity and conciseness, and to complete the exposition of his subject with reasonable speed. He seeks clarity through the use of Roman terms, and of specially selected examples; he seeks conciseness by keeping practical needs always in view, by scrupulously avoiding irrelevant matter, and by presenting methods and principles, not a host of particular illustrations of a given point (vii).

The *Ad Her.* identifies three types of public speaking, namely the epideictic (or the praise or censure of someone), the deliberative (discusses some issue and aims at persuading or dissuading), and the judicial (taking place in a legal context) (*Ad Her.* 1:2, 2). According to this classification James 2 would fit into the category of a deliberative speech in that it aimed at arguing a particular perspective. While *Ad Her.* gave attention to the examination of a juridical speech in Book Two, what is said has application to the deliberative as well. Mack notes how "the distinction between judicial and deliberative types of speech has broken down" ([1989b] 56). The author of *Ad Her.* presents two outlines for an argumentation: the complete argument and the seven-part development of a theme (thesis). He argues that the most complete and perfect argument comprises five parts: the *propositio* (proposition), the *ratio* (reason), the *rationis confirmatio* (proof of the reason), the *exornatio* (embellishment), and the *conplexio* (résumé). He describes these in this manner:

> Through the Proposition we set forth summarily what we intend to prove. The Reason, by means of a brief explanation subjoined, sets forth the causal basis for the Proposition, establishing the truth of what we are urging. The Proof of the Reason corroborates, by means of additional arguments, the briefly presented Reason. Embellishment we use in order to adorn and enrich the argument, after the Proof has been established. The Résumé is a brief conclusion, drawing together the parts of the argument (*Ad Her.* 2:18, 28).

Book 4 of *Ad Her.* uses this structure of the complete argument in the development of a theme he presents, also in seven parts: the statement of the theme *(res)*, the rationale *(ratio)*, the paraphrase of the theme *(pronuntio)*, a statement of the contrary *(contrarium)*, a comparison *(simile)*, an example *(exemplum)*, and finally the conclusion *(conclusio)* (*Ad Her.* 4.43, 56–44.56). Wesley Hiram Wachob ([2000] 59–113) has made an excellent application of these criteria to Jas 2:1-13. He is to be commended in his attempt to illustrate how James does conform to the details of rhetorical argumentation in the Mediterranean world as evinced by the evidence in the *Ad Her.*

Application to James 2: An examination of James 2 shows that the argumentation of both passages clearly draws upon knowledge of Greco-Roman rhetoric that was the common property of the Mediterranean world. Without doubt the author of James must have been educated in the art of rhetoric. This author shows an application of this rhetoric that is very close to what has been outlined in the *Ad Her.*, as illustrated by Wachob's treatment of 2:1-13. However, it is clear that James did not have the *Ad Her.* in front of him, as it is a Latin work written for Romans. Still, its usefulness is that it gives us an illustration of how universal the art of rhetoric was and how the formalizations and structures that the Greeks developed were faithfully used and adapted in similar ways by the Romans and by James, who has adapted the rhetorical styles and structures to his own argument. For this reason my examination of the two passages of James 2 is limited to the basic structure of the complete argument as indicated by the *Ad Her.* (2:18, 28). This outline differs from the more detailed and developed structure formalized by Wachob, who produced a compendium of the two examples provided by *Ad Her.*, namely that of the complete argument and its application to the development of a theme or thesis (see Wachob [2000] 63).

The structure of the perfect argument (outlined by *Ad Her.* 2:18, 28) is at the heart of every argumentation and this structure helps one to understand James's argument more clearly. It appears to me that James is using a very similar structure in this way:

The *theme* or the *proposition (propositio)*;

The *reason (ratio)*;

The *proof* of the reason *(rationis confirmatio)*;

The *embellishment (exornatio)*;

The *conclusion (conplexio* or *résumé)*.

An examination of *Jas 2:1-13* reveals the following outline:

Theme (propositio): Not to make distinctions among people (2:1)

Reason (ratio): Example of discrimination in the community between rich and poor (2:2-4)

Proof (rationis confirmatio): God has chosen the poor to be rich (2:5-7)

Embellishment (exornatio): Argument from Scripture: fulfillment of the royal Law (2:8-11)

Conclusion (conplexio): Judgment is without mercy (2:12-13).

An examination of *Jas 2:14-26* reveals the following outline:

Theme (propositio): Faith without works cannot save you (2:14)

Reason (ratio): Example of faith without works in the community (2:15-17)

Proof (rationis confirmatio): Argument against an imaginary opponent (2:18-19)

Embellishment (exornatio): Argument from Scripture: Abraham and Rahab (2:20-25)

Conclusion (conplexio): Faith without works is dead (2:26).

Interpretation of Jas 2:1-13

Using the structure outlined above, James considers two arguments concerning his community's faith. The first is about the imitation of the faith of Jesus Christ, which demands that there be no discrimination against the poor in favor of the rich (2:1-13). The second concerns the conviction that true faith is alive and demonstrates itself in actions (2:14-26).

(a) Theme (propositio): Not to Make Distinctions among People (2:1)

This announcement dominates everything that follows in this passage. The command not to discriminate is a theme that captures the essence of the faithfulness of Jesus. The background to this command not to discriminate, or not "to show acts of favoritism" (2:1), lies clearly, as the Notes have shown, with the way God treats human beings: God has no favorites (Deut 10:17). The New Testament extended this concept to emphasize God's universal judgment of all equally. As Paul says in Rom 2:11: "For God shows no partiality *(prosōpolēmpsia)*." Another New Testament tradition, 1 Pet 1:17, also supports this understanding of God's impartial judgment: "If you invoke as Father the one who judges all people impartially *(aprosōpolēmptōs)* according to their deeds, live in reverent fear during the time of your exile." Oecumenius, in his commentary on the letter of James, explains the verse in this way: "For whoever does something by showing favoritism heaps upon himself great shame and much reproach, bringing disdain on his neighbor and even much more on himself" *(Comment. in Epist. Cathol. Jacobi, MPG* 119:473-74).

While the biblical background to the prohibition against showing acts of favoritism rested on the way God acts toward humans, James develops the foundation in a christological direction. In a writing that only names Jesus Christ twice we discover one of the most expressive titles attributed to Jesus in the entire New Testament, "the faith of our glorious Lord Jesus Christ" (2:1). As the Notes have argued, this expression is to be seen as a subjective genitive emphasizing the faithfulness of Jesus Christ rather than the more familiar Pauline expression of "faith in Jesus Christ" (as an objective genitive) (e.g., Gal 2:16; see James D. G. Dunn, *Romans 1–8*. WBC 38 [Dallas: Word Books, 1988] 1:166–67, 177–78). However, other recent studies on this expression *dia/ek pisteōs Iēsou Christou* (see Hays [1983] 170–74; Wall [1997] 109–10) have argued, to my mind convincingly, that Paul's usage is also that of a subjective genitive, "the faith of Jesus Christ" (see *Excursus 7: Faith and Works in James and Paul*). The stress here lies on the faithfulness of Jesus to his relationship to the Father and the carrying out of the Father's will, a faithfulness that culminates in his death and ultimate vindication in his resurrection. For Paul the emphasis in the justification process remains on Jesus' action of faithfulness, epitomized in this sacrifice on the cross. Both James and Paul focus on the faithfulness of Jesus. However, where they differ is that Paul sees the faithfulness of Jesus illustrated in his sacrifice on the Cross, whereas for James, Jesus' whole life becomes an example of faithfulness for the believer to emulate. This is a very different vision for James. Jesus' life and teaching bore witness to an undeniable commitment to the poor and marginalized within society. Jesus' life demonstrated an obedience to the Torah as exemplified above all in Leviticus 19, with its call to show a love of neighbor that was situated in the context of the call not to show partiality to poor or rich (Lev 19:15-18). While Paul's focus rested on the salvific death of Jesus, James's focus is on the life of Jesus. That life bore witness to someone who cared for the needs of the poor. This is exactly what James's definition of true religion demanded (1:27). James clearly lies in the tradition of the vision of the narrative gospels that portray Jesus' life being led in conformity to God's will. This fidelity to God's will brought him into association with the poor and outcasts of society, to whom Jesus communicated God's love.

The perspectives of Paul and James are not meant to be exclusive. It is not a matter of *either . . . or*, but rather of *both . . . and*. Both Paul and James give different insights into the faithfulness and obedience of Jesus: both the salvific nature of Jesus' death and the exemplary quality of Jesus' life provide direction for the life of the believer. The value of James's approach lies in providing a direction for Christianity that values the ethical direction of Jesus' life as of fundamental importance. It challenges the believer to become involved in issues related to social justice in the manner in which Jesus did. As Wall says so succinctly: "Further, the profoundly ethical matter of Jesus' faithfulness helps to form an ethical Christianity that is not only made more aware of social injustice but compels a rejection of it as a requirement of eschatological religion" ([1997] 110).

In this context Jesus Christ is referred to as "Lord" (2:1). Throughout the letter of James the term "Lord" is used either for God the Father or for Jesus. Only the context can help us decide. This dual usage in James shows no hesitation in applying to Jesus Christ a title that was reserved for God in the Hebrew Scriptures. This acknowledgement of Jesus as Lord can be seen as in line with Paul's beautiful hymn to Jesus in Phil 2:6-11, where through Jesus' obedience to God's will he is raised to a position in which all creation acknowledges him as Lord. In like manner, for James the faithfulness of Jesus to God's will is acknowledged through this title of Lord.

Along with the ascription of lordship to Jesus Christ, James adds the further adjectival description "of glory" (2:1). While the Notes show that the word can be translated in various ways, without doubt the clearest understanding is to see it as an adjectival description of Jesus in reference to his lordship: "the glorious Lord Jesus Christ" (2:1). In the biblical tradition "glory" *(doxa)* refers to the manifestation of the divine, the way in which God is revealed to humanity. "The glorious Lord Jesus Christ" points to the revelation that Jesus is the one who has risen and ascended to the Father: it refers to his exaltation as Lord with the Father in line with other New Testament traditions such as Phil 2:6-11; Col 1:15-20; Heb 1:1-4 ("He is the reflection of God's glory . . ."); and Rev 1:13-18. While James has in mind the faithfulness of Jesus as referring to Jesus' life-response to God's will, he combines it with his acknowledgment of Jesus now as "the resurrected one." As Johnson says: "To define faith as that proclaimed by Jesus does not preclude James also from confessing Jesus as the resurrected one" ([1995] 221). This confession in Jesus and reminder of his memory and outreach to the poor provides the context for the example that follows.

(b) Reason (ratio): Example of Discrimination in the Community between Rich and Poor (2:2-4)

This section develops through the use of a contrast that highlights the two opposites, namely rich and poor. The whole section consists of one long sentence. The previous sentence had provided the thesis that the faith of Jesus cannot be equated with partiality or discrimination. The connecting phrase "for if" *(ean gar)* provides the reason *(ratio)* in order to illustrate the thesis with an example (2:2). The illustration runs through v. 4. What is provided here takes its origin, as I have argued above, from a concrete life-situation within the community. However, James does not provide full details regarding exactly what happened. The reader is left to surmise many things. James provides a general illustration to offer instruction concerning the way to emulate Jesus' faith by avoiding partiality.

The reference to *synagōgē hymōn* ("your synagogue") is unusual, given the fact that this is the only occasion in the New Testament in which the phrase is used to refer to a Christian gathering (2:2). This undoubtedly draws attention once again to James's Jewish roots. The world the letter addresses reflects its Jewish heritage; its places of gathering are viewed as identical to Jewish gathering places. As the Notes have indicated, the term "synagogue" embraces many different functions. The function here is that of a judicial gathering of the congregation. This view has been strongly and convincingly championed by Roy Bowen Ward ([1969] 87–97). His examples taken from rabbinic tradition support James's context of a judicial meeting of the community gathering to settle a legal dispute. This is further supported by the references to Lev 19:18 and particularly the context of Lev 19:15 that forbids showing favoritism within a judicial context. Elsewhere in the New Testament there is evidence that Christians did settle their disputes by means of such judicial gatherings (see Matt 18:15-20; 1 Cor 5:3-5; 6:1-8; 1 Tim 5:19-24).

The rhetorical function of this illustration is important. It aims at providing an example of partiality or discrimination for the hearers/readers so shocking that they will spontaneously agree that such action runs counter to the ethical way of life inspired by Jesus. The description of discrimination is painted vividly. The best places in the assembly are offered to the rich person, whose ostentatious dress illustrates his position and power within society. He is welcomed with a tone of voice that betrays a sense of groveling before the rich and powerful. While whether the rich person is understood as a member of the community or as an outsider remains a point of discussion, it seems more logical to see the rich person as an outsider. This is supported by what follows in 2:6-7, where the contrast is made in terms of *they (the rich)* and *you (the poor)*. In contrast, the poor person is insulted by being told either to stand or to accept a place symbolic of subservience and reserved for enemies (see, e.g., Ps 110:1: "Sit at my right hand until I *make your enemies your footstool"*). The physical description of the scene lends weight to the injustice this assembly is about to perform. Preferential seating immediately indicates a prejudice in favor of the rich. An impartial decision cannot be expected. Instead, a decision in favor of the rich against the poor is a foregone expectation. The poor came expecting to receive justice, but this is now impossible, given the partiality the assembly exudes. This is not a matter of being inhospitable toward the poor. Rather, it is a matter of evil, where injustice dominates. James had shown a commitment to following the justice of God and of Jesus in 2:1. Here justice is perverted.

Without doubt James reflects the way in which honor/shame operated within a Mediterranean society (see *Excursus 6: Honor and Shame, Patronage and Grace: Cultural Scripts behind the Letter of James*). Honor is afforded those with wealth and power, while those without do not deserve any. The description of the wealthy person here could also be a sign of patronage. The patron is due this honor from his very status. James shows a strong critique of this culturally accepted way of life. His critique is in harmony with some of the philosophical criticisms that were expressed against a system of honor/shame based on wealth. They argued for a greater honor that rested upon virtue. Lucian ridiculed those philosophers who promoted virtue yet at the same time sought riches (*Dial. Mort.* 20:368-74).

The concluding verse of this section (2:4) asks two rhetorical questions requiring affirmative answers that reject the above behavior. "Have you not made distinctions among yourselves?" truly runs counter to the way Jesus embraced the poor and treated everyone with equality. The second rhetorical question, "Have you not become judges with evil thoughts?" is clearly reminiscent of Lev 19:15: "You shall not render an unjust judgment; you shall not be partial to the poor or defer to the great: with justice you shall judge your neighbor" (see Laws [1980] 102). This way of judging clearly runs counter to the very foundation of the purity laws. The purpose of the Torah was to define boundaries between the insiders and those outside. The purity laws defined the way those who belong to this community act, in distinction from those who are outside its society. As Jas 1:27 expresses it: "Religion that is pure and undefiled in the sight of God (who is) also Father is this: to care for orphans and widows in their affliction, and to keep oneself unstained from the world." By discriminating against the poor, James's community defiles itself because it has betrayed the values of its own society as defined through the Torah and the example and teaching of Jesus.

(c) Proof (rationis confirmatio):
God has Chosen the Poor to be Rich (2:5-7)

In support of the illustration in the previous verses James offers an argument based on the way God acts: God has chosen the poor to be rich in faith and heirs of God's kingdom. Rhetorically this is a very powerful argument. In contrast to the way God acts, the hearers/readers are criticized for dishonoring the poor. The contrast appears in this way: "God has chosen the poor . . . but you have dishonored the poor." As the Notes make clear, the language of the synoptic beatitudes seems to lie behind James (Matt 5:3-5; Luke 6:20). God honors the poor in that God has made them heirs of the kingdom: their status has been elevated. Surely this is a reminder to the hearers/readers of what 1:9-11 had already stated: a reversal of fortunes would occur, with the lowly raised up and the rich brought low. See Lucian, who envisages in his *Dialogues of the Dead* an interesting equality between rich and poor in the afterlife: "And tell the poor, my Spartan friend, who are many, displeased with life and pitying themselves for their poverty, not to cry and moan; describe to them our equality here, telling them how they'll see the rich on earth no better here than they are themselves" (*Dial. Mort.* 1:334-35).

God's election was the very foundation for Israel's existence as a people and for Jesus' followers as their heirs. This same God extended election to embrace those whom the world has shunned (the poor). James charges his hearers/readers with the crime of dishonoring the poor. While God honors them with God's choice, James's hearers/readers refuse to accord them a similar honor. Instead of embracing God's values and virtues, James's hearers/readers continue to operate according to the values of this world. God has reversed the honor/shame system, but James's hearers/readers refuse to emulate God's pattern of behavior. Instead of living according to God's standards (God's Torah), they continue to embrace the standards of the world.

The promise of the inheritance of the kingdom "for those who love God" (2:5) is a reminder of the promise in 1:12 of "the crown of life" for "those who love God." Seen in this way the kingdom and the crown of life become parallel concepts. The kingdom takes on an eschatological concept as the reward of eternal life reserved for those who love God. The test of loving God is demonstrated in one's way of life, in the carrying out of the love of neighbor (2:8) that embraces above all a love for the poor. The future blessing of eternal life for James's hearers/readers is threatened because of their refusal to imitate God's honor of the poor.

Augustine, in his *Book on the Predestination of the Saints*, comments on Jas 2:5 by saying: "By choosing (the poor) God makes them rich in faith and heirs of the kingdom. It is indeed rightly said that he chose this (faith) in them because he chose them so that he might produce it in them" (*Praed.* 17 (34), *MPL* 44:985-6).

The second part of James's argument is an indictment against the rich and their treatment of the members of James's community. James asks three rhetorical questions that expect an affirmative reply and that again show the absurdity of demonstrating a preference for the rich. Their treatment of the community has deteriorated, ranging from oppression through persecution to the ultimate of blasphemy against God. Do not the rich oppress you? Do they not drag you before the court? Do they not blaspheme the excellent name invoked over them (2:6b-7)? While the first two charges against the rich as outsiders involve social oppression, the third brings the situation into the religious sphere: they blaspheme or revile the name of Jesus. This is the most serious of all. The charge is not only leveled against the rich; it also has implications for the community. They have sided with rich outsiders against the poor members of the community. In effect they support what the rich outsiders are doing to the people of their own community. Not only do they support the oppression and persecution of their poor brothers and sisters; they also lend support to blasphemers!

The community claims to be shaped by the faith of Jesus. His life showed fidelity to God's will and above all an imitation of God's preferential option for the poor. However, James charges the community with betraying that faith through their "acts of favoritism" (2:1). The values of the world have defiled their community. By not honoring the poor within their community they have broken the purity laws. James's tone is strident, for it goes to the very heart of the nature of the community. It has betrayed itself by adopting the world's values instead of God's values. The choice before it is always the same: friendship with God or friendship with the world (4:4). By dishonoring the poor the community aligns itself with the world.

(d) Embellishment (exornatio):
Argument from Scripture: Fulfillment of the Royal Law (2:8-11)

These verses do not introduce a new topic: rather, they continue or embellish the argument presented in the thesis of 2:1 and the reason provided by the example of 2:2-4. Stylistically there are many similarities and connections between these verses and the preceding ones. In particular a number of words establish a direct connection. The words "do not show favoritism" *(prosōpolēmptein)* (2:9) are a direct link back to the thesis of 2:1. The identification of the Law as "the royal *(basilikos)* Law" (2:8) is a reminder of the promise in 2:5 of being heirs of the kingdom *(basileia)*. Further, the law of love of neighbor quoted in 2:8 is a development of the reference to those who love God in 2:5a.

The thesis of this whole section, expressed in 2:1, was a call to follow the faith of Jesus by not showing partiality among people. In particular it was Jesus' concern for the treatment of the poor that captured James's attention. The call now to love one's neighbor continues the theme of avoiding partiality by positively showing love for all, regardless of who they are. It reflects Jesus' faith and reminds the hearers/readers of Jesus' teaching in Matt 22:36-40, where Jesus quotes the *Shema Israel* ("Hear, O Israel: The LORD is our God, the LORD alone. You shall love the LORD your God with all your heart, and with all your soul, and with all your might" [Deut 6:4-5]) and connects that with Lev 19:18c ("You shall love your neighbor as yourself"). James shows a reflection of Jesus' fundamental message on love of God and neighbor. This is no new teaching: as the quotations from the Hebrew Scriptures reveal, Jesus is expressing the essence of God's will as recorded in the Torah.

When James speaks of fulfilling the "royal Law" (2:8) he has in mind, as the Notes indicate, the whole Law *(nomos)*, not a single commandment *(entolē)*. James sees the Torah as an expression of God's will. The carrying out of God's will in obedience to Jesus' teaching brings the inheritance of the kingdom (2:5) and the promise of eternal life. The command to love one's neighbor is the center of God's will for God's people. In a sense it embraces the various other laws expressed in the Torah.

If one fulfills the whole Law (in particular the command to love one's neighbor), one does well (2:8). However, to show partiality (2:9) breaks the command to love and is a betrayal of the faith of Jesus Christ (2:1): it also means that one "commits a sin" (2:9). This is very forceful language. James refers to committing sin on a number of occasions (4:17; 5:15, 16, 20). He explains more carefully what he means by this by adding a further explanation: "you are convicted by the Law as transgressors" (2:9). The Law is personified and acts as Judge. The charge that one has become a transgressor *(parabatēs)* of the Law is especially serious in the context of the world of Israel. Transgression of the Law was tantamount to an act of rebellion against God (which is the essence of sin), and meant that one rejected God's rule for the sake of one's own independence (see Davids [1982] 116).

James 2:10-11 develops in great detail what being a transgressor of the Law entails. In this James again demonstrates that his thought is totally at home in the world of Judaism, as the Notes have demonstrated. One is called to carry out the whole Law. James spells this out very clearly by saying that even if one abides *(tēreō* [see Matt 19:17; Acts 15:5]) by the whole Law, but breaks one command, one is guilty and is a transgressor of the Law. The world of Judaism demonstrates this clearly: "Cursed be every person who does not abide by *all the words of this law* by doing them . . ." (Deut 27:26 LXX). The Qumran community had a similar conviction: "And anyone of the men of the Community, the covenant of the Community, who insolently shuns anything at all commanded, cannot approach the pure food of the men of holiness" (1QS 8:16-17). The teaching of Jesus reflects this same vision of the importance of upholding the whole Law: "Do not think that I have come to abolish the law or the prophets; I have come not to abolish but to fulfill. For truly, I tell you, until heaven and earth pass away, not one letter, not one stroke of a letter, will pass from the law until all is accomplished" (Matt 5:17-18). At issue here is not a certain type of casuistry or scrupulous adherence to every one of the minutiae of the Law. Rather, it is the vision of what the Law is about in the first place. The Law, the Torah, as we have emphasized, is the expression of God's will for humanity. That one must keep the whole Law means that one's whole life must be oriented to carrying out God's will in its totality. This certainly was the vision of Jesus' life and it is the same vision that James promulgates. Given this context of the fulfillment of God's will in its entirety, every command becomes important because it is an expression of carrying out God's will.

In explaining this point Augustine, writing to Jerome, showed how the law of love embraces the fullness of the law:

> However, no one loves his neighbor unless he loves God, and, by loving him as himself to the limit of his ability, he pours out his love on him so that he, too, may love God. But, if he does not love God, he loves neither himself nor his neighbor. In this way, whoever shall keep the whole law but offend in one point becomes guilty of all because he acts against charity on which the whole law depends. Thus, he becomes guilty of all by acting against that virtue on which all depends (*Epistola 167 ad Hieronymum* 16 [Fathers of the Church 12:46 {Parsons}]).

Paul's vision differs from that of James. James and Paul are not arguing against each other. Rather, they view things from two very different standpoints (see *Excursus 7: Faith and Works in James and Paul*). Paul knows of the Jewish tradition to abide by the whole Law, but he distances himself from it: "Once again I testify to every man who lets himself be circumcised that he is obliged to obey the entire law" (Gal 5:3). Paul's concern stems from his understanding of the path of justification. No one is justified by his own efforts; justification is an action of God worked through Christ. For Paul it is a simple choice: do you rely on works of the law for your justification and salvation; or do you rely on the justification wrought by Jesus Christ? "For all who rely on the works of the law are under a curse; for it is written, 'Cursed is everyone who does not observe and obey all the things written in the book of the law. . . .' Christ redeemed us from the curse of the law by becoming a curse for us—for it is written, 'Cursed is everyone who hangs on a tree'—. . . so that we might receive the promise of the Spirit through faith" (Gal 3:10-14). For Paul, salvation is a result of Jesus' actions: the believer attains salvation through the death and resurrection of Jesus and not through his or her own efforts.

James's concern is rather to stress the ethical wisdom dimension of following Jesus: the will of God is to be obeyed in all its dimensions. This is illustrated through the carrying out of the Torah as the expression of God's will for humanity. For James the Law is understood in its totality rather than its individuality. Since the Law is the expression of God's will, James's major concern is that God's will be obeyed in its fullness. James captures this well in his stress on God's *speaking* the law: "For *the one who said* 'Do not commit adultery,' *also said . . .*" (2:11). God, the Lawgiver, spoke his Law and in this way communicated his will to his hearers.

James's choice of these two prescriptions against adultery and murder is noteworthy. In James's mind, to show contempt for the poor is equivalent to committing adultery or even murder. Hilary of Arles, while explaining this verse in his commentary on the letter of James, posed this question: "Why does James support his argument with these two commandments?" He answered immediately: "Because these two commandments chiefly pertain to loving or hating one's neighbor" (*Incipit Tractatus in Epistola Jacobi, MPL* Supp. 3:71). In the Sermon on the Mount Matthew's Jesus uses the same two examples (Matt 5:21-26, 27-30) to illustrate Jesus' fulfillment of the law. Later in the letter James refers to both prescriptions, but in a symbolic way: 4:2 and 5:6 contain references to murder, but seen in the context of the greed of the rich who exploit the poor. In 4:4 adultery is envisaged in the biblical symbolic sense of turning away from God: choosing friendship with the world in place of friendship with God. Both in their own way embrace actions that discriminate against the poor.

(e) Conclusion (conplexio):
Judgment is without Mercy (2:12-13)

The conclusion, in fact, provides a fourth and final argument in support of the command not to make distinctions among people:

- Has not God chosen the poor? (2:5)

- Do not the rich oppress you? (2:6)

- Whoever fails in one point of the law fails in all of it (2:10)

- Judgment is without mercy (2:12-13)

James exhorts his hearers/readers to speak and act as those who will be judged by the law of liberty. James had described the Torah in this way previously in 1:25, where he expressed his understanding that the Law or Torah brought with it the experience of freedom. The Torah was a marker giving the community its identity as God's people. By carrying out the Law the people realized their identity, setting the boundaries between themselves and the world around them. In this community they enjoyed freedom to be in relationship with God and the rest of the community. The judgment that the law of liberty brings is its measure of whether in their action and in their speech they truly have abided by the Law that gives them their identity. To have failed in one law means to have rejected the entirety of the Law that gave them their freedom and made them who they are. Jesus also gave expression to the law of liberty in his teaching and actions, in his exposition of the law of love of God and neighbor. As followers of Jesus the hearers/readers recognize that it is in the faith of Jesus (2:1) that the law of liberty receives its fullest and finest expression.

To the concept of judgment James adds the notion of mercy (2:13). In what almost appears to be a proverb James states that "Judgment will be administered without mercy to the one who has shown no mercy." This echoes the teaching of Jesus: "For if you do not forgive others, neither will your Father forgive your trespasses" (Matt 6:15; see also 18:23-35). James further adds that mercy triumphs over judgment: for those who practice mercy there is no need to fear judgment. Hilary of Arles, in his *Tractate on the Letter of James*, comments on Jas 2:13 in this way: "Mercy triumphs over judgment . . . if you are merciful and lenient to the poor in judgment, you will not fear the judgment of God when each one of you presents his works before God" (*Incipit Tractatus in Epistola Jacobi*, MPL Supp. 3:71). This was pointed out by Jesus in the parable of the final judgment: the Son of Man will invite those who have really shown mercy toward the least of their brothers and sisters to enter the promised kingdom (Matt 25:34). James's thought has progressed from considering the faithfulness of Jesus as an example that embraces all people and avoids every form of discrimination to the enunciation of principles for the community that deal with judgment and mercy. This prepares for the next section, which has as its core the illustration of putting faith into action.

For Reference and Further Study

Boyle, Marjorie O'Rourke. "The Stoic Paradox of James 2:10," *NTS* 31 (1985) 611–17.

Bultmann, Rudolf. *Der Stil der paulinischen Predigt und die kynisch-stoische Diatribe.* FRLANT 13. Göttingen: Vandenhoeck & Ruprecht, 1910.

Countryman, L. William. *The Rich Christian in the Church of the Early Empire: Contradictions and Accommodations.* Texts and Studies in Religion 7. New York: Edwin Mellen, 1980.

Eisenstadt, S. N., and Luis Roniger. *Patrons, Clients and Friends: Interpersonal Relations and the Structure of Trust in Society.* Cambridge: Cambridge University Press, 1984.

Frankemölle, Hubert. "Gesetz im Jakobusbrief: Zur Tradition, kontextuellen Verwendung und Rezeption eines belasteten Begriffes," in Karl Kertelge, ed., *Das Gesetz im Neuen Testament.* Freiburg: Herder, 1986, 175–221.

Hays, Richard B. *The Faith of Jesus Christ: An Investigation of the Narrative Substructure of Galatians 3:1–4:11.* SBLDS 56. Chico: Scholars, 1983.

Hengel, Martin. *Property and Riches in the Early Church.* London: SCM, 1974.

Hock, Ronald F., and Edward N. O'Neil. *The Chreia in Ancient Rhetoric. Volume 1: The Progymnasmata.* Atlanta: Scholars, 1986.

Johnson, Luke Timothy. *Sharing Possessions; Mandate and Symbol of Faith.* Overtures to Biblical Theology. Philadelphia: Fortress, 1981.

Keck, Leander E. "The Poor among the Saints in the New Testament," *ZNW* 56 (1965) 100–29.

_____. "The Poor among the Saints in Jewish Christianity and Qumran," *ZNW* 57 (1966) 54–78.

Kilpatrick, G. D. "Übertreter des Gesetzes, Jak. 2,11," *TZ* 23 (1967) 433.

Mack, Burton L., and Vernon K. Robbins. *Patterns of Persuasion in the Gospels.* Sonoma, Calif.: Polebridge Press, 1989a.

Mack, Burton L. "Elaboration of the Chreia in the Hellenistic School," in idem and Vernon K. Robbins, eds., *Patterns of Persuasion in the Gospels.* Sonoma, Calif.: Polebridge Press, 1989b, 31–67.

Marconi, Gilberto. "La Struttura di Giacomo 2," *Bib* 68 (1987) 250–57.

Montefiore, Hugh. "Thou Shalt Love The Neighbour as Thy Self," *NovT* 5 (1962) 157–70.

Robbins, Vernon K. "Chreia and Pronouncement Story in Synoptic Studies," in idem and Burton L. Mack, eds., *Patterns of Persuasion in the Gospels.* Sonoma, Calif.: Polebridge Press, 1989, 1–30.

Schneider, Johannes. *"parabainō,"* *TDNT* 5:736–44.

Ward, Roy Bowen. *The Communal Concern of the Epistle of James.* PhD diss. Harvard University, 1966.

_____. "Partiality in the Assembly: James 2:2-4," *HTR* 62 (1969) 87–97.

Watson, Duane F. "James 2 in Light of Greco-Roman Schemes of Argumentation," *NTS* 39 (1993a) 94–121.

EXCURSUS 6:

HONOR AND SHAME, PATRONAGE AND GRACE
(CULTURAL SCRIPTS BEHIND THE LETTER OF JAMES)

The Concepts of Honor and Shame

The full implications of 2:1-13 only emerge when these verses are read against the cultural scripts of honor, shame, patronage, and grace that lay at that society's foundation. For this reason we will give a brief overview of these concepts before showing how they help to illuminate 2:1-13. Honor refers to the way in which individuals are held in esteem insofar as they embody the values and way of life of the group to which they belong. Honor embraces the value the individual has in his/her own eyes as well as the value the group assigns to him or her (Malina [1993] 31). Honor above all shows concern for the way others evaluate worth. First-century Mediterranean society was oriented toward maintaining honor and avoiding dishonor. There were two ways in which honor was attained: it could be ascribed or aquired. *Ascribed honor* comes to one in a passive way through birth or power. One is born into an honorable family and thus shares in the honor of that family, or one receives honor from a powerful person who can ensure that this honor is acknowledged by others. As Jerome Neyrey says: "The Psalms contain many examples of ascribed honor, such as the oath that establishes the priesthood of Melchizedek: 'The Lord has sworn . . . Thou art a priest forever' (Ps 110:4//Heb 7:21), or the adoption of the king: 'He said to me, You are my son, today have I begotten you' (Ps 2:7)" (Neyrey [1998] 16). *Acquired honor* is attained through one's own efforts as a result of interaction with others through the game of challenge and response (Malina [1993] 34).

Honor is the overarching virtue that embraces the behavior and values that give identity to a particular culture and distinguish that culture from another. Those who belong to a society will endeavor to live out the values of that society. The culture of the first-century Mediterranean was by no means monolithic. Within the Greco-Roman culture there was the sub-culture of Judaism as well as many voluntary associations and minority cultures, including various philosophical schools as well as Christian communities. It was imperative within society to define the boundaries of one's group by indicating clearly the values that all the adherents of that group accepted. The honor in which one is held by that particular group is what matters, not the way in which one is esteemed outside the group.

A constant tension arose, in the nature of things, between the dominant and the minority culture. The interaction between Greco-Roman society and the early Christian communities illustrates this tension graphically, witnessed by many of the persecutions to which the New Testament writers refer. The persecution is not state-sponsored suppression, but a matter of pressure and ridicule exerted on individual communities and individuals to conform to the values of the dominant culture. First Peter reflects this very well: "Beloved, I urge you as aliens and exiles to abstain from the desires of the flesh that wage war against the soul. Conduct yourselves honorably among the Gentiles, so that, though they malign you as evildoers, they may see your honorable deeds and glorify God when he comes to judge" (2:11-12; see also 1 Pet 4:1-4; Heb 10:32-34). The Gentiles malign and ridicule Christians because their actions do not conform to what was identified as honorable in their society. Peter exhorts his hearers to remain true to the values they hold as honorable. In this way they bear witness among the wider society to their honorable character. All groups defined what was honorable/dishonorable in different ways. What really matters to the group is the way the members of their group define what is honorable. When one lives in the midst of a dominant culture (Jewish or Greco-Roman) one experiences all types of pressures to conform to the values (what is considered honorable) of that dominant society.

Shame is not simply the opposite of honor. It conveys at least three different meanings, depending on the context. Neyrey ([1998] 30–32) provides an excellent survey of these three meanings and I acknowledge my dependence on him. In the first instance shame has a positive sense when referring to the concern an individual or a group has regarding what others think or say about them. Contrasted to this is the "shameless person" who does not respect the opinion of others or uphold the social boundaries (Malina [1993] 51). In this second sense shame has a strongly negative connotation that embraces the loss of value and worth in the eyes of others. As Aristotle says:

> Now men esteem those who admire them and those whom they admire, those by whom they wish to be admired, those whose rivals they are, and whose opinion they do not despise. They desire to be admired by those, and admire those who possess anything good that is greatly esteemed. . . . They are also more ashamed of things that are done before their eyes and in broad daylight; whence the proverb, The eyes are the abode of shame. That is why they feel more ashamed before those who are likely to be always with them or who keep watch upon them, because in both cases they are under the eyes of others (*Rhet.* 2:6, 15-18 [Freese, LCL]).

In the third sense the concept of shame is used in the context of the gender roles assigned to the Mediterranean society of that day. Men and women were assigned specific roles within their society to which they had to remain faithful. The man's role was in the *public forum*, where his honor was reflected in fidelity to his public roles. The woman's role, on the other hand, was in the home, in the *private world* of the household. When women were true to the role society assigned them they were said to have shame. As Neyrey ([1998] 32) says: "'Shame' in this third sense, then, sums up the broad social expectations about females in antiquity. Thus it has a positive meaning, namely, that females have 'honor' when they have this kind of 'shame.' That is, they are judged positively in the court of reputation when they live up to the social expectations encoded in the gender stereotype."

Limited Resources and Patron-client Relationships

Another important social script of first-century Mediterranean society was the social relationship of patron and client. The importance of this relationship can only be understood against the background of society's belief in the limited supply of economic resources (see George M. Foster, "Peasant Society and the Image of Limited Good," *American Anthropologist* 67 [1965] 293–315). The concrete consequence of this concept of limited supply of resources was that if someone within the society acquired wealth or honor there was less to go around for the rest of society. Individuals could only enhance their positions within society at the expense of others. The natural reaction was one of envy, because it meant that there was less wealth or honor for others.

In a society in which a small number of the population possessed the greatest share of the wealth most people were poor and in need of assistance. One way of acquiring support was through a patron and establishing a "patron-client relationship." The patron in turn might introduce the client to another patron who was able to help the client more fully. In such a case the first patron is referred to as a broker or mediator.

These concepts of patron—client—broker emerge very clearly in the New Testament world: Jesus Christ is the mediator, the broker who brings his followers, his clients, into relationship with God, the Patron. David deSilva expressed this in another way: "God, the Patron, accepts Christ's clients (i.e., the Christians) on the basis of the mediator's merit" ([2000c] 767).

A term frequently used within the context of the relationship between patron and client was "grace" *(charis)*. For the Mediterranean world this term had a threefold reference that was primarily secular rather than religious (deSilva [2000a] 104). It meant first of all the favorable attitude the patron or benefactor adopted toward the client or recipient in his or her willingness to grant a favor to the recipient. Second, it referred to the actual gift that was bestowed. Finally, it embraced the response of gratitude the client showed toward the patron for the gift (deSilva [2000a] 104–105). From the perspective of the patron nothing was to be expected in return for the gift; nevertheless, from the perspective of the client a suitable response of gratitude was expected. Gratitude was a sacred obligation (deSilva [2000c] 768). Seneca uses the beautiful image of an unbroken circle to describe how each of these "graces" flows into the other: ". . . passing from hand to hand [grace] returns nevertheless to the giver; the beauty of the whole is destroyed if the course is anywhere broken; and it has most beauty if it is continuous and maintains an uninterrupted succession" (*Ben.* 1:3, 2-4 [Basore, LCL])

Besides *charis* ("grace") the concept of *pistis* ("faith") also played an important role in the patron-client relationship. Again the dominant meaning was secular rather than religious. From the perspective of the patron *pistis* meant "dependability." The patron showed that he or she was dependable or trustworthy in giving what had been promised. From the perspective of the client *pistis* meant that the client placed *trust* in the patron that he or she would carry out what was promised. It also captures the quality of the *loyalty* the client owed the patron for the gift.

Honor and Shame, Patronage and Grace in the New Testament

To express the values Christian groups shared in common, early Christian writers made use of the concepts of "honor and shame" in their own way. So much of New Testament language reflects these ideas: glory, honor, purity, esteem, etc. The community of believers became the primary focal point and the values this group espoused became the all-important values. However, these values were not always the values of the wider society. For Christian believers honor was sought not in paying attention to what the wider society endorsed, but rather in what the members of their own community accepted.

A reflection on the death of Jesus shows how members of the Christian community and the wider society saw their honor system very differently. From the perspective of the wider society the death of Jesus was viewed as shameful: that of a common criminal executed in the way in which a political prisoner would be put to death, on a cross. For Christian believers the death of Jesus did not end on the cross. His victory was demonstrated through his triumphal resurrection from the dead. The resurrection of Jesus brought Jesus to the right hand of the Father: honor and power were restored through his resurrection. The resurrection of Jesus guarantees that those who follow Jesus and emulate his values and way of life will also experience a reversal of fortunes at the end of time or the end of their lives.

The community of faith becomes the center to which the believer turns for his or her values and in which he or she seeks honor. This has many implications for Christian communities. Individual members of the community show concern for one another and attempt to strengthen each other's faith. This is illustrated well in Jas 5:19-20: "My brothers (and sisters), if anyone of you wanders from the truth, and is turned back by another, know that whoever turns back a sinner from the way of error will save that soul from death and will cover a multitude of sins."

All New Testament writers had a rhetorical purpose: to form the identity of the group to whom they were writing and to inculcate the values at the heart of their communities. While the New Testament letters clearly show this perspective and aim, the gospels and other writings demonstrate a similar intent. Matthew, Mark, Luke, and John all wish to show that Jesus' values were countercultural. Discipleship meant imitating Jesus' life by adopting his way of life. In essence it meant seeking honor according to Jesus' lifestyle, an honor that was contrary to what the wider society promulgated.

It is chiefly in the area of wealth and poverty that one sees a distinct reversal of values. While the wider society proclaimed wealth to be valuable and deserving of honor, and poverty the path to shamelessness and degradation, Jesus, James, and Paul all reversed this condition. In the community of the followers of Jesus honor came from faith in God (see Jas 1:9-11) rather than wealth and status in society. Christians receive their honor from being part of God's own people.

In the context of both the Hebrew Scriptures and the New Testament writings God is seen as Patron. The concept of God as Patron of Israel clearly helps to define the relationship that exists between God and God's people. What is especially noteworthy about this relationship is God's enduring loyalty to the bond between God and people. When the Israelites turn from the relationship God may punish them, but never renege on the enduring bond.

The New Testament writers draw on both their Israelite and their Greco-Roman background to apply the concept of God as Patron to define this relationship. God promises to be the benefactor of all who trust in God's favor. "And without faith it is impossible to please God, for whoever would approach him must believe that he exists and that he rewards those who seek him" (Heb 11:6). God's role as Patron is reflected especially in the New Testament teaching on prayer. There the believer requests God's favor and is assured that his or her prayer will be answered: "Do not be afraid, Zechariah, for your prayer has been heard. Your wife Elizabeth will bear you a son, and you will name him John" (Luke 1:13; see also Luke 11:9-13). "Let us therefore approach the throne of grace with boldness, so that we may receive mercy and find grace to help in time of need" (Heb 4:16). The songs of Mary (Luke 1:46-55) and Zechariah (Luke 1:68-79) capture a number of aspects essential to the cultural script of patronage and grace: they are hymns of praise and gratitude to God for what God has done for God's people Israel in the past, as well as gratitude for God's enduring love and protection for the future. The image of God as the Patron who specially champions the cause of the poor and the weak lies behind this presentation: "My spirit rejoices in God my Savior, for he has looked with favor on the lowliness of his servant. . . . He has brought down the powerful from their thrones and lifted up the lowly; he has filled the hungry with good things and sent the rich away empty" (Luke 1:46-47, 52-53). Not only does God give freely; God is also generous to those who reject God: "(For God) makes his sun rise on the evil and on the good, and sends rain on the righteous and on the unrighteous" (Matt 5:45).

At times Jesus is also viewed in the role of patron. In so many of the miracles worked by Jesus, people come to him requesting the grace of healing. In the narrative of the healing of the centurion's servant the Jewish leaders approach Jesus and say: "He is worthy of having you do this for him, for he loves our people . . ." (Luke 7:4-5). In effect they are saying: "He is an honorable person whose honor calls upon you to respond in a positive way." Jesus responds to the centurion's words: "I tell you, not even in Israel have I found such faith" (Luke 7:9). Jesus shows that the centurion's faith *(pistis)*, his trust in Jesus' power to heal, is so remarkable that it moves him to perform the miracle. As the patron, Jesus responds to the trust placed in him. Likewise in the New Testament letters Jesus is presented as the patron of the Christian community who cares for all the members: "He did not come to help angels, but the descendants of Abraham" (Heb 2:16-18). But Jesus' role in relationship with his followers is more like that of a broker or mediator: he makes it possible for believers to come into relationship with God, the Father. Jesus is the broker who mediates the relationship between God the Father and believers: "Therefore, my friends, since we have confidence to enter the sanctuary by the blood of Jesus . . . let us approach with a true heart in full assurance of faith, with our hearts sprinkled clean from an evil conscience and our bodies washed with pure water" (Heb 10:19-22). For the New Testament writers Jesus is the one who mediates God's grace: "For there is one God; there is also one mediator between God and humankind, Christ Jesus . . ." (1 Tim 2:5).

As indicated above, Mediterranean society required a response of gratitude from those who received a gift. The same is true within the Christian community: to God's generosity the Christian believer must respond with faith *(pistis)*, loyalty, and service *(diakonia)*. As the Markan Jesus instructs his disciples: ". . . it is not so among you; but whoever wishes to become great among you must be your servant, and whoever wishes to be first among you must be slave of all" (Mark 10:43-44).

The leaders of the Christian communities also function in the role of patrons with regard to their own communities. They are concerned that their communities adhere to the values that give them identity. For example, Paul, as the founder of most of the communities to whom he writes, is the one who has brought them the gift of the Christian faith. When Paul writes to Philemon he reminds him of the debt he owes him: "I, Paul, am writing this with my own hand: I will repay it. I say nothing about your owing me even your own self. Yes, brother, let me have this benefit from you in the Lord!" (Phlm 19-20).

How Do These Cultural and Social Scripts Feature in James 2:1-13?

It is not possible to understand the letter of James and particularly 2:1-13 without a clear understanding of the cultural and social scripts outlined above. In the opening verse (2:1) the role of Jesus is clearly that of the broker or mediator between God the Father and us believers. The "faith" *(pistis)* that Jesus demonstrates is that of obedience to and trust in God. In his way of life and in his teachings he demonstrates to his followers how they are to emulate him in showing obedience to and trust in God's Patronage. The further description of Jesus as "our glorious Lord Jesus Christ" uses the language of honor very directly: the glory that is attributed to Jesus is the honor in which he is held. It is an honor ascribed to him from his very position as the Messiah, the Christ.

In writing this letter to his community, James's rhetorical intention, like that of the other New Testament letters, was to strengthen the identity of his hearers/readers by inculcating the values that were at the center of their community. Above all, as v. 1 indicates, the believers are to emulate Jesus, his faithfulness, and in particular his honor and the values that stem from this. James singles out the value or virtue of "not showing acts of favoritism" (2:1). Immediately the countercultural nature of the way of life of Jesus and his followers comes to the fore. Mediterranean society was based on patron-client relationships in which "acts of favoritism" were a prerequisite for success and survival. Contrary to the wider society, James is showing that in the voluntary association that is their community the core value is that of equality: all people are made in God's likeness (3:9). The consequence is that all must be treated equally with honor and dignity.

The concepts of honor and shame permeate this whole section. In the example given (2:2-4) to support the basic thesis of this passage (2:1), James shows how acting according to the values of the outside society is, in fact, shameful behavior. The wider society embraced the actions of showing favoritism to those who have wealth and shunning those who are poor: according to its value system the man "with gold rings and fine clothes" is honorable while "the poor man in squalid clothes" is shameful.

James categorizes this type of behavior that shows favoritism to people on the basis of their wealth as "evil" or dishonorable (2:4).

James goes on to provide *arguments in support* of his conclusion that such action is dishonorable. *In the first argument (2:5-7)* he cites the way in which God, the Patron, acts. God has shown a choice of the poor and in doing so God reverses the values of society. The poor in fact become "rich in faith and heirs of the kingdom." James challenges his hearers/readers to see that by slighting the poor they have failed to imitate the action of God, and so they "dishonored the poor person" (2:6). *In a further argument (2:8-9)* James shows how following the Law is what establishes true honor. The Law provides the boundaries for the community and separates them from those outside (see *Excursus 5: The Perfect Law of Liberty*). The Law spells out what is honorable behavior. Central to that behavior is the law of love of neighbor (Jas 2:8; Lev 19:18c). Acts of favoritism in discriminating against the poor are a breach of the virtue of honor and are thoroughly shameful (2:9). *In a final argument (2:10-11)* James shows that honorable behavior demands that one keep the entire Law, the whole Law, while shameful behavior includes the breaking of one of the commands. Finally, in the conclusion (2:12-13) James shows again that honorable behavior conforms to the law of liberty, the ultimate judge of what one does.

Without doubt the rhetoric James employs in this section (and in the rest of the letter) runs counter to the culture of the prevailing dominant society. In this passage the example portrays the picture of a patron entering the assembly and shows how the community fawns over him. Instead, James offers a way of behaving that locates the community's honor in Jesus' faith. Central to this faith is the awareness of the equality of all and the carrying out of the love commandment (2:8) as the fulfillment of the Law. James has replaced the figure of the rich patron with that of God as the true Patron. God's actions become normative for the community (2:5). God as Patron, in choosing the poor to be heirs of the kingdom, reverses the position the poor hold in the eyes of the dominant society and shows that in James's community true honor is located in the way the poor are treated. This is not the first time the letter has employed the imagery of God as Patron. In 1:17 God is the Patron who communicates to the followers of Jesus the fullness of grace *(charis):* "Every good act of giving and every perfect gift is from above, coming down from the Father of lights, with whom there is no variation or shadow of change." God the Patron supplies everything that is lacking "without hesitation and without reproach" (1:5). The greatest gift God communicates to those who accept God is the grace of rebirth into a new community, a new family that has its own values and honor stemming from their Patron God and Jesus who mediates the Father to believers. "Because he freely decreed it, he gave us birth by the word of truth, so that we might be a kind of first fruits of his creatures" (1:18).

David deSilva applies this passage to today very succinctly when he writes: "When a church fails to make a visitor welcome (or worse, tries to make someone feel unwelcome) on account of a difference in race, attire and the like, then Jesus' designs have been defeated in favor of the world's classification lines. The result is that we find *ourselves* on the outside again, living at home in the world's maps rather than enacting Jesus' program" ([2000a] 313).

FOR REFERENCE AND FURTHER STUDY

Chow, John K. *Patronage and Power: A Study of Social Networks in Corinth.* JSNTSup 75. Sheffield: Sheffield Academic Press, 1992.

deSilva, David A. *Honor, Patronage, Kinship and Purity: Unlocking New Testament Culture.* Downers Grove, Ill.: InterVarsity Press, 2000a.

_____. "Honor and Shame," in Craig A. Evans and Stanley E. Porter, eds., *Dictionary of New Testament Background.* Downers Grove, Ill.: InterVarsity Press, 2000b, 518–22.

_____. "Patronage," in Craig A. Evans and Stanley E. Porter, eds., *Dictionary of New Testament Background.* Downers Grove, Ill.: InterVarsity Press, 2000c, 766–71.

Edgar, David Hutchinson. *Has God Not Chosen the Poor? The Social Setting of the Epistle of James.* JSNTSup 206. Sheffield: Sheffield Academic Press, 2001.

Malina, Bruce J. *The New Testament World: Insights from Cultural Anthropology.* Rev. ed. Louisville: Westminster John Knox, 1993.

Neyrey, Jerome H., "Honor and Shame in Luke-Acts: Pivotal Values of the Mediterranean World," in idem, ed., *The Social World of Luke-Acts: Models for Interpretation.* Peabody, Mass.: Hendrickson, 1991, 25–66.

_____. *Honor and Shame in the Gospel of Matthew.* Louisville: Westminster John Knox, 1998.

Robbins, Vernon K. "Rhetoric and Culture: Exploring Types of Cultural Rhetoric in a Text," in Stanley E. Porter and Thomas H. Olbricht, eds., *Rhetoric and the New Testament: Essays from the 1992 Heidelberg Conference.* Sheffield: Sheffield Academic Press, 1993, 443–63.

Roberts, Keith A. "Toward a Generic Concept of Counter-Culture," *Sociological Focus* 11 (1978) 111–26.

5. *Doers of the Word/Faith and Works* (2:14-26)

14. My brothers (and sisters), what good does it do if someone claims to have faith but does not have works? Is faith able to save that person? 15. If a brother or sister is going naked and lacking daily food, 16. and if someone should say to them, "Go in peace! Be warmed and filled (with food)," but you do not give them what is necessary for the body, what good does it do? 17. So also faith by itself, if it does not have works, is dead.

18. But, someone will say, "You have faith and I have works." Show me your faith apart from your works, and by my works I will show you my faith. 19. You believe that God is one. You do well! Even the demons believe—and shudder!

20. Do you wish to know, you empty person, that faith apart from works is ineffectual? 21. Was not our father Abraham proved to be right-eous (as shown) through his works when he offered (in sacrifice) his son Isaac on the altar? 22. You see that faith was active together with his works, and by the works faith was brought to perfection. 23. And the Scripture was fulfilled that says, "And Abraham believed God, and it was reckoned to him as righteousness," and he was called God's friend. 24. You see that a person is proved righteous by works and not by faith alone. 25. And likewise, was not Rahab, the prostitute, also proved right-eous by works when she received the messengers and sent them out by another road? 26. For just as the body apart from spirit is dead, so faith apart from works is also dead.

NOTES

14. *what good does it do if someone claims to have faith:* This verse contains two rhetorical questions each expecting a negative answer (hence the use of the negative particle *mē*). The style clearly resembles that of a diatribe. The phrase *ti to ophelos* ("what good is it") captures the traditional argumentative style of the diatribe (Ropes 203). See, e.g.: "For of what use is it *(ti gar ophelos)* to say what is excellent, but to think and to do what is most shameful?" (Philo *Post.* 86; *Migr.* 55); see also "What good does he get *(to oun ophelos)*, then, from acting right?—What good does the person get *(ti d'ophelos)* for writing the name 'Dio' as it ought to be written?" (Epictetus *Diatr.* 3:24, 51); see also Sir 20:30; 41:14; 1 Cor 15:32). All the citations (except 1 Cor 15:32) omit the article *(to)*, as does Codex Vaticanus (see Aland [1997] 35). The lack of the article in this manuscript is probably due to a scribe conforming James's text to that of the popular idiom. A similar expression occurs in Matt 16:26 (and parallels in Mark 8:36 and Luke 9:25): *ti gar ōphelēthēsetai anthrōpos* ("For what will it profit a person"). The claim to have *faith* connects back to the opening theme of 2:1. The phrase "If someone claims" *(ean legē tis)* does not mean that this hypothetical example (as in 2:2-4) is not drawn from a real situation within the context of James's community. In the second part of the clause the use of the subjunctive

echę instead of the infinitive *echein* affirms that this part of the clause is not a continuation of what the person says, but is rather an observation by the author. Hence the person claims to have faith, but the author comments that he or she does not. The *erga* ("works") to which James refers are understood as "good deeds" (see, e.g., Matt 5:16; John 3:21) and not *erga nomou* ("works of the law").

Is faith able to save that person? It appears that the answer to this question is self-evident: "No!" The contrast between being a doer of the word and not just a hearer (1:22-25) is echoed here in the contrast between faith and works. One has to put faith into action: one must be a doer of faith. A similar stress on the importance of good works is found in 2 *Bar.* 14:12; 51:7.

15. *If a brother or sister is going naked and lacking daily food:* The same stylistic construction is followed here as in 2:2-4: *ean* + subjunctive introduces a hypothetical illustration that is wrong and should be avoided. Interestingly, James refers to both a "brother and a sister" *(adelphos ē adelphē)*. This is one of the rare occasions in the New Testament where the term "sister" *(adelphē)* is used in reference to a community member (see Rom 16:1; 1 Cor 7:15; 1 Tim 5:2; Phlm 2). The word *gymnoi* does not indicate complete nakedness: a person who was clad only in an undergarment was considered naked: e.g., Saul in 1 Sam 19:24, who has taken off his outer garments *(himatia)*, is called *gymnos;* so is Peter in John 21:7 who is "without an outer garment" *(gymnos)* (see BDAG 208). People who are poorly clothed (see also Job 22:6; Isa 20:2-3; 58:7) are clearly those who are in desperate need of immediate help. It is reminiscent of Matt 25:36: "I was naked and you gave me clothing." To be naked illustrates one's situation of poverty ("You do not realize that you are wretched, pitiable, poor, blind, and naked" [Rev 3:17]) or of shame ("and white robes to clothe you and to keep the shame of your nakedness from being seen" [Rev 3:18]). Noticeable here grammatically is the use of plural verbs, *hyparchōsin kai leipomenoi ("is going* naked and *lacking* daily food") with singular subjects connected by *ē,* ("and"). This is not uncommon in Hellenistic writers (see BDF 74:135). The phrase *leipomenoi tēs ephēmerou trophēs* ("lacking daily food") continues to describe the urgency of the situation. An immediate response is demanded ("Give some of your food to the hungry, and some of your clothing to the naked" [Tob 4:16]). The word *ephēmeros* ("daily") is a *hapax legomonon* in the New Testament. While it also does not occur in the LXX, the phrase does appear in classical Greek (see, e.g., Dionysius of Halicarnassus, "he went out of the house alone . . . without taking . . . even food for the day" *[ephēmeros] [Ant. Rom.* 8:41, 5]; see also BDAG 418).

16. *"Go in peace! Be warmed and filled (with food)":* The farewell greeting "Go in peace" *(hypagete en eirēnę)* is based on the biblical expression: "Walk (or go) in peace" *(lĕki lĕšālôm* [MT] or *poreuou eis eirēnēn* [LXX]: 1 Sam 1:17; see also Judg 18:6; 1 Sam 20:42; and in the New Testament Mark 5:34; Luke 7:50; Acts 16:36). This prayer is offered at parting, that God will grant the gift of *šālôm,* a blessing on every dimension of one's being. The actual prayer "Be warmed and filled" is hypocritical: the statement reflects the needs that were identified in the previous verse, but the speaker refuses to do anything about them.

what is necessary for the body: The words *ta epitēdeia* ("the things that are necessary") does not occur elsewhere in the New Testament, though it does appear occasionally in the LXX (see 1 Macc 14:34; 2 Macc 2:29) and more frequently in other writers (see, e.g., "For Josephus, seeing the abundance of the city's other supplies *[tōn allōn epitēdeiōn]* . . ." [Josephus, *B.J.* 3:183 {Thackeray, LCL}]). The expression *ti to ophelos* ("What good does it do?") acts as an inclusion with 2:14, where the same expression occurs. It is a way of drawing the example together more forcefully and reiterating the hollowness of such behavior.

17. *So also faith by itself, if it does not have works, is dead:* The phrase *houtōs kai* ("so also") draws a conclusion from the example (see also 1:11; 2:26; 3:5): faith without works is dead. The use of *pistis* (faith) connects back again to 2:1 and "the faith of Jesus Christ." The phrase *kath' heautēn* means "by itself" or "on its own" (Martin 85; see also Mayor 99). It is not faith and works that James contrasts here, but rather a living faith and a dead faith.

18. *But someone will say, "You have faith and I have works":* Dibelius claims that this is "one of the most difficult New Testament passages in general" (154). The difficulties do not concern the text itself, but the interpretation of the text. Two main problems emerge. (1) Is the speaker of v. 18a a supporter of James (see Mayor 99–100; Mussner [1982] 136–38) or an opponent (Ropes 213–14; Dibelius 154–56)? The style of the verse supports an adversarial stance: as in a diatribe, the speaker is an imaginary opponent who presents an objection the author will then counter in order to advance his argument. We see Paul using rhetoric in this way in Rom 9:19; 11:19; 1 Cor 15:35 (see also 4 Macc 2:24; *Barn.* 9:6). (2) What is the actual meaning of the objection raised? As it reads, the statement appears to agree with what James himself would say: "You have faith and I have works." If it were the words of the objector, they would surely be "I have faith and you have works." So the question arises: Why are these words placed on the lips of the objector? Ropes (208–10) and Dibelius (155–58) provide the best solution to the problem by interpreting "you" *(sy)* and "I" *(kagō)* not as referring to James ("you") and his opponent ("I"), but rather in a generalized sense to "one person . . . another." Both Ropes (209) and Dibelius (156) quote the example of the Cynic Teles (Stobaeus, *Anthologium Graecum* 3:1, 98) in support of this interpretation; there "the author is not concerned about exact identification of the 'you' and the 'I'" (Dibelius 156, n. 35). In effect James is saying: "One person has faith and another has works." (The more natural Greek expression would have been *allos . . . allos.*) James rejects this position and in effect goes on to add: "You are quite mistaken: works cannot be deduced from faith, yet faith can be deduced from works." (see Dibelius 156).

Show me . . .": James begins his reply to the objector, providing both a challenge and an offer. He first of all challenges his opponent to show his faith without works. For an example of this combination of challenge and offer see Epictetus: "And yet, though I can show you that you have resources and endowment for magnanimity and courage, do you, pray, show me what resources you have to justify faultfinding and complaining!" (*Diatr.* 1:6, 43 [Oldfather, LCL]). James makes the offer to his opponent to demonstrate his faith from his works. The chiastic structure of the sentence shows James's linguistic ability: *pistin—erga; ergōn—pistin.*

19. *You believe that God is one. You do well!* James continues with his argument that a living faith is essential. "You believe" *(sy pisteueis)* is taken as an affirmative statement rather than a question. There are many textual variants relating to the phrase "God is one," mainly involving the presence or absence of the article before "God" *(theos)* (Metzger [1975] 681). Codex Vaticanus lacks the article and reads "there is one God" *(heis theos estin),* which is similar to Paul's confession in 1 Cor 8:6: "yet for us there is one God *(heis theos),* the Father. . . ." This is a general monotheistic statement. On the other hand, 𝔓⁷⁴ and Codices Sinaiticus and Alexandrinus contain the article and read "God is one" *(heis estin ho theos).* This form of expression conforms to the Jewish monotheistic profession of faith in God as one and would be a deliberate attempt to remind the reader of this confession of faith (Deut 6:4; Philo, *Opif.* 171; *Decal.* 65). From a theological perspective the second alternative is in conformity with James's consistent attempt to preserve his Jewish background. The phrase *kalōs poieis* ("You do well") in itself is not ironic (as Mark 12:32 demonstrates), but from its context here it certainly is (as also in Mark 7:9).

Even the demons believe—and shudder: Ta daimonia has many nuances, depending on the context. In the Greco-Roman world it was a term used for pagan divinities, as in Acts 17:18 "foreign divinities" *(xenōn daimoniōn).* See Herodotus, *Hist.* 5:87 (Godley [LCL]): "but the Argives say that it was they, and the Athenians that it was divine power *(daimoniou),* that destroyed the Attic army," and Plato, *Apol.* 26B. In the LXX *daimonia* was used for pagan gods: "For all the gods of the peoples are idols *(daimonia)*" (Ps 96:5 [95:5 LXX]; see also Deut 32:17). In the context of the synoptic gospels it is a phrase often used to refer to "demons," also identified as "unclean spirits" *(pneumata akatharta)* (see also Matt 7:22; Mark 3:22; Luke 4:33). The synoptic gospels also testify to such spirits' belief as well as their fear: e.g., the man Legion who is possessed by many "unclean spirits" cries out to Jesus: "What have you to do with me, Jesus, Son of the Most High God? I adjure you by God, do not torment me" (Mark 5:7; see also Mark 1:24; Acts 16:17; 19:15). Legion shows his belief through acknowledging who Jesus is and his willingness to take an oath in the name of God. He also shows his profound fear. The verb *phrissein* ("to shudder") is used to describe the physical reaction of fear such as the hair standing on end, as in Job 4:14-15: "Dread came upon me and trembling, which made all my bones shake. A spirit glided past my face; the hair of my flesh bristled *(ephrixan).*" Jewish literature showed how all of creation shuddered *(phrissousin)* before God ("For myself, I shudder *(phrittō)* at recounting the works of God to unworthy ears" [Josephus, *B.J.* 5:378 {Thackeray, LCL}]). Materials from the Hellenistic world such as the Greek magical papyri show that the power of God's name causes demons to shudder (see Dibelius 160). The Christian world continued this tradition: e.g., Justin (*Dial.* 49:8), who speaks about shuddering at the power of God demonstrated in the crucified Christ, and Clement of Alexandria, *Strom.* 5:125, 1. The important thing James expresses in this verse is that while the demons know who God is, this knowledge does not bring salvation; instead, it awakens fear and terror and causes them to shudder—at the same name of God that can be used to exorcise them!

20. *Do you wish to know, you empty person:* James introduces a new argument based on Scripture. "Do you desire a proof?" (Ropes 216). This question is a frequent element of the diatribe (see Jas 4:4; Rom 11:2). The direct address to an imaginary opponent ("O empty person") also conforms to the style of the diatribe (Bultmann [1910] 58–61). A harsh tone is another characteristic feature (Ropes 216): e.g., Seneca, *Ira* 3:28,1: *"Age infelix ecquando amabis?"* ("Act, O unhappy one! Will you ever love?"). James's choice of this expression shows his strong feelings (see also Paul: *ō anoētoi Galatai* ("You foolish Galatians!") (Gal 3:1; see also L&N 1:812, 91.14). James continues the address consistently in the singular (see 2:14, 19, 22). The word *kenos* indicates "foolishness" and in this context "a foolish advisor" (Mussner [1981] 140; see Epictetus, *Diatr.* 2:19, 8) as well as moral failure (Judg 9:4). It has the same connotation as the word *raka* ("empty simpleton") in Matt 5:22; see *TDNT* 3:660.

   that faith apart from works is ineffectual: The Greek word *argē* ("ineffectual") is strongly supported by Codex Vaticanus. A number of manuscripts read *nekra* ("dead," as in Codices Sinaiticus and Alexandrinus) while $\mathfrak{P}^{74}$ has *kenē* (see Aland [1997] 42). As Metzger ([1975] 681) notes, it seems that *nekra* was introduced through the influence of 2:17, 26. Further, the use of *argē* would be in line with James's affinity for creating a play on words: *ergōn—argē (a + ergē)*. Literally James would be saying that "faith apart from works is 'work-less' *(a + ergē)*."

21. *our father Abraham:* In Gen 17:4 God had made the promise to Abraham that he would be "the father *(patēr)* of many peoples." This tradition is continued throughout the biblical heritage: see Isa 51:2; Sir 44:19; 4 Macc 16:20; 17:6; Matt 3:9; Luke 1:73. This again points to the writer's Jewish background: James sees himself and his community as part of those promises in that they can claim Abraham as their father.

   proved to be righteous (as shown) through his works: This is the central aspect of the verse. The difficulty with understanding the verb *dikaioun* ("proved to be righteous") comes from its rich range of meanings and the fact that it is used in different ways in different contexts. In the writings of Paul the term *dikaioun* is used to oppose a faith that is achieved by one's own efforts through carrying out the works of the law. In Rom 4:1-3 Paul claims that Abraham was justified by faith and not by works (of the law). He goes on to use a biblical quotation that James also uses: "Abraham believed God, and it was reckoned to him as righteousness" (Rom 4:3; Gal 3:6; 2:23; see Gen 15:6). In Paul's usage the term *dikaioun* captures God's action that produces a transformation within the life of the believer so that he or she is brought into a right relationship with Christ. All this occurs through the transforming gift of Jesus Christ's faithfulness (Rom 3:23-26) (see *TDNT* 2:208–10; *Excursus 7: Faith and Works in James and Paul*). In James the concern is very different. Works (that is, good deeds) show that one's faith is living and that one is in a right relationship with God. Hence *dikaioun* in the context of James bears the meaning "demonstrates righteousness." I translate it "proved to be righteous (as shown) through his works." See other translations, e.g., "wasn't Abraham proved righteous (as demonstrated) by his deeds" (Martin 91); or "shown to be righteous on the basis of deeds" (Johnson [1995] 242). James and Paul are not opposing each other; they have different visions of concern: James's is with a living faith that is demonstrated through deeds, while Paul is concerned with the gift of faith that does not come through works of the Law.

when he offered (in sacrifice) his son Isaac on the altar: James has in mind the LXX account in Gen 22:1-19. Some words from this LXX account are observable in James: *thysiasterion* ("altar") (Jas 2:21; Gen 22:9) and *anenengkas* (from *anapherein*, meaning "to offer [in sacrifice]" [Jas 2:21 and Gen 22:2, 13]). The offering of Isaac in sacrifice was limited to the ʿ*Aqedah*, the "binding of Isaac" (*sympodisas Isaak ton hyion*, Gen 22:9) upon the altar. The testing of Abraham's faith was a key concept of the Hebrew tradition: e.g., "Was not Abraham found faithful when tested . . ." (1 Macc 2:52); ". . . and when he was tested he proved faithful" (Sir 44:20); "And the Lord was aware that Abraham was faithful in all of his afflictions" (*Jub.* 17:17 [*OTP* 2:90]). The Epistle to the Hebrews continues the same tradition as James: "By faith Abraham, when put to the test, offered up Isaac" (Heb 11:17).

22. *You see that faith was active together with his works:* "You see" (*blepeis*) is a statement, not a question, drawing out the conclusion from the illustration. It would be similar to the particle *oun:* "then, therefore." It is singular, continuing the dialogue with the opponent (2:18, 19, 20). While the Greek word *synērgei* is common in classical Greek, it appears in the LXX only in 1 Esdr 7:2 and 1 Macc 12:1, and in the New Testament in Mark 16:20; Rom 8:28; 1 Cor 16:16; 2 Cor 6:1. It has the meaning of "to cooperate with; to work together with; to be active together with." The use of the imperfect tense of the verb instead of the present (as some manuscripts indicate, including Codices Sinaiticus and Alexandrinus; see Aland [1997] 43) is appropriate here: it captures the ongoing actions that demonstrated the faith of Abraham. The "offering" of Isaac was only one of such works.

by the works faith was brought to perfection: The verb *teleioun* means "to bring to perfection," where perfection is understood as "completeness, totality, or wholeness" (Hartin [1999] 63). It clearly connects back to 1:3-4, where faith is brought to perfection through works of testing and suffering, while in 2:22 Abraham's faith is perfected through the testing he endured in being asked to offer his son. James illustrates the unfinished state of faith: works bring faith to maturity and keep it alive.

23. *the Scripture was fulfilled:* As in 2:8, *graphē* refers to a passage of Scripture. The verb *plēroun* ("fulfill") is used in the sense of how a later event (usual in the context of the New Testament) brings to completion a passage of Scripture: the scheme of promise/fulfillment is evident in this way of reading the Scriptures. The Gospel of Matthew above all gives expression to this understanding of the relationship between the Hebrew Scriptures and the events that have occurred in the birth and ministry of Jesus (e.g., Matt 1:22; 2:15, 18; 3:3;

4:15-16; 8:17; 12:18-21; 13:14-15; 21:5; 26:56; 27:9). However, James shows an interesting understanding of this promise-fulfillment connection: here he sees the fulfillment of Gen 15:6 occurring in Gen 22:1-19.

Abraham believed God, and it was reckoned to him as righteousness: This is a direct quotation from Gen 15:6 (LXX). James replaces *kai* ("and") in the Greek text with the particle *de*. He also uses the name Abraham in place of the LXX Abram (the change of name only occurs in Gen 17:5). James is simply using the customary form of the name. The passive use of the verb *logizomai* ("to reckon, calculate, consider") indicates that the judgment of Abraham's righteousness was given by God on behalf of Abraham. "God declares and qualifies Abraham in this passage of Scripture to be righteous because of his faith" (Mussner [1981] 144). Again the faith of Abraham must be seen to incorporate his works, which illustrate this faith as alive.

he was called God's friend: This is not part of the biblical quotation and is not a biblical phrase in itself, though it is similar to the biblical description of Abraham as "the one loved by God" in the LXX texts of 2 Chr 20:7; Isa 41:8. Many extratestamental writings also designate Abraham in a similar way: e.g., *Jub.* 19:9: "and he (Abraham) was recorded as a friend of the Lord in the heavenly tablets" (*OTP* 2:92); Philo, *Abr.* 273: ". . . no longer conversing with him as God might with man, but as one friend with another"; 4 Ezra 3:14: ". . . you chose for yourself one of them, whose name was Abraham; and you loved him . . ." (*OTP* 1:528). For James it is a significant designation because later, in 4:4, he demands that his hearers/readers make a choice: friendship with the world or with God. In later Christian writings the identification of Abraham as "a friend of God" was often made (*1 Clem.* 10:1; 17:2).

24. *You see that a person is proved righteous by works and not by faith alone:* James changes to the plural address to direct his attention now to the community at large, away from addressing the opponent. In this way he introduces his conclusion and provides a summary of his position. For the phrase "proved righteous" see 2:21. James's whole concern is that faith must be demonstrated by means of works. The phrase *ek pisteōs monon* ("not by faith alone") is equivalent to "without the aid and cooperation of works" (Ropes 223). James formally answers the question he raised in 2:14. The faith of a believer must automatically blossom forth into a demonstration of good works. Faith illustrates its true nature through the works it performs. The addition of the adverb "alone" *(monon)* indicates that in James's mind faith is essential to salvation, but he cannot accept a view that sees a faith divorced from a life that illustrates its faith through actions. Such a concept of faith is not opposed to Paul's view, but very much in harmony with Paul's perspective (see Gal 5:6: "the only thing that counts is faith working through love"; 1 Cor 13:2: "and if I have all faith, so as to remove mountains, but do not have love . . .").

25. *And likewise . . . Rahab, the prostitute:* A second example is offered in addition to Abraham, this time a woman. Johnson raises the interesting question: "Is it accidental that the figures of Abraham and Rahab correspond to the needy 'brother and sister' in 2:15?" ([1995] 245). The identification of Rahab as a

"prostitute" *(pornē)* corresponds to the picture presented of her in Josh 2:1-21; 6:15-25. James accepts much in this biblical description: the account in Joshua shows that her hospitality to the Israelites stems from her faith. In Josh 2:11 she confesses: "The LORD your God is indeed God in heaven above and on earth below." James presumes this faith and goes on to stress her deeds of kindness in helping the Israelites. In Jewish and Rabbinic tradition, extending over many centuries, the figure of Rahab appeared prominently: She became a proselyte who married Joshua and was the ancestor of eight prophets (including Jeremiah and Ezekiel). Her faith and deeds of hospitality are also mentioned: "By faith Rahab the prostitute did not perish with those who were disobedient, because she had received the spies in peace" (Heb 11:31); and "for her faith and hospitality Rahab the harlot was saved" (*1 Clem.* 12:1 [Lake, LCL]).

26. *just as the body apart from spirit is dead:* This is a summary of James's argument. The *sōma/pneumatos* ("body/spirit") reference clearly illustrates a Jewish anthropology that is exemplified in the Genesis creation narration (Gen 2:7), where the human being is constituted from body and breath. The word *pneuma* is without an article, indicating the life-giving force within the human being. As Ropes defines it, it is "the vital principle by which the body is animated" (225).

so faith apart from works is also dead: This forms an *inclusio* with 2:17. James's main point in the whole argument emerges here. A living faith by its very nature expresses itself in works, and the actions become a demonstration of the living nature of the faith.

INTERPRETATION

Contrary to the view of Dibelius (149), a careful examination of this pericope shows a connection to and a continuation of the line of thought presented in the previous passage (2:1-13). There James had stressed that Jesus' faith precluded any discrimination against others. The focus rested on the faith of Jesus and the challenge was to put that faith into action through the practice of the command of love. The faith of Jesus Christ (2:1) demanded that one show no partiality and demonstrate love. Now, in this paragraph (2:14-26), this faith is examined in more detail. Its character again demands that faith express itself in action. This is a further illustration of the practical wisdom of this writing.

The structure of this pericope is almost identical to the previous one. A fivefold structure like the one we described in the Interpretation to 2:1-13 is also discernible here.

(a) *Theme (propositio):* Faith without Works Cannot Save You (2:14)

(b) *Reason (ratio):* Example of Faith without Works in the Community (2:15-17)

(c) *Proof (rationis confirmatio):* Argument against an Imaginary Opponent (2:18-19)

(d) *Embellishment (exornatio):* Argument from Scripture: Abraham and Rahab (2:20-25)

(e) *Conclusion (conplexio):* Faith without Works is Dead (2:26).

(a) Theme (propositio):
Faith without Works Cannot Save You (2:14)

This opening verse presents the theme of the whole pericope and introduces an imaginary dialogue between the author and his projected opponent. As participants in this dialogue, the hearers/readers are addressed as "my brothers and sisters" *(adelphoi)*. The center of consideration is the theme that faith must demonstrate itself through works. From the outset James's use of the noun "faith" *(pistis)* connects back to the theme of 2:1: "the faith of Jesus Christ." In the previous pericope James showed that true faith demonstrated itself in brotherly love. Now he argues that a faith that is alive is one that demonstrates itself in works of love. That is the type of faith that saves. In some ways this pericope is an illustration of Jesus' statement in the Sermon on the Mount: "Not everyone who says to me, 'Lord, Lord,' will enter the kingdom of heaven, but only the one who does the will of my Father in heaven" (Matt 7:21; Luke 6:46).

Rhetorically, James's thesis lies at the heart of Jewish faith and piety. His aim is to persuade his hearers/readers to put their faith into action. Neither a person's profession of faith nor his or her ritual actions is sufficient. What is required is a life of deeds that embrace love and concern for others. The prophets above all criticized the faith and ritual actions of their fellow Israelites because they neglected their social responsibilities (Isa 1:11-17). James lies within this tradition as well. His message is also in line with Jesus' teaching (e.g., in the parable of the judgment of the nations in Matt 25:31-46, the separation between the "sheep and goats" is dependent on the way they demonstrated concern for others).

(b) Reason (ratio):
Example of Faith without Works in the Community (2:15-17)

James provides a reason for his thesis by means of an example that illustrates what faith without works would be like. While this is a hypothetical example, that is not to say that such examples did not exist within the context of the communities to whom he writes. His description is such that the members of his community could see themselves and their responses reflected clearly. The analysis in the Notes of the terms James uses (*gymnos* and *tes ephēmerou trophēs*) has shown that James is not painting a scene of utter destitution. Nevertheless, the example does reflect the real poverty that was the common experience of most people in the Mediterranean world. To such everyday experiences of poverty the members of James's communities are called to respond, not with wishful remarks but with real actions. "Go in peace!" (2:16) is not meant to portray callousness (Laws [1980] 121), but rather to capture the attitude of a person of faith whose reaction is limited to uttering a prayer with good wishes. Without doubt such a response runs counter to the very definition of religion James provided earlier: "to care for orphans and widows in their affliction . . ." (1:27).

This illustration would have shocked his hearers/readers just as it would have shocked any Jewish audience of his day. A person who could act in this way had never absorbed the central teaching of the message of Jesus, let alone the basic message of the prophets. He or she has a false understanding of what faith is all about. James concludes with a terse summary he repeats again later: faith apart from works is dead (2:17; 2:26). For James the major contrast is between a living faith and a dead faith. Works help to demonstrate the nature of faith as alive, but they do not replace it.

(c) Proof (rationis confirmatio):
Argument against an Imaginary Opponent (2:18-19)

An imaginary opponent is conjured up to present an objection, enabling the author to state his argument. The Notes have discussed the difficulties inherent in this verse. The best way to understand the passage is to see James providing both a challenge and an offer to his opponent. His challenge: "Show me your faith apart from your works" (2:18). The implication with which James leaves the reader is that of course his approach cannot do that. His offer: to demonstrate his own faith through works of love.

The absurdity of making a separation between faith and works is painted brilliantly with the example of profession of faith in God. "You believe that God is one" is a confession of belief expressed in terms of the *Shema Israel* (Deut 6:4). The profession that God is one embraces the understanding that God is all-powerful and demands total allegiance. The punch in James's argument comes at the end, when he says that even demons make such an acknowledgment that God is one. Laws has rightly argued that such a profession demands more than giving an "intellectual assent to a proposition" ([1980] 126). The belief the demons have includes more than just the understanding that God, the all-powerful one, demands total allegiance. This understanding provokes a response: they shudder in fear! So even with demons faith includes a response!

The very profession of belief in God as one, as expressed in the *Shema Israel*, requires a response of love: "You shall love the LORD your God with all your heart, and with all your soul, and with all your might" (Deut 6:5). In Jesus' teaching this profession of faith also requires a responsive love of neighbor (Matt 22:36-40). The traditions on which James relies (Israel and Jesus) are clear in presenting a vision that true faith requires a response. James builds on these traditions to argue that faith needs to demonstrate itself in action if it is to remain alive, and he refuses to concede the possibility that faith and works can be neatly separated into two independent compartments. Faith, if it is true faith, has to flower forth in actions. Any other kind of faith is dead.

(d) Embellishment (exornatio):
Argument from Scripture: Abraham and Rahab (2:20-25)

The argument is now embellished with support gleaned from the Hebrew Scriptures. In fact, a double application is developed, first through Abraham (2:20-23) and then through Rahab (2:25). Noteworthy, as well, is the intended reference to male and female examples. In 2:15 James deliberately referred to a "brother or sister" within the community. Now it is as though he is providing a biblical illustration for each (Johnson [1995] 249).

The selection of Abraham is no mere chance. The essence of James's concern in his choice of Abraham as an example is to reflect upon faith. Abraham is the "father" of the Jewish nation, and James's community continues to see itself as heir to the traditions of Israel, a heritage that incorporates the role of Abraham as their father. Abraham demonstrates his faith through his willingness to sacrifice his son on the altar. This is part of the testing of Abraham's faith and is surely a graphic illustration of the point with which James opened his letter (1:3-4): the testing of faith leads to endurance, which ultimately culminates in perfection: maturity, integrity, and completeness in a relationship with God. The similarity in thought between 1:3-4 and 2:22 is obvious. In 1:3-4 faith comes to perfection through works of testing, while in 2:22 Abraham's faith is perfected through his works, which embraced testing his willingness to offer his son in sacrifice on the altar. Since the actual sacrifice of his son never occurred it was not the sacrifice that demonstrated Abraham's faith, but rather the ᶜ*Aqedah*, the binding of Isaac. A circular movement occurs in the interaction between faith and works: faith inspires the works and is active together with the works, and in this interaction faith is brought to completion and maturity (2:22).

Is there an inconsistency between the reference to the "works" of Abraham and the single "work" (the *ʿAqedah,* the binding of Isaac) that is quoted by way of illustration? Ward thinks there is: "It is somewhat strange that the offering of Isaac should be referred to by the plural, *erga* (2:22)" ([1968] 286). He argues further that in the tradition the examples of Abraham and Rahab demonstrate their works of faith through hospitality ([1968] 283–90). This is clearly evident in *1 Clem.* 10–12. Ward's argument is that, since James reflects the same tradition, the works to which he refers should embrace Abraham's hospitality as well: "May not this also be the case for Abraham's *erga*—that is, James used Abraham as a well-known example of hospitality, but without referring explicitly to the famous story of his reception of the three travelers [Gen. 18] or to the other lore based on this incident?" ([1968] 286). However, I think the plural "works" (as is also the case with Rahab) is more stylistic than factual. Throughout the pericope James has been intent on contrasting faith and works (plural), so it is natural for him when illustrating his argument with the examples of Abraham and Rahab to use the plural "works," even though he provides only one example in each case.

James makes an interesting use of the promise/fulfillment scheme. Normally we see this schema operating between the Hebrew Scriptures and the New Testament. In this instance the promise/fulfillment occurs within the Hebrew Scriptures themselves, specifically within the Torah. James views the *ʿAqedah,* the binding of Isaac, in Gen 22:1-19 as the fulfillment of Gen 15:6. James is above all concerned to show that the faith of Abraham comes to fulfillment, to completion and perfection in the *ʿAqedah.* Abraham's faith is demonstrated through his actions. This is the heart of James's argument as outlined in 2:18: "by my works I will show you my faith." In applying the quotation (Gen 15:6) to this action James states that God considers Abraham to be righteous. Abraham's faith is shown to be alive through works. His righteousness is not based on works, but upon the quality of his faith, which is demonstrated to be alive.

To this quotation James adds the characterization that Abraham "was called God's friend" (2:23). As the Notes indicate, not only is that an important description in the tradition, but it is highly significant in the context of James's letter. One of the central motifs running throughout the letter is the contrast between those who belong to James's community and those who are outside. This contrast is laid out clearly before his hearers/readers in the choice they have to make between "friendship with the world" and "friendship with God." The opposition between the world and its values on the one hand, and God and God's values on the other is central. James 1:27 defines the very core of religion as comprising such values: "caring for orphans and widows in their affliction" and "keeping oneself unstained from the world." As a friend of God, Abraham acted in a way that showed that his fidelity to God's will was central to his life. His faith in action was a demonstration of his friendship with God. This surely was the example *par excellence* for James's hearers/readers. They too had to choose between friendship with God and friendship with the world. Like Abraham, they had to put their faith into action: they had to demonstrate by their works that their faith was alive.

James provides a further illustration in the person of Rahab (2:25). While the biblical narrative (Josh 2:1-21) makes a strong connection between Rahab's faith and her actions of hospitality (see especially Josh 2:9-13; Heb 11:31), James's text makes no direct mention of her faith. Undoubtedly James does presume Rahab's faith, because this is the foundation for his argument, but he wishes to focus attention on her work of hospitality.

Why did James choose Rahab as an example? There are two answers to this question. First of all, as has been indicated, Rahab became an important figure within the tradition, both biblical and Rabbinic. In *1 Clem.* 12:1 Rahab is praised because of "her faith and hospitality" (see also Heb 11:31). Both Clement (10–12) and Hebrews (11:1-40) show that they are clearly dependent on traditions that contain lists of people of faith. The tradition shows many examples of such lists (Sirach 44–50; 1 Macc 2:51-60; 3 Macc 6:2-8). Without doubt James is drawing on such lists in his mention of both Abraham and Rahab. The second reason for James's reference to Rahab has to do with her work of hospitality. Having provided the basis of his argument with the Abraham example, James refers briefly to Rahab, and in doing so gives specific attention to her hospitality to the Israelite messengers. It is possible that James holds up this action for admiration because it reflects something of his own world. Just as Rahab made the Israelite messengers welcome and sent them off safely, in a similar manner the communities to whom James writes should also extend hospitality to wandering missionaries and see them safely on their way. In this way Rahab could be a symbol for the Christian community. Once again we have an insight into the nature of James's communities: they would be situated at an early stage of the Christian movement when wandering missionaries moved from community to community. Stephen J. Patterson (*The Gospel of Thomas and Jesus* [Sonoma: Polebridge Press, 1993] 178–88) supports this perspective:

> I would suggest that it is not accidental that when the author of James addresses the question of faith and works, he or she chooses to illustrate the point using three examples relating to hospitality. He or she is focused so explicitly here on the hospitality theme that one must surely conclude that the reason the author brings up the subject of faith and works at all is that he or she feels it will be useful in treating what he or she perceives as a problem in the churches: the refusal of hospitality to travelers. (184)

At the heart of the concern for hospitality lies the obligation to care for the poor. Throughout ch. 2 James has been at pains to demonstrate the believer's responsibility to reach out to the less fortunate members of the community. It is again a concrete illustration of his definition of religion in 1:27.

(e) Conclusion (conplexio): Faith without Works is Dead (2:26)

James sums up his argument with a final phrase that acts as an *inclusio* with 2:17. In this way he ties together his argument with his main thesis (2:14) that faith apart from works is dead. James makes it clear that he is not contrasting faith and works, but rather a faith that is dead (without works) with a faith that is alive and brought to perfection (through works). James refuses to acknowledge that faith and works can be separated from each other. This was the position of his opponent in 2:18. For James the only true faith is one that expresses itself in works. The works are a natural outcome of faith and point to the quality of faith as alive. In reality, for James there is only one kind of faith, and that is faith demonstrated through works.

The rhetorical function of this whole section is clear: to persuade the hearers/readers that faith that comes to perfection is a faith demonstrated to be alive. James shows clearly that there is an unbreakable bond between ethics and faith: you cannot have one without the other. The words of James are equally applicable to our world, where some Christians see their faith as a purely private matter embracing solely a confession of faith. The message of James is undoubtedly a corrective to such individualistic and private notions of religion by reminding the community that faith, to be saving, must be alive.

FOR REFERENCE AND FURTHER STUDY

Bacon, Benjamin Wisner. "Doctrine of Faith in Hebrews, James and Clement of Rome," *JBL* 19 (1900) 12–21.

Baird, William. "Abraham in the New Testament," *Int* 42 (1988) 367–79.

Donker, Christaan E. "Der Verfasser des Jak und sein Gegner: Zum Problem des Einwandes in Jak. 2:18-19," *ZNW* 72 (1981) 227–40.

Hanson, Anthony Tyrrell. "Rahab the Harlot in Early Christian Tradition," *JSNT* 1 (1978) 53–60.

Longenecker, Richard N. "The 'Faith of Abraham' Theme in Paul, James, and Hebrews: A Study in the Circumstantial Nature of New Testament Teaching," *JETS* 20 (1977) 203–12.

McKnight, Scot. "James 2:18a: The Unidentifiable Interlocutor," *WTJ* 52 (1990) 355–64.

Siker, Jeffrey S. *Disinheriting the Jews: Abraham in Early Christian Controversy.* Louisville: Westminster John Knox, 1991.

Soards, Marion L. "The Early Christian Interpretation of Abraham and the Place of James within that Context," *IBS* 9 (1987) 18–26.

Ward, Roy Bowen. "The Works of Abraham: James 2:14-26," *HTR* 61 (1968) 283–90.

Windisch, Hans. "Zur Rahabsgeschichte," *ZAW* 35 (1917/8) 188–98.

EXCURSUS 7:

FAITH AND WORKS IN JAMES AND PAUL

In the course of the history of interpretation this pericope (2:14-26) has prompted intense discussion regarding its relationship to Paul's theology. Is there a contradiction between James's teaching on the necessity of good works for justification and Paul's teaching on justification by faith apart from works? The difficulty arises from the fact that James and Paul share a vocabulary that is similar, but at the same time acquires a unique meaning in each of their theological visions: e.g., justification *(dikaiosynē)*, to save *(sōzein)*, faith *(pistis)*, law *(nomos)*, and works *(erga)*. Different answers have been proffered to this question (see, e.g., Luther's negative evaluation in the *Introduction: 2. Text and Canonicity*). The position adopted by this commentary is that there is in reality no opposition between James and Paul since they are merely stressing different aspects.

Justification

In the Scriptures the term "justification" is used to refer to a situation in which people are declared to be in a right relationship with God. The concept of justification emerges from a legal context where "to be justified" (from the verb *dikaioun*, "justify") means that one is legally demonstrated to be in the right. The English words "justification, justify" translate the same root terms represented by the English word "righteousness."

The Hebrew Scriptures

In the world of Israel and the Hebrew Scriptures the concept of justification was used above all in the context of God's covenant with Israel. One is said to be in a right relationship with God insofar as one is a member of the covenant people and abides by the stipulations of the covenant. Genesis 15:6 (which both Paul and James quote) illustrates this well: "And he (Abram) believed the LORD and the LORD reckoned it to him as righteousness." The author is aware that the Mosaic covenant had not yet occurred, and that righteousness only came through God's covenant with Moses. Consequently he writes that Abraham's relationship with God was considered as though he were a member of the Mosaic covenant.

God is always faithful to this covenant relationship, a fidelity referred to as God's righteousness. Consequently, in reference to God the term righteousness refers to God's actions in upholding the covenant relationship and coming to the support of Israel.

Early Christianity

In the context of early Christianity the concept of justification and God's righteousness endured. The early Christians developed this concept and theology found in the Hebrew Scriptures by giving it their own specific understanding in relation to the person, death, and resurrection of Jesus. It is especially through reflection on the hopes of the Psalms that some New Testament writers developed an understanding of the fulfillment of Israel's hopes in God's actions in the death and resurrection of Jesus: e.g., "In you, O LORD, I seek refuge; do not let me ever be put to shame; in your righteousness deliver me" (Ps 31:1); "In you, O LORD, I take refuge; let me never be put to shame. In your righteousness deliver me and rescue me; incline your ear to me and save me" (Ps 71:1-2). The hope of God's righteous actions in the deliverance of Israel is now focused on the vindication of Jesus' death. God's ultimate deliverance of Jesus from death through the resurrection is the greatest demonstration of God's righteousness. In this vein the famous hymn quoted in 1 Tim 3:16 (obviously reflecting a liturgical tradition far more ancient than the letter itself [see *JBC* 2:355]) refers to Jesus, dead and risen, as "justified *(edikaiōthē)* (by God) in the spirit."

Paul

In Paul's letters the concept of justification/righteousness acquires special importance. Paul sums up his thought and position succinctly when he says: "We ourselves are Jews by birth and not Gentile sinners; yet we know that a person is justified not by the works of the law but *through faith in Jesus Christ.* And we have come to believe in Christ Jesus, so that we might be justified by faith in Christ, and not by doing the works of the law, because no one will be justified by the works of the law" (Gal 2:15-16). What is significant here is that Paul begins by appealing to a common faith, namely that salvation and justification occur through the community's *"faith in Jesus Christ."* It is this common understanding of justification that unites Jews and Gentiles in the new people of God.

An interesting new proposal has been advanced for the interpretation of the phrase "through faith in Jesus Christ" (*dia/ek pisteōs Iēsou Christou;* see Gal 2:15-16; 3:22; Rom 3:22). Most scholars and translators see it as an *objective genitive:* faith in Jesus Christ, where Jesus is the object of the faith of the believers. However, in more recent studies (such as those of Williams [1980] 241–90; [1987] 431–47; Johnson [1982] 77–90; Hays [1983]; [1987] 268–90; [*ABD*] 3:1129–33) the phrase *dia/ek pisteōs Iēsou Christou* is understood as a *subjective genitive* and translated as "through Jesus Christ's faithfulness" (Hays [1992] 1131). In this understanding of justification the stress is placed on the action of Jesus, his faithfulness and obedience to his relationship with his Father's will. In Gal 2:16 the contrast is drawn not between the believer placing faith and trust in Jesus as opposed to placing trust in his or her own efforts at obeying the Jewish Law. Rather, the contrast is between the faithfulness of Jesus Christ, whose sacrifice on the cross attained salvation for humankind, and humankind's efforts to acquire salvation through themselves and their obedience to the stipulations of the Jewish Law. As Hays notes:

> (T)his interpretation would be consistent with the view of justification articulated in Rom 5:18-19: "Then just as the trespass of one [Adam] led to condemnation for all, so also the righteous act *[dikaiōma]* of one [Christ] leads to the justification *[dikaiōsis]* of life for all. For just as by the disobedience of one [Adam] many were made sinners, so also by the obedience of one [Christ] will many be made righteous *[dikaioi]*" (*[ABD]* 1131).

Two things still remain essential for Paul's perspective: justification rests on God's action within Jesus' death and resurrection, making people righteous; second, Paul sets up an opposition with regard to those who strive to earn their own justification through works of the Mosaic Law. Paul remains true to the basic understanding of righteousness/justification expressed throughout the Hebrew Scriptures, namely that it is God's action of remaining faithful to the covenant. God brings people into this covenant relationship now through the death and resurrection of Jesus rather than through the biblical Torah.

James

In the letter of James the language of justification is used relatively frequently for such a short writing: the verb *dikaioun* occurs on three occasions (2:21, 24, 25); the noun *dikaiosynē* also appears three times (1:20; 2:23; 3:18) while the adjective *dikaios* occurs twice (5:6; 16) and the noun *adikia* once (3:6). Differently from Paul, James sees salvation predominantly in terms of the future rather than as a present reality. As Jeremias says: "James, when speaking of justification, has in mind the last judgment" ([1954/55] 371). However, this vision is not exclusively future, as James does envisage a present dimension for the concept of salvation. In 1:18 he states that "(God) gave us birth by the word of truth, so that we might be a kind of first fruits of his creatures." James speaks in terms of community. He sees individuals undergoing a transformation into a new birth as God's creatures. Just as the language of justification envisages the action of God bringing the believer into the context of God's covenant people, in like manner James sees the individual being brought through God's action into a community of those who are God's new creation.

In the context of salvation the focus for James rests on what God has done and is doing. The new creation (1:18) is God's work according to God's own purpose. God is the one who grants the "crown of life . . . to those who love him" (1:12). God too is the one who grants forgiveness of sins and the gift of healing (5:15). In everything God is the cause and origin of all salvation. Humanity does not earn this: human beings are the recipients of God's generous gifts.

As indicated in the interpretation of 2:1, the concept of "the faith of Jesus Christ" *(pistis Iēsou Christou),* found in Paul as a subjective genitive, also appears in James 2:1. While Paul stresses the faithfulness of Jesus, culminating in his salvific death, James draws attention to the importance of the faithfulness of Jesus' whole life and ministry. For James the believer has to follow Jesus' example. The stress lies on the imitation of a faithfulness that is demonstrated in the works of Jesus.

Consequently, James's main concern is to argue that faith must be demonstrated by works of love: faith on its own has no justifying power. Faith is true faith when it demonstrates itself in action with works of love (2:22). These works of love show that faith is alive. Faith is brought to perfection through the works of obedience to God and kindness to one's neighbor (2:21-22). "You see that a person is proved righteous by works and not by faith alone" (2:24) expresses James's thesis. James is just as opposed to "works alone" as he is to "faith alone" in attaining justification. Works have to be demonstrated through actions of love before they are accepted by God as demonstrating that a person's faith is alive.

Essentially James and Paul have two very different visions of the relationship between faith and works. One can describe the relationship as something akin to the "before and after" scenario. Paul is concerned about the situation of a person before she or he comes to faith and justification. According to Paul, works of the Law do not lead to faith and justification. For James, on the other hand, the perspective is rather that of a believer who already has faith and is in a justifying relationship with God. James stresses that it is vital for that person to express his or her faith in actions, or good deeds. The different concerns of the two authors can be represented in this way:

Paul's concern	James's concern
Works of the Law	**Faith**
(do not lead to)	(expresses itself in)
Faith	**Works of Faith**

This is, in effect, the way Augustine saw the relationship between James and Paul. He expressed their concerns in this way: "Therefore the opinions of the two apostles, Paul and James, are not opposed to each other when the one says that man is justified by faith without works, and the other says that faith without works is useless: because the former (Paul) speaks about works that precede faith, while the latter (James) speaks about those that follow faith; as even Paul shows in many places" (*De diversis quaestionibus LXXXIII Liber Unus* 76 [*MPL* 50:89]). Augustine further distinguished between a dead faith that demons have and the justifying faith that works through love:

> It is this same kind of faith which separates the faithful ones of God from the unclean devils, since even these, as the Apostle James says, "believe and tremble," (2:19) though they do not perform good works. Theirs, then, is not that faith by which the just man lives, namely, a faith which so works through charity that God requites it with eternal life in accordance with its works. But as these same good works also come from God, who bestows faith and charity upon us, this same Teacher of the Gentiles has accordingly spoken of "eternal life" itself as a grace (*Grat.* 7:18 [Russell]).

Works

Paul

For an excellent and detailed treatment of the concept of "works" in both Paul and James see Mussner ([1981] 152–57). I acknowledge my debt to and dependence upon him for many of the insights here. In the letters of Paul the term *ergon/erga* is very common (some sixty-seven times in all the writings attributed to Paul). His varied use of the term betrays a clear theological vision. A survey of Paul's usage reveals the following as the most significant aspects:

"Works of the Law" *(erga tou nomou):* This is the most significant use of the term for Paul's understanding of the justification process. According to Paul, in the new dispensation that began with the death and resurrection of Jesus the works of the Mosaic Law have no value for justification. The main concern, as indicated above, was to place the emphasis on God's actions in Jesus rather than on human actions. People cannot earn their own justification through fulfilling the requirements of the Law: a new path was opened up through the death and resurrection of Jesus. Paul constantly speaks in this context of "works of the Law" in the plural (see Rom 3:20, 27; 4:2, 6; 9:12, 32; 11:6; Gal 2:16[3x]; 3:2, 5, 10; Eph 2:9).

"Good work" *(ergon agathon):* Paul deliberately uses the singular in place of the plural to avoid confusion with the negative "works of the Law." This is understood in a positive sense as referring to human actions that are pleasing to God: "to those who by patiently doing good *(ergou agathou)* seek for glory and honor and immortality, he will give eternal life" (Rom 2:7). Paul also uses this phrase to refer to "God's good work": "I am confident of this, that the one who began a good work *(ergon agathon)* among you will bring it to completion by the day of Jesus Christ" (Phil 1:6). God's work is God's gift of salvation, which will ultimately be brought to completion at the end-time. The emphasis is decidedly on what God has done. God's work can also be identified with the person of Jesus Christ: in the letter to the Philippians, Epaphroditus is described as coming "close to death for the work of Christ" (Phil 2:30).

Paul's work of ministry (ergon diakonias): Again Paul uses the singular, *ergon:* e.g, "For to me, living is Christ and dying is gain. If I am to live in the flesh, that means fruitful labor *(karpos ergou)* for me; and I do not know which I prefer" (Phil 1:21-22); and "to equip the saints for the work of ministry *(eis ergon diakonias),* for building up the body of Christ" (Eph 4:12).

What is significant in Paul's use of these terms *ergon/erga* is the dividing line he draws between "works of the Law" and other positive uses of the term work/works. While there are times when Paul consistently goes out of his way to use the singular form *(ergon)* in order to avoid confusion with "the works of the Law," he is not always successful in maintaining this distinction. In Rom 2:6 he writes: "For he will repay according to each one's deeds *(kata ta erga autou).*" Here Paul is not referring to the "works of the Mosaic Law," but rather to the actions of the individual believer in the course of his or her life. He is in fact quoting Ps 62:12 (61:13 LXX).

James

The terminology *ergon/erga* appears some fifteen times in the letter of James (1:4, 25; 2:14, 17, 18[3x], 20, 21, 22[2x], 24, 25, 26; 3:13). One of the clearest illustrations of James's intent in the use of this vocabulary is 3:13:

"Show by your good way of life your works in wisdom's meekness." Clearly James demonstrates the understanding that "works" are an outgrowth of the life of the believer: they illustrate the quality and nature of the life of faith. James 2:14-26 uses the term *erga* frequently to embrace acts of love toward community members.

James's vision embraced an understanding of works that occurred in the context of one's whole life of faith. Works of love were beacons of light demonstrating the quality of faith, a faith that owes its origin to God's new creating action (1:18). Once again this understanding of works in relation to the demonstration of one's faith and love is a direct continuation of the teaching of Jesus, particularly in the Sermon on the Mount. "In the same way, let your light shine before others, so that they may see your good works *(kala erga)* and give glory to your Father in heaven" (Matt 5:16). For Jesus one's actions, one's good works, must be a demonstration of one's faith that ultimately brings glory to God. The conclusion to the Sermon on the Mount highlights the importance of faith expressed in action. Jesus stresses that it is not the confession of faith but rather the carrying out of his Father's will that is important: "Not everyone who says to me, 'Lord, Lord,' will enter the kingdom of heaven, but only the one who does the will of my Father in heaven" (Matt 7:21). Jesus' saying is later echoed in James's statement: "So faith by itself, if it has no works, is dead" (2:17). The contrast Matthew's Jesus draws between good and bad fruit is another attempt to assert the importance of good works as a demonstration of the nature of one's faith: "In the same way, every good tree bears good fruit, but the bad tree bears bad fruit. . . . Thus you will know them by their fruits" (7:16-20). Finally, the parable of the house built on rock is a further reminder of the necessity that works put into practice one's faith in Jesus: "Everyone then who hears these words of mine and acts on them will be like a wise man who built his house on rock . . ." (Matt 7:24-27). This also finds an echo in James's teaching on the need to be a doer of the word and not a hearer only (1:22-23).

Consequently, James's vision that faith must be alive and demonstrate itself through works or actions is not on the periphery of the New Testament writings. His vision conforms to the message of the Jesus of the Sermon on the Mount, which undoubtedly is one of the central visions of early Christianity and has remained so until today. Even Paul embraces this vision in his own way. He often expresses the desire that those to whom he writes should bear fruit through lives whose actions demonstrate their faith: ". . . so that you may lead lives worthy of the Lord, fully pleasing to him, *as you bear fruit in every good work* and as you grow in the knowledge of God" (Col 1:10). This spirituality of works-demonstrating-faith so beautifully describes James's position and shows ultimately that Jesus, James, and Paul are on the same page. While they each speak to different contexts and audiences, and have different perspectives in mind, they nevertheless uphold a common message of the importance of faith being put into action.

Conclusion

The above examination has demonstrated that much posited opposition or contradiction between James and Paul has little foundation in the reality of their writings. One of the difficulties encountered is that there are thirteen letters attributed to Paul and from these one can build a comprehensive picture of Paul's theology related to justification, faith, works, and the law. However, as far as James's thought is concerned there is really only one writing on which to construct his ideas related to these same concepts.

Both authors give the role of faith a primary position in the context of salvation. Paul's major concern was the battle he waged against those who wanted Christians to continue to observe the Jewish Torah with its traditions and rituals, such as male circumcision and the Jewish dietary laws. For Paul this approach was in essence a denial of the role Christ played in salvation. It was indeed a rejection of God's gift of Christ. At heart Paul saw the conflict with these Judaizers in terms of either/or: salvation is attained either through works of the Law or through faith in Christ.

An examination of the reference made to the example of Abraham in Paul and James demonstrates the differences in their context and vision. Paul refers to the example of Abraham in Gal 3:6-9. In doing so, he quotes Gen 15:6 and gives it a particular understanding. He shows that God justified Abraham on the basis of his faith in God and God's message. Thus Abraham becomes an example for all who are on the path to justification, especially the Gentiles: God effects the justification of a sinner on the basis of faith and not on works of the Law.

James (2:21-23) refers to Abraham and uses the same scriptural quotation as Paul does (Gen 15:6), although in a different way. As the Interpretation showed, James sees Gen 22:1-19 (the account of the binding of Isaac) as the scriptural fulfillment of Gen 15:6. Abraham manifested his faith in this action of offering his son on the altar. By referring to the quotation (Gen 15:6) in the context of this action James states that God considers Abraham's faith to be true faith, a faith shown to be alive through works. On this basis God considers Abraham righteous. His righteousness is not based on works of the Law but on the quality of his faith, which is demonstrated to be alive. Abraham emerges for all as an example of what true faith is. While Paul's concern was to argue that justification does not rest on works of the Law but on faith, James's concern is very different. He opposes an empty faith with one that is alive in God and in Christ Jesus. He demonstrates that a person is shown to be righteous through a living faith, a faith that flowers forth into action. Paul and James each have their own concerns. They are not addressing each other, but give attention to issues that are dominant within their own communities.

A failure to read James and Paul within the context of their visions and concerns has been the leading cause for scholars to see an opposition between them. Far more agreement exists between Paul and James than is generally acknowledged (as Johnson [1995] 58–64 also argues). One point of important agreement is the value they both attach to the Torah. For Paul and James the Torah is the moral universe in which they live and operate, giving expression to God's moral will for the way humans are to act. Paul refers to the Law as holy, just, and good (Rom 7:12) and spiritual (7:14), while James characterizes it as the perfect law of liberty (1:25). A further remarkable similarity appears in their teaching on being not just a hearer but also a doer. Paul relates this teaching to the Law, while James brings it into the context of the word: "For it is not the hearers *(akroatai)* of the law who are righteous in God's sight, but the doers *(poiētai)* of the law who will be justified" (Rom 2:13); and "But become doers *(poiētai)* of the word, and not merely hearers *(akroatai)* who deceive themselves" (Jas 1:22).

This is not to deny that James and Paul do emerge from different traditions and communities within early Christianity. That there was diversity among and within those communities is something present-day scholarship acknowledges and celebrates more, especially since the discovery of the Nag Hammadi tractates, and the Gospel of Thomas in particular. James and Paul represent different and diverse streams within the early Christian movement, but this does not mean that their diversity necessarily implies opposition. This is a mistaken conclusion scholars often tend to draw. As Martin says: "Those who see James and Paul as being in irreconcilable antagonism look to this passage as part of the diversity of New Testament Christianity" (82). But why should diversity necessarily imply antagonism? While James had a theology different from that of Paul, this does not mean that James was against Paul (see Johnson [1995] 114). It is the position of this commentary that James's diversity must be respected and celebrated, and that James's voice must be read in its own right as a witness to its own vision and theology without placing it within a straitjacket that views it through the eyes of Paul's universe.

FOR REFERENCE AND FURTHER STUDY

Bultmann, Rudolf. *"Dikaiosyne Theou,"* JBL 83 (1964) 12–16.
Cosgrove, Charles H. "Justification in Paul," JBL 106 (1987) 653–70.

Hays, Richard B. "Have We Found Abraham to be Our Forefather According to the Flesh?" *NovT* 27 (1985) 76–98.

_____. "Christology and Ethics in Galatians: The Law of Christ," *CBQ* 49 (1987) 268–90.

_____. "Justification," *ABD* 3:1129–33.

Jeremias, Joachim. "Paul and James," *ExpTim* 66 (1954/5) 368–71.

Johnson, Luke Timothy. "Romans 3:21-26 and the Faith of Jesus," *CBQ* 44 (1982) 77–90.

Reumann, John H. P., et al. *Righteousness in the New Testament: "Justification" in the United States Lutheran-Roman Catholic Dialogue.* Philadelphia: Fortress, 1983.

Soards, Marion L. "The Righteousness of God in the Writings of the Apostle Paul," *BTB* 15 (1985) 104–109.

Stendahl, Krister. "The Apostle Paul and the Introspective Conscience of the West," *HTR* 56 (1963) 199–215.

Williams, Sam K. "The 'Righteousness of God' in Romans," *JBL* 99 (1980) 241–90.

_____. "Again *Pistis Christou*," *CBQ* 49 (1987) 431–47.

Ziesler, J. A. *The Meaning of Righteousness in Paul: A Linguistic and Theological Enquiry.* SNTSMS 20. Cambridge: Cambridge University Press, 1972.

6. *The Tongue and Speech* (3:1-12)

1. Let not many of you become teachers, my brothers (and sisters), since you know that we will receive a more severe judgment. 2. For we all fail often. If anyone does not fail in speech, this person is perfect, able to hold the whole body in check with a bridle. 3. And if we place bits into the mouths of horses to make them obey us, we guide their whole bodies as well. 4. See also the ships: although they are so large, they are driven by strong winds; yet they are guided by a tiny rudder wherever the impulse of the pilot directs. 5. Likewise the tongue is a small member, yet it boasts of great things. See how large a forest a little fire sets ablaze! 6. And the tongue is a fire. The tongue is the world of iniquity placed among our members: it stains the whole body and sets on fire the cycle of existence and is itself set on fire by Gehenna. 7. For every species of animal and bird, of reptile and sea-creature, is being tamed and has been tamed by humankind. 8. But no human can tame the tongue—a restless evil, full of death-dealing poison! 9. With it we bless the Lord and Father, and with it we curse human beings made in God's likeness. 10. From the same mouth come blessing and curse. My brothers (and sisters), things like this ought not to happen! 11. Surely a spring does not pour forth from the same opening both sweet and bitter water? 12. Can a fig tree, my brothers (and sisters), produce olives, or a grapevine figs? No more can a salt spring produce sweet water.

NOTES

1. *Let not many of you become teachers:* The term "teacher" *(didaskalos)* translates the term "rabbi" in the Jewish world. In Christian Jewish churches undoubtedly the teacher would occupy the position the rabbi exercised in the synagogue. Again James shows his roots in the heritage of Judaism. All the gospel traditions present Jesus as being frequently called "Teacher (Rabbi)" (Matt 8:19; Mark 4:38; Luke 9:38; John 13:13-14). Within the early Christian movement the term "teacher" reflected a specific ministry. In Antioch we hear of "prophets and teachers" (Acts 13:1). They are included among Paul's lists of church ministries: "Are all apostles? Are all prophets? Are all teachers?" (1 Cor 12:29), and "The gifts he gave were that some would be apostles, some prophets, some evangelists, some pastors and teachers . . ." (Eph 4:11). In the *Didache* teachers are again mentioned together with prophets *(Did.* 13:2; 15:1-2).

   since . . . we will receive a more severe judgment: James presents a reason for not seeking the office of teacher. By using the first person here James associates himself among the teachers. The word *eidotes* ("you know") is often found in Paul's letters to indicate traditional Jesus teaching (Rom 5:3; 6:9; 13:11; 1 Cor 15:58). This shows that James is using a familiar instruction coming from tradition. Since teachers have a deeper understanding and knowledge they bear a greater responsibility. James indirectly makes reference to judgment on the last day. Does the judgment *(krima)* refer to receiving a greater punishment (see Laws [1980] 144), or being judged according to a higher standard or "responsibility"? (see Ropes 227). Both meanings are possible. It is not necessary to choose between them; rather, one should see both concepts as intended in the judgment. Paul also reflects the seriousness of the teacher's role: "(B)ut I punish my body and enslave it, so that after proclaiming to others I myself should not be disqualified" (1 Cor 9:27).

2. *we all fail often:* The reason for the advice is the weak human condition. Sins of the tongue are the hardest to avoid. The verb *ptaiō* ("fail") occurs in the New Testament only here and at Jas 2:10; 2 Pet 1:10; and Rom 11:11. In James it bears the sense of moral failure, though in general usage it can simply mean "lose one's footing, stumble, trip" (see BDAG 894). Undoubtedly James is using proverbial language. Similar thoughts or expressions commonly occur in the Hebrew Scriptures (Job 4:18-19; Prov 20:9); in the LXX (Sir 19:16); and throughout Greek literature: e.g., Seneca writes: "We have all sinned—some in serious, others in trivial things; some from deliberate intention, some by chance impulse . . ." *(Peccavimus omnes, alii gravia, alii leviora; alii ex destinato, alii forte impulsi . . .)" (Clement.* 1:6, 3 [Basore, LCL]); and Philo states: ". . . there has never been a single man who, by his own unassisted power, has run the whole course of his life, from the beginning to the end, without stumbling . . ." *(Deus* 75; see also Sophocles, *Ant.* 1023).

   this person is perfect, able to hold the whole body in check with a bridle: For the use of *teleios* ("perfect") see 1:4. Wholeness and integrity are the dominant idea here. To tell the truth means that one's thought and speech are in harmony and one conforms "to the way God has created them" (Hartin [1999] 152). As

in 1:12, *anēr* occurs in a way that evokes an example with universal application. For this reason the translation is "person." See Jas 1:26 for the use of the
Greek verb *chalinagōgēsai* ("hold in check with a bridle"). James deliberately
wishes to recall the previous usage in 1:26 and to provide an opening for the
use of *chalinos* ("bit") in the next verse. The figure of using a bridle in the
mouth of a horse to guide and direct the horse at will is further extended to
the image of how we can direct our whole being by controlling our tongue.
The phrase *holon to sōma* ("the whole body") is a reference to the "whole person." It is repeated again at 3:3 and 3:6. Israel's wisdom literature reflected
often on the uncontrolled use of the tongue (e g., "A person may make a slip
without intending it. Who has not sinned with his tongue?" [Sir 19:16; see also
Prov 10:8, 11, 19; 16:27-28; 18:7-8; 21:23; Sir 20:1-8]).

3. *And if we place bits into the mouths of horses:* It is difficult to decide how James
intended to open this verse. There are two possible readings: *ide* ("behold") or
ei de ("and if"). The manuscript evidence is very unclear (see Aland [1997]
48–49). Metzger comments that the problem probably arose since "(t)he
itacistic confusion between *ei* and *i* being extremely common, it is possible
that a copyist wrote *ide* but meant *ei de*, or vice versa . . ." ([1975] 681–82).
The problem of itacism is that in Greek *ei* is pronounced like *i*, and in Codex
Vaticanus *i* often replaces *ei*. While commentators are divided on the issue, the
twenty-seventh revised edition of Nestle-Aland's *Novum Testamentum Graece*
and the fourth revised edition of the UBS *The Greek New Testament* adopt the
reading *ei de*. I have opted for this reading, *ei de* (translated "and if") on the
basis of the principle of *lectio difficilior:* grammatically it is an awkward conditional clause. The reading *ide* could be the result of a scribe creating a harmo-
nization with *idou* (v. 4) either consciously or unconsciously (Metzger [1995]
682). Further, an examination of James's stylistic features shows that he uses *ei
de* on five more occasions, while *ide* never occurs again (although *idou* also
appears five times). This verse begins a series of analogies that capture the
power of the tongue despite its small size. Many of these analogies were
common in the Greco-Roman world, such as the image of a charioteer using a
small bit to control horses or the pilot guiding the ship with a small rudder.
See, e.g., Plutarch: "'Tis character persuades, and not the speech.' 'No, rather it
is both character and speech, or character by means of speech, just as a horse-
man uses a bridle, or a helmsman uses a rudder, since virtue has no instrument so humane or so akin to itself as speech'" (*Mor.* 33F [Babbitt, LCL]); and
Philo: "And so the Creator has made man to be as it were a charioteer and
pilot over all other animals, in order that he may hold the reins and direct the
course of every thing upon earth . . ." (*Opif.* 88; see also *Legat.* 2:104; 3:223-24;
Spec. 4:79). Plato compared the soul to "the natural union of a team of winged
horses and their charioteer" (*Phaedr.* 246B-247C [Nehamas & Woodruff]).

4. *See also the ships:* James continues the double image found in the Greco-Roman
tradition of the charioteer and the helmsman (see examples above as well as
Mayor 110–11; Ropes 231). Dibelius argued that James here is making free use
of established metaphors: "Therefore, he seems to be dependent upon tradition here also, and consequently it seems that all of the metaphors which have

been mentioned are ones which James has borrowed. Indeed, James may have also borrowed a fixed association of these metaphors" (189-90). That James is using commonly known oral proverbs in the illustration of his argument seems to be supported as well by the fact that many of the words in these verses are *hapax legomena* in the New Testament. This is further evidence for James's familiarity with Greek literature and culture. James has woven these metaphorical sayings into his argument very well, for they lead naturally into the next verse. For the phrase "strong winds" *(anemōn sklērōn)* see Prov 27:16 LXX. The adjective strengthens the contrast with the tiny rudder.

impulse of the pilot directs: The word *hormē* ("impulse" or "will") occurs only here and in Acts 14:5 in the New Testament. BDAG (724) defines it as: "a psychological state of strong tendency, impulse, inclination, desire." Mayor notes that the word *hormē* "is used of the origin of motion either moral or physical" (111–12). In James what is intended is the moral will of the pilot, not the guiding force of his hand (Dibelius 190).

5. *the tongue is a small member, yet it boasts of great things:* This restates the argument made above that control can be exercised through small things. Though the tongue is small, its boast is great. In the New Testament boasting was seen as a vice because it replaces trust in God with trust in one's own abilities. "Faith implies the surrender of all self-glorying. But for those who stand in faith there may open up a new possibility of boasting, namely, in terms of their achievements in the propagation of faith (Gl. 6:13)" *(TDNT* 3:649 [Bultmann]). James uses the phrase *megala auchei* ("boast of great things"): such usage of this verb + accusative is unknown in the LXX and the rest of the New Testament, but it is common in Hellenistic literature (see Josephus, *C. Ap.* 1:22; *Vita* 340; Herodotus, *Hist.* 7:103). A textual variant, *megalauchei,* occurs in a number of manuscripts, including Codex Vaticanus and $\mathfrak{P}^{20}$. This verb *megalauchein* appears in the LXX in Ezek 16:50; Sir 48:18; 2 Macc 15:32 in the sense of "to be haughty." Perhaps this variant arose through a scribe mistaking *megala auchei* for the more familiar *megalauchei.* James also achieves a skillful alliteration in this verse: *mikron—melos—megala* ("small member—great things").

See how large a forest a little fire sets ablaze: This begins the discussion (extending to 3:12) on the destructive power of the tongue. There is an interesting play on words here: *hēlikon . . . hēlikēn.* Literally *hēlikos* has the meaning "of what size" (Martin 112). James uses it in two contrasting ways: "how great . . . how small." Both meanings are attested in Hellenistic literature: e.g., the meaning "how great" can be seen from Josephus: "Or what proof was brought against them so convincing ('so great,' *hēlikos*) as that which establishes this traitor's guilt?" *(B.J.* 1:626 [Thackeray, LCL]; see also *A.J.* 8:208), while "how small" can be seen from Lucian: "Goodness, Hermotimus! How small *(hēlikous)* you make us, not as big as pygmies!" *(Hermot.* 5 [Kilburn, LCL]; see also BDAG 436). The exact contrast is captured well in Philostratus, where Damis comments on a thirteen-year-old boy riding an elephant: "For it seems to me a super-human feat for *such a tiny* mite to manage *so huge* an animal" *(to gar thēriŏ tēlikoutŏ epitetachthai tēlikonde onta . . .)* *(Vit. Apoll.* 2:11 [Conybeare,

LCL]; see also Dibelius 191). Classical literature abounded in references to forest fires that had been started by a small flame. The Greek noun *hylē* can have the meaning "a forest" or "the stuff out of which a thing is made, material, matter, stuff" (BDAG 1027). Given James's context, where he has been comparing something small to something great (ship-rudder; bit-horse), the contrast of flame-forest makes more sense (see also Dibelius 191–92). There are many biblical references to the tongue as a fire/flame: Pss 39:1-3 (38:2-4 LXX); 120:2-4 (119:2-4 LXX); Prov 16:27 LXX; 26:21; Isa 30:27; Sir 28:13-26 (especially v. 22: "It [the tongue] has no power over the godly; they will not be burned in its flame"). Dibelius (192–93) gives many examples of the use in Hellenistic literature, where the passions are frequently compared to a fire. Philo (*Decal.* 173) illustrates this well: ". . . nothing ever escapes desire, but, like a fire in a wood, it proceeds onward, consuming and destroying everything." However, James's comparison lies between the tongue and a fire, and not between the passions and fire (as both Davids [1982] 141 and Martin 113 also indicate). For this reason it seems more likely that James is dependent here on the biblical tradition for this image. Many of the words are unique or nearly unique to James in the New Testament: *anaptō* ("set ablaze") occurs elsewhere only in Luke 12:49; *hēlikos* is found in Gal 6:11 and Col 2:1; *hylē* ("fire") is a *hapax legomenon*. This appearance of vocabulary that is unusual in the New Testament may point to James's use of a familiar proverb.

6. *And the tongue is a fire. The tongue is the world of iniquity placed among our members:* The Greek *kai* ("and") makes the connection by applying the comparison in the preceding verses. The meaning of this half verse is clear, but grammatically it is difficult to follow because of the numerous nominative expressions (five in all) connected with only one finite verb (*kathistatai*, from the verb *kathistanai*, "to place or set"). Because of the difficulties, some commentators have argued that the text is corrupt. For example, Dibelius writes: "In fact, there are few verses in the New Testament which suggest the hypothesis of a textual corruption as much as this one does" (194). Consequently he argues that the phrase "the tongue . . . among our members" (*hō kosmos . . . hēmōn*) is actually a gloss added by some scribe by way of explanation (Dibelius 195). Davids's advice is important: "Before one resorts to the expedient of changing the text, he should be sure the given text does indeed make no sense" ([1982] 142). Further, Metzger's *Textual Commentary* (1975) in the section on James makes no mention of this verse, which I think is informative. By making no comment the editors of the *United Bible Societies' Greek New Testament* text indicated that they thought the text as it stands does make sense (Aland [1997] 53–57 supports this conclusion). The best approach is to take the text as it stands. One must not lose sight of the author's rhetorical intent in this verse. He uses metaphors taken from popular and common usage, stringing them one after another for rhetorical effect. A sermon develops by building on images to achieve the desired effect among the hearers (Davids [1982] 144). A period is to be understood after *pyr* ("fire"), with the verb "to be" *(estin)* implicitly understood. The phrase *kai hē glōssa pyr* is then taken as a complete sentence: "And the tongue is a fire." The difficult phrase *ho kosmos tēs adikias*

("the world of iniquity") is to be read in connection with the second use of the word "tongue" (*glōssa*) (see Martin 115). Mussner translates it in this way: "And the tongue exists among our members as a fire, (yes) as the unjust world" ([1982] 163). However, the phrase "the world of iniquity" is more than the simile Mussner takes it to be. It is a metaphor, as Johnson ([1995] 259) correctly identifies it. Consequently, the phrase is the predicate of the verb *kathistanai* ("place or set"): "the tongue is the world of iniquity placed . . ." The meaning is grasped from the use of the term *kosmos* ("world") elsewhere in James: in 1:27 religion demands that one keep oneself "unstained from the world"; in 2:5 the world is set in opposition to the kingdom; and in 4:4 a clear opposition is set up between friendship with the world and friendship with God. In fact, in 4:4 the same verb, *kathistanai,* is used to identify those who make the choice of friendship with the world: "they are now placed as enemies of God." In the context of our verse it is the tongue that establishes the world of iniquity (that is opposed to God) among our bodies. The phrase "among our members" is a metaphor that refers to our bodies; the part is used for the whole.

It stains the whole body: The use of the verb *spiloun* ("stain, defile") is significant in that it reminds one of the reference to religion in 1:27 where one is called to "keep oneself unstained (*aspilon*) by the world." What 1:27 has warned against has now occurred. The world from which one is called to protect oneself has actually entered the body through the tongue.

sets on fire the cycle of existence and is itself set on fire by Gehenna: The noun *trochos* can mean either "wheel" or "course," depending on where the accent falls. Commentators have found the use of this phrase, *ton trochon tēs geneseōs* ("cycle of existence"), troubling (see Mayor 116–18; Ropes 235–39; Dibelius 196–98). The meaning of the phrase becomes clear: James indicates the tongue's destructive power for evil. It affects all existence from the cradle to the grave. However, the problem comes when one notes that the concept of "the cycle of nature" was a technical term used in the Orphic mystery religions (see Dibelius 196–97 for a detailed exposition of this term in Greek literature). In the belief system of Orphism the soul is imperishable and so there is the constant "cycle" of coming into a new earthly existence and then passing out of it into another one. The only way to escape this never-ending cycle of transmigration is through salvation, which the Orphic mysteries offer the initiates (Dibelius 196). While the usual term they employ is *kyklos* ("circle"), there is one reference from Simplicius where the phrase "wheel of becoming" is used: ". . . appointed to the wheel of fate and becoming (*geneseōs trochō*) by the demiurge god . . ." (*In Arist. de cael.* 2:168b, 25). Since the literature in which this phrase is used is very early, over time it entered popular speech without maintaining its original context. Examples of its use in a nontechnical sense can be seen in Virgil ("All these, when they have rolled the wheel through a thousand years . . ." [*has omnes, ubi mille rotam volvere per annos . . .] [Aen.* 6:748]) and Philo ("After that he puts on a golden necklace, a most illustrious halter, *the circlet and wheel* of interminable necessity . . ." [*Somn.* 2:44]). It is likely that by the time of James the phrase had become so much a part of common speech that it had lost its technical identification with its origins in the Orphic mystery religions. For James, then, the image of the wheel captures the cyclical nature of human existence: in every aspect of this cycle the tongue has the power to inflame with evil. The same verb *phlogizō* ("set on fire, inflame") is used for both phrases in this half-verse (see Exod 9:24), which intends to strengthen the originating point of the evil, namely "Gehenna." The exact Greek word is *geenna,* a term that does not occur in the LXX except for the form *gaienna* in Josh 18:16. The Greek form *geenna* ("Gehenna") is from the Hebrew *gê ḥinnōm* ("the valley of Hinnom," or "the valley of the son of Hinnom"; see MT of Josh 15:8; Neh 11:30). This valley or ravine south of Jerusalem was once used for pagan fire sacrifices (2 Kgs 23:10). Jeremiah viewed it as a place for divine punishment on Jerusalem (7:31-34). It became associated with the last judgment in apocalyptic literature from the second century B.C.E. onward (*1 En.* 27:1; 54:1; 56:3-4; 90:26; see *TDNT* 1:657–58). In the gospels it appears as a place of punishment (Matt 5:22, 29, 30; 10:28; 18:9; 23:15, 33; Mark 9:45, 47; Luke 12:5) and of fire (Matt 5:22; 18:9). The point of James's imagery is to show that evil emanates from "Gehenna" itself and gives the tongue its all-consuming power.

7. *For every species of animal and bird, of reptile and sea-creature*: *Gar* ("For") connects this sentence with the previous one, giving the reason why the tongue is full of evil: human beings have been able to control everything except the tongue. The argument continues in the following verse, since vv. 7-8 are really one sentence. *Physis* ("species") refers to the nature or kind of creatures as distinct from each other (see Philo, *Spec.* 4:116, for a similar usage). The fourfold classification of "animal and bird, reptile and sea-creature" is common in the Hebrew Bible (Deut 4:17-18; 1 Kgs 4:33; Acts 10:12; 11:6), tracing its origin back to Gen 1:20-26. The list and sequence in James is similar to Gen 9:2, where God blesses Noah after the flood: "The fear and dread of you shall rest on every animal of the earth, and on every bird of the air, on every thing that creeps on the ground, and on all the fish of the sea. . . ." This categorization of four groups is intended to include all created beings. The Greek word *enalios* ("sea-creature") is a *hapax legomenon* in the LXX and the New Testament. It is found in Philo, *Decal.* 54. The language of creation is preparatory for the reference to human beings as created in God's likeness in 3:9.

is being tamed and has been tamed by humankind: The ability of humans to control the natural world as a divine gift was a universal belief in the Greco-Roman world. See Philo, *Opif.* 88: "And so the Creator has made man to be as it were a charioteer and pilot over all other animals, in order that he may hold the reins and direct the course of every thing upon earth, having the superintendence of all animals and plants, as a sort of viceroy of the principal and mighty King" (see also Philo, *Decal.* 13; *Legat.* 2:104). See as well Seneca (*Ben.* 2:29, 4 [Basore, LCL]): "consider what great blessings our Father has bestowed upon us, how much more powerful than ourselves are the creatures we have forced to wear the yoke, how much swifter those that we are able to catch, how nothing that dies has been placed beyond the reach of our weapons," and Cicero, *Nat. d.* 2:60, 151. It is also a common Hebrew belief, as is reflected in the classic texts of Gen 1:28; 9:2; Ps 8:6-8; Sir 17:4. James creates a play on the word *damazō* ("to tame") by using the present and perfect tenses. While this is a redundancy, the effect is to stress the control human beings have exercised on the animal world from the very beginning.

8. *But no human can tame the tongue:* The particle *de* is used in an adversative sense to provide a contrast with the preceding. The subject has changed from the tongue to the human person. James creates a deliberate alliteration with the phrase *damasai dynatai* ("can tame"). He demonstrates a pessimistic attitude: the tongue alone among all created things is impossible to control.

a restless evil, full of death-dealing poison! These two phrases in the nominative express an exclamation, with the tongue as its object: *akatastaton kakon, mestē iou thanatēphorou!* The adjective *akatastatos* ("restless") occurred before in 1:8 (there translated as "vacillating") and appears later in 3:16 in the form of a noun, *akatastasia* ("disorder") that identifies a vice of unspiritual people. The picture of the restlessness of the tongue develops the other images, namely that of blazing fire or untamed nature. In this context the noun *ios* means "poison" and has a possible allusion to a serpent's tongue (Ropes 241). As Mayor (121) notes, the metaphor possibly comes from Ps 140:3: "They make their tongue sharp as a snake's, and under their lips is the venom of vipers" (also quoted in Rom 3:13). The adjective *thanatēphoros* literally means "death-bearing" and is translated here as "death-dealing" (BDAG 442). The tongue's death-bearing qualities are also referred to in Sir 28:17-23.

9. *we bless the Lord and Father . . . we curse human beings made in God's likeness:* To bless and praise God is the most important prayer one can make in the Jewish and Christian traditions (see Ps 16:7; Eph 1:3). Some textual witnesses (including the *Textus Receptus*) read "God and Father." However, the strength of witnesses is in favor of the reading "Lord and Father" (e.g., $\mathfrak{P}^{20}$; Codices Sinaiticus, Alexandrinus, and Vaticanus). Metzger ([1975] 682) argues convincingly for the reading "Lord" *(kyrion)* on the basis that it is the *lectio difficilior,* as it is the only place in the Bible where the phrase "Lord and Father" occurs. A copyist would more probably change the phrase "Lord and Father" to the more usual "God and Father" than the other way around. Perhaps James is reflecting here the Jewish formula of blessing that opens "Blessed are you, Lord God" (see, e.g., Gen 9:26; 24:27). The combination of Lord and Father occurs in Isa 63:16 and Sir 23:1, 4. The theme of the tongue performing a contradictory role appears in both Greek and Jewish literature (see Laws [1980] 154–55). See, for example, *T. Benj.* 6:5: "The good set of mind does not talk from both sides of its mouth: praises and curses, abuse and honor, calm and strife, hypocrisy and truth, poverty and wealth, but it has one disposition, uncontaminated and pure, toward all men" *(OTP* 1:827). Philo writes in the context of the taking of oaths: "for it is an impiety for any disgraceful words to be uttered by that mouth by which the most sacred name is also mentioned" *(Decal.* 93). The theme of uttering a curse on someone was characteristic of the Hebrew Scriptures. See Gen 12:3: "I will bless those who bless you, and the one who curses you I will curse. . . ." Here James provides the motivation for not cursing another: he or she is created in God's image and likeness.

10. *things like this ought not to happen!* James uses the phrase *ou chrē* and the accusative + infinitive to express a negative necessity. Literally it means "that which should not be/happen" (see BDAG 1089). This is the only use of this phrase in the New Testament.

11. *Surely a spring does not pour forth:* The first of a series of three questions using three metaphors that show how incomprehensible it is for the tongue to be inconsistent. The interrogative particle *mēti* expects a negative answer. The Greek noun *pēgē* ("spring") has the article "as the representative of its class" (Ropes 242). The verb *bryein* ("pour forth") does not occur elsewhere in the LXX or the New Testament. It means "something that is teeming with a substance" (BDAG 184) and generally refers to "plants bursting into bud and flower, or . . . the land in spring" (Mayor 124). Here it captures the image of water bursting to overflowing, gushing forth.

from the same opening sweet and bitter water: The noun *opē* refers to the crevice or opening in a rock (see also Heb 11:38). The two accusative adjectives *glyky* ("sweet" or "fresh") and *pikron* ("bitter") both presume the neuter noun *hydōr* ("water"). The adjective *pikros* only occurs here and at 3:14 in the entire New Testament. The more common term is *halykos* (see 3:12). James has probably chosen *pikros* because it can be used metaphorically in a moral sense (see 3:14).

12. *Can a fig tree, my brothers (and sisters), produce olives, or a grapevine figs?* Again we meet a question expecting a negative answer. This time James uses the particle *mē*. The fig tree *(sykē),* the olive *(elaia),* and the vine *(ampelos)* are typical of Palestine and the Mediterranean climate. Similar to this metaphor of the fig tree and the grapevine is Jesus' saying in Matt 7:16-17: "You will know them by their fruits. Are grapes gathered from thorns, or figs from thistles? In the same way, every good tree bears good fruit, but the bad tree bears bad fruit" (see also Luke 6:44). Dibelius (204–205) has demonstrated the popularity of these images in Stoic thought to express the notion that each person has to do what is proper to him or her: e.g., Plutarch used the threefold images of fig, olive, and vine: "But as it is, we do not expect the vine to bear figs nor the olive grapes . . ." *(Tranq.* 13 [472E]). Seneca used the metaphors of the fig and the olive to express the impossibility of good arising from evil: "Therefore, good is not born from evil nor evil from good, any more than figs come from olive trees" *(non nascitur itaque ex malo bonum neque ex bono malum, non magis quam ficus ex olea) (Ep.* 87:25). Marcus Aurelius Antoninus also used images of the fig tree and the vine producing their natural fruit: "Remember that it is as absurd to be surprised that the world brings forth the fruits with which it teems as that the fig-tree should bear figs" *(Med.* 8:15 [Farquharson]), and "Nothing can happen to any human being which is not an incident appropriate to man, nor to an ox which is not appropriate to oxen, nor to a vine which is not appropriate to vines . . ." *(Med.* 8:46 [Farquharson]; see also Epictetus, *Diatr.* 2:20, 18). James is not necessarily borrowing Stoic thought directly, but the wide diffusion of these images points to the author's access to them from the wider Greek world. James borrows these metaphors from the world with which he is familiar to express the idea that inconsistency in

human speech should be just as inconceivable for a believer as it is for a tree to produce a fruit different from its type or species.

No more can a salt spring produce sweet water: There are many textual variants to this clause (see Aland [1997] 59). Since the revised fourth edition of the United Bible Societies text follows the more difficult reading and is based on the important manuscripts (Codices Alexandrinus and Vaticanus), and because it does prepare for the thought of 3:13-18, this translation remains with the established text. The adverb *oute* ("and not") is used in place of the more usual *oude* (BDAG 740). Instead of judging this to be a mistake, Ropes notes that these words were constantly interchanged and it is "hard to be sure that good ancient writing did not exercise more freedom in the use of them than the grammarians would sanction" (243). Finally, James uses the neuter adjective *halykon* as a noun ("salt spring") instead of *pikron* (3:11) to vary his vocabulary.

INTERPRETATION

The Structure of James 3:1-12

James turns to a topic introduced in the opening chapter. As argued, the function of the opening chapter was to announce themes that would be developed further in the course of the letter. The theme of speech occurred twice in the introduction. James 1:19 gave the admonition "Let every person be . . . slow to speak," while 1:26 argued that uncontrolled speech ran counter to the very concept of religion: "If any think they are religious, and do not bridle their tongues, but deceive their hearts, their religion is worthless." This passage takes up the need for controlling speech or the tongue.

James 3:1-12 is more than just a loose configuration of sayings. As in 2:1-13 and 2:14-26, James has structured a well-balanced argument on the control of the tongue. The argument is subsumed under the theme "Let not many of you become teachers" (3:1). The office of teacher is the one most affected by the universal inability to control the tongue. While some thoughts from this passage do flow over into the following section (3:13-18), such as the importance of consistency in one's actions, 3:13-18 really looks to the following section (4:1-10), thus shaping the larger rhetorical unit of 3:13–4:10.

Once again the structure of the perfect argument, as illustrated in the two passages of ch. 2, is evident here. The development unfolds in this way: (1) James 3:1 presents the *theme* of the argument: "Let not many of you become teachers. . . ." (2) In 3:2 the *reason* for not becoming teachers is presented: we all often fail in speech. (3) The *proof* for the need to control the tongue is offered in 3:3-5a: it has a tremendous power and produces great things. (4) The *embellishment* on the destructive power of the tongue occurs in 3:5b-10. Here James becomes much more pessimistic. Within this section he provides theological support for control. Uncontrolled speech is inconsistent: it curses a fellow human being who is created in God's likeness while at the same time blessing God. (5) The argument *concludes* in 3:11-12 with examples chosen from the world of nature. These examples imply that the situation of uncontrolled speech ought not to exist.

Duane F. Watson ([1993b] 48–64) has also examined this passage according to the structure of the perfect argument and has provided a division somewhat different from the one I propose. His division is as follows: *propositio* (v. 1a), *ratio* (v. 1b), *confirmatio* (v. 2), *exornatio* (vv. 3-10a), *conplexio* (vv. 10b-12) (see Watson [1993] 64). Where I differ from his detailed analysis is chiefly in identifying the *ratio* in James's argument. According to the flow of the argument, the reason why many should not become teachers is not that teachers will receive a greater judgment (as Watson evaluates it): that is still part of the *theme* or *propositio*. Rather, the reason is that we humans all make many mistakes, especially in speaking, and since the whole ministry of teachers depends on speaking, the judgment of teachers will be greater than it will be for others. *Ad Her.* 18:28 expresses it as follows: "The Reason, by means of a brief explanation subjoined, sets forth the causal basis for the Proposition, establishing the truth of what we are urging" (Caplan, LCL). The truth of the proposition as to why many should not become teachers resides in the universal failure humans experience in what they say.

Consequently, the structure of James's argument develops as follows:

(a) *Theme (propositio):* Do not become teachers (3:1)

(b) *Reason (ratio):* We all fail in speech (3:2)

(c) *Proof (rationis confirmatio):* The power of the tongue (3:3-5a)

(d) *Embellishment (exornatio):* The dangers of the tongue (3:5b-10)

(e) *Conclusion (conplexio):* One nature cannot produce two contradictory effects (3:11-12)

Not only is 3:1-12 a well-structured argument; one can also observe many of its striking stylistic features, to which attention has been drawn in the Notes. One of the characteristic features of this passage is its use of alliteration: *polla ptaiomen . . . hapantes* (3:2); *mikron melos . . . megala* (3:5); *phlogizousa . . . phlogizomenē* (3:6); *damazetai . . . dedamastai* (3:7); *damasai dynatai* (3:8). Also noteworthy in this passage is the use of concepts and thoughts from Greek philosophy that had become the common stock of popular thought and speech, such as the "cycle of existence" (3:6) and the metaphors of the fig, olive, and grapevine (3:12).

(a) Theme (propositio): Do Not Become Teachers (3:1)

James initiates a reflection on the tongue and the need to keep it under control. It challenges all people ("for we all fail often"), including members of James's community ("my brothers [and sisters]"). However, it is a topic that is especially relevant for those who exercise the role of teacher within the community. That is why James prefaces his instructions on the tongue by referring to the responsibility the teacher has within the community. The ministry of instruction was exercised chiefly through speaking rather than through the written word. The function teachers exercised within the early Christian communities was vital for the growth and development of the community. Their role could be either positive (the building up of the community) or negative (the undermining and destruction of the community).

Of the fifty-eight uses of the term *didaskalos* ("teacher") in the New Testament some forty-eight occur in the gospels (*TDNT* 2:152). The usage of the term is explicable against the background of the Jewish and Christian worlds rather than the Greek world. In the Jewish world the rabbi or teacher is the one who above all interprets and explains the Law and sees to it that people are able to carry it out correctly. Jesus is frequently addressed as "Rabbi." The identification of rabbi and teacher is made explicit in John 1:38: "When Jesus turned and saw them following, he said to them, 'What are you looking for?' They said to him, 'Rabbi' *(Rabbi)* (which translated means Teacher [*Didaskale*]), 'where are you staying?'" Within the context of the early church the term "teacher" is also applied to those whose main function is to instruct the community. Paul and Barnabas are both identified by this term in Antioch (Acts 13:1). What is important to note here is that the reference is to the role or function certain believers are called to exercise, not to an office. James D. G. Dunn insightfully notes the difference between the functions of prophet and teacher in this way: "In short, the teaching function provided an indispensable complement to prophecy; the normative role of the gospel and of Jesus' words provided an invaluable control on charismatic excess. . . . Teaching preserves continuity, but prophecy gives life; with teaching a community will not die, but without prophecy it will not live" ([1975] 284). In light of James's discussion earlier on the role of the Law and the importance of the fulfillment of the whole Law, the teacher has an important role within the community. The focus is not on status, but rather on function and the ability to be an official interpreter of the Law. The teacher has the task of ensuring the guidance of the community through the correct interpretation of these traditions. The author is indeed carrying out this function through the way in which he applies the Torah and the sayings of Jesus to the new context of his own community.

James's instruction not to become teachers is reminiscent of Jesus' command in Matt 23:8: "But you are not to be called rabbi, for you have one teacher, and you are all students." Just like Jesus, James is against any tendency to seek positions of authority for the sake of prestige, power, or domination over others. James is not attacking the office of teacher, but draws attention to the function or responsibility of the one who teaches. The judgment against which James warns occurs not in the court of human opinion but rather "in the eyes of God." The judgment on the last day is what he envisages.

(b) Reason (ratio): We All Fail in Speech (3:2)

The human condition of weakness is given as the reason in support of the theme of not becoming teachers. Sins of the tongue are the hardest to avoid. James intends more here than just the unrestrained use of the tongue. In the context of what he has said about the teacher this statement is a warning against leading others astray from the truth. This can have serious repercussions on the community as a whole. James has in mind the responsibility teachers bear in upholding the faith of the community. As with all James's instructions, the focus goes beyond the personal and individual level to embrace the community as well. This is further strengthened by his references within this section to "the body" or "the whole body" (vv. 2, 3, 6). While the immediate reference is to the physical body, it also takes on a metaphorical application to the Christian community. He has in mind the way both leaders as well as ordinary believers use their speech in ways destructive to the community as a whole.

According to James the "perfect person" is able to keep his or her speech in check. Once again he introduces the theme of perfection or wholeness. Speech and thought are brought into harmony, so that one is simply the outgrowth of the other. The believer strives for wholeness or integrity, which is the exact opposite of the dividedness James has so frequently opposed in the letter.

(c) Proof (rationis confirmatio): The Power of the Tongue (3:3-5a)

In developing his argument James provides proof to support his call to control the tongue. Although small, the tongue holds great power. James builds his argument through the use of popular images current in Hellenistic culture and literature (see the Notes). Using these oral Greek proverbs, he builds a strong descriptive case to illustrate the tongue's power. Like a charioteer who controls a horse with a bridle or bit, and like the pilot who steers the ship using a tiny rudder, the small tongue is able to produce great things, both good and evil. This is the essence of the challenge. Good and evil are within the tongue's ability. James, as teacher, urges his hearers/readers to ensure that their control of the tongue results in good being effected. However, James is very pessimistic, as the following verses show.

(d) Embellishment (exornatio): The Dangers of the Tongue (3:5b-10)

James now develops or embellishes his argument for the power of the tongue and the consequent need to control it. He offers proof to show the tongue's potential destructive powers. This is an extremely pessimistic description. Johnson ([1990] 329–39) has shown how this passage differs radically from the traditional Greek *topos* on speech. The major difference stems from their different evaluations of the dangers of speech. While Greek moralists did paint a picture of speech's destructive effects, James's vision appears more bleak and the possibility of actually controlling the tongue, in James's mind, appears virtually nil. James 3:8 does state that no one can tame the tongue!

Using two metaphors, James paints a vivid picture of the tongue's destructive power: The tongue is a fire! The tongue is a cosmic force! Each metaphor builds on the other and is a further extension of the other. The imagery is very frightening. The picture of a fire immediately communicates a sense of danger. Just as a small flame can rampage through a whole forest, so the devastation of the tongue knows no limits. It can enflame the whole body, whether of the individual or the community. Once the fire is ignited, the devastation is impossible to stop. James extends the imagery of the fire by adding another metaphor: the tongue is "the world of iniquity" (3:6). The tongue brings the individual and the community into relationship with the "world." To put it another way, the tongue brings the world within the person or group. The concept of world, as the Notes observe, is that which is set in opposition to God and the kingdom. James 4:4 expresses this opposition in the starkest terms: it is a clear choice between friendship with God and friendship with the world. The world is evil, it is set against God, and through speech the tongue brings this opposition within the very being of the individual or the community. The values that belong to the world become part of the inner being of the individual and the community. They seep into everything. The real evil of the tongue is that it verbalizes the values inherent in the world and, as Wall expresses it, "speech patterned after the protocols and perquisites of the world order shape a people who live contrary to God's will" ([1997] 169). In this sense the metaphor ("the tongue is the world of iniquity") has cosmic dimensions. The forces of evil enter the life of the believer and the community. These forces are further enhanced by the powers of "Gehenna" that enflame the "world of iniquity." Since evil emanates from "Gehenna," it ultimately gives the tongue its destructive power.

The tongue's power is twofold: First of all, "it stains the whole body" (3:6). Using the root of the same word as in 1:27 *(aspilos—spilousa)*, James shows that what he warned about earlier has come to pass through the tongue's power. True religion demanded that one keep oneself "unstained *(aspilon)* from the world" (1:27). Now through the power of the tongue this evil world "stains *(spilousa)* the whole body." Second, it "sets on fire the cycle of existence" (3:6). As the Notes have indicated, James uses philosophical language that had become part of popular speech to indicate the evil influence the tongue exerts on human existence at every stage of development. Through these two images James shows the cosmic dimensions of the destructive power of the tongue: its evil seeps not just into the individual and the community, but into all creation.

James's embellishment adds further weight to his argument for the need to control the tongue. As he has done previously in 2:1-13 and 2:14-26, he solicits examples from Scripture to support his viewpoint. In particular he turns for support to the creation story. The first reference is with the well-known phrase "every species of animal and bird, of reptile and sea-creature" (3:7). This is the standard fourfold classification of the animal world (Gen 1:26-31; 9:2). Part of God's creative plan was for humanity to bring the created world under control; in other words, humanity was charged with taming the created world: "God said to them, 'Be fruitful and multiply, and fill the earth and subdue it; and have dominion over the fish of the sea and over the birds of the air and over every living thing that moves upon the earth'" (Gen 1:28). James indicates that humanity has carried out this instruction faithfully: "every species . . . is being tamed or has been tamed by humankind" (3:7). The startling thing James acknowledges is that there is one area where humanity is unable to exercise control, and that is the human tongue. James uses hyperbole when he says that no human can tame the tongue. This is a surprising statement, given the starting point in 3:2, where he acknowledges that the person who is able to control speech is perfect. The contradiction is ultimately resolved in the next section (3:13-18). God's wisdom enables the believer to tame the tongue. On one's own that cannot be done. As Robert W. Wall says: "The believer's 'ability' to respond to spiritual testing in ways that are pleasing to God is conditioned by the believer's dependence upon divine wisdom" ([1997] 172).

Further images from the creation narrative occur in the development of James's argument. The tongue is "full of death-dealing poison" (3:8). The image of a serpent is implicit in this metaphor, a clear reminder of the serpent of Genesis (Gen 3:1-24). The serpent was the tempter of the first parents and brought about the change in their relationship with God. As a consequence death entered the world: ". . . you are dust and to dust you shall return" (Gen 3:19). The tongue exercises the same function as the serpent of Eden. As tempter and destroyer it ultimately brings death. In line with the previous metaphor of "Gehenna" setting the tongue on fire (3:6), one can see that ultimately behind the tongue's deadly power lies the serpent, the devil, who enflames the tongue in its hostility to God and humanity. The division between friendship with God and friendship with the world becomes ever more acute and its consequences ever more serious. The ultimate result of not allowing divine wisdom to control the tongue is that control is ceded to the serpent, with the inevitable consequence of spiritual death.

James deliberately continues to allude to the creation story in 3:9-10 with the description of the human being "made in God's likeness" (a reference to Gen 1:26-27). The Greek word used *(homoiōsis)* does not occur elsewhere in the New Testament and is also very rare in the LXX. It is found in Gen 1:26 LXX, where it is used together with the better-known term "image": "Then God said, 'Let us make humankind in our image, according to our likeness . . .'" *(kai eipen ho theos Poiēsōmen anthrōpon kat' eikona hēmeteran kai kath' homoiōsin . . .)*. A difference in the meaning of these two terms "image and likeness" has long been proposed. For example, Philo sees *eikōn* ("image") as referring to the mind of the human being: "for the mind which exists in each individual has been created after the likeness of that one mind which is in the universe as its primitive model" *(Opif. 69)*. On the other hand, the phrase "in his likeness" was added "to prove that it means an accurate impression, having a clear and evident resemblance in form" *(Opif. 71)*. It is impossible to demonstrate whether James had these more nuanced distinctions in mind. However, it seems to me that the view that James deliberately chose the little used *homoiōsis* in order to draw attention to Gen 1:26 (Laws [1980] 156) makes perfect sense. The contradictory action of the tongue in blessing and cursing takes on a heightened seriousness. Admirably, the tongue praises and blesses God, and conversely, something as reprehensible as the other is admirable, the tongue curses "human beings made in God's likeness" (3:9). James provides the motivation for not cursing another: he or she is created in God's likeness. It makes the charge more serious and is ultimately connected with cursing God. Jervell (240, 295–96) makes the argument that Gen 1:27 lies behind this admonition as well as behind all the ethical instructions in James. It explains why the prohibition of murder is so serious: "Whoever sheds the blood of a human, by a human shall that person's blood be shed; for in his own image God made humankind" (Gen 9:6). It accounts for the two references to the prohibition against murder in 2:11 and 4:2.

Not only is the theme of creation the background to all the ethical injunctions in James: it is also central to James's whole vision. The communities to whom James writes are viewed as the "twelve tribes in the

Dispersion." James's Jewish-Christian hearers/readers, as the reconstituted twelve-tribe kingdom, are the fulfillment of Israel's messianic hopes. As the beginnings of this new people of God they are identified as "the first fruits of his (God's) creatures" (1:18). James reminds his hearers/readers of this tremendous role and the position they occupy in God's dealings with humanity. They are God's special re-creation, to whom the gift of divine wisdom has been communicated. They, then, have the gift that enables them to overcome the evil power of the tongue and to tame it.

(e) Conclusion (conplexio):
One Nature Cannot Produce Two Contradictory Effects (3:11-12)

James brings his treatment of the tongue to a conclusion with three rhetorical questions that expect an automatic negative response. The theme of creation continues. An observation of God's created order reveals a simple axiomatic fact: one nature can only produce one effect consistent with its nature. One spring produces either sweet or bitter water (never both); fig trees produce figs; olive trees produce olives; grapevines produce grapes. In the created order all things conform to the principle of God's created order: one nature, one effect. God's creation is orderly and stable; there are no fluctuations or changes since God is a God who is "the Father of lights, with whom there is no variation or shadow of change" (1:17). The implications are clear. The tongue, which is also a created entity, must conform to its nature and produce a single effect: blessings and cursing cannot result from the same source. The point James makes is clear: just as it is against nature for one kind of tree to yield a different kind of fruit, so human speech should not utter what is inconsistent. The law of creation and the law of nature demand uniformity.

Some Final Reflections

James has developed his advice on the basis of the biblical tradition as well as from the popular language and idiom of the wider Greek world. This essay on speech deviates in many ways from what one would identify as a straightforward or standard *topos* on the subject. Johnson defines Hellenistic *topoi* of moral instruction in this way: "These are standard treatments of a subject, usually consisting in a loose agglomeration of clichés, propositions, examples, and other statements organized around a central theme and frequently drawn together by a process of association" ([1995] 28). What James has constructed here is more developed than a loose collection of sayings. He has presented a well-conceived argument, as I have endeavored to illustrate, patterned on what was considered to be the construction of a perfect argument. He clearly was aware of the *topoi* in existence in the biblical and the Greek worlds, but he has developed a much more powerful and pessimistic assessment of the ability to control the tongue.

James's reflection on the power of the tongue and its effects can be viewed on three levels: the individual, the community, and the cosmic. Each is not independent of the others but in some ways, like a spiral, each leads into the others.

On the individual level James's admonition is dire. A tongue that goes unchecked acts like a flame that soon fans out into a forest fire engulfing the individual and those around. The starting point in his reflection is the advice for the teacher to see the grave responsibility she or he bears in teaching others. Yet the advice is not restricted to the teacher alone; it calls all believers to be conscious of the effects and power of speech. James is conscious of the forces of evil that exist outside the individual and these also incite the tongue to further evil.

On the community level the effects of irresponsible speech are equally disastrous. It can lead others astray, which is contrary to James's rhetorical purpose for his letter. The whole aim of the letter is to show his hearers/readers the way in which the perfect law of freedom is to be implemented. He concludes his letter with the injunction that "My brothers (and sisters), if anyone of you wanders from the truth, and is turned back by another, know that whoever turns back a sinner from the way of error will save that soul from death and will cover a multitude of sins" (5:19-20). James has in mind more than simply the disastrous effects of speech on the individual. His reference to "the whole body" (3:2, 3, 6) can be understood as an allusion to the whole community of believers. Teachers especially have to give careful attention to what they say, as it influences the spiritual well-being of the entire community. James's letter develops a strong community ethic and responsibility by demanding an awareness of the need to control the tongue.

The power of the tongue also plays itself out *on the cosmic level*. The power of "Gehenna" feeds the tongue. The tongue shares in the effects of fallen humanity. Just as the serpent, the devil, introduced death and disunity between God and humanity, and within the human community, so James sees the tongue (itself infected by the power of the serpent) continuing to bring discord and death to the human community. This corresponds to the golden thread that runs throughout the letter. The fundamental choice set before the believer is between friendship with God and friendship with the world (4:4). The choice is clear and simple. Such is the power that the world and the forces of evil exert upon the human person that it is impossible to control the tongue. The only path is through the power of wisdom from above (3:13-18). Friendship with God empowers the believer to control the tongue and attain the perfection, the wholeness and integrity God intended for each human being at creation.

FOR REFERENCE AND FURTHER STUDY

Bratcher, Robert G. "Exegetical Themes in James 3–5," *RevExp* 66 (1969) 403–13.

Bultmann, Rudolf. *"kauchaomai," TDNT* 3:645–54.

Dunn, James D. G. *Jesus and the Spirit: A Study of the Religious and Charismatic Experience of Jesus and the First Christians as Reflected in the New Testament.* Philadelphia: Westminster, 1975.

Eliott-Binns, Leonard E. "The Meaning of HYLĒ in James 3,5," *NTS* 2 (1955/6) 48–50.

Jeremias, Joachim. *"geenna," TDNT* 1:657–58.

Jervell, Jacob. *Imago Dei. Gen 1,26f. im Spätjudentum, in der Gnosis und in den paulinischen Briefen.* FRLANT 76. Göttingen: Vandenhoeck & Ruprecht, 1960.

Milikowsky, Chaim J. "Which Gehenna? Retribution and Eschatology in the Synoptic Gospels and in Early Jewish Texts," *NTS* 34 (1988) 238–49.

Rengstorf, Karl Heinrich. *"didaskalos," TDNT* 2:148–59.

Watson, Duane F. "The Rhetoric of James 3:1-12 and a Classical Pattern of Argumentation," *NovT* 35 (1993b) 48–64.

Zimmermann, Alfred F. *Die urchristlichen Lehrer.* WUNT 2nd ser. 12. Tübingen: J.C.B. Mohr [Paul Siebeck], 1984.

7. Call to Friendship with God (3:13–4:10)

13. Who is wise and understanding among you? Show by your good way of life your works in wisdom's meekness. 14. But if you have bitter jealousy and selfish ambition in your heart, do not boast and lie against the truth. 15. This is not the wisdom that comes down from above, but is earthly, unspiritual, demonic. 16. For where there is jealousy and selfish ambition, there is disorder and everything that is evil. 17. But the wisdom from above is first of all pure, then it is peaceable, gentle, obedient, full of mercy and good fruits, without a trace of partiality or hypocrisy. 18. But the fruit that is righteousness is sown in peace by those who make peace.

4:1. From where do wars and from where do battles among you come? Do they not come from this, namely your desires that are at war within your members? 2. You desire and you do not have, so you murder. And you are filled with envy and you cannot obtain, so you fight and wage war. You do not have because you do not ask. 3. You ask and you do not receive because you ask wickedly in order to spend it on your desires. 4. You adulteresses! Do you not know that friendship with the world is enmity with God? Therefore whoever wishes to be a friend of the world becomes an enemy of God. 5. Or do you think that in vain the Scripture says: "Does the spirit that God made to dwell in us yearn enviously?" 6. Rather, he gives a greater grace; therefore it says: "God resists the proud, but gives grace to the humble." 7. Therefore submit to God. But resist the devil and he will flee from you. 8. Draw near to God and he will draw near to you. Cleanse your hands, you sinners, and purify your hearts, you double-minded! 9. Lament and mourn and weep! Let your laughter be turned into mourning and your joy into dejection. 10. Humble yourselves before the Lord and he will exalt you.

NOTES

13. *Who is wise and understanding among you?* The interrogative pronoun *tis* introduces a rhetorical question similar to the clause that occurs in the Jesus saying: "What father among you *(tina de ex hymōn ton patera)* if his son asked for a fish would hand him a snake instead of a fish" (Luke 11:11; see also Deut 20:5-8; Pss 34:12 [33:13 LXX]; 107:43 [106:43 LXX]; Isa 50:10; Sir 6:34 *[tis sophos]*). These brief interrogative questions are typical features of the diatribe (Bultmann [1910] 13). In Jewish usage the rabbi (teacher) was the wise person *(sophos)* whose teaching embraced practical moral wisdom based on the Torah, both written and oral (Sir 9:17; 21:13; Wis 7:15). This connects back to the opening of ch. 3 in the reference to the teacher. The term *epistēmōn* ("understanding") refers to someone who has an expertise in some field in contrast to the person who has no training. It is a *hapax legomenon* in the New Testament, although in the LXX it appears in conjunction with the word *sophos* in Deut 1:13, 15; 4:6; Sir 21:15.

Show by your good way of life your works in wisdom's meekness: Literally the text reads: "Let him show by his good way of life his works. . . ." I have translated this in the second person to achieve an inclusive translation, for that is certainly what James intends insofar as his instruction is directed to the community at large, as one can see from the preceding and following sentences, both in direct address. In 2:18 above ("Show me your faith apart from your works . . .") James asked that the hearer/reader demonstrate faith by means of works. Now the hearer/reader is asked to show wisdom by works that illustrate a whole life. The noun *anastrophēs* refers to one's whole way of life. Paul uses the same noun in Gal 1:13 to embrace his way of life before his call (see also 1 Pet 1:15; 2:12; 3:2, 16; Heb 13:7 [see *TDNT* 7:715–17]). Characteristic of Hebrew teaching is the view that a person should demonstrate by conduct the wisdom that comes from the Torah. While the adjective *kalēs* is translated as "good," in this context it embraces above all a moral quality in the sense of "good, noble, praiseworthy, contributing to salvation" (BDAG 504). Grammatically, the genitive construction of the phrase *prautēti sophias* ("in wisdom's meekness") is awkward (see Davids [1982] 150; Martin 129). It is probably a Semitism, with the genitive "of wisdom" used in place of an adjective, "in meek wisdom" (Dibelius 209). By preserving the two nouns James gives a stress to both concepts, of wisdom and of meekness. The translation "in wisdom's meekness" endeavors to capture this nuance. For James, wisdom is the most important gift that comes down from above (1:5; 3:17). By this gift one shares in God's wisdom and is shown how to act. Wisdom is above all characterized by James as "meekness." The type of life that a follower of Jesus is to embrace is one that emulates Jesus' lifestyle and is characteristically identified as being meek: "Take my yoke upon you, and learn from me; for I am gentle (literally "meek") and humble in heart *(hoti praus eimi kai tapeinos tē kardią)* . . ." (Matt 11:29). The virtue of "meekness" *(prautēs* [noun] or *praus* [adjective]) is distinctively Christian, for it captures the essence of trust in God rather than in oneself. For Paul it is one of the fruits of the Spirit: *prautēs engkrateia* ("meekness and self-control") (Gal 5:23). Paul and the Pauline school refer to it often: 1 Cor 4:21; Eph 4:2; 2 Tim 2:25; Titus 3:2. See also Jas 1:21; 1 Pet 3:16; Sir 3:17: "My child, perform your tasks with humility *(en prautēti)* (literally 'meekness')." In the Greek and Roman world *prautēs* was not necessarily looked upon as a vice, as Osborn (32) and Laws ([1980] 159-60) contend. "Among the Greeks gentle friendliness *(prautēs)* is highly prized as a social virtue in human relationships, though it needs compensation if it is not to be a fault. . . . Hence the gentleness of leading citizens is constantly extolled in encomiums, and it has a prominent place in depictions of rulers" (*TDNT* 6:646 [Hauck/Schulz]). In the Qumran writings the concept of "meekness" (Hebrew *ănāwā*) occurs frequently (see 1QS 2:24; 3:8; in 1QS 4:3 it appears in a catalogue of virtues to capture the spirit of those who place their trust in God's actions).

14. *But if you have bitter jealousy and selfish ambition in your heart:* James begins with a catalogue of vices that is in direct contrast to his topic sentence of 3:13. He could have introduced this sentence in like manner by saying: "Who has bitter envy and selfish ambition among you?" The effectiveness of the *ei de* ("but if") sets up a stronger contrast between this verse and "wisdom's meekness," which was praised in 3:1. The meaning of *zēlos* is neutral. It can be used in a positive sense: "intense positive interest in something, zeal, ardor, marked by a sense of dedication" (BDAG 427). Or it can express "intense negative feelings over another's achievements or success, jealousy, envy" (BDAG 427). It is used here in the latter sense (*contra* Ropes 245; Davids [1982] 151) as a synonym for *phthonos* ("jealousy; envy") (used in 4:5) to give expression to the main theme that runs throughout this section (Johnson [1995] 271). The adjective *pikron* connects this verse to 3:11, identifying the jealousy as "bitter." Just as evils perpetrated by speech leave, as it were, a harsh taste in the mouth, so too does jealousy. The noun *eritheia* does not occur in the LXX. Before its use in the New Testament it is found only in Aristotle (*Pol.* 1302B, 1303A) "where it denotes a self-seeking pursuit of political office by unfair means" (BDAG 392). In James its meaning embraces the use of unworthy means in order to promote one's own self-interest to the detriment of others, particularly the community (see its use again in 3:16). In this sense it is also found in Rom 2:8; 2 Cor 12:20; Gal 5:20. In the phrase *en tē kardią hymōn* ("in your heart") the

noun *(kardia)* is singular while the pronoun *(hymōn)* is plural. This is a typical biblical expression referring to the seat of the emotions: "And the LORD said to Moses, 'When you go back to Egypt, see that you perform before Pharaoh all the wonders that I have put in your power; but I will harden his heart . . .'" (Exod 4:21). It occurs again in James in 4:8. The basic meaning is: even if you have these emotions within you, do not express them (Ropes 246).

do not boast and lie against the truth: See 2:13 for the use of the verb *katakauchao-mai*, which appears there with a different nuance. In 2:13 it captures the concept of "to triumph over," while in 3:14 it expresses "to boast or to brag" (BDAG 517). With the use of the prefix *kata* one expects the concept of "boasting over someone or something." That is why some manuscripts (e.g., Codex Sinaiticus) have changed the text to read *katakauchasthe kata tēs alētheias kai pseudesthe* ("boast against the truth and lie") (see Aland [1997] 61). Accepting the text as it stands means reading it in the absolute sense, as in Jer 27:11 LXX ("to boast"). The phrase "to lie or speak against the truth" occurs in *T. Gad* 5:1. It is used here in the practical sense of the manner of life the community leads. Its members must not be seen to betray or deny the message of salvation they have received (see 1:18 and 5:19 for the use of the word *alētheias*). "The truth" refers especially to the practical knowledge one gains on how to lead one's life.

15. *This is not the wisdom that comes down from above:* James describes the type of wisdom these opponents possess. It certainly cannot be identified with that "wisdom that comes down from above." James expresses the central understanding of wisdom in the biblical tradition, where its origin lies in the one God (Prov 2:6; 8:22-31; Wis 7:24-27; 9:4-18; Sir 1:1-4; 24:1-12). See also 1:17, where James speaks of "every perfect gift that comes down from above," using a similar expression, *anōthen estin katabainon* ("is from above, coming down . . .").

but is earthly, unspiritual, demonic: James uses three adjectives arranged in an ascending order of intensity to contrast the wisdom from above. The first term, *epigeios* ("earthly"), is not found in the LXX, but its use in the New Testament is quite common in the sense of "pertaining to what is characteristic of the earth as opposed to heavenly; earthly" (BDAG 368). It occurs in this sense in 1 Cor 15:40; 2 Cor 5:1; John 3:12. It bears a morally negative understanding in the context of Phil 3:19, "their minds are set on earthly things," which closely resembles James's understanding here. The second characterization is *psychikē* ("unspiritual"). In the New Testament writings besides Jas 3:15 this adjective occurs in 1 Cor 2:14; 15:44, 46; Jude 19 with the meaning "pertaining to the life of the natural world and whatever belongs to it, in contrast to the realm of experience whose central characteristic is *pneuma*, natural, unspiritual, worldly" (BDAG 1100; see also Pearson 13–14). Dibelius in an excursus on the term *psychikos* (211–12) argues that James and Paul are using a Gnostic term that has become part of common popular speech without endorsing the technical meaning, just as James had done before with other terminology such as "cycle of existence" (3:6). Finally, the climax is reached with the adjective *daimoniōdēs* ("demonic"). This adjective does not occur in the LXX, or in Hellenistic literature, or elsewhere in the New Testament besides here in James.

The term can have the meaning of making a comparison with the devil in the sense of "like a demon's" (Laws [1980] 161). Given the allusions within James to demons (2:19) who acknowledge the existence of God, to Gehenna that inspires the tongue to evil (3:6), and to the exhortation within this section to "resist the devil" (4:7), it makes sense to see this term as referring to the devil, who inspires a way of life contrary to the wisdom that comes from God.

16. *there is disorder and everything that is evil:* James has used the adjective *akatastatos* twice before: in 1:8 he spoke of the double-minded person as being *akatastatos* ("vacillating"), while in 3:8 the tongue was described as a "restless *(akatastatos)* evil." Here he uses the noun *akatastasia*, understood in the sense of "disorder" to express the concept of being "in opposition to established authority" (BDAG 35). In 2 Cor 12:20 Paul uses this word *akatastasia* together with *zēlos* ("jealousy") and *eritheiai* ("selfishness") just as does James here. This does not argue for any form of dependency, but it does show that New Testament lists of vices tended to embrace the same habits. To this disorder or anarchy James adds the expression *pan phaulon pragma* ("everything that is evil"), an all-encompassing phrase used to include the evils that result from disorder within the community. See the use of *phaulon* in this same sense of moral evil in John 3:20 "For all who do evil *(pas gar ho phaula prassōn)* hate the light. . . ."

17. *first of all pure, then it is peaceable, gentle, obedient, full of mercy and good fruits, without a trace of partiality or hypocrisy:* James lists the characteristics of true wisdom through a series of seven adjectives. They could be called "the 'fruits' of wisdom" (Martin 133). These adjectives are introduced with the marker *prōton men . . . epeita* ("in the first place . . . then") introducing a sequence of words [see BDAG 630, 2(c)]. James's literary ability is clearly evident once again. He uses alliteration: four of the adjectives begin with the vowel *e*, as do the verb *estin* and the adverb *epeita (estin, epeita eirēnikē, epieikēs, eupeithēs . . . eleous).* Further, assonance is used on two occasions achieving a certain rhythm with the endings *-eikēs/-eithēs* (the two adjectives *epieikēs* and *eupeithēs*) as well as the ending *-kritos* (the final two adjectives *adiakritos* and *anypokritos*). James opens this list with the word *hagnē* ("pure"). This is extremely important because it places the whole list in the context of the purity laws. After this opening virtue, *hagnē,* James's list of virtues falls into three groups. The first comprises three adjectives *(eirēnikē, epieikēs, eupeithēs)* that directly oppose the spirit of the wisdom of the world that brings disorder (3:16). Wisdom is *eirēnikē* ("peaceable"): this adjective appears only in Heb 12:11 in the rest of the New Testament. Proverbs 3:17 presents one of the results of the gift of wisdom as peace: "Her ways are ways of pleasantness and all her paths are peace *(eirēnē).*" The virtue *epieikēs* ("gentle") was a "distinctively Greek virtue; . . . its derivatives are found a few times in LXX, e.g. Ps 86[5], 2 Macc 9[27]" (Ropes 249). BDAG defines it in this way: "not insisting on every right of letter of law or custom, yielding, gentle, kind, courteous, tolerant" (371). This word captures the nuance of "gentleness" that also occurs elsewhere in the New Testament, especially in Phil 4:5 and in the lists of virtues in 1 Tim 3:3 and Titus 3:2. Finally, the quality *eupeithēs* ("obedient") continues a similar meaning. It only

occurs here in the New Testament. Laws argues that the latter two adjectives both express an attitude of reasonableness: "They may be seen as a complementary pair, two sides of a coin: wisdom is reasonable or gentle both in a dominant and a subordinate position" ([1980] 163). The second group of virtues in James's list comprises *mestē eleous kai karpōn agathōn* ("full of mercy and good fruits"). "Mercy" *(eleos)* is the attitude whereby one shows concern through help and compassion. In this context it is not the emotion of pity as implied in 2:13, 15-16. The language "of good fruits" *(karpōn agathōn)* prepares for the reference to the "fruit of righteousness" *(karpos dikaiosynēs)* in 3:18. The final group of virtues in James's list contains the pair of alliterative adjectives *adiakritos* and *anypokritos*. The first adjective, *adiakritos*, is only found here in the New Testament. In the LXX it occurs only in Prov 25:1, where its meaning is uncertain (see Ropes 250; Mayor 132). It comes from the verb *diakrinein*, with its various meanings of "to separate, to make a distinction, to differentiate, to evaluate, to judge" (BDAG 231). In 2:4 this verb is used with the meaning "to make distinctions" in the context of showing partiality for the rich against the poor. Consequently it is best to interpret this occurrence in a similar sense as "impartial" (BDAG 19). I have translated it as "without a trace of partiality" in order to preserve James's literary connection with the following adjective, *anypokritos*, translated here as "without hypocrisy." In the LXX it appears in Wis 5:18, and in the rest of the New Testament at Rom 12:9; 2 Cor 6:6; 1 Tim 1:5; 2 Tim 1:5; and 1 Pet 1:22 with the meaning of genuine or sincere.

18. *But the fruit that is righteousness:* Dibelius (214–15) sees this as an isolated saying. While it may have originated independently within the tradition, James has undoubtedly woven it inextricably into the development of his argument in 3:13–4:10. It brings together the spirit of the virtues outlined above with the focus on the virtue of peace. At the same time it prepares for 4:1, where James demonstrates the need for harmony within the community. The meaning and translation of the phrase *karpos dikaiosynēs* is much disputed. The genitive "the fruit of righteousness" can be interpreted as "the reward which righteous conduct brings" (Ropes 250). More likely it is a genitive of definition: "the fruit which is [i.e., consists of] righteousness" (Martin 135; Davids [1982] 155). As an expression it appears in the LXX (Amos 6:12; Prov 11:30) and in the New Testament (2 Cor 9:10; Phil 1:11). The meaning conveyed is that actions of peacemaking demonstrate righteousness.

is sown in peace by those who make peace: The phrase *en eirēnē* (literally "in peace") can be translated: "by means of acts of peace." The imagery of sowing continues James's agricultural language (his reference to "fruit"). Moral action is often described in the biblical writings through the imagery of sowing and reaping (Prov 22:8; Sir 7:3; 1 Cor 9:11; Gal 6:7-8). Righteousness is the outcome of the actions of peace. Those who perform these acts of peace are the peacemakers: "by those who make peace *(tois poiousin eirēnēn)*." While some see this as a dative of advantage ("for those who make peace" [Dibelius 215; Laws {1980} 165]), it is best to see it as a dative of agent ("by those who make peace") as James deliberately uses a certain repetition here "for rhetorical effect" (Davids [1982] 155). This reminds one of the saying of Jesus in the Sermon on the Mount: "Blessed are the peacemakers, for they will be called children of God" (Matt 5:9).

4:1 *From where do wars and from where do battles among you come?* The interrogative *pothen* ("from where") is repeated twice: a further illustration of James's liking for repetition (see 1:19; 3:9). The interrogative that opens this sentence is a favorite stylistic feature in this letter: 2:4, 5, 6, 7, 14, 15, 16, 20, 21, 25; 3:11, 12, 13; 4:4, 5, 12, 14. This question continues the discussion from 3:13-18 and does not open a new section. The two words *polemoi* and *machai* ("wars and battles") often occur in conjunction with each other (see Homer, *Il.* 1:177; Epictetus, *Diatr.* 3:13, 9). The question of why James should refer to wars and battles in this context has been examined by Johnson and shown to stem from the traditional language and imagery associated with the typical *topos* on envy: "(I)t should be seen as one of the standard features of that *topos*, based less on the supposed activities of his hearers/readers than the logic of the argument" (Johnson [1995] 276).

your desires that are at war within your members: The noun *hēdonē* means "state or condition of experiencing pleasure for any reason, pleasure, delight, enjoyment, pleasantness" (BDAG 434). In this context it has the sense of "cravings" (NRSV) or "desire for pleasure" (Johnson [1995] 276). This interpretation is reinforced from the context of the next verse, where James specifically speaks about "desiring" *(epithymein)*. The imagery of a war occurring within the human being is found elsewhere in the New Testament, although the specific vocabulary may be different: e.g., "Beloved, I urge you as aliens and exiles to abstain from the desires of the flesh that wage war against the soul" (1 Pet 2:11). Romans 7:21-23 envisages two laws at war within Paul's body. The writings of Qumran imagine the struggle between two spirits within each individual (1QS 3:17-21; 4:20-23). The concept of desires being responsible for wars and battles is a common theme in Hellenistic literature. Plato identifies the desires of the body as a cause of wars: "Whence come wars, and fightings, and factions? Whence but from the body and the lusts of the body?" (*Phaed.* 66C [Jowett]). Cicero speaks of wars arising from within the desires of the human being: "Hatred, discord, disagreements, seditions, wars are all born from desires . . ." (*Ex cupiditatibus odia, discidia, discordiae, seditiones, bella nascuntur . . .) (Fin.* 1:44).

2. *You desire and you do not have, so you murder. And you are filled with envy and you cannot obtain, so you fight and wage war:* There are two major difficulties with this verse. The first concerns the punctuation. The Greek text of the fourth revised edition of the *UBS Greek New Testament* and the twenty-seventh revised edition of *Nestle-Aland* punctuates it with commas dividing the sentence into three statements: "You desire and do not have, you murder and are filled with envy and you cannot obtain, you fight and wage war." The punctuation adopted in this translation follows the NRSV translation, which breaks the sentence into two statements, each containing a cause and effect: "You desire and do not have, so you murder. And you are filled with envy and you cannot obtain, so you fight and wage war." The main reason for adopting this second

option stems from the understanding of the reference made to murder. In the first translation the reference to "you murder" is viewed as a statement on its own: it is one among a number of unrelated vices that are identified within the community. In the second translation the statement "you murder" is viewed as a consequence of the vice of inordinate desiring, which undoubtedly is the central theme in this section. The further question, however, needs to be answered: How can "murder" be understood to occur within the community? It is hard to imagine that in a Christian community people would be perpetrating murders and killing. This led to the suggestion, going back to Erasmus's second edition of the Greek New Testament (1519), that the Greek word *phoneuete* ("you murder") should be emended to read *phthoneite* ("you envy, you desire"). In support of this emendation it is argued that a copyist's error could easily have occurred with these verbs. There is much to be said in support of this emendation, especially from the internal logic of the statements. It would support the first suggested translation, producing an internal logic within the second series of statements: "You desire and you are filled with envy and you cannot obtain." In this way the concept of envy and desiring would be strengthened which, as we have shown, is central to this section. This emendation is favored by Mayor (136–37) and accepted by Dibelius, who says this suggestion "is really a rather obvious solution" (217). However, the biggest objection still remains: there is absolutely no textual evidence in support of such an emendation. It is irresponsible to accept a reading for which there is no concrete textual evidence. For this reason one must make sense of the text as it stands. As I have argued, following Johnson ([1995] 28) and Laws ([1980] 171), James has adopted here the Hellenistic literary *topos* on envy. The concepts of murder, war, and battles are standard features of this *topos*. James is simply drawing upon these traditional elements that make up the *topos*. The connection between envy, jealousy, and murder can be seen not only in Hellenistic writings (see Plato, *Leges* 869E-870A), but also in the biblical tradition (e.g., in the stories of Cain and Abel [Gen 4:1-25], Ahab and Naboth [1 Kgs 21:1-29]; see also Wis 2:24; Mark 15:10; Matt 27:18; Acts 5:17-18; *1 Clem.* 4:1–5:2). Speaking in reference to the murder of Abel by Cain, *1 Clement* says: "You see, brethren—jealousy and envy wrought fratricide" (*1 Clem.* 4:7 [Lake]). "Be not proud, for pride leads to murder, nor jealous, nor contentious, nor passionate, for from all these murders are engendered" (*Did.* 3:2 [Lake]).

You do not have because you do not ask. 3. You ask and you do not receive: The end of v. 2 runs into the beginning of v. 3. God is the giver of all gifts, so the request is being made of God. This harks back to 1:5. What is noticeable is the interchange of the active and middle voices of the verb *aitein* ("to ask"). In vv. 2 and 3 James uses the middle voice twice (*aiteisthai*) and the active voice once (*aiteite*) (James 1:5 also used the active voice [*aiteitō*]). Dibelius (219, n. 63) says that no change in meaning is intended. This is supported by the variation also evident in other passages such as Matt 20:20-22 and John 16:23-26. No distinction is to be drawn between these two uses: "Without any real distinction between active and middle: the distinction between active ('ask' outright) and middle ('ask' as a loan) found by ancient grammarians has only very limited validity for our literature" (BDAG 30). The best solution is to see the differences in this usage as simply a stylistic variation by James.

3. *because you ask wickedly in order to spend it on your desires:* The adverb *kakōs* ("wickedly") is explained by the following clause: your requests are based on securing selfish motives (your desires) rather than securing God's wisdom. *Kakōs* communicates a very strong condemnation of evil. This is akin to "the world of iniquity" (3:6). Here one is using the tongue not to pray, but to make evil requests of God in prayer. These evil requests are identified as "your selfish desires." The next verse will give a more forceful illustration of this opposition between the service of God and of the world.

4. *You adulteresses! Do you not know that friendship with the world is enmity with God?* The word *moichalides* ("adulteresses") is used in the figurative sense of the biblical tradition, where Israel is the bride of God who is constantly unfaithful to God's ever-loving faithfulness (Jer 3:20; Ezek 16:23-26; Hos 9:1). Matthew's Jesus uses the same language in condemning his own generation: "An evil and adulterous *(moichalis)* generation asks for a sign . . ." (12:39). The relationship of God to Israel as a bride is carried into the New Testament and applied to the relationship between Christ and the church (2 Cor 11:1-2; Eph 5:24-28; Rev 19:7; 21:9). The feminine form alone is explicable from the imagery of the bride as Israel or the church. The harshness of the language prepares for the accusation that is contained in the rest of the verse. "Do you not know" *(ouk oidate)* implies that what follows is common knowledge to the hearers/readers. It is a further condemnation: although they know this, they refuse to act upon it. Regarding "friendship with the world" see 2:23 for the reference to friend. Basic to the concept of friend in the Greco-Roman world was the view that friends saw things from the same perspective: e.g., "We shared the one element indispensable to friendship, a complete agreement in aims, ambitions, and attitudes" (Cicero, *Amic.* 4:15 [Copley]). The word *echthra* ("enmity") expresses the opposite of friendship. Although the contrast of friendship and enmity does not occur in the rest of the New Testament, a number of aspects lend support to James's perspective. For a similar usage of *echthra* see Rom 8:7: "Therefore the mind of the flesh is at enmity toward God *(echthra eis theon)."* First John 2:15-16 uses the language of love in a way similar to James's understanding of friendship: "Do not love the world or the things in the world. The love of the Father is not in those who love the world; for all that is in the world . . . comes not from the Father but from the world."

whoever wishes to be a friend of the world becomes an enemy of God: Grammatically the phrase *hos ean* in place of the more usual *hos an* (translated as "whoever") was frequently used in the New Testament and in the Greek of the first two centuries C.E. For James there is no middle ground. This corresponds to Jesus' teaching in Matt 6:24: "No one can serve two masters; for a slave will either hate the one and love the other, or be devoted to the one and despise the other. You cannot serve God and wealth" (see also Luke 16:13). The verb *kathistatai* ("becomes") indicates a state of permanency (literally "is constituted") (Mayor 140). The verb refers back to 3:6: "The tongue is the world of iniquity placed *(kathistatai)* among our members." Being an enemy of God parallels the world of iniquity.

5. *Or do you think that in vain the Scripture says: 'Does the spirit that God made to dwell in us yearn enviously'?* The particle *ē* ("or") is used here to introduce an interrogative sentence in the form of a rhetorical statement that calls for agreement (see, e.g., Matt 12:29; 1 Cor 6:16). There are many problems with this verse, making it one of the most disputed in the letter of James. A way forward is to start from what is certain. The phrase *hē graphē legei* ("the Scripture says") is used in the New Testament to refer to a passage of Scripture that is quoted. As Davids says: "the *hē graphē legei* formula introduces a direct quotation, not a sense quotation, allusion, or reference to scripture in general" ([1982] 162). This has occurred twice already in James (2:8, 23). The problem stems from the fact that the source of this quotation has not been identified. Many different explanations have been given to account for what is expressed here. One common proposal has been to see James referring not to an actual quotation of Scripture, but to Scripture in general. The two sentences are then taken as two parallel questions: "Do you think that Scripture speaks in vain? Does the spirit that God made to dwell in us yearn enviously?" Johnson ([1995] 280) and Laws ([1973/74] 210–15) have offered a form of this solution. While the proposal is attractive, two major problems still remain: (1) The first relates to the formula *hē graphē legei*. This expression always introduces a quotation and not simply a reference to Scripture in general. Johnson delays the actual scriptural quotation to v. 6, but this still does not explain the unusual usage of *legei* as "speaks" instead of "says." Two further solutions are possible: James could be referring to an apocryphal work that he considered Scripture in the way in which Jude quoted from the *Assumption of Moses* and the book of Enoch (Jude 9 and 14-15 respectively), or he is quoting a version of the Hebrew Scriptures that is unknown to us. As has been demonstrated, James usually quotes from the LXX. The closest quotation that can be identified in the Hebrew Scriptures is from Exod 20:5 ". . . for I the LORD your God am a jealous God. . . ." Ropes identifies James's quotation as possibly a "poetical rendering of the idea of Ex 20⁵" (262). Whatever the solution, James considered this to be a quotation from Scripture and the audience would have heard it in a similar way. Consequently we should treat it as such. (2) The second problem related to this quotation is how to translate it. The difficulty really arises from the fact that since we do not have the origin of the quotation we lack the help of its context (Davids ([1982] 163). Two issues need to be resolved in order to translate the quotation. The first relates to the reading of two possible verbal forms attested in the manuscripts. Because of itacism these forms were pronounced in the same way although they had different meanings (Metzger [1975] 683): the first form, *katōkisen* (the causative form of *katoikizō*) gives the translation: "the spirit that (God) made to dwell in us." The second form, *katōkēsen* (the intransitive indicative form of the verb *katoikein*) is translated as: "the spirit (Spirit) that dwells in us" (see BDAG 534). The form *katōkisen* has stronger attestation from the better manuscripts such as 𝔓⁷⁴ and Codices Sinaiticus, Alexandrinus, and Vaticanus (see Metzger [1975] 683).

Since this verb *katoikizein* occurs nowhere else in the New Testament it is more likely that copyists would have replaced it with the more usual *katoikein*. Consequently I opt for the following translation: "the spirit that God made to dwell in us." The second issue concerns the translation of the first part of the sentence. What is the subject of the verb *epipothei?* (BDAG 377: "yearns"). Does God (understood) yearn jealously? Or, is it the spirit (human or divine) that yearns jealously? Both readings are possible. However, as Laws ([1980] 177) argues, a close examination of the Greek phrase *pros phthonon epipothei* ("yearns jealously") shows that it would be very difficult to attribute it to God as the subject. Since James has an excellent knowledge of Greek and of the LXX, as has been shown, his use of this phrase should conform to what can be established from the way these words are used, particularly in the LXX. The verb *epipothein* is never used to refer to God. Further, the noun *phthonos* is always used in reference to a vice. While *zēlos* has a positive ("zeal, ardor") and a negative meaning ("jealousy, envy"), *phthonos* always has a negative connotation (see BDAG 427; 1054; see also the use of *phthonos* in Wis 2:24; 6:23; 1 Macc 8:16; Rom 1:29; 1 Pet 2:1). This then argues for the spirit as being the subject of the verb, rather than God: "the spirit yearns enviously."

6. *Rather, he gives a greater grace:* The Greek text of the fourth revised edition of the *UBS Greek New Testament* and the twenty-seventh edition of *Nestle-Aland* punctuates this as a question that forms part of the preceding. However, since the particle *de* ("rather") marks a strong contrast, it is best to see this verse as starting a new statement in sharp distinction to the previous verse. God is understood to be the subject of *didōsin* ("gives"). The phrase *meizona charin* (the "greater grace") to which James refers contrasts this with the previous verse, where the human spirit yearns jealously. God's grace is such that it has the power to overcome those vices to which the human spirit tends. The phrase is influenced by the quotation that follows. This conforms to James's previous statements that God is the one who gives gifts generously (1:5; 3:17).

therefore it says: "God resists the proud, but he gives grace to the humble": The phrase *dio legei* ("therefore it says") connects back to *hē graphē legei* (v. 5). Hence the subject of *dio legei* is understood to be *graphē* ("the Scripture says"). As indicated before, this is the technical form for the introduction of a quotation (see the same formula in use in Eph 4:8; 5:14; Heb 3:7). The quotation comes from the LXX and is identical to the LXX text of Prov 3:34 except for the subject: while the LXX has *kyrios* (Lord), James has *theos* (God). First Peter 5:5 and *1 Clem.* 30:2 have the identical quotation, with the same subject, *theos*. They are all probably drawing from a common tradition. God's choice of the humble *(tapeinos)* is one of James's basic themes (1:9). James 4:10 returns to the theme of the humble: "Humble yourselves before the Lord and he will exalt you." This offers an echo of Prov 3:35: "The wise will inherit honor, but the ungodly will exalt disgrace." Consequently 4:7-9 is bracketed between the two references to the humble being exalted by the Lord. Proverbs 3:34-35 provides the background to this passage (Wall [1997] 205–206). This spirit of humility is the exact opposite to the spirit of envy and jealousy that has been the topic of this passage.

7. *Therefore submit to God:* The particle *oun* ("therefore") establishes the connection to the preceding by showing that the following ten imperatives in 4:7-10 bring the previous instructions (3:13–4:6) to a conclusion. The imperative *hypotagēte* (from *hypotassein*) is a call to submit to God and sets the direction for all the other commands. It is a plea to return to the covenant relationship with God. This verb is a favorite word for 1 Peter; however, James and Peter show a difference in nuance: for James submission is to God alone, while for Peter submission embraces civil authority as well (1 Pet 2:13, 18; see also submission to church authorities [1 Pet 5:5]).

But resist the devil and he will flee from you: The LXX uses the Greek word *diabolos* ("devil") to translate the Hebrew *haśśāṭān* (e.g., Job 1:6-12; 2:1-7). The theme of resisting the devil appears also in 1 Pet 5:8-9 and Eph 6:11-12. In all three passages the thought is the same but the expression is different. This shows again that a common tradition lies behind them. The idea of resisting the devil is one found elsewhere, particularly in the *Testaments of the Twelve Patriarchs* (see *T. Sim.* 3:5; *T. Iss.* 7:7; *T. Dan* 5:1; *T. Naph.* 8:4; *T. Ash.* 3:2). This theme of resisting the devil also occurs in many New Testament traditions (e.g., Matt 4:1-11; Luke 4:1-13; Matt 25:41; Eph 4:27; 6:11; 1 Tim 3:7; 1 Pet 5:8-9).

8. *Draw near to God and he will draw near to you:* The language of the cult and purity is clearly operative in this verse. The phrase *eggisate tō theō* ("draw near to God") was a technical term used to refer to the work of priests in the Temple: "Even the priests who draw near *(eggizontes)* to the LORD God must make themselves holy . . ." (Exod 19:22 LXX; see also Ezek 44:13). Thereafter it began to take on a spiritual or figurative meaning: e.g., "Moses alone shall come near *(eggiei)* the LORD; but the others shall not come near *(eggiousin)*, and the people shall not come up with him" (Exod 24:2 LXX; see also Hos 12:7 LXX). While the Greek verbs differ, the thought in Zech 1:3 is identical to that of James: "Return *(epistrepsate)* to me, says the LORD of hosts, and I will return to you . . ." (see also Mal 3:7; Heb 7:19).

Cleanse your hands, you sinners, and purify your hearts, you double-minded! The phrase *katharisate cheiras* ("cleanse your hands") refers to the ritual washing that was necessary prior to service in the Temple (see Exod 30:17-21, in particular v. 19: "Aaron and his sons shall wash their hands *[nipsetai . . . tas cheiras]* and their feet"). This ritual was then adopted by Israelites as a daily usage before meals, etc. As part of their purity rules and rituals it was a clear demonstration of their separation from the world and their connection with God's realm. See Mark 7:3: "For the Pharisees, and all the Jews, do not eat unless they thoroughly wash their hands *(nipsōntai tas cheiras)*, thus observing the tradition of the elders." In the prophets the concept acquired a spiritual, figurative sense insofar as it applied to moral purity (see Isa 1:16; Jer 4:14; Job 22:30). In place of his customary "brothers and sisters" *(adelphoi)* James uses the harsh term *hamartōloi* ("sinners") to draw attention to the urgency of his call. The *hamartōloi* are essentially those who break the Law, the Torah (see Ps 1:1-5). They refuse to carry out the purity rules that maintain the covenant relationship with God and the people. It is a frequent term in the gospels, often in the phrase: "tax collectors and sinners" *(telōnai kai hamartōloi:*

e.g., Matt 9:10). James adds a parallel term of address (*dipsychoi* ["double-minded"]), one he has used before (see 1:8). Since they are the ones who want to be friends with God and the world they have divided loyalties.

9. *Lament and mourn and weep!* A further series of three imperatives occurs here. The verb *talaipōrein* ("lament, feel miserable") is a *hapax legomenon* in the New Testament. It is found in Josephus (*C. Ap.* 1:237) and is a favorite word of Jeremiah (e.g., "woe to us, for we are ruined *[talaipōroumen]*" [4:13]). It gives expression to a physical or general state of wretchedness (see Tob 13:12: "and love those within you who are wretched *[talaipōrous]*"). James's language has shifted from the cultic and priestly to the prophetic. He deliberately adopts this word in order to call his hearers/readers to turn away from seeking pleasure by demonstrating repentance through deliberate actions that reflect a state of feeling miserable. James uses the noun *talaipōria* ("misery") at 5:1. The attitude of "feeling miserable" is given expression through mourning *(penthein)* and weeping *(klaiein)*. These two terms are often joined in the biblical writings (e.g., 2 Sam 19:1; Neh 8:9 [2 Esdras 18:9]). Matthew's beatitudes speak of blessings on those who mourn: "Blessed are those who mourn *(makarioi hoi penthountes)*, for they will be comforted" (Matt 5:4). The two words are joined in Luke 6:25: "Woe to you who are laughing now, for you will mourn and weep *(penthēsete kai klausete)*" and in Rev 18:11: "And the merchants of the earth weep and mourn *(klaiousin kai penthousin)* for her" (see as well Rev 18:15, 19).

Let your laughter be turned into mourning and your joy into dejection: The noun *gelōs* ("laughter") is a *hapax legomenon* in the New Testament although the verb *gelan* ("to laugh") occurs in Luke 6:21, 25. The verb *metatrepein* ("turn into") is also a *hapax legomenon* in the New Testament. In the LXX it occurs only in 4 Macc 6:5. Turning from one state ("laughter") to another ("mourning") is a graphic illustration of the state of repentance. Because of the large number of *hapax legomena* in this passage (*talaipōrein, gelōs, metatrepein,* and *katēpheia)*, some scholars, such as Seitz ([1944] 131–40), postulate that James could be using a written source, specifically a lost apocryphal writing. In support of this contention he cites *1 Clem.* 23:2-4, which he argues is also using an apocryphal source: "Wherefore let us not be double-minded, nor let our soul be fanciful concerning his excellent and glorious gifts. Let this Scripture be far from us in which he says 'Wretched are the double-minded, who doubt in their soul and say "We have heard these things even in the days of our fathers, and behold we have grown old, and none of these things has happened to us"'" (Lake, LCL). Seitz concludes his argument in this way: "We have good reason to believe that he (James) may have derived it, as did also I and II Clement and Hermas, from the anonymous literary source, herein referred to as 'the prophetic message,' which says: 'Miserable are the double-minded, who doubt in their heart'" ([1944]) 140). On the other hand, *1 Clement* (as well as *2 Clem.* 11:2-3; Herm. *Vis.* 3:7, 1; Herm. *Sim.* 1:3, all of which use the term *dipsychos* or different variations of the word) could simply be dependent on the letter of James, since the first known use of this term appears in James and its usage only becomes evident in early Christianity after the letter of James (see Notes 1:8 and the Introduction). Finally, James states that joy must be turned into "dejection" (*katēpheia*, another *hapax legomenon*). A good description of this state of "dejection" is the attitude of the publican in Luke 18:13, although the word itself is not used: "But the tax collector, standing far off, would not even look up to heaven, but was beating his breast and saying. . . ."

10. *Humble yourselves before the Lord and he will exalt you:* James returns to the thought of 4:6 with the verb *tapeinoun* ("to humble") and the theme he introduced in 1:9. The Hebrew Scriptures, especially the prophets, often speak about God humbling the proud: e.g., ". . . the pride of everyone shall be humbled *(tapeinōthēsetai);* and the LORD alone will be exalted in that day" (Isa 2:11). On the other hand James calls on his hearers/readers to be the ones who humble themselves. The theme of the reversal of fortunes is reminiscent of the Jesus saying in Matt 23:12: "All who exalt themselves will be humbled, and all who humble themselves will be exalted" (see also Luke 14:11; 18:14). First Peter 5:6 also shows a marked similarity to this verse: "Humble yourselves *(tapeinōthēte)* therefore under the mighty hand of God, so that he may exalt *(hypsōsē)* you in due time." While the two verbs are the same in both James and 1 Peter, there is a difference in meaning. James is concerned with humbling oneself in repentance while 1 Peter speaks from the context of "submissiveness to God" (Ropes 272).

INTERPRETATION

James 3:13–4:10: One Rhetorical Unit

The examination of 3:13–4:10 from the perspective of a Greek *topos* helps us appreciate this section's unity as well as the rhetorical function it exercises in the context of James's letter. In his insightful studies on the letter of James, Johnson ([1990] 329–39; [1983] 327–47) has drawn attention to the letter's usage of *topoi.* He has demonstrated the development of *topoi* especially on two occasions: in 3:1-12 on the topic of speech and in 3:13–4:10 on the topic of envy.

The term *"topos"* refers to a theme or subject that an ancient speaker/writer addressed by way of argument (Malherbe [1986] 144; see also [1992] 267–333). Malherbe indicates that the term is used by scholars in a variety of ways:

- To express "clichés" or commonly accepted sayings or maxims: "An eye for an eye and a tooth for a tooth" (Matt 5:38). This is the way Hans Dieter Betz uses it (*Galatians* [Philadelphia: Fortress, 1979] 220–37 on Gal 4:12-20).

- The treatment of a virtue or vice in a more developed form than just a simple maxim (see Bradley: "treatment in independent form of the topic of a proper thought or action, or of a virtue or a vice" (240).

- The systematic development of a recurring topic or theme in a "standardized way" (Malherbe [1986] 144).

It is in the third sense that the term *topoi* is used here. Malherbe defines it as "traditional, fairly systematic treatments of moral subjects which make use of common clichés, maxims, short definitions, and so forth, without thereby sacrificing an individual viewpoint" ([1986] 144): e.g., Plutarch's treatise *How to Tell a Flatterer from a Friend* draws upon *topoi* such as friendship to present his ideas on frank speech (*Adul. Amic.* 70D–71C; 73C–74E). Three important points are observable in the development of these conventional moral subjects. (1) While drawing upon the traditionally accepted wisdom circulating in the form of the maxims etc., individual speakers/writers would incorporate this wisdom within their own individual philosophical or religious framework. Consequently, a Stoic or Epicurean treatment on friendship might draw upon the same traditional wisdom, yet the perspective presented could be decidedly different or even totally opposite. This would lend itself well to New Testament writers who themselves could draw upon the traditional Greek wisdom circulating within their societies, yet at the same time could give it their own perspective. (2) The *topoi* generally do not speak to concrete situations, but more frequently tend to foresee them and give instructions on how to approach them should they arise (Malherbe [1986] 144). (3) The development of the *topoi* is related to the variety of rhetorical functions to which they can be put: e.g., they can form part of protrepsis, or paraenesis, or even of a sustained argument (*contra* the formalized approach of Mullins 541–47). The form of presentation of the *topoi* varies according to the purpose or function for which it is being developed. Malherbe has rightly called for more attention to be devoted to "the need to determine the function to which the *topos* is put by a writer" ([1992] 325).

An examination of the letter of James shows the clear use of *topoi* on at least two occasions: the *topos* of speech (3:1-12; see Johnson [1990] 329–39) and the *topos* of envy (3:13–4:10; see Johnson [1983] 327–47).

On the topos of speech: An examination of 3:1-12 has shown that while using the form of the perfect argument as the structure for his own, James drew on the *topos* of speech to construct his argument. From among the many elements common to this *topos* found in Greek writers, James has chosen a number of metaphors such as the ship's rudder, the horse's bit, and the taming of wild animals (Johnson [1990] 336–37). See also Dibelius (185–90) for a detailed survey of Hellenistic writings illustrating these examples.

At the same time James constructs his argument in his own way, adapting the *topos* within his own perspective, as Malherbe ([1986] 144) has indicated. This James did in a number of ways: most importantly, the development of James's argument and the foundation for the *topos* rest on his distinct religious and theological outlook. While Johnson does acknowledge the "religious valuation of speech" in the letter of James, he surprisingly expresses the difference between James and Hellenistic moral rhetoric in this way: "he (James) entirely lacks the religious motivations found in those writings" ([1990] 337). This is certainly not the case. James has as much religious motivation as the Delphic Oracle, except that he expresses it in his own way in harmony with his tradition. James roots the whole evaluation of the need to control speech in the covenantal relationship between God and God's people: "With it we bless the Lord and Father, and with it we curse human beings made in God's likeness" (3:9). The whole theme of God the creator underlies James's argumentation and provides the religious motivation for controlling the tongue. God has created nature in such a way that each species acts according to its nature: fig trees produce figs, olive trees produce olives. So the tongue should produce blessings of God and of human beings (3:12).

Second, James radiates the worldview of his Jewish heritage by drawing a distinct contrast between good and evil, God and the world. The world is the scene where the forces of evil assail adherence to God. In particular the symbolism of "Gehenna" becomes very intense: it is the root cause of all the evils the tongue perpetuates. The tongue is drawn into this cosmic battle between God and the forces of evil; the tongue "is the world of iniquity" that is "set on fire by Gehenna" (3:6).

Finally, as indicated above, James's assessment of the possibility of controlling the tongue appears more pessimistic than that of his Hellenistic counterparts: "But no human can tame the tongue—a restless evil, full of death-dealing poison" (3:8; cf. Plutarch, *Garr.* 502B–E; 511F–512C). James does acknowledge at the outset of his argument that "If anyone does not fail in speech, this person is perfect . . ." (3:2). On the human level it is impossible to control the tongue, but with the help of the wisdom from above (3:17) it is possible. Since speech is involved in the cosmic struggle, it is only through the power of God's wisdom that the destructive power of "Gehenna" can be overcome.

On the topos of envy: Johnson's examination of this *topos* in its application to 3:13–4:10 is insightful. His thesis is: "We can begin by regarding James 3:13–4:10 as a single literary unit, namely, as a call to conversion which employs the Hellenistic *topos* on envy *(peri phthonou)*" ([1983] 332). This is, as Johnson ([1995] 268) shows, contrary to the dominant perspective established by Dibelius's commentary, where this section is judged to be a loosely connected series of isolated sayings and small collections. As Dibelius summarizes his position: "So the whole section breaks down into the two admonitions in 3:13-17 and 4:1-6, between which stands the isolated saying 3:18, and to which is joined the series of imperatives in 4:7-12" (208).

The problem relates, as Johnson ([1983] 328–29) indicates, to the concept of paraenesis with which Dibelius operated, which precluded any form of structure in the work. All the unconnected sayings were thought to be strung together without developing any specific logic or thought: ". . . *we may designate the 'Letter' of James as paraenesis*. By paraenesis we mean a text which strings together admonitions of general ethical content" (Dibelius 3). Rather than force a preconceived view upon the text, the opposite approach should be adopted where the text itself determines its genre (see Johnson [1983] 329).

Johnson's study of the *topos* of envy in Hellenistic moral literature as well as in Hellenistic Judaism (particularly the *Testament of Simeon*) helps to shed light on this rhetorical unit in 3:13–4:10. What Johnson says in this regard is worth quoting in full:

> In addition to the coherent thematic framework provided James 3:13–4:10 by the Testaments as a whole, then, the *Testament of Simeon* offers eight separate points of similarity: (1) the explicit call to conversion; (2) the synonymous use of *zēlos* and *phthonos*; (3) the attribution of envy to a *pneuma* which is a deceiver; (4) the tendency of envy toward murder; (5) the role of envy in generating societal unrest and war; (6) the turning from the evil spirit to God by prayer and mourning; (7) the giving of grace by God to those who turn from envy (or Beliar) and turn to the Lord; (8) the portrayal of envy's opposite as simplicity of soul and goodness of heart. ([1983] 345)

Johnson's study has shown that James is clearly building upon the *topos* of envy. Words such as *pikros, epieikēs, adiakritos,* and *akatastasia* are all connected to the *topos* of envy *(phthonos)* (Johnson, [1983] 346). The scriptural quotation in 4:5 provides the climax for James's rhetorical address: "Does the spirit that God made to dwell in us yearn enviously?" Surely, this is not what God intended. The rhetorical function is clear: God did not intend the spirit God placed in the human being to be envious. This is contrary to God's creative intent. Even more: God intended for the human being to seek friendship, not enmity with God *(echthra tou theou)* (4:4).

I contend that in order to make this argument James has used once again the structure of the perfect argument that was identified in the three previous sections. If James has used this structure before in presenting an argument, it is logical to expect that he would do so again. It is here that I differ from the way Johnson understands the structure of this passage. Johnson sees that 3:13–4:10 divides into two clear rhetorical sections: 3:13–4:6 presents *a denunciation of envy* as a prelude to 4:7-10, which issues *a call to conversion or a change in the way of life* ([1995] 287). I see this section instead as demonstrating a unity that develops through the structure of the perfect argument. As is clear from this exposition, I acknowledge my debt to Johnson's insights with regard to James's dependence on the Greco-Roman *topos* of envy. However, I am convinced that James has used the structure of the perfect argument to communicate this *topos*. This is in conformity with the observation of Malherbe, who sees that the *topoi* are always used in different ways and brought into conformity with the function they intend to serve ([1992] 325). In this section James calls his hearers/readers to make a choice for a life of friendship with God that embraces the wisdom that comes from above. They are to turn away from friendship with the world that entices one along false paths. To achieve his rhetorical function James uses the *topos* of envy while constructing his argument, together with the structure of a perfect argument.

An examination of James 3:13–4:10 reveals the following outline:

(a) *Theme (propositio):* Demonstrate your way of life by works in wisdom's meekness (3:13).

(b) *Reason (ratio):* Bitter envy leads one to act against the truth (3:14).

(c) *Proof (rationis confirmatio):* Wisdom from above brings true righteousness (3:15-18).

(d) *Embellishment (exornatio):* Envy brings disharmony into the community. Argument from scripture: "Does the spirit that God made to dwell in us yearn enviously?" (4:1-6).

(e) *Conclusion (conplexio):* Call to submit to God (4:7-10).

Using the above features of the perfect argument, I will show how James has woven the *topos* of envy into this structure. When James's hearers/readers heard/read this letter they would surely have perceived the structure of the perfect argument, since it was so widespread in the ancient world. At the same time they would have understood his references to envy and the way in which he developed them through their familiarity with that *topos*.

(a) Theme (propositio):
Demonstrate Your Way of Life by Works in Wisdom's Meekness (3:13).

This verse announces the theme that runs throughout this section. James wishes to argue that a believer's whole way of life will demonstrate works or deeds that are inspired by wisdom from above. Chapter 3 opened with a reference to the teacher within the community. Now this section opens with a question: "Who is wise and understanding among you?"

(3:1). The rabbi (or teacher) was the characteristically wise person in the Jewish world. So the immediate response to James's question would be to identify the wise person with the rabbi. However, the answer James gives to this question broadens the whole understanding of who is wise. Throughout this section James contrasts two types of wisdom. There is *a false wisdom* inspired by the world and influenced above all by jealousy and envy. There is also *a wisdom that comes down from above,* whose fruits bring righteousness and peace. One's way of life is clearly influenced by one of these two types of wisdom. James's point is that the truly wise person is the one who allows life to be inspired by a wisdom James characterizes as "in wisdom's meekness." This is a very important description of wisdom, for it shows the type of wisdom James has in mind. Meekness, as the Notes have shown, is the virtue that places trust in God rather than in oneself. Applied to wisdom, it shows that the source of wisdom's inspiration comes from God, not from oneself or any other place, such as the world. In effect James is saying: "The truly wise and understanding person is the one whose life and actions are inspired by the wisdom that comes from above, from God." James will proceed to illustrate this theme in what follows.

(b) Reason (ratio):
Bitter Envy Leads One to Act against the Truth (3:14).

Following the structure of the perfect argument, James offers the *ratio* or reason for his thesis. He does this by presenting a contrast: if your life is inspired by envy and selfish ambition, you cannot claim that you are inspired by the wisdom that comes from above. This manner of arguing is characteristic of the letter of James, as Wall notes: "Typically, James follows a statement of principle with a direct address. In this case, the familiar 'But if' (*ei de;* cf. 1:5; 2:9; 3:3; 4:11) introduces the contrasting characteristics of the wise and understanding teacher as a statement of rational fact. That is, 3:14 is a first-class conditional that describes a matter of fact" ([1997] 183). All traditional wisdom bears witness to the conviction that envy and selfish ambition show that people are inspired by their own self-serving desires and not by the true wisdom that comes from above.

The concept of envy is only understandable against the background of James's worldview. A social-scientific analysis of the world of the New Testament has shown that its economic system operates within the framework of a closed system or society (see *Excursus 6: Honor and Shame, Patronage and Grace. Cultural Scripts behind the Letter of James*). Foster explains it very well: "By 'Image of Limited Good' I mean that broad areas of peasant behavior are patterned in such a fashion as to suggest that peasants view their social, economic, and natural universes—their total environment—as one in which all of the desired things in life such as land, wealth, health, friendship and love, manliness and honor, respect and status, power and influence, security and safety, *exist in finite quantity and are always in short supply,* as far as the peasant is concerned" (296).

What the concept of limited supply of resources meant in reality was that individuals could only increase their position within society at the expense of others. The natural reaction to this was one of envy, because it meant that there was less wealth or honor to be distributed among others. Envy was judged to lie behind every form of competition among people. Envy was also responsible for all the strife and discord that infected society. These were the thoughts this *topos* communicated within the context of ancient moral rhetoricians. Going hand in hand with envy was *eritheia* ("selfish ambition"), the attitude that used unworthy means to overcome rivals and promote oneself.

Contrasted to this concept of the limited supply of resources is God's realm, where God bestows grace lavishly on all who ask (1:5). There is no limit to God's supply of grace. This explains the ongoing contrast that develops within this passage between the world and God.

James says that those whose actions are dominated by envy and selfish ambition "boast and lie against the truth" (3:14). This way of life influenced by jealousy and rivalry over others actually betrays and denies the truth of the message of salvation they have received. Given "birth by the word of truth" (1:18), they are called to establish a community of equals as "the first-fruits of his (God's) creatures" (1:18). Instead, they are only interested in themselves.

The rhetorical effect of James's use of this *topos* of envy explains why his hearers/readers cannot claim to have the wisdom from above. It is not just a matter of using the word envy or similar words on a number of occasions. Rather, it is a matter of seeing the effect James achieves through the use of this *topos.* Envy leads to murder, strife, and war (see 4:1-6).

(c) Proof (rationis confirmatio):
Wisdom from Above Brings True Righteousness (3:15-18).

In proof of his thesis that wisdom inspires a specific way of life, James contrasts two types of wisdom: wisdom that comes from above and wisdom that comes from the earth. In other words, James shows the fruits each type of wisdom generates by illustrating the virtues or vices that emerge. Behind this contrast lies James's fundamental contrast between God and the world. He begins by describing the fruits of the wisdom that come from the world, and his description intensifies inexorably: it is *epigeios, psychikē, daimoniōdēs* ("earthly, unspiritual, demonic") (3:15). The final adjective shows the real center for the opposition between the two types of wisdom. One is inspired by God, the other by the devil. What James said before about the tongue being inspired by "Gehenna" (3:6) is now developed to show that the source of all evil, the devil, inspires evil within one's way of life. In continuing to describe the fruits of the wisdom from below James returns to the *ratio*. Jealousy and selfish ambition are responsible for the disorder within the community and in society at large. James uses the *topos* of envy to further illustrate how all-pervasive is the evil inspired by the devil (3:16). The effects of this false wisdom on society are significant, whether they be in the community or in the wider society. False wisdom reaps disorder and chaos *(akatastasia)*. Wall expresses this dimension very clearly: "In support of this pastoral concern is the tacit connection between the 'demonic' and social chaos in Jewish teaching. Already in James, the adjectival form of 'chaos' conjoins the duplicitous person (1:8) and duplicitous tongue (3:8). Each results in spiritual anarchy; each characterizes the spiritually immature; each prevents wisdom from having its intended result; each imperils eschatological blessing" ([1997] 186–87).

In contrast to this false wisdom from below, James describes the fruits of the wisdom that comes from above (3:17-18). He opens this list with the word *hagnē* ("pure"), which places the whole list in the context of the purity laws. The concept of "pure" is more than just a characterization of a moral absence or lack of defilement. To be pure means that one is "unstained from the world," as James had defined true religion in 1:27. It sets one on the side of God against the world, as one tries to imitate God and God's ways and laws in all that one does. See the discussion on purity and purity laws in *Excursus 4: James and the Heritage of Israel.* Malina's description of purity rules is very relevant to James's reference to purity in this particular context:

> (I)f purity rules are to facilitate access to God, and if the God to whom one wants access has human welfare as the main priority in the divine will for the chosen people, it follows that proper interpretation of purity rules must derive from giving primary consideration to relationships with one's fellows. This is what righteousness is about. For righteousness means proper interpersonal relationships with all those in one's society, between God and covenanted human beings and between human beings and their fellow beings ([1993] 174).

In this context James refers to a wisdom that comes down from above. The believer is in a relationship with the God who inspires every action. Life's aim is to remain within this covenanted relationship. While God always remains faithful to the covenant, human beings are fickle and in constant need of God's gifts and grace to remain faithful. Those who allow this wisdom from above to permeate their lives and their community truly do experience righteousness (3:18). Righteousness is the fruit, the result that emerges from the wisdom from above. At the same time this righteousness is demonstrated through actions of peacemaking (3:18). Since the whole purpose of the purity rules is to maintain access to God as well as to renew one's relationships with one's fellow human beings, the wisdom from above communicates the ability to retain these relationships. This wisdom enables the believer to know how to act in interpersonal relationships. James enumerates six more attributes that are important manifestations of wisdom from above and are essential for maintaining these interpersonal relationships. Each in its own way is an expression of what the purity rules are all about: maintaining relationship with God and one's fellows, especially the members of one's own community. The word *eirēnikē* ("peaceable") expresses the essence of human relationships. True peace comes from God and is spread by those who carry out God's law. The adjective *epieikēs* ("gentle") gives expression to the virtue in interpersonal relationships that puts the other person first. The adjective *eupeithēs* ("obedient") expresses that conciliatory attitude in which one is willing to listen to another, especially in the context of a community where one respects the views and positions of those who exercise any form of authority. The expression *mestē eleous kai karpōn agathōn* ("full of mercy and good fruits") continues to express concern for the essential community values: Mercy demonstrates the virtue of compassion. So serious is the responsibility to show this type of compassion that those who fail to do so stand under God's judgment (2:13). *Good fruits* foreshadows the reference to "fruit of righteousness" in 3:18. It is a reminder of the Jesus saying in Matt 7:17-18 of the need to produce good fruit. For James this language reflects his basic concern: like faith, wisdom must also be demonstrated in good works. Finally, the two adjectives *adiakritos* and *anypokritos* ("without a trace of partiality or hypocrisy") again reinforce virtues that concern honesty and sincerity in relationship with others.

"To be holy, according to James, is to be whole—with respect to personal integrity, communal solidarity, and religious commitment" (Elliott [1993] 78). The purpose of the Law was to define the boundaries for the believing community in order to maintain access to God and to keep its wholeness. The wisdom that has come down from above provides the context for the search for wholeness and purity. The first fruit of this wisdom is that it is pure: this comes from having access to God, from being in a wholehearted relationship with God. Each of the virtues listed here illustrates that the fruits of wisdom are recognized in those deeds that foster relationships of harmony within the community.

(d) Embellishment (exornatio):
Envy Brings Disharmony in the Community.
Argument from Scripture:
"Does the Spirit That God Made to Dwell in Us Yearn Enviously?" (4:1-6).

In filling out his argument James continues to work within the *topos* of envy. The language of wars and battles is characteristic of that *topos*. In the context of this language and of the biblical tradition James illustrates for his hearers/readers the inevitable outcome of the vice of envy: it leads to murder and war. James is not necessarily pointing to events that have recently occurred within the community. His use of the present indicative is a rhetorical device, more along the lines of issuing a warning to them: "If you desire and do not have, you will murder" (4:2). In the biblical tradition certainly the clearest illustration of this connection of envy-jealousy-murder is found in the narrative of Cain and Abel (Genesis 4).

While desire and envy are the characteristic features of the world, James charges that envy has infected the religious piety of his community. Even their prayer life has been contaminated by envy: "You ask and you do not receive because you ask wickedly in order to spend it on your desires" (4:3). This again betrays the closed system of Hellenistic society that views everything as being in limited supply. They use prayer to God in order to attain what they envy in others. It is as though they are asking that God take from others and give to them. They have failed to understand that the society God has inaugurated is an open one in which God bestows graces abundantly and freely: there is an unlimited supply of God's grace.

James's statement is a further reflection of a Jesus saying in the Sermon on the Mount: "Ask, and it will be given you; search, and you will find; knock, and the door will be opened for you" (Matt 7:7; Luke 11:9). James balances the unqualified statements of Matt 7:7 and Luke 11:9 with experience: not every request is gratified. James attributes apparently unanswered prayer to the fault of the human person, not to God. The proper object of prayer is wisdom (1:5), not the gratification of one's desires.

The pulsating heart of the letter emerges here in 4:4, with the contrast drawn between friendship with the world and friendship with God. This polarity has been in evidence on many occasions, e.g., in the very definition of religion in 1:27 and in the contrast between the wisdom from above and the false wisdom from the earth (3:13-18). A clear choice now lies before the hearer/reader: a choice for God against the world. This gives expression to the community's very identity. In the context of the thesis of this section (3:13) their way of life will demonstrate the choice they have made. This choice is presented against the background of the covenantal relationship between God and God's people. In sharp language reminiscent of the biblical prophets (see Ezek 23:45; Mal 3:5) James challenges his hearers/readers: *"Moichalides"* ("adulteresses"). Against the background of the marriage imagery this phrase recalls the covenant relationship between God and Israel. The image of adultery represents the breaking of this covenant bond between God and God's people, Israel.

The heart of the challenge lies in the choice between friendship with God and friendship with the world. The same alternative is expressed by Matthew's Jesus: "You cannot serve God and wealth" (6:24). Divided loyalty is not possible, as James's reprimand against the double-minded person has shown (1:7-8).

James deliberately uses the concept of friendship to capture the exclusive bond that exists between God and God's people. In the Greco-Roman world friendship was a deeply valued relationship and much reflection and discussion was accorded the topic in its writings. Given the lack of exact parallels in the language of friendship in the New Testament, it is quite likely that the appeal to the concept of friendship is James's own contribution to the common tradition.

Fundamental to the concept of friendship in the Greco-Roman world was the perception that friends viewed reality in the same way. Euripides (*Orest.* 1046) used the phrase "one soul" (*mia psychē*) to capture the unity of spirit in friendship. Cicero described Laelius's friendship with Scipio as "a complete agreement in aims, ambitions, and attitudes" (*Amic.* 4:15 [Copley]). Cicero went further when he wrote later in the same work: "Now friendship is just this and nothing else: complete sympathy in all matters of importance, plus goodwill and affection, and I am inclined to think that with the exception of wisdom, the gods have given nothing finer to men than this" (*Amic.* 6:20 [Copley]). In the context of friendship, then, the choice is decisive: it lies between attaining oneness with God or with the world.

James opened this section with the theme that the believer's way of life will demonstrate deeds that are inspired by the true wisdom from above. The concept of friendship with God gives concrete expression to this: one's way of life demonstrates oneness with God. The gift of friendship with God is the fruit of the wisdom from above. At the same time it establishes a unity among the community of those who have embraced the same way of life, one that is influenced by the wisdom from above. Friendship with God gives an identity to all those who live out their faith in the same way. While the community lives in the world, its values are inspired by the wisdom from above and its members lead their lives in awareness of their friendship with God.

As James has done previously when developing the embellishment *(exornatio)*, he turns to Scripture for support to illustrate his argument. In this instance he gives two quotations from the Scriptures. The Notes have drawn attention to the problems associated with the first quotation, and tried to provide a solution by reading it in this way: "Does the spirit that God made to dwell in us yearn enviously?" (4:5). Fundamental to the discussion is the fact that James uses a technical form for the introduction of quotations, namely *hē graphē legei* ("the Scripture says"). James (as well as his hearers/readers) clearly believes that he is using a quotation from Scripture. This quotation makes a contribution to James's argument, especially when one identifies "the spirit" to which the quotation refers. It cannot refer to the Holy Spirit, as the same arguments for rejecting God as the subject of evil jealousy would apply. Johnson ([1995] 281) argues convincingly that it should be interpreted in light of the *Testaments of the Twelve Patriarchs,* which speak about the two spirits that dwell within the human person: "So, understand, my children, that two spirits await an opportunity with humanity: the spirit of truth and the spirit of error. In between is the conscience of the mind which inclines as it will. The things of truth and the things of error are written in the affections of man, each one of whom the Lord knows" (*T. Jud.* 20:1 [*OTP* 1:800]). This division corresponds well to James's understanding that within the human person there are two competing forces: one comes from the "world of iniquity" that consumes the tongue and is inspired by the devil and "sets on fire the cycle of existence" (3:6); the other is from the wisdom from above that God communicates to those who ask (1:5). Given this understanding, the best interpretation of this quotation is to see it as a question that expects a negative answer: "Does the spirit that God has made to dwell in us yearn enviously?" As both Ropes (264) and Johnson ([1995] 282) observe, the one difficulty with this interpretation is that a question is usually introduced by the particle *mē.* However, the fact that it is a quotation might account for this strange usage. This interpretation does offer more solutions than other projected interpretations (Johnson [1995] 282).

James uses the quotation in the context of this passage to contrast envy with the true spirit within the human person. If envy permeates the individual, then it is not the true spirit from God that is directing the person or the community. Once again it is the *topos* of envy to which James turns to highlight what is wrong with the type of life they are leading.

Finally, James turns to another Scripture quotation for further support: "God resists the proud, but gives grace to the humble" (Prov 3:34 LXX). Augustine, in exhorting his readers to humility, says: "For there is hardly any page of the Sacred Scriptures that does not speak about God resisting the proud and giving grace to the humble" (*Doctr. chr.* 3:23 [*MPL* 34:78]). Again James's quotation reinforces and illustrates his argument further. The proud and the envious are those whose lives surely do not reflect the meekness and humility of dependence on God (3:13). God's gifts are bestowed on those who are open to receive them. Meekness and humility are the greatest virtues that foster openness to the reception of God's wisdom from above.

(e) Conclusion (conplexio): Call to Submit to God (4:7-10).

This section brings to a conclusion James's argument about being open to the wisdom from above to give direction to one's way of life. Throughout this passage James has built contrasts between:

- wisdom from above—wisdom from the earth
- friendship—enmity
- friendship with God—friendship with the world
- humble—proud

These contrasts all illustrate two realms: of God and of the world. Their way of life will demonstrate to which one belongs. That is why James ends this section with an impassioned plea containing a further direct opposition:

- Submit to *God*—resist the *devil*

Turning to the language of purity and of the cult, James expresses the call for a change in their way of life. The purity laws and rules are designed to show how one is to maintain access to God (see *Excursus 4: James and the Heritage of Israel*). They set the individual and the community off from the wider society. In effect they identify those who have access to God, who belong to the sphere of the sacred, in distinction from those who belong to the world of the profane. That is why James calls out to them: "Draw near to God and he will draw near to you. Cleanse your hands, you sinners, and purify your hearts, you double-minded" (4:8). This is in line with James's definition of religion in 1:27, which expresses the essence of the purity laws: keeping yourself undefiled from the world and its values.

The ritual of washing one's hands was a way to remove the dirt of the world and to purify oneself for the realm of God. The prophets adopted the phrase to give it a spiritual meaning in reference to moral purity: e.g., "Wash yourselves; make yourselves clean; remove the evil of your doings from before my eyes; cease to do evil; learn to do good; seek justice, rescue the oppressed, defend the orphan, plead for the widow" (Isa 1:16; see also Jer 4:14; Job 22:30). The prophets made a strong connection between inner purity and external concern for the poor and oppressed. James is certainly at home in this tradition, for his whole letter shows a radical option for the poor. Note the combination of hands and hearts in Ps 24:4 (23:4 LXX) as in James: "innocent in hands and pure in heart" *(athǫos chersin kai katharos tę kardią)*. The combination of these two expressions is meant to symbolize the external and the internal. "Hands" is used in a symbolic way for deeds and actions, while the word "hearts" symbolizes thoughts and intentions: e.g., "Give up your faults and direct your hands rightly, and cleanse your heart from all sin" (Sir 38:10). The second imperative, *hagnisate* (from the verb *hagnizein,* "to purify") and its related noun *hagnismos* ("purification"), are generally associated with cultic ritual acts of purification. E.g, "Go to the people and purify *(hagnison)* them today and tomorrow" (Exod 19:10). It is also used in a figurative and spiritual sense (as here in James) in 1 Pet 1:22: "Now that you have purified *(hēgnikotes)* your souls by your obedience to the truth . . ." and 1 John 3:3: "And all who have this hope in him purify *(hagnizei)* themselves, just as he is pure *(hagnos).*" They need single-minded devotion to God and for this reason they must purify their hearts. The purity rules take on extreme importance, for they are the means of maintaining friendship with God.

James concludes his appeal with a saying that reflects the Jesus tradition: "All who exalt themselves will be humbled, and all who humble themselves will be exalted" (Matt 23:12; see also Luke 14:11; 18:14). It is parallel to 4:6 and is an appropriate way to draw the argument to a conclusion. Humility and meekness are the exact opposites of envy and pride. The humble person is the one who opens up in trust to God and God's control of his life. In the lives of the meek (3:13) the wisdom from above finds a true resting place.

FOR REFERENCE AND FURTHER STUDY

Bertram, Georg. *"anastrephō," TDNT* 7: 715–17.

Bradley, David G. "The *Topos* as a Form in the Pauline Paraenesis," *JBL* 72 (1953) 238–46.

Foster, George M. "Peasant Society and the Image of Limited Good," *American Anthropologist* 67 (1965) 293–315.

Hauck, Friedrich, and Siegfried Schulz. *"praus, prautēs," TDNT* 6:645–51.

Johnson, Luke Timothy. "James 3:13–4:10 and the Topos *PERI PHTHONOU," NovT* 25 (1983) 327–47.

_____. "Friendship with the World/Friendship with God: A Study of Discipleship in James," in Fernando F. Segovia, ed., *Discipleship in the New Testament.* Philadelphia: Fortress, 1985, 166–83.

Laws, Sophie. "Does Scripture Speak in Vain? A Reconsideration of James 4.5," *NTS* 20 (1973/4) 210–15.

Malherbe, Abraham J. *Moral Exhortation: A Greco-Roman Sourcebook.* Philadelphia: Westminster, 1986.

_____. "Hellenistic Moralists and the New Testament," *ANRW* 2.26.1 (1992) 267–333.

Marconi, Gilberto. "La 'Sapienza' nell'esegesi di Gc 3,13-18," *RivB* 36 (1988) 239–54.

Mullins, Terence Y. "Topos as a New Testament Form," *JBL* 99 (1980) 541–47.

Osborn, Eric F. *Ethical Patterns in Early Christian Thought.* Cambridge: Cambridge University Press, 1976.

Pearson, Birger A. *The Pneumatikos-Psychikos Terminology in 1 Corinthians.* SBLDS 12. Missoula: Scholars, 1973.

Perkins, Pheme. "James 3:16–4:3," *Int* 36 (1982) 283–87.

Schmitt, John J. "You Adulteresses! The Image in James 4:4," *NovT* 28 (1986) 327–37.

Seitz, Oscar J. F. "Relationship of the Shepherd of Hermas to the Epistle of James," *JBL* 63 (1944) 131–40.

8. *Speaking Evil against Another* (4:11-12)

11. Do not speak evil against another, brothers (and sisters). The person who speaks evil against a brother or sister or judges a brother or sister speaks evil against the Law and judges the Law. If you judge the Law, you are not a doer of the Law, but a judge. 12. There is one Lawgiver and Judge who is able to save and to destroy. But who are you who are judging your neighbor?

NOTES

11. *Do not speak evil against another:* These verses return to the theme of speech first announced in 1:26 and taken up again at 3:1-12. The verb *katalalein* means to "speak ill of, speak degradingly of, speak evil of, defame, slander" (BDAG 519). The command not to speak evil of others (particularly members of the Israelite community) is frequent in the context of the Hebrew Scriptures: e.g., "One who secretly slanders *(katalalounta)* a neighbor I will destroy" (Ps 101:5 [100:5 LXX]; see also Ps 50:20 [49:20 LXX]; Prov 20:13; Wis 1:11). It often occurs as well in New Testament lists of vices in various forms as verb, noun, or adjective (e.g., Rom 1:30; 2 Cor 12:20; 1 Pet 2:1), as well as in the early Church writers (such as *1 Clem.* 30:1-3; Herm. *Mand.* 2:2-3; Herm. *Sim.* 6:5, 5). James addresses his readers with the familiar word *adelphoi* ("brothers [and sisters]"), marking the beginning of a new section. This is in stark contrast to the condemnatory address *moichalides* ("adulteresses") in 4:4, and the accusatory "sinners and double-minded" in 4:8. In fact, James repeats this word *adelphoi* three times in this sentence in order to appeal to their bonds as members of the same community.

The person who speaks evil against . . . judges the Law: the concept of judging parallels the concept of speaking evil against someone. This implies that judging *(krinein)* is "to pass an unfavorable judgment upon, criticize, find fault with, condemn" (BDAG 567). Again this reflects the Jesus saying in Matt 7:1. Luke 6:37 has a variation of this saying that includes an interpretation of the act of judging similar in meaning to that of James: "Do not judge, and you will not be judged; do not condemn *(katadikazein),* and you will not be condemned." The Law referred to here is again the Torah, whose essence is expressed in Lev 19:18 in the law of love of neighbor. James considers that this type of action, speaking evil of another, is at the heart of condemning another and is above all a violation of the law of love.

not a doer of the Law, but a judge: James 1:22 speaks of a "doer of the word." This phrase "doers of the law" *(poiētēs nomou)* is found in only three places in the Bible: here, in Rom 2:13 ("For it is not the hearers of the law who are righteous in God's sight, but the doers of the law *[hoi poiētai nomou]* who will be justified"), and in 1 Macc 2:67 ("You shall rally around you all who observe the law *[pantas tous poiētas tou nomou],* and avenge the wrong done to your people"). In classical Greek the phrase refers to the "lawgiver" rather than the "doer of the law" (see Mayor 148; Ropes 274). The attitude of criticizing or finding fault with the Law shows a wrong spirit with regard to the Law. Rather than adopting a rebellious attitude, one should approach the Law with humility and a willingness to carry out God's will.

12. *There is one Lawgiver and Judge who is able to save and to destroy:* The sentence opens with the Greek word *heis* ("one"), emphasizing that there is only one lawgiver. This recalls the Israelite profession of faith in the oneness of God (Deut 6:4; 32:39). God is the "Lawgiver" *(nomothetēs).* This word is a *hapax legomenon* in the New Testament, although the words *nomothetein* ("to receive the law" [Heb 7:11] and "a covenant that has been [legally] enacted . . ." [Heb 8:6]) and *nomothesia* ("the giving of the law" [Rom 9:4]) also occur. God is "Lawgiver and Judge" *(kritēs).* The concept of God as judge is fundamental to the tradition of Israel ("For the LORD is our judge" [Isa 33:22]) and the New Testament ("Who are you to pass judgment on servants of another? It is before their own lord that they stand or fall" [Rom 14:4]). The two verbs "to save and to destroy" *(sōsai kai apolesai)* are not found together in the Hebrew Scriptures. Nevertheless, this is a description of God that is basic to Israelite thought and theology: e.g., "See now that I, even I, am he; there is no god besides me. I kill and I make alive; I wound and I heal; and no one can deliver from my hand" (Deut 32:39); "The LORD kills and brings to life; he brings down to Sheol and raises up" (1 Sam 2:6); "When the king of Israel read this letter, he tore his clothes and said, 'Am I God, to give death or life, that this man sends word to me to cure a man of his leprosy?'" (2 Kgs 5:7); "Our God is a God of salvation" (Ps 68:20). In the New Testament we find, for example, Matt 10:28: "Do not fear those who kill the body but cannot kill the soul; rather fear him who can destroy *(apolesai)* both soul and body in hell," as well as Jas 1:21: "the implanted word that is able to save *(sōsai)* your souls." See also the Shepherd of Hermas: "Listen, therefore, to me, and fear him who has all power, 'to save

and to destroy' *(sōsai kai apolesai)* . . ." (Herm. *Mand.* 12:6, 3 [Lake, LCL]); and ". . . shall man who is mortal and full of sin bear malice against man, as though he were 'able to destroy or to save him?' *(apolesai ē sōsai auton)"* (Herm. *Sim.* 9:23, 4 [Lake, LCL]).

But who are you who are judging your neighbor? The use of the rhetorical question as well as the present participle *krinōn* ("who are judging") implies that this is a vice occurring presently within the community. James has changed from speaking in terms of general advice to identifying the actual vice as present among his hearers/readers. The reference to "neighbor" *(plēsion)* recalls 2:8 and the law of love of neighbor (Lev 19:18). For the form of this question, "But who are you . . ." *(sy de tis ei)* see "But who indeed are you *(sy tis ei)*, a human being, to argue with God?" (Rom 9:20). As Davids expresses it: "Who indeed do humans think they are?" ([1982] 170).

INTERPRETATION

In this passage James turns to a topic he had introduced in the opening chapter. As has been argued, the function of the opening chapter was to introduce the main themes that would be addressed throughout the letter. The theme of speech is one of the letter's main preoccupations (see 1:19, 26; 3:1-12).

The relationship of this passage to what precedes and what follows is one of the important questions to be addressed at the outset. Almost every commentator approaches the division differently. The relationship of 4:11 to what precedes in 4:10 is the easier question to answer. The discussion of 3:13–4:10 showed that this passage was an entity in its own right that conforms to the structure of the perfect argument. James 4:10 brings the passage to a conclusion through the use of a saying from the Jesus tradition: "Humble yourselves before the Lord and he will exalt you." This is similar to what he has done frequently at the end of a section, using a saying, a maxim, or a proverb to draw the argument to a conclusion (see, e.g., 2:13; 2:26; 3:12). The saying made an appropriate conclusion to his discussion, since it contrasted humility to envy, the theme that had been the *topos* of the entire passage: humility and meekness are the opposites of envy and pride. The next verse, 4:11, clearly introduces a new section through the use of the marker *adelphoi* ("brothers and sisters"). James has employed this marker consistently throughout the letter to draw attention to a new topic or passage he is introducing (see, e.g., 1:2; 2:1, 14; 3:1; 4:11; 5:7, 12, 19). The form of James's argument also changes at this point. In 4:7-10 he had a series of direct positive imperatives arranged one after the other. Now, in 4:11, he uses the negative command to convey his argument. All this indicates that 4:11 is introducing a new section and a new topic for consideration.

The further question is more difficult to answer: How far does this new section extend? Johnson sees 4:11–5:6 comprising one unit because, as he says, "an identifiable thematic thread can be seen to run through it" ([1995] 292). Johnson sees the theme of arrogance as the common link that runs through all the sayings in these verses. While Johnson has made an arguable case, I feel that the attempt to focus on arrogance forces the material into a structure the author did not have in mind. From a formal point of view these verses do not present a unity. Dibelius noted this in his discussion on their structure. Speaking about the relationship between 4:11-12 and 4:13-16, he wrote: "4:13-16 is unquestionably an independent section. . . . There is no connection between this passage and the preceding series of imperatives" (Dibelius 230). On the one hand 4:11-12 seems to form a unity. These verses have a common theme that addresses the issue of speech once again. At the same time 4:13 contains the opening address *age nyn* ("Come now") that appears to begin a new topic: an address of condemnation against merchants who lead lives independently of God. Because both form and content are distinct between 4:11-12 and 4:13-17 I take them as separate units or sections. The unit in 5:1-6 opens with an address similar to 4:13, *age nyn* ("Come now"). While 4:13-17 is directed against the merchants, 5:1-6 is aimed at the rich. Both sections are similar in form. They imitate for rhetorical effect the prophetic oracle that addresses those who are outside the community. They show the conviction that God is the champion punishing those who act in such a way. At the same time they act as a motivation for the community: in the case of the prophets it is the Israelites; in the case of James it is the members of his community. Because of the similarity in form and content between 4:13-17 and 5:1-6 I shall approach them as a unified section in which James addresses those who demonstrate a love of the world as opposed to a love for God. That was the basic choice set before the readers in 4:4, and in these verses James clearly shows how a life of friendship with the world is opposed to a life led in friendship with God. Consequently I read 4:11-12 as an independent unit, while I take 4:13–5:6 as a unified section dealing with the results of friendship with the world.

The address of 4:11-12 shows a marked change in tone from the previous section. From the accusatory address "adulteresses" (4:4) James turns to the personal and more intimate "brothers and sisters." This puts these words into a new context: an appeal to the bonds between the community and the author rather than an oracular address in the manner of the prophets. James is intent throughout his letter on giving the members of the community direction on how to forge their identity as "the first fruits of his (God's) creatures" (1:18). He gives his community markers to show them the type of life that is characteristic of members of this new community in new relationships with one another and with God. One of the key features of this new creation relates to the realm of speech.

This is the third time James has addressed this theme of speech. In 1:19 he first announced the theme: "You must understand this, my beloved; let everyone be quick to listen, slow to speak, slow to anger." A few verses later he connected this theme with the very heart of religion: "If any think they are religious, and do not bridle their tongues, but deceive their hearts, their religion is worthless" (1:26). The very identity of this religious community is characterized by its members' speech. Hence the need to "bridle" one's speech.

In 3:1-12 James takes up the topic again and sets it within the context of his major vision of the call to perfection or embracing a life of integrity. While James acknowledges that as humans we all fail in many ways, it is the person who is acknowledged to be perfect who ensures that he does not sin with the tongue (3:2). A person of integrity is one who is whole and sound in nature, whose speech and thought are in harmony. James introduced an important concept into this reflection on the tongue by showing how evil permeates speech: "The tongue is a world of iniquity placed among our members: it stains the whole body and sets on fire the cycle of existence and is itself set on fire by Gehenna" (3:6). Through the tongue and speech the forces of evil that are opposed to God influence the human person. Speech is a graphic marker that identifies the choices one has made either for the world or for God. In the cosmic struggle between God and world, speech illustrates the choice the human person has made.

James 4:11-12 addresses the theme of speech a third time and continues to illustrate speech's evil nature through a reflection on the implications of slander (falsely imputing to another something supposedly done or said). He urges both the community and the individual not to speak evil against one another. Behind the evil that slander and gossip generate lie the implicit judging and condemnation of another in secret: "The person who speaks evil against a brother or sister or judges a brother or sister speaks evil against the Law . . ." (4:11). By means of parallelism James equates slander and judgment. One sets oneself up as a judge over another, giving oneself an importance and power not possessed in reality. As Johnson ([1995] 306–307) shows, it is "a form of arrogance" that reflects again the theme of envy that permeated the previous section. Envy and jealousy are behind the motivation of putting another down and raising oneself: this gives one importance at the expense of another. Within a community where all are held as equal (the "brothers and sisters" James evokes so frequently), slander is a violation of the very nature of the profession one makes to live in a community where all treat each other as brothers and sisters.

How does slander against another (4:11) lead to slander against the Law and become a judgment on the Law? Slander against another is a clear violation of the law of love of neighbor (2:8) that has Lev 19:18 in mind. Within the context of Leviticus 19 slander is seen as a direct violation of the law of love of neighbor: "You shall not go around as a slanderer among your people . . ." (Lev 19:16). Consequently, slandering is a most serious violation against the royal Law of love (2:8). According to James's principle, a violation of one command is a violation against the whole Law, the Torah (2:10). By slandering one sets oneself above the Law in deciding what commands to obey and what not to obey. In effect one claims for oneself God's role as the ultimate Lawgiver. This surely is the greatest arrogance. In classical Greek the phrase "doer of the law" (*poiētēs nomou*) indicates a lawmaker (Mayor 148; Ropes 274; Laws [1980] 187). It seems that James had this in mind because in the next verse (4:12) he identifies God as the Lawgiver. This further supports the charge that the slanderer is claiming a position reserved for God as the true Lawgiver.

In describing God as the Lawgiver (4:12) James provides a glimpse into his understanding of God that shows again how rooted it is in the tradition of Israel. That God is the Lawgiver is a fundamental assumption of Israel's Scriptures. In Ps 9:21 LXX God is identified as *nomothetēs* ("lawgiver") (see also Ps 83:7 LXX where the participle is used). As indicated in the Notes, the structure of this sentence reflects the fundamental belief in the oneness of God (see also 2:19). That God is one also means that God is the one and only Lawgiver and Judge. In turn this means that God's role embraces salvation and destruction ("to save and to destroy"), something to which the Hebrew Scriptures consistently testify. From this understanding of the unique position God holds in the world of Israel and the early church James draws out the implications for his community. In effect he says: "Who do you think you are? God alone is the one to make the law, to judge according to the law, to exercise the role of salvation and destruction based on the law." Whenever anyone judges, or worse, slanders another, one is claiming a prerogative and role that is God's alone (see Wall [1997] 214). Such claims and such actions are the height of all arrogance. Not only do they lead to "lowering my neighbor and elevating me" (as Johnson [1995] 306 so aptly describes arrogance), but they also lead to abrogating God's position in order to claim it for myself! Speaking evil has the double consequence of breaking the law of love and claiming God's role for oneself (see Martin 170).

FOR REFERENCE AND FURTHER STUDY

Baker, William R. *Personal Speech-Ethics in the Epistle of James.* WUNT 2nd ser. 68. Tübingen: J.C.B. Mohr (Paul Siebeck), 1995.

9. *Judgment on the Rich Because of Friendship with the World* (4:13–5:6)

13. Come now, you who say, "Today or tomorrow we will go into such and such a town and will spend a year there and will carry on business and make a profit." 14. You are people of such a nature who do not know what will happen tomorrow. What will your life be like? For you are a mist that appears for a little while and then vanishes. 15. Instead of this you ought to say, "If the Lord wishes, we will both live and do this or that." 16. But now you boast in your arrogance; all such boasting is evil. 17. Therefore, for everyone who knows the right thing to do and does not do it, for that person it is a sin.

5:1. Come now, you rich! Weep and wail for the miseries that are coming upon you! 2. Your riches have rotted, and your clothes have become moth-eaten! 3. Your gold and silver have rusted, and their rust will be proof against you, and it will eat your flesh like fire. You have stored up treasure in the last days. 4. Behold! The wages of the laborers who mowed your fields—which you held back by fraud—are crying out. And the cries of the harvesters have reached the ears of the Lord of hosts. 5. You have led a life of self-indulgence on earth, and have lived in pleasure. You have fattened your hearts for a day of slaughter. 6. You have condemned and murdered the righteous one who offers you no resistance.

NOTES

13. *Come now, you who say:* The phrase *age nyn* ("come now") occurs again in 5:1. As a harsh term of address it introduces a new topic suddenly and abruptly. It would conform to the biblical prophets' address of "Woe to you . . ." (see Isa 5:8). As a form of address it is not found elsewhere in the New Testament. The use of *age* only appears in the LXX in the following passages: Judg 19:6 (Codex Vaticanus); 2 Kgs 4:24; Isa 43:6. However, it is found in ancient Greek sources such as Epictetus, *Diatr.* 1:2, 20, 25; 1:6, 37; 3:1, 37. "*You who say*" *(legontes)* raises the question: Are these members of the community or outsiders? James usually addresses the community in a positive way as "brothers and sisters," though he did call them "sinners and double-minded" in 4:8. It is hard to imagine the Christian community of that early stage being made up of business people. This address would correspond more to the way the prophets singled out nations around Israel for condemnation. The prophet did not expect the nation addressed to hear the oracle. The rhetorical purpose was for Israelites to hear the message and change their actions accordingly. In a similar way James addresses merchants with the intention that his own community would hear the message and respond.

"Today or tomorrow we will go into such and such a town and will spend a year there and will carry on business and make a profit": These words are translated as a

quotation expressing the business intentions of the merchants. "Today or *(ē)* tomorrow" is the reading better attested by the manuscripts Codex Sinaiticus and Codex Vaticanus, instead of the reading given by some manuscripts (e.g., Codex Alaexandrinus): "today and *(kai)* tomorrow" (see Aland [1997] 76). All the verbs are in the future, which makes more sense than the aorist subjunctive that occurs in some manuscripts. The verb *poiein* plus an accusative of time means "to spend or stay" (BDAG 841): e.g., "the righteous will spend . . . many years *(dikaioi poiēsousin . . . etē polla)*" (Prov 13:23 LXX). The phrase "into such and such a town" is a colloquial way of speaking (see Zerwick 531). The purpose of the travel was financial gain: "to carry on business" *(emporeusometha,* which implies buying and selling) and "to make a profit" *(kerdēsomen).* James criticizes the attitude of doing everything in the secular realm without reference to God.

14. *You are people of such a nature who do not know what will happen tomorrow. What will your life be like?* The pronoun *hoitines* is used in the classical sense "of such a nature" (as BDAG 729 says: "to indicate that persons [or things] belong to a certain class *[such a one] who . . .").* It refers back to 4:13, "those who say" and who speak about their plans for the future. The phrase *to tēs aurion* (literally "that concerning tomorrow") is translated here as "what will happen tomorrow." The textual witnesses give many variations of this form, such as *ta tēs aurion* ("the things concerning tomorrow") (see Metzger [1975] 683–84; Aland [1997] 77). The reading given by the Greek text *(to tēs aurion)* found in the twenty-seventh revised edition of *Nestle-Aland* and the fourth revised edition of the *UBS* is followed here. As Metzger observes, it is represented "by a wide diversity of witnesses" ([1975] 684). The interrogative pronoun *poia* ("of what kind?") agrees with the noun *zōē* ("life"), giving the expression "of what kind is your life?" Since *poios* introduces a question, I translate it here as "What will your life will be like?" The theme of the uncertainty of life is common in Philo as well as Greek and Latin writers (see Ropes 277). Marcus Aurelius expressed this concept when he wrote: "Of man's life, his time is a point, his existence a flux, his sensation clouded, his body's entire composition corruptible, his vital spirit an eddy of breath, his fortune hard to predict, his fame uncertain" *(Med.* 2:17 [Farquharson]).

For you are a mist that appears for a little while and then vanishes: This answers the question posed in the previous phrase. Again there are several variations in the readings of the manuscripts (see Metzger [1975] 684). This translation again follows the Greek text *(atmis gar este hē* ["for you are a mist that . . ."]) of the fourth revised edition of the *UBS* and the twenty-seventh revised edition of *Nestle-Aland.* The noun *atmis* means vapor, steam, smoke "typical of what passes away" (BDAG 149). In the LXX the word appears in Lev 16:13; Sir 22:24; 24:15; Hos 13:3 with the nuance "smoke." This image expresses the concept of the brevity of life, as *1 Clement* expresses it: "But I am as smoke *(atmis)* from a pot" (17:6 [Lake, LCL]). This theme was common to the Hebrew writings as well: e.g., "Remember that my life is a breath . . ." (Job 7:7) and "You have made my days a few handbreadths, and my lifetime is as nothing in your sight. Surely everyone stands as a mere breath" (Ps 39:5; see also Wis 2:1-2;

1QM 15:1-11). It also appears as a common theme in Greek and Roman writings: e.g., Seneca: *Quam stultum est aetatem disponere ne crastini quidem dominum!* ("How foolish it is to arrange one's life, when [one is] not even master of tomorrow!" [*Ep.* 101.4-6]). This brevity of life is also captured in the following contrast, which is deliberately drawn with participles that have a similar sound: *phainomenē—aphanizomenē* ("appears—vanishes").

15. *Instead of this you ought to say: "If the Lord wishes":* The expression *anti tou* ("instead of this; rather than this") sets up a contrast with v. 13, where the merchants expressed their ability to lead their lives independently of God. Verse 14 interrupts the logic of the contrast: "Come now, you who say (v. 13) . . . instead of this you ought to say (v. 15). . . ." While the phrase *anti tou legein* is correct Greek, Mayor notes that a classical writer would probably have written *deon legein* ("one ought to say") (151). The expression "If the Lord wishes" has been called the *"conditio Jacobaea."* However, the phrase was not coined by James, as there is ample evidence to show it was a common expression in the Greco-Roman world *("deo volente"):* e.g., Plato's Dialogue, *Alcibiades I,* contains an interesting exchange:

> *Socrates*: And do you know how to escape out of your present state . . . ?
>
> *Alcibiades*: Yes, I do.
>
> *Socrates*: How?
>
> *Alcibiades*: By your help, Socrates.
>
> *Socrates*: That is not well said, Alcibiades.
>
> *Alcibiades*: What ought I to have said?
>
> *Socrates*: *By the help of God.*
>
> *Alcibiades:* I agree . . . (Plato, *Alc.* 1:135d [Jowett]; see also Plato, *Phaed.* 80d).

A similar thought and expression are found in other New Testament writings: e.g., "But I will come to you soon, if the Lord wills . . ." (1 Cor 4:19; see also 1 Cor 16:7; Acts 18:21; Heb 6:3). This shows that James is using a popular phrase from the culture of his world, be it Hellenistic or Christian. "The Lord" *(ho kyrios)* is to be understood as referring to God the Father, who is in control of life.

we will both live and do this or that: The connecting markers *kai . . . kai* ("both . . . and") join together the two verbs *zēsomen* and *poiēsomen* ("to live . . . to do"). God's will embraces the gift of life and the gift of action. The expression *touto ē ekeino* ("this or that") continues the generality James had embraced earlier ("such and such a town") in order to give his teaching a more universal application.

16. *But now you boast in your arrogance; all such boasting is evil:* The verb *kauchasthai* ("to boast") has occurred before in James (1:9; 2:13; 3:14). Boasting is evil if one boasts in one's abilities and possessions (e.g., "Your boasting is not a good thing" [1 Cor 5:6]; see also Rom 3:27; 4:2). If boasting is in Christ, or God, it is praiseworthy (e.g., "Let the brother [or sister] in humble circumstances boast in exaltation" [Jas 1:9] and "and we boast in our hope of sharing the glory of

God" [Rom 5:2]). In James's context the merchants' boasting is evil because it excludes God from their activities and places confidence in their own abilities. The phrase *en tais alazoneiais* ("in arrogance") expresses the manner in which the boasting is done. In the New Testament this noun occurs only here and in 1 John 2:16. The adjective *alazōn* also occurs only twice, but in connection with *hyperēphanoi* in Rom 1:30 and 2 Tim 3:2. *First Clement* 21:5 expresses what James says here in a very similar way: "Let us offend foolish and thoughtless men, who are exalted and boast in the pride of their words *(egkauchōmenois en alazoneią tou logou autōn)*, rather than God." James specifies the nature of this boasting by identifying it as *ponēra* ("all such boasting is *evil*"): it is without reference to God, hence its evil nature.

17. *Therefore, for everyone who knows the right thing to do and does not do it, for that person it is a sin:* The verse appears as a proverb or saying that attempts to sum up what has been stated in the previous verses. The origin of the saying is unknown. It is a familiar feature of James's style to conclude his arguments with a popular saying or maxim (see, e.g., 2:13; 3:18). The use of the particle *oun* ("therefore") denotes "that what it introduces is the result of or an inference from what precedes" (BDAG 736). James intends this maxim to sum up what he has said. Knowing what to do and acting accordingly is one of the main themes of the letter (see 1:22-27; 2:14-26). A parallel is drawn between *hamartia* ("sin") and *ponēra* ("evil") in the previous verse: sin and evil are one and the same.

5:1. *Come now, you rich!* For *age nyn* ("Come now") see above at 4:13. As in the previous address to the merchants, James does not consider the rich to be members of the Christian community, but outsiders who oppress the members of the community. There is a strong biblical tradition of criticism of the rich: e.g., "Those who trust in their riches will wither, but the righteous will flourish like green leaves" (Prov 11:28; see also Isa 5:8; Amos 6:4-6; Luke 6:24; 1 Tim 6:9-10). The rhetorical language and style are reminiscent of the prophets. Wisdom 2 shows some parallel thoughts to this passage in James: namely, the brevity of life and the unjust treatment of the righteous.

Weep and wail for the miseries that are coming upon you! The same verb *klausate* ("weep") was used in 4:9, but with a different purpose. In 4:9 the weeping was a sign of repentance for sin, while here the weeping is for those who are awaiting condemnation. Revelation 6:15-17 gives a graphic description of the punishment that befalls the rich. The participle *ololyzontes* ("wail") is used effectively as an imperative (Mussner [1981] 193). It appears only here in the New Testament. In Homer it is used in a very positive sense of the joy of women shouting in worship: "Then, with ecstatic cries *(ololygē)* they all lifted up their hands to Athene . . ." (*Il.* 6:301 [Murray, LCL]; see also Herodotus, *Hist.* 4:189). In the LXX it occurs only in the negative sense in the prophets, to express howling or crying out in fear and terror: e.g., "Wail *(ololyzete)* for the day of the LORD is near" (Isa 13:6; see also 14:31; 15:3). The word is clearly onomatopoetic, as is the similar Latin word *ululatus*. The reference to *talaipōriais* ("miseries") indicates the punishments that await those who have done evil (e.g., Amos 3:10; Joel 1:15). The impending approach of these miseries *(eperchomenais)* places James's considerations within the context of the expectation of the imminent end or the coming of the Lord, an essential feature of the vision of earliest Christianity.

2. *Your riches have rotted, and your clothes have become moth-eathen!* Verses 2-3 provide the first of four charges against the rich (see also vv. 4, 5, and 6). The noun *ploutos* ("riches") refers to the wealth or "abundance of many earthly goods" (BDAG 832). While the verb *sēpein* ("to rot or decay") is a *hapax legomenon* in the New Testament, it is found in the LXX (e.g., "Every work decays *(sēpomenon)* and ceases to exist" [Sir 14:19] and "From the purple and linen that rot *(sēpomenēs)* upon them" [Bar 6:72 {Letter of Jeremiah LXX 71}]). The second image of decay is the phrase "your clothes have become moth-eaten." The adjective *sētobrōtos* ("moth-eaten," made up of *sēs* ["moth"] and *bibrōskein* ["to eat" or "to consume"]) is a further *hapax legomenon* in the New Testament. It is found in the LXX only in Job 13:28: "One wastes away like a rotten thing, like a garment that is moth-eaten *(sētobrōton)*." While it is possible that James was influenced by Job's text, it is more likely that he is using a traditional image (e.g., "Like a moth *(sēs)* in clothing or a worm in wood" [Prov 25:20]; see also Sir 42:13; Isa 50:9; 51:8). James's statement again seems to reflect the Jesus saying in Matt 6:19-20: "Do not store up for yourselves treasures on earth, where moth *(sēs)* and rust consume and where thieves break in and steal; but store up for yourselves treasures in heaven, where neither moth *(sēs)* nor rust consumes and where thieves do not break in and steal" (see also Luke 12:33). The verbs in 5:2 are in the perfect tense: *sesēpen . . . gegonen* ("have rotted . . . have become") as well as *katiōtai* (v. 3, "have rusted"). This construction is, as Davids describes it, "a prophetic anticipation of the event" ([1982] 175). See also Mayor, who defines it as "a prophetical perfect" [154]. In imitation of the prophets, James describes these events as though they had already occurred: e.g., Isaiah's reference to the hope for God's ingathering of the dispersed people of Israel: "Arise, shine; for your light has come; and the glory of the LORD has risen upon you" (Isa 60:1).

3. *Your gold and silver have rusted, and their rust will be proof against you:* Again James uses the perfect tense with the same prophetic effect. Interestingly, he uses the singular form of the verb *katiōtai* ("have rusted") for the two nouns "gold and silver." The preposition *kata-* gives the verb an intensive sense (Mayor 154). This is a *hapax legomenon* in the New Testament and is found only in the LXX in Sir 12:11. Baruch 6:11-12 (The Letter of Jeremiah LXX 10) speaks about the rusting of gold: ". . . these gods of silver and gold and wood that cannot save themselves from rust and corrosion." See also Bar 6:24 (The Letter of Jeremiah LXX 23) where the reference to rusting actually implies simply the tarnishing of the metal (see Ropes 285). James, however, does not intend the concept of tarnishing of the precious metal. His image is bold and conveys the understanding that no treasure has any permanency: all things are subject to perishing. The second phrase of this verse uses an expression that appears in the New Testament in many varied contexts: *eis martyrion hymin* (e.g.,

". . . but go, show yourself to the priest, and offer the gift that Moses commanded, as a testimony to them *[eis martyrion autois]*" [Matt 8:4]; see also Matt 10:18; 24:14). It could also be translated as "a witness to you." In this sense the rust will be a sign to them calling them to repentance. In effect the image of the rust witnesses to what will happen to them if they do not repent. On the other hand, since the context of this passage has been set in apocalyptic terms of the imminence of the end and final judgment, it is best to interpret it in the sense of "a witness or a proof against you." In the final judgment the worthlessness of what the rich have trusted in will demonstrate how worthless their lives have been. The "rust" acts as a judgment against them.

and it will eat your flesh like fire. You have stored up treasures in the last days: There is a question of punctuation here. Does "like fire" *(hōs pyr)* belong to the first phrase, or to the second phrase and begin a new sentence? Ropes interprets it in the second sense: "Since you have stored up fire . . ." (287) and gives as his reason the fact that the verb *thēsaurizein* requires a direct object. However, the object is actually contained within the meaning of the verb: "to store up treasure" (e.g., "So it is with those who store up treasures *(thēsaurizōn)* for themselves" (Luke 12:21). This translation follows the punctuation of the text of the *Greek New Testament* of the fourth revised edition of the *UBS* and the twenty-seventh revised edition of *Nestle-Aland* where "like fire" belongs to the first phrase and acts as a comparison for how their flesh will be devoured. The verb *phagetai* ("it will eat") is the future of *esthiō* in the New Testament and the LXX. Classical writers also used *esthiō* in the context of devouring by fire (e.g., "Twelve noble sons of the great-hearted Trojans, all these together with you the flame devours *[pyr esthiei]*" [Homer, *Il.* 23:182 {Murray, LCL}]). The meaning of *ethēsaurisate* in this context can be seen on a number of levels. In the first instance James refers to how the rich have stored up treasures for their retirement ("in the last days"). However, he uses this metaphorically and in an ironic sense. While they were storing up wealth in riches they ignored the true source of riches, namely God. So "in the last days," namely at the end of time, they end up with nothing: their wealth has disintegrated and they have not placed their confidence in God. It is very similar to Luke's parable of the rich fool in 12:13-21: "So it is with those who store up treasures for themselves *(thēsaurizōn)* but are not rich toward God." The phrase "in the last days" clearly has eschatological connotations. However, it embraces more than just a reference to the fact that Christians are living in the last days (see Davids [1982] 177). From James's context and the way the phrase is used both in the singular and plural in the Hebrew writings as well as the rest of the New Testament it refers to the end of time and the day of God's judgment: e.g., "In the last days *(ep' eschatōn tōn hēmerōn)* the mount of the Lord's house shall be established . . ." (Mic 4:1). A similar understanding occurs with Paul's reference to the "day of wrath": "But by your hard and impenitent heart you are storing up wrath for yourself on the day of wrath, when God's righteous judgment will be revealed" (Rom 2:5).

4. *Behold! The wages of the laborers who mowed your fields—which you held back by fraud—are crying out:* This is the second accusation against the rich: they have

defrauded the laborers. James uses the particle *idou* ("behold") to draw close attention to the importance of what follows (3:4-5; 5:7, 9, 11). The word *misthos* ("wages") in this context refers to the remuneration that is owed for work that is done (BDAG 653). It is a matter of justice that "the laborer deserves to be paid" (Luke 10:7). The noun *ergatōn* (genitive plural of *ergatēs*, "laborer") is a term that reflects the cultural and social world of first-century Palestine, where day laborers would work on the large estates of mainly absent land-lords. This explains why the word occurs only in the later writings of the LXX such as Wis 17:16; Sir 19:1; 40:18; 1 Macc 3:6. The parables of Jesus often reflect this social context (e.g., Matt 18:23-34; 20:1-16; 21:33-44). The verb *aman* ("to mow") is another *hapax legomenon* in the New Testament and has the meaning of mowing or cutting fields, particularly the reaping of the grain. It also occurs in this sense in the LXX (e.g., "When you reap [*amēsēs*] your harvest in your field and forget a sheaf in the field . . ." [Deut 24:19]). The keeping back of wages was judged to be very serious: it was one of the major evils that cried *(krazei)* to heaven: "You shall pay them their wages daily before sunset, because they are poor and their livelihood depends on them; otherwise they might cry to the LORD against you, and you would incur guilt" (Deut 24:15) (see Gen 4:10, where the blood of Abel cried out to heaven).

And the cries of the harvesters have reached the ears of the Lord of hosts: The noun *boai* ("cries") is another *hapax legomenon* in the New Testament. It is found in the LXX (e.g., "their cry [*hē boē*] went up to God from their works" [Exod 2:23]); 1 Sam 9:16. The name for God, "Lord of hosts," is a translation of the Hebrew term YHWH Sabaoth. At first it referred to God's role as commander of the forces of Israel, then took on the extended meaning of Lord or ruler of the heavenly world with its forces. The LXX usually translated this word by the term *pantokratōr* ("almighty" or "all powerful"; e.g., 2 Sam 5:10 LXX). However, in Isaiah the LXX simply transliterated it as *sabaoth* (e.g., Isa 5:9), as James does here. The meaning here is that God will use divine almighty power to support the defrauded laborers.

5. *You have led a life of self-indulgence on earth, and have lived in pleasure:* This is the third accusation against the rich. The verb *tryphan* ("to lead a life of self-indulgence," BDAG 1018) is a *hapax legomenon* in the New Testament. It can have a positive or a neutral sense as in "they ate, and were filled and became fat, and delighted themselves *(etryphēsan)* in your great goodness" (Neh 9:25 [2 Esdr 19:25]; see also Isa 66:11; Sir 14:4). However, in this context it has a pejorative sense. This negative judgment is further strengthened by the next verb, *spatalan,* which BDAG defines as "to indulge oneself beyond the bounds of propriety, live luxuriously/voluptuously" (936) (see Ezek 16:49; Sir 21:15). The lifestyle of the rich man in the parable of Luke 16:19-31 is a graphic illus-tration of what James condemns here. What is implied is that the rich lead a luxurious life while ignoring the needs of the poor. This theme of condemna-tion of the rich is characteristic of the prophets (see Amos 2:6-8).

You have fattened your hearts for a day of slaughter: While the phrases in this sentence are not found exactly in the rest of biblical literature, they do reflect biblical imagery. The comparison is clear: indulgence before destruction. Just as an animal is force fed before it is killed, so the rich are feeding themselves for the day of judgment. The phrase "day of slaughter" is reminiscent of the biblical imagery of God carrying out judgment upon God's enemies: e.g., "That day is the day of the Lord GOD of hosts, a day of retribution, to gain vindication from his foes. The sword shall devour and be sated, and drink its fill of their blood. For the Lord GOD of hosts holds a sacrifice in the land of the north by the river Euphrates" (Jer 46:10; see also Isa 30:33; Rev 19:17-21). The picture of the slaughter of the rich is also found in *1 En.* 94:7-9, which is very close to James's description: "Woe unto you, O rich people! For you have put your trust in your wealth. You shall ooze out of your riches, for you do not remember the Most High. In the days of your affluence, you committed oppression, you have become ready for death, and for the day of darkness and the day of great judgment" (*OTP* 1:75; see also *1 En.* 97:8-10). "Hearts" (*kardias*) is a term symbolizing the seat of the emotions and pleasures (e.g., "For out of the heart come evil intentions, murder, adultery, fornication, theft, false witness, slander" [Matt 15:19]).

6. *You have condemned and murdered the righteous one who offers you no resistance:* This is the fourth accusation against the rich. The verb *katadikazein* ("to condemn") reflects the legal context of a court where a judgment of condemnation is meted out (see Schrenk, who stresses its forensic nature [*TDNT* 3:621–22]). It reflects a context similar to the one in 2:2, where the rich exercised their undue influence in a legal setting. The image that James conveys is that of the rich using (or abusing) their power to influence the law to the detriment of the poor, who have no power or status to protect themselves from this misuse of power. See Jesus' saying in Matt 12:7: "But if you had known what this means, 'I desire mercy and not sacrifice,' you would not have condemned (*katedikasate*) the guiltless." "The righteous one" (*ton dikaion*) need not necessarily refer to Jesus, as some early Christian commentators (such as Oecumenius, Cassiodorus and Bede) argued, and in more recent times Feuillet (275). This title *ho dikaios* ("the righteous one") was used to refer to Jesus in the New Testament (see Acts 3:14; 7:52; 22:14; 1 Pet 3:18; 1 John 2:1, 29; 3:7). However, there is no reason to see it as a title for Jesus here, even less given the fact that there is no tradition where the death of Jesus is blamed on the rich. Nor should it be taken as a reference to James, who is called "the Just" (as Greeven argued in editing Dibelius [240, n. 58]). Instead, one should see this reference in a collective sense, with the meaning not limited to one individual. It describes the type of person the rich oppress and kill. James is probably influenced here by Wis 2:10-20: "Let us oppress the righteous poor man (*dikaion*) (v. 10). . . . Let us lie in wait for the righteous man (*ton dikaion*) (v. 12). . . . Let us condemn him (*katadikasōmen*) to a shameful death, for according to what he says he will be protected (v. 20)." Not only in this passage is there reference to the "righteous one" (*dikaios*), but there is also the reference to condemning the righteous and the way they plan to kill him. Both James and Wisdom use the same verb (*katadikazein*). First Enoch also contains the theme of the innocent, righteous person being subjected to oppression by the rich: e.g., "Woe unto you who carry out oppression, deceit, and blasphemy. . . . You who coerce the right-

eous with your power, the day of your destruction is coming! In those days, at the time of your condemnation, many and good days shall come for the righteous ones" (*1 En.* 96:7-8 [*OTP* 1:77]; see also *1 En.* 100:7). The final phrase of this verse, *ouk antitassetai hymin* is translated in various ways. Ropes interprets it as a question: "Does not he (sc. *ho dikaios*) resist you?" (292). Johnson also reads it as a question, but interprets the understood subject as God: "Does (God) not oppose you?" ([1995] 305). Among the reasons he adduces is the prior use of this verb *antitassein* in 4:6 as part of a quotation, where the subject is God who opposes the proud. Most scholars, however, interpret the phrase as a statement rather than as a question, and assume that it continues the thought of the sentence. Mayor interprets it in its more logical sense: "The subject here is *ho dikaios*. A more regular construction would be *ouk antitassomenon*, but the abrupt change to direct statement is a far more graphic way of putting the fact" (160). He goes on to explain the change from aorist to present tense as focusing on the central issue: that the righteous one does not resist the rich. It strengthens the generic nature of the "righteous one" and makes a clear application for hearers/readers of every generation. I follow the direction of Mayor and have translated the phrase as: "the righteous one who offers you no resistance." It is in line with the thought of Matt 5:39: "But, I say to you, Do not resist an evildoer," as well as Rom 12:19: "Beloved, never avenge yourselves, but leave room for the wrath of God; for it is written, 'Vengeance is mine, I will repay, says the Lord.'" See also Herm. *Mand.* 8:10: "to resist none (*mēdeni antitassesthai*)." This statement speaks to the context of a community of the poor that has experienced the power of the rich, as the rest of the letter has implied (see especially 2:1-7). The contrast between rich and poor reaches its climax here, with the power of the rich being extended over the powerlessness of the community.

INTERPRETATION

The Unity of James 4:13-17 and 5:1-6

I have argued for the independence of the previous section (4:11-12) as a separate unit. Its position within the letter of James, however, showed connections to many themes that ran like golden threads throughout the letter. The theme of speech and the importance of the Law were important connections. The theme of arrogance continued the thought from the previous section, which had focused on the consequences of envy (3:13–4:10).

In this new section (4:13–5:6) James turns to another major theme that runs throughout the work: the choice between friendship with God and friendship with the world. In particular these verses illustrate by means of two examples what consequences the love of the world entails. This section focuses particularly on the rich. Its rhetorical function is to show how their choice of the world and its values leads them to evil and sin.

The theme of arrogance continues on into the thought of this section as well, with the reference to the way merchants rely on themselves and their own efforts rather than trusting in God. The section addresses two important groups within first-century Mediterranean society: merchants and landowners. Some scholars treat these as independent units (see Laws [1980] 189–218; Mussner [1981] 189–99; Martin, 157–84). Although two paragraphs are identifiable here, some markers demonstrate bonds that show the author intended the paragraphs to be taken as a unity. Each paragraph opens with an identical phrase: *age nyn* ("Come now"); both paragraphs treat the same theme and topic, namely the judgment on the rich for their choice of the world and its values; and then finally the marker *adelphoi* ("brothers and sisters") in 5:7 shows that James is beginning a new section (see Davids [1982] 171).

(a) Judgment on Rich Merchants (4:13-17)

The rich businessmen or merchants are condemned for their attitude to the way they are leading their lives. Their efforts are directed solely to the attainment of more and more wealth. Their sin lies in their arrogance, in that they rely on themselves and their own efforts without acknowledging that their lives and activities depend upon the Lord.

In the manner of the prophets James raises a voice of judgment against the merchants, business people, or traders. Scholars are divided over whether these merchants are Christian business people and consequently members of James's community. Two strong reasons militate against the view that they are Christians. Given the world of early Christianity, it is hard to imagine a social context in which many wealthy business people or traders were members of Christian communities. The merchants are not just people who are wealthy, such as local traders in a particular town; they are people of great means who travel around the Mediterranean conducting business. They are the "mercantile class" (as Laws [{1980} 189–90] identifies them) of the big cities of the Mediterranean basin such as Antioch, Jerusalem, and Ephesus. Laws goes on to offer an important observation in connection with James's vocabulary. James identifies these people through their activity. He uses the verb *emporeuesthai* (4:13), which has the nuance of traveling for the purpose of conducting commercial business or trading. Hence they would be identified as *emporoi* in contrast to the *kapēloi*. A distinction can be drawn between these two groups in this way: *emporos* is "one who travels by ship for business reasons, merchant . . . [the word] denotes *wholesale dealer* in contrast to *kapēlos*, 'retailer'" (BDAG 325). Given this distinction, it is hard to imagine in the context of early Christianity a group or a large number of these wealthy traders forming such a significant part of the Christian movement that James would be required to intervene and condemn them in the way he does. Second, James is speaking in the manner of the prophets of Israel, who would single out a country, a city, or a group of people and direct their invective there. Their rhetorical purpose was not that the particular country or group would actually hear their message and repent. The message was intended instead for the Israelites. The prophet used this rhetoric as a foil to challenge his own audience to conform to a particular way of life by identifying those outside the community who disregard that way of life. James acts similarly. His hearers/readers would immediately know the group about whom he is speaking and would clearly see what was wrong with their way of life. It functions rhetorically as a means for challenging his community, to identify what is essential in their own approach to living in the world. As Dibelius says: "4:13-16 is delivered in the style of a prophetic address. The prophet cries out his words among the masses, unconcerned about whether his accusations reach the ears of those whom he accuses" (231).

James's invective against the merchants shows two aspects of concern. First, their plans operate solely on the level of the world without any reference to God or God's will. The concern here is not against doing business, or even with making a profit. As Davids ([1982] 172) observes, this type of activity was completely normal and occurred throughout the Mediterranean world. Of concern to James is the way business is conducted. While planning is an essential ingredient of any business undertaking, all plans should occur under the auspices of God's will. Life must be viewed as subject to and guided by God's sovereign rule of the world. The theme of the uncertainty of tomorrow is common to all peoples. "You are a people of such a nature who do not know what will happen tomorrow" (4:14). Faced with this universal uncertainty and the frailty of human existence, James shows that the proper response is to open oneself up to God's guidance and providence in the world. In other words, all plans should be made subject to the divine will. This leads James to use a phrase that was not essentially biblical, but rather one that was common to the Greco-Roman world: "If the Lord wishes."

The Hebrew Scriptures also warned against boasting about plans for tomorrow: "Do not boast about tomorrow, for you do not know what a day may bring. Let another praise you, and not your own mouth—a stranger, and not your own lips" (Prov 27:1-2). James is concerned not just with the fragility of human existence. His major concern is the practical atheism of the merchants who act without acknowledging God's will or control. This is illustrated chiefly in the arrogance they show in their boasting: "You boast in your arrogance" (4:16). In this way James continues the thought of the previous section, which focused on the call to "Humble yourselves before the Lord, and he will exalt you" (4:10). Paul, too, was opposed to all boasting or the placing of trust in oneself (see Rom 3:27; Phil 3:3-11). However, Paul shows that there is a type of boasting that is acceptable: "'Let the one who boasts, boast in the Lord.' For it is not those who commend themselves that are approved, but those whom the Lord commends" (2 Cor 10:17-18). James makes a further point that is in line with his whole vision on the relationship between faith and action. One's actions must demonstrate their foundation: trust in God or in oneself. "If the Lord wishes, we will both live and do this or that" (4:15). Not only is life in God's hands, but actions will demonstrate God's moral guidance.

The second aspect of James's invective against the merchants is his concern for what they do with their wealth. As noted, James is not attacking profit taking. But what do the merchants do with that profit? It seems their sole concern is with making a profit: they show little or no concern for any responsibility for doing good with what they have. In a sense James reflects an awareness of the thoughts of the parable of the rich fool in Luke 12:13-21, which condemns not just the action of storing up possessions, but also the failure to use wealth responsibly. James's final statement, "for everyone who knows the right thing to do and does not do it, for that person it is a sin" (4:17) implies responsibility for ensuring that actions reflect faith or knowledge. This is a reminder of the constant challenge to show concern for the poor (2:1-7). It is an appropriate way to end this paragraph on the note of bearing responsibility for one's actions, and it prepares the way for the next invective against the rich landowner who oppresses the poor and the righteous.

It is important to see James's vision against the cultural-anthropological perspective of the first-century Mediterranean world. I am indebted to Johnson's insights ([1995] 307) in this regard. He draws the distinction between two systems of reality: a closed and an open system. In a world of limited resources, the amassing of more and more wealth as the merchants were doing meant that there was less for others. This would add to James's concern that the merchants give no thought to anyone except themselves. Friendship with the world implied the acceptance of this vision of a world with limited resources. On the other hand, as indicated before, friendship with God brought a totally different vision. God is the source of all gifts (1:5) that are unlimited. This means that those who belong to the realm in which God is in control do not live in a world of limited resources, but rather one of unlimited resources because of the nature of God. By opening oneself up to God's will and placing oneself under God's supremacy one also opens oneself up to a new vision of reality in which human beings are no longer in competition with one another (Johnson [1995] 308), but in which God's magnificence gives the possibility for all to coexist in harmony and prosperity.

(b) Judgment on the Rich Landowners (5:1-6)

The focus changes to a condemnation of the landowning class. The tone is harsh and is again reminiscent of the prophetic oracles of denunciation. The rich landowners stand condemned because of their treatment of the poor and the righteous. Two traditions circulating at the time of James adopted a similar tone of condemnation: *1 En.* 94–97 and the Jesus sayings of Luke 6:20-26. As the Notes have indicated, the address is rhetorical and aimed at the hearers/readers rather than the rich themselves, who act as a foil for the message James is communicating. The judgment leveled against the rich stems from their attitude toward the poor, whom God chose as heirs of the kingdom (2:5).

James reflects the social situation of Palestine during the first century C.E. The amassing of large tracts of land in the hands of a few wealthy and powerful individuals was a phenomenon throughout the Roman world. The Roman philosopher and writer, Seneca, also refers to this problem. Reflecting on the evils of greed or *avaritia,* he shows how it has led to landowners seizing more and more property at the expense of the poor: "(Greed) adds fields to fields, expelling a neighbor either by purchasing (the field) or by harming (him)" (*Ep.* 90:39). This situation was evident in Palestine as well and conditions had been deteriorating over many centuries. In the account of Naboth's vineyard (1 Kgs 21:1-29), Ahab (king of Israel during the ninth century B.C.E.) and his wife Jezebel seize Naboth's vineyard and have him killed in the process, simply to satisfy their own greed. It is a good illustration of the power of the king and the way many of these large estates developed. Isaiah, e.g., reflects a situation in the eighth century B.C.E., where the wealthy were adding more and more estates to their land: "Ah, you who join house to house, who add field to field, until there is room for no one but you, and you are left to live alone in the midst of the land" (Isa 5:8). Horsley (207–16) shows how the development of large estates throughout Palestine was largely due to the powerful rulers annexing land for their own use or granting land as favors for political reasons. He comments:

> We can see how the system worked when Herod took over from the Hasmoneans. He simply killed the Hasmonean family and officers, expropriated their land and property, and then granted his own family members and high-ranking officers various estates (*B.J.* 1.358; *Ant.* 15.5-6; 17.305-7). It seems likely that, after he murdered the last Hasmonean high priest, he would also have provided the new high priests he brought from Babylon and Egypt with estates near Jerusalem (213).

This conforms to what Gerhard E. Lenski has shown in his study *Power and Privilege: A Theory of Social Stratification:* "To win control of the state was to win control of the most powerful instrument of self-aggrandizement found in agrarian societies. By the skillful exercise of the powers of the state, a man or group could gain control over much of the economic surplus, and with it at his disposal, could go on to achieve honor and prestige as well" ([1966] 210). Since Palestine was a temple-state, important officials were able to expand their wealth through power and positions. The aristocracy of first-century Palestine comprised both the religious leaders and the political rulers: very often they were one and the same. To a large extent these people belonged to the Sadducees or priestly class.

The confiscation of much property by the rulers led to situations in which the former owners were now reduced to the status of tenant farmers working for the large landowners, many of whom did not live on their estates, but were absent landlords. Further, the more power the rich landowners had, the less the power of the smaller landowners was. The consequence was a situation in which the smaller landowners were forced to go into debt and ultimately give up their farms and work for the larger landowners as day laborers. These day laborers were the mowers and harvesters about whom Jas 5:4 speaks. James reflects the hardships and oppression they experienced at the hands of the rich landowners. Deuteronomy 24:14-15 condemns in very strong terms such exploitation of the day laborer: "You shall not withhold the wages of poor and needy laborers, whether other Israelites or aliens who reside in your land in one of your towns. You shall pay them their wages daily before sunset, because they are poor and their livelihood depends on them; otherwise they might cry to the LORD against you, and you would incur guilt." When James condemns the oppression of mowers and harvesters by the rich landowners he clearly has this text in mind: he speaks of the wages of these laborers crying out to God for justice.

James reflects well the social injustices of first-century Palestine and the wider Roman world. He acts as the voice of the powerless (in this case the day laborer) and lays out in fine detail the evils committed and the charges against the rich landowners. The four accusations James levels in 5:1-6 against these rich landowners can ultimately be reduced to two charges: they lived a life of excessive luxury, and they oppressed the poor.

The first charge: leading a life of excessive luxury. James 5:1-3 paints the picture of the rich hoarding their riches, described in terms of fine clothes and precious metals. James also shows in 5:5 that self-indulgence and pleasure have been the dominant driving forces. Their lives have aimed at self-gratification with no thought given to others, especially the poor. This shows the choice they have made for "friendship with the world." As such they have become wise in the ways of the world and have learned how to use the world's values for their own self-aggrandizement. The graphic imagery of the rich "fattening themselves up" for the day of slaughter is analogous to the fattening of a calf. James 5:3c ("You have stored up treasure in the last days") and 5:5b ("You have fattened your hearts for a day of slaughter") are parallel, showing that the "day of slaughter" refers to the end-time. The rich will experience destruction at the end of time, which is imminent: "The judge is standing at the doors" (5:9). James's vision situates him and his community in that time period leading up to the last days. Again it is a concept that shows the relatively early date of this letter's theology and thought.

The second charge: oppression of the poor. The rich landowners withhold the wages of the day laborers—the mowers and the harvesters (5:4). Given the context of society of that time, this is a very serious charge. The day laborer depended on the daily wage to support himself or herself and his or her family. Peasant society was not geared toward the storing up of money, food, or clothing for a later time. One lived from hand to mouth. Not to earn a wage for the day would lead to a situation of starvation for the worker and his or her family. Sirach reflects the seriousness of this failure to pay the day laborer: "The bread of the needy is the life of the poor; whoever deprives them of it is a murderer. To take away a neighbor's living is to commit murder; to deprive an employee of wages is to shed blood" (34:25-26). The arrogance of the rich landowners is clearly evident in these verses: they are assuming for themselves the role God exercises of "saving and destroying" (4:12). They hold the lives of the poor in their hands. This leads James to make the strongest accusation to date against the rich: "You have condemned and murdered the righteous one" (5:6). As the Notes have demonstrated, "the righteous one" is used in a collective sense and refers to the ordinary, innocent, just person. James envisages not only that the righteous experience oppression from the rich, but also that some form of violence occurs. The concept of killing the righteous person should be taken seriously and literally. It conforms to the wisdom tradition that lies behind this letter: e.g., "Let us condemn him (the righteous person) to a shameful death . . ." (Wis 2:20). It is clear that by depriving the poor of their land, their wages, and all the elements necessary to lead their lives the rich condemn the poor to starvation and ultimately to death. It is tantamount to actually killing them.

Despite what the rich do to the poor, James says that the righteous person "offers no resistance" (5:6). Once again James shows how close he is to the Jesus sayings in the Sermon on the Mount: "You have heard that it was said, 'An eye for an eye and a tooth for a tooth.' But I say to you, Do not resist an evildoer . . ." (Matt 5:38-41). The reason for not resisting is that it is God's prerogative to mete out justice. By not resisting oppressors one is handing judgment over to God. Believing in the imminence of the *parousia*, James expects that this judgment will occur soon. The opening of this section with the call "Come now, you rich! Weep and wail for the miseries that are coming upon you!" (5:1) shows his expectation that judgment on the rich is to happen soon: the end-times are quickly approaching. James's imagery is in line with that of the apocalyptic tradition, which foresees and describes horrendous afflictions befalling the evil at the end-time: e.g., the graphic descriptions of the prophet Zephaniah:

> On that day, says the LORD, a cry will be heard from the Fish Gate, a wail from the Second Quarter, a loud crash from the hills. The inhabitants of the Mortar wail, for all the traders have perished; all who weigh out silver are cut off. . . . Their wealth shall be plundered, and their houses laid waste. . . . The great day of the LORD is near, near and hastening fast; the sound of the day of the LORD is bitter, the warrior cries aloud there. That day will be a day of wrath, a day of distress and anguish, a day of ruin and devastation, a day of darkness and gloom, a day of clouds and thick darkness, a day of trumpet blast and battle cry . . . (Zeph 1:10-16).

The intertestamental literature contains much apocalyptic imagery and many descriptions of the end-time. *First Enoch*, a writing that was well used during the course of the first century C.E., contains much descriptive imagery that closely parallels the descriptions in James. This is not to say that either James or *1 Enoch* is borrowing from the other. What these similarities do indicate is that they are both steeped in common imagery, thought, and a vision they both embrace. Both James and *1 Enoch* draw from an apocalyptic worldview and language in order to communicate their message to hearers/readers who themselves are steeped in that vision and understand their message within that framework.

While James does look toward the imminent future for the judgment and punishment of the rich and uses images and descriptive language that are among the harshest in the New Testament, his message is also directed toward the present and has relevance for every age. James's message, and by implication Jesus' message, that he is applying to his community is one that has social relevance and proclaims a message of social justice (see Maynard-Reid 97). His main concern is to draw attention to unjust situations that act as paradigms for every age and context. As indicated, the attack on the rich landowners was not directed toward their conversion, but rather to give his hearers/readers comfort and encouragement in the face of oppression. He gives his hearers/readers the assurance that God hears the cry of the poor. James proclaims that God truly is on the side of the poor. His message remains true to Jesus' message and heritage. Concern for the poor characterized his whole ethos. Maynard-Reid sums up James's perspective very well: "(I)t is clear that James equates true religion with social concern and that for him one's personal religion is not all that counts in the final reckoning. As in Matthew 25:31-46, James reveals that one's social involvement in the present is as important as one's personal religious practices and that, in fact, personal religion is meaningless without social commitment. This in essence is the profound meaning of James's statement that 'faith by itself, if it has no works, is dead' (2:17)" (98).

As one looks back over the letter of James one sees that James has developed a theology of the poor in a way that is unique in the entire New Testament. In the introductory section (1:9-11) James introduced the important themes of the letter. He shows that in the new society or kingdom a reversal of situations takes place. Two different responses to reality are contrasted. There is the response of the rich who have made an option for the world and so trust in themselves, their own abilities, and their achievements. Since the poor, on the other hand, have nothing within themselves in which to trust, they place their confidence in God. It is all a matter of honor, status, and power. As Malina argues: "On a morally neutral level, as frequently in the Wisdom books, the rich and poor simply mark the extremes of the social body in terms of elite and non-elite status. But in a moral context, rich meant powerful due to greed, avarice, and exploitation, while poor meant weak due to inability to maintain one's inherited social station. . . . In this context rich and poor characterize two poles of society, two minority poles—the one based on the ability to maintain elite status, the other based on the inability to maintain one's inherited status of any rank" [1987] 357–58). Without honor or status, the poor turn to God to be their champion and support. God responds.

James's definition of religion in 1:27 shows that his understanding of it centers on social action and justice. Religion demands a way of life that expresses itself in a concern for "orphans and widows"—metaphors for the powerless in society. Since God is their champion, those who seek friendship with God must act in like manner and champion the cause of the poor.

James 2:1-7 proclaimed that faith in Jesus Christ excluded a way of life that embraced any form of discrimination, chiefly exemplified in discrimination against the poor in favor of the rich. Again it is God's action that forms the foundation for the believer's way of life: "Has not God chosen the poor in the world to be rich in faith and heirs of the kingdom that he has promised to those who love him?" (2:5). James portrays a way of life based on the way God approaches reality. If one claims to be a friend of God (4:4), one has to act in like manner. Actions must illustrate faith. Above all, James proclaims a spirituality that embraces the equality of all people, with a special love for the poor.

Finally, 5:1-6 takes up the cause of the poor, attacking their oppression by the rich and powerful. That God champions the poor is once again illustrated: "The cries of the harvesters have reached the ears of the Lord of hosts" (5:4). The oppressed do not resort to violence (5:6). Instead, having addressed their cause to God they are confident that God will redress the injustices at the imminent end of time.

The Scriptures present God's vision as a basic "option for the poor" (Maynard-Reid 98). James has embraced this option, and through the letter appeals to his community to make that choice their own. The social equality of all members of James's community is what gives them their equality and their identity, and distinguishes them from the wider world.

FOR REFERENCE AND FURTHER STUDY

Alonso Schökel, Luis. "James 5,2 and 4,6," *Bib* 54 (1973) 73–76.

Blevins, William L. "A Call to Repent, Love Others, and Remember God: James 4," *RevExp* (1986) 419–26.

Felder, Cain Hope. *Wisdom, Law and Social Concern in the Epistle of James.* Ph.D. diss. Columbia University, 1982.

Feuillet, André. "Le Sens du Mot Parousie dans l'Evangile de Matthieu," in David Daube and William D. Davies, eds., *The Background of the New Testament and Its Eschatology.* Cambridge: Cambridge University Press, 1964, 261–80.

Horsley, Richard A. *Galilee: History, Politics, People.* Valley Forge, Pa.: Trinity Press International, 1995.

Lenski, Gerhard E. *Power and Privilege: A Theory of Social Stratification.* New York: McGraw-Hill, 1966.

Malina, Bruce J. "Wealth and Poverty in the New Testament and Its World," *Int* 41 (1987) 354–67.

Schrenk, Gottlob. *"katadikdazō," TDNT* 3:621–22.

10. *Call to Patient Endurance* (5:7-11)

7. Be patient, then, my brothers (and sisters), until the coming of the Lord. Look! The farmer waits for the precious crop of the earth, being patient with it until it receives the early and late rain. 8. You also be patient! Strengthen your hearts, because the coming of the Lord is near. 9. Brothers (and sisters), do not grumble against one another, so that you may not be judged. Look! The judge is standing at the doors! 10. As an example of suffering and patience, brothers (and sisters), take the prophets who spoke in the name of the Lord. 11. Look! We call blessed those who showed endurance. You have heard of the endurance of Job and you have seen the outcome accomplished by the Lord, because the Lord is compassionate and merciful.

NOTES

7. *Be patient, then, my brothers (and sisters), until the coming of the Lord:* This is the first of three direct references to "brothers (and sisters)" in this passage. James changes from the harsh denunciations of the *plousioi* ("rich") he had addressed in the previous two paragraphs (4:13-17; 5:1-6) to speak to his community directly as "brothers (and sisters)" *(adelphoi)* with a tone of affection. The address to the rich in the above two paragraphs was used as a foil to communicate with the community. Here in 5:7-11 the community is addressed directly. The particle *oun* ("then, therefore") shows the transition to a new topic that develops from what has been argued previously. In 5:1-6 James had spoken about the end days. Now, in 5:7-11, he writes of "the coming of the Lord." Whereas the previous section dealt in strong terms with judgment as "a day of slaughter" (5:5), here it is more positive and hopeful: "the Lord is compassionate and merciful" (5:11). The imperative *makrothymēsate ("be patient")* introduces a major theme of these verses expressed by the verb-noun combination *makrothymein/makrothymia* (5:7[2x], 8, 10) as well as the combination of *hypomenein/hypomonē* ("to show endurance" [5:11{2x}]). While the verb *makrothymein* is seldom found in classical Greek, it appears in all forms, as noun, verb, adjective in the LXX and the New Testament to express a quality of God: e.g., "But you, O Lord, are a God merciful and gracious, full of patience *(makrothymos)* and merciful love and faithfulness" (Ps 86:15: [85:15 LXX]); "The Lord is not slow about his promise . . . but is patient with you *(makrothymei)* . . ." (2 Pet 3:9). In the LXX it also expresses a virtue human beings are called to emulate (e.g., "Be patient with someone in humble circumstances *[plēn epi tapeinǭ makrothymēson] . . .*" [Sir 29:8]; "Love is patient *[makrothymei] . . .*" [1 Cor 13:4]).

The phrase *heōs tēs parousias tou kyrios* ("until the coming of the Lord") contains a number of important concepts. The term *parousia* has a rich meaning developing out of the basic sense of "presence" or the "state of being present" (BDAG 780) (e.g., "Therefore, my beloved, just as you have always obeyed me, not only in my presence *[en tǭ parousiǭ] . . .*" [Phil 2:12]). From this develops the meaning "coming, arrival, advent," which refers in general to the arrival of any person (e.g., Paul speaks of his arrival in Philippi: "through my coming to you again" *(dia tēs emēs parousias palin pros hymas* [Phil 1:26]). It is worth noting that the word *parousia* occurs five times in the LXX (Neh 2:6 [LXX Codex Alexandrinus, 2 Esdr 12:6]; Jdt 10:18; 2 Macc 8:12; 15:21; 3 Macc 3:17). Its usual meaning was that of the arrival of a king in one of his cities. It was never used to refer to the coming of the Messiah or of God. In the New Testament the word *parousia* took on a technical meaning to refer to the coming or arrival of Jesus Christ at the end of time to inaugurate his messianic kingdom (see, e.g., Matt 24:3, 27, 37, 39; 1 Cor 15:23; 1 Thess 2:19; 2 Thess 2:8; 2 Pet 3:4; 1 John 2:28). In these instances the *parousia* is either said to be the "coming of the Son of Man" or the "coming of the Lord *(kyrios),*" where Lord refers unequivocally to Jesus. This shows that many different traditions within earliest Christianity used the phrase "coming of the Lord" as a reference for the second coming of Jesus (see *TDNT* 5:865–71). While 5:4 used the term Lord *(kyrios)* to refer to God as the judge, here in 5:7 the phrase speaks of the advent of Jesus Christ at the end of time. The concept of judgment is not necessarily connected with Jesus' role, but probably should be reserved for God, as 5:4 indicates.

Look! The farmer waits for the precious crop . . . until it receives the early and late rain: The demonstrative particle *idou* ("look, behold, see") draws attention to what follows (Mayor 161; BDAG 468). It occurs three times in this passage (see also 3:4, 5). James introduces a brief parable showing the farmer's patience. The word *geōrgos* (literally *gē* + *ergon* = "work of the earth") refers to a farmer, as distinct from the hired laborer of 5:4 *(ergatēs)* (Martin 190). The language of 2 Tim 2:6 is close to this verse of James: "It is the farmer *(geōrgon)* who does the work who ought to have the first share of the crops *(karpōn)*." While James stresses the farmer's patience, he also draws attention to *timion karpon* ("the precious crop"). The adjective *timios* refers to something of great value, hence "precious" (e.g., "the precious blood *[haima]* of Christ" [1 Pet 1:19]; or the "precious promises *[epangelmata]*" [2 Pet 1:4]). It gives the reason for waiting. For a farmer whose existence depends on the harvest, the crop is truly "precious." "Early and late rain" *(proimon kai opsimon)* refers to a phenomenon distinctive to the climate of Palestine and southern Syria.

8. *You also be patient! Strengthen your hearts:* Some MSS (see 𝔓⁷⁴ and Codex Sinaiticus; cf. also Aland [1997] 89) add *oun* ("therefore, then"). This appears to be an attempt by a copyist to clarify James's grammar. The lack of a particle would be the more difficult reading. In any event, the meaning is clear: James draws a conclusion by repeating the imperative from 5:7 (*makrothymēsate* ["be patient"]). He adds a further imperative: *stērixate tas kardias hymōn* ("strengthen your hearts"). This is a biblical expression that means to stand firm in the faith and not be overcome by doubt (see *TDNT* 7:655–57; see also 2 Thess 2:17: "Comfort your hearts and strengthen them in every good work and word" *[parakalesai hymōn tas kardias kai stērixai . . .]*). Usually God is the one who "strengthens the heart" (e.g., "And may he [Jesus] so strengthen your hearts *[eis to stērixai hymōn tas kardias]* in holiness that you may be blameless before our God and Father at the coming of our Lord Jesus with all his saints" [1 Thess 3:13]; see also 1 Pet 5:10).

because the coming of the Lord is near: James reflects again the belief that the *parousia*, the coming of the Lord, is near *(ēngiken)*. This expression is used often in the synoptics to express the nearness of God's kingdom (e.g., Matt 3:2; Mark 1:15). It continues in use to refer to the nearness of the *parousia* (e.g., Rom 13:12; Heb 10:25; 1 Pet 4:7). The important point, as Davids ([1982] 184) notes, is not so much the length of the time of the waiting, but rather remaining faithful during this time.

9. *do not grumble against one another, so that you may not be judged:* According to Dibelius this verse "is quite isolated, so there is no need to find some sort of connection between the warning not to 'grumble against one another' and the preceding saying" (244). However, one can certainly see a connection between the thought of this verse and its context. James has been intent on stressing patience in difficult times. Consequently one can see that the grumbling could be connected to the difficulties his hearers/readers were experiencing in an-

ticipation of the *parousia* (Davids [1982] 184). The verb *stenazein* means "to express oneself involuntarily in the face of an undesirable circumstance, sigh, groan" (BDAG 942). This takes on the figurative meaning of "to complain" in this verse. The biblical writings commonly speak of groaning in response to difficult circumstances, showing it to be an acceptable response (see Job 30:25; Isa 59:10; Lam 1:22; 1 Macc 1:26; Mark 7:34; Rom 8:23; 2 Cor 5:2, 4). In all instances the verb *stenazein* is used in the sense of either giving visible expression to feelings in the context of difficulties or making known feelings toward God. The best illustration occurs in the groaning of the people of Israel to God: "The Israelites groaned *(katestenaxan)* under their slavery, and cried out. Out of the slavery their cry for help rose up to God. God heard their groaning *(stenagmon)* and God remembered his covenant with Abraham, Isaac, and Jacob" (Exod 2:23-24). James does not challenge this traditional understanding of "groaning or complaining," but he does oppose making others, namely members of the community, the object of the complaint or the grumbling *(kat' allēlōn* ["against one another"]). James's concern is that they remain in harmony with the community (see 4:11, where he also discusses "speaking evil against another"). In effect James is arguing that his hearers/readers should not blame others for their difficulties. Instead they ought to practice patience (see Ropes 297). Criticizing others is tantamount to passing judgment on them. Consequently, James issues his warning that if they judge others they will have the same done to them: "so that you may not be judged." God is the ultimate judge. This is reminiscent of Matt 7:1-2: "Do not judge, so that you may not be judged. For with the judgment you make you will be judged, and the measure you give will be the measure you get."

The judge is standing at the doors! In some New Testament traditions Jesus does exercise the role of judge at the end of time (e.g., the parable of the judgment of the nations [Matt 25:31-46]). While the judge in James's context of the *parousia* may probably be Christ (Davids [1982] 185; Martin 192), I agree with Laws ([1980] 213) that one should rather see the judge as God, in line with James's statement in 4:12 that "there is one Lawgiver and Judge. . . ." While James does not elaborate his eschatological expectations in detail, it does seem that his vision embraces two elements: the coming of Christ and the judgment of God. The expression *pro tōn thyrōn* (literally "before the doors") is translated here as "at the doors." This is a traditional phrase that Mark's gospel used in an eschatological context: "So also, when you see these things taking place, you know that he is near, at the very gates *(hoti engys estin epi thyrais)*" (Mark 13:29). Matthew 24:33 repeats these words verbatim. While the English translation gives the verb the pronoun "he," implying Jesus, the Greek text is ambiguous: it could be "he" or "it." Notable too is the fact that Luke reproduces the Markan text in this way: "So also, when you see these things taking place, you know that *the kingdom of God is near*" (Luke 21:31). All this indicates a fluctuation in the eschatological details of the coming Day of the Lord.

10. *As an example of suffering and patience . . . take the prophets:* The phrase *hypodeigma labete* is literally "take as an example." Although the letter of James has provided numerous examples in the course of its moral exhortations, this is

the only occasion when the letter uses this noun *hypodeigma* ("example"). This word can refer either to a *positive example* (e.g., "Enoch pleased the Lord and was taken up, an example *[hypodeigma]* of repentance to all generations" [Sir 44:16]; see also 2 Macc 6:28; John 13:15), or to a *negative example* (e.g., "Therefore, let us strive to enter into that rest, so that no one may fall after the same example *[hypodeigmati]* of disobedience" [Heb 4:11 NAB]; 2 Pet 2:6). James provides two positive examples in both this and the following verses, namely the prophets and Job. The two nouns "suffering and patience" create a type of hendiadys and are properly understood as "patience in hardship" (Ropes 298). The New Testament shows an awareness of a developing tradition about the martyrdom of the prophets (e.g., Matt 5:12; Luke 6:22-23; 11:49-51; Acts 7:52; 1 Thess 2:15). In the Hebrew Scriptures the only prophet to be martyred was Zechariah the son of Jehoiada (2 Chron 24:20-22). However, in the inter-testamental literature there are many accounts of the death of prophets, for example in the *Ascension of Isaiah.* Still, James makes no reference to the death of the prophets. He is interested in the hardships they endured with patience. The word *kakopathia* ("suffering") is a *hapax legomenon* in the New Testament and reflects the aspect of passive suffering (Johnson [1995] 318). The second word, *makrothymias,* on the other hand is more dynamic: it captures their active endurance or patience. The stress in James's example is not on the prophets' suffering but rather on their patient endurance.

spoke in the name of the Lord: This is a biblical idiom used to indicate that the prophets act and speak through God's power or inspiration. The life of Jeremiah is a good illustration of this suffering in the Lord's service (see Jer 20:7-9). James implies that the suffering of the prophets arose from their fidelity in carrying out the Lord's message. The life and message of the prophets are at the service of the Lord. In their life and suffering they demonstrate that they truly are examples of patience (Laws [1980] 214).

11. *Look! We call blessed those who showed endurance:* The use of the particle *idou* ("look") again draws attention to what follows. The verb *makarizein* introduces a beatitude in which those who endure are considered "blessed," endowed by God the creator with every blessing on their lives (see 1:12 for the first beatitude to be introduced in James). It is possible that James is quoting some well-known saying. The theme of endurance continues with James using another series of words: *hypomeinantas tēn hypomonēn* ("who showed endurance . . . endurance"). These words capture the nuance of enduring passively what happens in distinction from the other series of words, *makrothymein/makrothymia,* which expresses the nuance of an active endurance. The concept of blessedness for those who have remained steadfast in the time of persecution is found in most of the traditions of the New Testament.

You have heard of the endurance of Job: This is the second example James provides to illustrate the principle of endurance with patience. Many commentators on the letter of James have noted that in the biblical picture Job hardly appears as someone who endures patiently. For the letter of James, however, Job is the example *par excellence* of the faithful believer showing the endurance of his faith under testing. The concept of the patience of Job developed in the intertestamental period, and James developed his thought out of these newer traditions. One of the more important intertestamental books that shows affinity with the letter of James is the *Testament of Job*. For example, the word *hypomonē* and related terms and forms appear frequently in *T. Job* (see, e.g., 4:5-6; 27:3-7). Job is celebrated from the outset as the one who expresses the virtue of patience (e.g., "I am your father Job, fully engaged in endurance *[hypomenē]* . . ." [1:5]). James 5:11 contains the only reference to Job in the New Testament, and the focus is on his patience as it is in *T. Job*. Having quoted the example of Job's patience, James now adds the phrase *to telos kyriou eidete* ("you have seen the outcome accomplished by the Lord" [5:11]). While commentators interpret *telos* in many ways, "the end" to which James refers embraces Job's restoration by God. It is, as Ropes describes it, "the conclusion wrought by the Lord to his troubles" (299). James refers to God's intervention in Job's life by restoring him to health and wealth.

the Lord is compassionate and merciful: James presents the reason for their hope: the concept they have of God that is stamped by God's compassion and mercy. The adjective *polysplagchnos* ("compassionate") is a *hapax legomenon* in the New Testament. Its usage continues in later church writers (e.g., Herm. *Mand.* 4:3, 5). It is possible that James was the one who introduced this word into the language of the early church. The description of God as *oiktirmōn* ("merciful") has deep roots within the Hebrew Scriptures and is basic to the Hebrew reflection on God (e.g., "The Lord is merciful and gracious *[oiktirmōn kai eleēmōn ho kyrios]*, slow to anger and abounding in steadfast love" [Ps 103:8 {102:8 LXX}]; see also Ps 111:4 [110:4 LXX]; Exod 34:6). *Oiktirmōn* occurs elsewhere in the New Testament only at Luke 6:36.

INTERPRETATION

James 5:7-20:
a Suitable Conclusion to the Letter of James

One of the strongest reasons scholars have used to reject James's epistolary nature is the form of its conclusion (e.g., Mitton, who argues that "the epistolary convention is observed only in the opening verse, and is not even followed up in the conclusion. Certainly there is nothing in the body of the writing to make it sound like a real letter. It is rather a book [or pamphlet] of precise Christian instruction . . ." [238]). James's conclusion is so different from the familiar endings of Paul's letters. The final greetings and blessings (so characteristic of Paul's letters) are missing. However, Francis in his detailed examination of Hellenistic letters has concluded that the omission of a closing formula containing blessings or greetings was a possible option:

> To begin with, attention must be called to the fact that many Hellenistic letters, both private (*P. Tebt.* 34, I BC) and public (*P. Tebt.* 29, II BC), both

secondary (*Ant.* VIII, 50-54; 1 Macc 10.25ff.) and primary (*P. Tebt.* 34), both early (*P. Tebt.* 29) and late (*P. Oxy.* 1071, V AD)—many Hellenistic letters of all types have no closing formulas whatsoever; they just stop. . . . This does occur in other letters with a double opening statement (*Ant.* VIII, 50-54; 1 Macc 10.25ff.) (125).

An examination of 1 Macc 10:25-45, to which Francis points, clearly shows similarities to the letter of James. Both letters begin with a brief identification of their author, readers, and greetings. Cf. James 1:1: "James . . . to the Twelve Tribes in the Dispersion: Greetings"; 1 Macc 10:25: "King Demetrius to the nation of the Jews, greetings." After listing the immunities and gifts he, the king, is willing to bestow on the Jews, he brings the letter to an abrupt end: "And let the cost of rebuilding the walls of Jerusalem and fortifying it all around, and the cost of rebuilding the walls in Judea, also be paid from the revenues of the king" (1 Macc 10:45).

The letter of James does not use the customary Pauline blessings and greetings; nevertheless, an examination of 5:7-20 shows that this passage does constitute a suitable ending to the letter. These final thirteen verses contain four brief paragraphs. Each in its own way brings together themes that were important throughout the letter and so draws it to a conclusion.

James 5:7-11 issues a call to patient endurance as the author provides the hearers/readers with a reminder of their hope in the "coming of the Lord." Eschatological themes are also observable in the endings of other New Testament letters (e.g., 1 Cor 16:22; 1 Thess 5:23; 1 Pet 5:10-11; 2 Pet 3:12-14; Jude 18-21 [see Francis 124 n. 47]). Within this context of eschatological hope in the Lord's return, the letter of James has taken up a theme introduced at the beginning, namely a call to patient endurance (1:2-4, 12). In a sense this theme of patient endurance operates in the manner of an *inclusio* for the entire letter. All the instructions of the letter are framed within the spirit of patient endurance. This is the characteristic feature that identifies the life of the "twelve tribes in the Dispersion" (1:1).

James 5:12 issues a call to avoid the taking of oaths. A formula that contains some expression of an oath is also found at the conclusion of Hellenistic letters (see Francis 125; Exler 127–32). James introduces this verse with the phrase *pro pantōn* ("above all") as a way of signaling that the letter is drawing to a close (see 1 Pet 4:8). Further, the discussion on the taking of oaths is another dimension of James's frequent consideration of the theme of speech (1:19, 26; 3:1-12; 4:11-12). This discussion culminates with the categorical statement: "Let your 'Yes' be yes, and your 'No' be no . . ." (5:12).

James 5:13-18 deals with the topic of prayer, while the final verses (5:19-20) treat the theme of bringing back a sinner. An examination of 1 John 5:14-21 and Jude 17-25 shows that both writings conclude with a focus on prayer offered to God on behalf of another so that they will turn away from evil. All three letters (James, 1 Peter, Jude) use similar themes at the end. This seems to indicate the use of a common epistolary tradition. Finally, James returns to another theme with which he opened the letter, namely that of prayer (1:5: "But, if any of you is lacking in wisdom, let him ask God . . .").

The final four paragraphs of James's letter (5:7-11, 12, 13-18, 19-20) capture many themes that were developed throughout the writing: patient endurance, speech, eschatology, and prayer. Davids gives a good reflection on the rhetorical effect produced by bringing together some of the major themes: "Thus there is a merging of themes in this summary section and some disjointedness as the redactor pulls materials together, yet there is a real sense of unity with the rest of the book as themes are resumed and brought into dynamic relationship with one another" ([1982] 181).

James 5:7-11:
Introducing the Conclusion

One of the functions of this paragraph is to connect the conclusion to the body of the letter. The particle *oun* ("then, therefore") establishes the connection by bringing to a conclusion what has been said not only in the preceding section (4:13–5:6), but also in the letter itself. James 5:7-11 continues the eschatological dimension introduced in 5:1-6. Attention was given to the judgment that was to befall the rich because of their friendship with the world and their treatment of the poor. Turning from offering a harsh judgment, James gives hope to his hearers/readers for the bestowal of God's blessings on those who endure patiently until the coming of the Lord.

James 5:7-11 calls the hearers/readers to a life of confident, patient endurance. Following the tradition of the prophets, the previous paragraph (5:1-6) had focused on God's punishment of those rich who had exploited the poor: "Weep and wail for the miseries that are coming upon you!" (5:1). In line with this prophetic voice, 5:1-6 also gives expression to the theme of divine retribution (Martin 196). The tone changes with 5:7-11 to offer positive hope and consolation to the community when faced with oppression. The address "brothers (and sisters)" that occurs on three occasions in this short section accomplishes this change of tone from a tirade against the rich to an exhortation and offer of hope for the community. In particular James advises them on the fundamental attitude they should adopt when faced with oppression from the rich and the onslaughts of the world. The attitude is one of patient endurance.

James's choice of words is significant. To capture the concept of patient endurance in this paragraph and throughout the letter he has used two separate word groups: *makrothymein/makrothymia* and *hypomenein/hypomonē*.

As the Notes have shown, James used the word group *makrothymein/ makrothymia* on four occasions in this short paragraph (5:7[2x], 8, 10) and the combination of *hypomenein/hypomonē* twice in 5:11. Johnson ([1995] 312–13) insightfully draws attention to a nuance in meaning between these synonyms. The distinction lies in the realms of activity and passivity. The word group *makrothymein/makrothymia* reflects the patience God adopts toward humanity in the sense of a superior toward an inferior, in which the superior God actively accepts or "puts up with" humanity's behavior (Johnson [1995] 313). Mayor offers the translation "long-tempered" in distinction to "quick-tempered" (161). The concept of *makrothymia* is undoubtedly the main theme of 5:7-11 (see *TDNT* 4:385). James challenges his community to imitate God by actively adopting a positive attitude of patience as they await the *parousia*, the coming of the Lord.

In contrast, the series *hypomenein/hypomonē* (v. 11) captures the nuance of passively enduring something. The difference in nuance expressed by these two word groups becomes clearer when one looks at the context in which the endurance occurs. The group *hypomenein/hypomonē* is used within the context of facing struggles, opposition, and persecution that come from the world. As Hauck expresses it: "James is also directed to Christians under affliction, and it has a sharp exhortation to steadfast endurance both at the beginning and at the end. . . . Job is the great example of this perseverance under affliction (5:11, cf. Job 1:21f.)" (*TDNT* 4:588). On the other hand, the group *makrothymein/makrothymia* has as its context the expectation of the *parousia* or coming of the Lord. In light of James's conviction that the Lord is to return soon, the virtue he desires to inculcate within the lives of the faithful is active endurance. One looks forward dynamically to the coming of the Lord. Horst expresses this understanding of *makrothymia* extremely well:

> Under the constraint of having to suffer unjustly, *makrothymia* comes to be orientated to perseverance, to expectation of the *parousia, makrothymēsate heōs tēs parousias*, v. 7, cf. v. 8. In connection with *kakopatheia*, (endurance of) affliction and *hypomonē*, persistence, it comes to suggest a triumphant steadfastness which does not come from the heroic depths of one's own heart but from certainty of the proximity of the *parousia* (*TDNT* 4:385).

In the opening of this letter James had urged his hearers/readers toward a spirit of heroic endurance *(hypomonē)* in the face of afflictions that tested their faith (1:3-4). The same exhortation to heroic endurance occurs throughout the letter (1:12; 4:6-10). At the end, then, James creates an inclusion by returning to this theme. Not only is one called to heroic endurance amidst the afflictions that befall one (5:11), but one must actively look forward to and embrace *(makrothymein/makrothymia)* the coming of the Lord that is imminent (5:7-10). This certainty in the coming of the Lord gives rise to patient endurance. The ability to endure comes from two sources. The first of these is one's faith, namely the way one looks at the world. Using the comparison of the farmer, James shows that the tiller of the soil demonstrates a patient endurance that stems from a faith conviction that God is the one who sends the rain and God will come through. This gives the farmer an ability to face the present moment and its attendant difficulties with the assurance that God is in control of nature. On the other hand, the ability to endure also stems from the certainty Christians have in the coming of the *parousia.* It provides a dimension of confident expectation in the future. There is hope that in the not too distant future Jesus will return to give the crown of life (1:12) to those who have endured patiently.

James's reference to the early and the late rain (5:7) has raised the question whether he was personally familiar with the land of Syria and Palestine. The early rain *(proimos* [the standard spelling is *prōimos,* BDAG 870]) usually begins in October to November. For the farmer this early rain is essential for the seed to germinate. The late rain *(opsimos)* of April to May is essential for the maturation of the harvest. If either of these were to fail, the crops would be lost despite good winter rains. This expression occurs in the LXX in Deut 11:14; Jer 5:24; Hos 6:3; Joel 2:23; Zech 10:1. Some scholars suggest that James is reliant on these textual witnesses for the expression and that it does not necessarily mean he has an intimate knowledge of the climate of Palestine-Syria (see, e.g., Laws [1980] 211–12). Dibelius (243–44) argues that since the image appears in Deut 11:14 as part of the *Shema Israel* recited in the synagogue, James's knowledge would derive from its liturgical usage. However, there are a number of reasons that support the view that James's knowledge here is based on personal awareness of the climate of Syria-Palestine. First of all, the expression *proimon kai opsimon* is somewhat ambiguous. The omission of the noun "rain" conforms to James's style rather than to his use of a textual source or quotation. Further, James's style in this passage demonstrates a vividness and familiarity that derives from a personal knowledge of the scene, as Ropes argues convincingly: "To suppose that to him and his readers this was a mere Biblical allusion to a situation of which they knew only by literary study would give a formal stiffness and unreality to the passage wholly out of keeping with the intensity and sincerity of the writer's appeal" (296). The way James refers to the climate presumes his hearers/readers were also familiar with this allusion. That later readers of the text were unfamiliar with his references is evident from the way in which copyists added a noun to the text in order to give it clarity: e.g., the noun "rain" *(hyeton)* was added by some texts (such as Codex Alexandrinus) to explain the meaning for the readers. On the other hand, in texts emanating from Egypt (such as Codex Sinaiticus), copyists unfamiliar with the climate of Palestine added the noun "crop" *(karpon)*. This produced a reading "he (the farmer) receives the early and late harvest" (see Metzger [1975] 685; Aland [1997] 88).

James 5:7-11 in the Context of James's Eschatological Expectations

The call to patient endurance in 5:7-11 occurs within the context of an eschatological worldview. This same connection between the eschatological hope and heroic endurance is evident at the opening of the letter. The joy expressed so clearly in 1:2, 12, is founded on eschatological hope: "Blessed is the person who endures testing, because such a person, having stood the test, will receive the crown of life. . . ." The joy is an "anticipated joy" *("eschatologische Vorfreude")* as Johannes Thomas (183–206) expresses it: a joy that permeates all tribulation because of the end one foresees and in which one hopes. In this way James situates his letter within an eschatological framework that operates as an *inclusio* embracing the whole letter within this eschatological context. In fact, one can say that eschatology provides both the context and the horizon for all James's admonitions (Davids [1982] 39).

James's opening immediately invoked an eschatological worldview by identifying his hearers/readers as the "twelve tribes in the Dispersion" (1:1). James presumes they share his worldview, as he does not feel the need to explain his eschatology; he presupposes it. As indicated in the discussion of 1:1, the letter sees the Christian-Jewish audience as the beginning of a restoration of the people of Israel that brings to fulfillment the centuries-old hope for a reconstituted nation. In fact, the beginning of the end-time now takes place in this Christian-Jewish community, the new twelve-tribe people. James employs creation imagery to give expression to the rebirth of this twelve-tribe kingdom God has inaugurated. They are also "the first fruits of his (God's) creatures" (1:18). God's creative activity begins with this Christian-Jewish community, but it does not end there. It is intended to continue. The "first fruits" demand that there will be others who will come afterward. Again this operates within an eschatological worldview in which all things will be brought to fulfillment. Creation imagery is used in the service of eschatology. In this sense the present is viewed as the beginning of the end-time. The letter's opening has established this as the horizon in which all the ethical admonitions within the letter operate. One's moral life is informed by the eschatological horizon in which one lives.

Not only is the present the beginning of the end-time; it also operates as a preparation for it. The clearest expression of James's eschatological vision is found in 5:7-11. Fundamental to this vision is the belief that the coming of the Lord is near (5:8) and that the judge is standing at the doors (5:9). James sees that believers are situated at the end of time and the response they should make is one of perseverance amid the onslaughts of evil to be faced. The previous paragraph (5:1-6) had paid attention to the judgment the rich will experience because of their behavior. Their unjust actions and their treatment of those who worked for them will reverberate to their judgment: "You have fattened your hearts for a day of slaughter" (5:5).

Although James uses apocalyptic imagery in these descriptions, he does not develop the images. It is rather a matter of speaking in a way his audience would understand to be part of their shared horizon and thought world. James does not resort to apocalyptic speculations in the manner of the book of Revelation or the apocalyptic passages in the synoptic gospels. Instead, he uses apocalyptic language to challenge his hearers/ readers to use the present to prepare for the future.

For James the "coming of the Lord" ushers in both judgment and salvation. Judgment is envisaged especially for the rich who have exploited the poor (5:4). Salvation is especially for the poor and those who have endured to the end (5:7-11). This positive and negative dimension runs throughout the letter. The theme of judgment first emerges in 1:11, where James envisages the rich wasting away in the midst of their activities. On the other hand, in 1:12 the theme of salvation is introduced with the promise of the "crown of life" being offered to those who have endured the testing. Finally, James promises to those who are ill the eschatological gift of the forgiveness of sins (5:15). "In effect, the Epistle of James shows that the whole life of the believer is orientated towards a future with an eschatological end resulting in either salvation (life) or judgment (condemnation)" (Hartin [1996b] 493).

In the letter of James the eschatological dimension acts as the motivation behind all the wisdom admonitions. This motivation envisages either judgment or salvation. On the negative side the possibility of judgment operates as a caution for his hearers/readers: "Let not many of you become teachers . . . since you know that we will receive a more severe judgment" (3:1). Since God alone is the judge, believers should not usurp God's position and authority by judging one another (4:12). On the positive side James holds out many prospects for salvation for believers:

- The crown of life is promised to those who endure testing (1:12).

- Those who persevere will be blessed in all they do (1:25).

- Those who are poor in the world will be heirs of the kingdom (2:5).

- Those who endure will be blessed: "We call blessed those who showed endurance" (5:11).

- Those who bring back a sinner "will save the sinner's soul from death and will cover a multitude of sins" (5:20).

Eschatology is an essential feature of this letter. It is the very air James and his hearers/readers inhale. Because they share this same worldview and imagination, James takes it for granted and does not find it necessary to explain his vision. James tends to reinterpret the apocalyptic imagination to conform to his experience of the present. Two reasons help to account for this apocalyptic reinterpretation (Hartin [1996b] 494). First of all, James is convinced that he and his community are living in the end-time. Since the traditional experience of the signs of the end-time is lacking, James reinterprets the sufferings of the present as signs of this end-time: e.g., Jas 1:27 uses the term *thlipsis* ("affliction"), the technical apocalyptic word for the tribulations that mark the eschatological age, to describe the sufferings of widows and orphans. As Laws notes:

> . . . elsewhere in the NT the noun *thlipsis* has almost the status of a technical term for the sufferings that precede the End, the 'Messianic Woes,' e.g. Mk xiii.19; 2 Thess i.4; Rev. ii.22; cf. Dan xii.1; Hermas, *Vis.* ii.2.7. In Col. i.24 Paul seems to see his own sufferings as contributing to the *thlipseis tou Christou*, the 'Messiah's affliction' which his people must bear ([1980] 89; see also *TDNT* 3:139–48).

For James the sufferings widows and orphans endure are indeed signs of the afflictions of the end-time. At the same time the sufferings ordinary believers undergo are also signs of the imminence of the end-time: "My brothers (and sisters) consider it nothing but an occasion of joy whenever you encounter various trials" (1:2).

A second reason why James distances himself from the traditional apocalyptic descriptions of destruction and fear stems from his view of the future. James engenders in his hearers/readers feelings of joy and hope rather than fear and trepidation. His wisdom advice aims at encouraging his hearers/readers to endure with the expectation that "our glorious Lord Jesus Christ" (2:1) will give "the crown of life" (1:12) to those who have remained faithful.

The *Epistle of Enoch* (92–105), as has already been observed (see 5:1-6), bears a number of similarities to the letter of James (see Hartin [1996b] 495–98). A brief comparison between the Letter of James and *1 Enoch* 92–

105 helps us understand the nature of the letter of James and its eschatological vision.

One of the closest parallels between the letter of James and *1 Enoch* 92–105 is that both writings are presented in epistolary form. Chapter 92 of *1 Enoch* identifies the writer with the ancient patriarch Enoch (Gen 5:18-24) "(Book) five, which is written by Enoch, the writer of all the signs of wisdom among all the people . . ." (*1 En.* 92:1 [*OTP* 1:73]). The community to whom it is addressed is viewed as the spiritual offspring of the faithful Enoch: "(It is written) for all the offspring that dwell upon the earth, and for the latter generations which uphold uprightness and peace" (92:1 [*OTP* 1:73]).

James's task is similar. The letter of James is also written by the "patriarch" James to the spiritual heirs of the people of Israel ("the twelve tribes in the Dispersion") to teach and provide his hearers/readers with guidance for their lives. He sees his community as the fulfillment of God's promises in the past and of Israel's hopes in the present.

Another major similarity between James and *1 En.* 92–105 is that both use similar literary forms to express their thought. First of all, they both utilize *the form of the woe:* "Woe unto those who build oppression and injustice! Who lay foundations for deceit. They shall soon be demolished; and they shall have no peace" (*1 En.* 94:6 [*OTP* 1:75]). This literary form is scattered frequently throughout these chapters of *1 Enoch.* The letter of James contains two woes directed against merchants and the rich, 4:13-17 and 5:1-6: "Come now, you who say. . . . Come now, you rich!" James's concern lies with the poor and in particular the way the rich oppress them. Divine judgment awaits them in the future. The author of *1 Enoch* also champions the cause of the poor and criticizes the rich for oppressing them: "Woe unto you, O rich people! For you have put your trust in your wealth. You shall ooze out of your riches, for you do not remember the Most High. In the days of your affluence, you committed oppression, you have become ready for death, and for the day of darkness and the day of great judgment" (*1 En.* 94:8-9 [*OTP* 1:75]).

Second, James and *1 Enoch* 92–105 contain a series of admonitions or exhortations to the hearers/readers to remain faithful. As we have indicated, the theme of perseverance is an important one for the letter as a whole, and more especially for Jas 5:7-11. Similarly, *1 Enoch* 92–105 exhorts the hearers/readers to continue to walk the path of righteousness: "Now, my children, I say to you: Love righteousness and walk therein! For the ways of righteousness are worthy of being embraced; (but) the ways of wickedness shall soon perish and diminish" (*1 En.* 94:1 [*OTP* 1:75]).

These similarities should not be overstressed. One major difference between the letter of James and *1 Enoch* 92–105 is the focus Enoch places

on the revelation of the future. Nickelsburg describes the genre of *1 Enoch*
92–105 in this way:

> Wherein does Enoch 92–105 cohere? How does the author perceive
> reality, and indeed his writing, within that context? I should express the
> message pervading the whole of these chapters as follows: The revela-
> tion of God's unseen world and future paradoxically calls the oppressed
> community to faith, courage, and joy in the present. The centrality of
> revelation to these chapters makes the adjective 'apocalyptic' altogether
> appropriate as a description of the author's message ([1977] 326).

In contrast, James focuses on the present rather than the future and offers no revelation or descriptions of future judgment. While James clearly
teaches that judgment will occur, he does not enter into a description of
that future judgment. This aspect of "revelatory literature" separates
James from the apocalyptic genre. John J. Collins has provided a definition for the genre of apocalypse that has become standard:

> (A)n apocalypse is defined as: a genre of revelatory literature with a nar-
> rative framework, in which a revelation is mediated by an otherworldly
> being to a human recipient, disclosing a transcendent reality which is
> both temporal, insofar as it envisages eschatological salvation, and spa-
> tial insofar as it involves another, supernatural world (1992 [1984] 4).

An application of this definition to the letter of James shows that this
writing lacks almost all the distinguishing features of the apocalyptic
genre. Fundamentally, the letter is not revelatory literature in that it
contains no narrative framework and no revelation is given by means of a
supernatural being. James's message is not constructed through the
medium of visions, dreams, or revelations coming from some supernatural, angelic, or heavenly being. Finally, the focus is not with the future
but with the present of which the future is an imminent outgrowth. While
the letter of James maintains a clear belief in the "coming of the Lord," it
provides no graphic description of that coming, or any description of the
judgment it will entail, or of the future world that will be established as a
result of that coming. Undoubtedly James's community is aware of this
vision and its details. While the letter presumes this worldview, it provides no speculation about the details of the "coming of the Lord." The
only point it makes is that it is a Day of Judgment. James's concern is more
with the present and how to live in expectation of that imminent end. For
this reason James's paraenetic advice gives attention to the role faith plays
in one's life: faith must be put into action. Faith in action is exemplified
above all in the relationship between rich and poor. The "faith of our

glorious Lord Jesus Christ" (2:1) demands the avoidance of every aspect of favoritism. All people are to be treated equally because they have been created in God's likeness (3:9). The law of love, "the royal Law" (2:8), becomes the defining feature of this community of "the twelve tribes in the Dispersion."

This comparison with *1 Enoch* 92–105 sheds light on the function and nature of the letter of James. While the letter does not belong to the apocalyptic genre, it certainly contains eschatological features belonging to a worldview shared with *1 Enoch*, James's community, and society at large. The eschatological outlook provides James with the horizon within which his ethical admonitions operate. The final coming of the Lord will bestow judgment and salvation on all (5:1-6, 7-11). The eschaton is the horizon and goal in which faith is put into action.

James 5:7-11 sets the tone for the concluding paragraphs of the letter. Having called the hearers/readers to perseverance and an expectation of the Lord's imminent coming for salvation and judgment, James concludes with a call to ensure that speech conforms to one's intentions (5:12). It reflects the call to avoid double-mindedness: one cannot serve both God and the world. Further, one is called to pray and to entrust one's life to God's direction (5:13-18). Faced with the imminence of Christ's return, every believer should be solicitous about the spiritual welfare of his or her neighbor (5:19-20).

Two Examples: the Prophets (5:10) and Job (5:11)

To illustrate a life that embraces endurance with patience James refers to two examples: the prophets (5:10) and the person of Job (5:11). While *the example of the prophets* refers to their "suffering and patience," it is actually their "patience in hardship" (Ropes 298) that is stressed. For James the focus rests on their patient endurance in the midst of trials and difficulties. A frequent question raised by commentators is: "why is there no reference to the suffering and death of Jesus in this context?" For a Christian author Jesus would be the obvious example of someone who endured suffering and death patiently. In fact, both the authors of 1 Peter (2:21-23) and Hebrews (11:1–12:2) turn to the example of Jesus' suffering to illustrate their teaching. For this reason some thinkers such as Augustine and Bede interpreted the phrase *to telos kyriou* (5:11; "the outcome accomplished by the Lord"; literally "the end of the Lord") to refer to Jesus' death. However, it would seem strange for James to refer to the death of Jesus in such an indirect way. Mayor comments on such an interpretation: "If *telos* is supposed to refer to the Resurrection and Ascension, the main point of the comparison (suffering) is omitted; if it refers to the Crucifixion, the encouragement is wanting" (164). The question why James did not refer to Jesus is in fact misleading. The picture of Jesus that James has drawn in the brief references to him in this letter is that he is "the glorious Lord Jesus Christ" (2:1). This points to his resurrection and second coming (5:8). The role of Jesus in his triumph, in his resurrection, and in his return is what James has in mind (see Laws [1980] 218). In the final analysis the answer is obvious: James is using traditional imagery and examples. The image of Job in this letter emerges from traditional interpretations of the person of Job handed on through the centuries in the context of the world of Judaism. The letter relies on these traditions to support James's argument relating to "patience in hardship." As Laws says: "What we have evidence for is not a rejection of the example of Jesus, but a use of the example of Job; and that in itself is perfectly understandable" ([1980] 218). Dibelius has also drawn attention to James's reliance on traditional Jewish material here. The lack of reference to Jesus and his death is nothing sinister. Instead, James simply repeats the traditions he embraces "without using the example of Jesus. The rigidity of the tradition itself was partly responsible for this" (Dibelius 247).

The example of Job is also intriguing. As the Notes have indicated, the biblical picture of Job is hardly that of a patient person (see also Cantinat 239). He cries out about his innocence and demands from God to be heard and to find the reason for his reversal of fortune and sufferings. The picture of Job as a man of patience developed in the course of the intertestamental period. The letter of James is clearly reflecting this intertestamental picture. There is further evidence to show that the intertestamental picture of Job resonates with the picture James wishes to invoke for the faithful believer. In the *Testament of Job* there is frequent use of the vocabulary of patience *(hypomonē: T. Job* 1:5; 4:6; 27:6-7). Characteristic of Job's life was a real concern for the poor and outcasts of society (*T. Job* 9-15). The testing of Job is seen to emanate from the hand of Satan. Faced with suffering, Job persevered and was ultimately rewarded by God. The letter of James draws on this picture of Job and calls its hearers/readers to a similar perseverance and patience in the midst of trials and sufferings.

In the wake of the example of Job, *to telos kyriou eidete* ("you have seen the outcome accomplished by the Lord") points to be the outcome God intended through the restoration granted to Job. James shows that endurance is not an end in itself, but is the path to the fulfillment of God's plans and one's hopes. The outcome of Job's endurance was the reward God gave Job by restoring his life and former fortunes because he had remained faithful. The implication for the hearers/readers is clear: they too can hope for an intervention of God in their lives at the end if they endure. In particular the coming of the Lord will bring salvation and blessedness for those who have endured the test (5:11), for to them will be given "the crown of life" (1:12). James encourages his hearers/readers by reminding them that the God in whom they trust is a God who is "compassionate and merciful" (5:11). There is nothing to fear if one endures to the end.

For Reference and Further Study

Collins, John J. *The Apocalyptic Imagination.* New York: Crossroad, 1984.
Doty, Williams G. *Letters in Primitive Christianity.* Philadelphia: Fortress, 1973.
Fine, Hillel A. "The Tradition of a Patient Job," *JBL* 74 (1955) 28–32.
Gordon, Robert P. *"kai to telos kyriou eidete* (Js 5,11)," *JTS* 26 (1975) 91–95.
Haas, Cees. "Job's Perseverance in the Testament of Job," in M. A. Knibb and P. W. van der Horst, eds., *Studies on the Testament of Job.* SNTSMS 66. Cambridge: Cambridge University Press, 1989, 117–54.
Harder, Günther. *"stērizō," TDNT* 7:653–57.
Hauck, Friedrich. *"hypomenō, hypomonē," TDNT* 4:581–88.
Horst, Johannes. *"makrothymia," TDNT* 4:374–87.
Nickelsburg, George W. E. "The Apocalyptic Construction of Reality in 1 Enoch," in John J. Collins and James H. Charlesworth, eds., *Mysteries and Revelations: Apocalyptic Studies since the Uppsala Colloquium.* JSPSup 9. Sheffield: Sheffield Academic Press, 1991, 51–64.
_____. "The Apocalyptic Message of 1 Enoch 92–105," *CBQ* 39 (1977) 309–28.
Oepke, Albrecht. *"parousia, pareimi," TDNT* 5:858–71.
Schlier, Heinrich. *"thlibō, thlipsis," TDNT* 3:139–48.
Thomas, Johannes. "Anfechtung und Vorfreude," *KD* 14 (1968) 183–206.

11. *Call to Avoid Taking Oaths* (5:12)

12. Finally, my brothers (and sisters), do not take oaths, either by heaven, or by earth, or any other oath. But let your "Yes" be yes, and your "No" be no, so that you may not fall under judgment.

Notes

12. *Finally, my brothers (and sisters):* The Greek phrase *pro pantōn* ("above all") indicates that what follows is connected to what precedes (see Moule 74; 1 Pet 4:8). But the question arises: To what exactly is it connected? Is it a reference to 5:7-11, or to a theme or topic that had been developed throughout the letter? Bo Reicke (56) argues for seeing a connection with what directly precedes. The taking of oaths shows an urgency to rectify a situation. In the context of 5:1-11 James would be calling on the poor for patient endurance. Douglas Moo (173), on the other hand, considers such attempts to connect to the preceding verses

"artificial." Instead one should see the phrase *pro pantōn* as bringing the argument of the letter to a conclusion. F. X. J. Exler (114) has demonstrated that *pro pantōn* was an expression found in the closing of some Hellenistic letters. He showed further that the formula of an oath was also characteristic of some Hellenistic letters (127–32). Although James does not adhere to the structure of the Pauline letter, he does show a certain awareness of other forms of the ending of Hellenistic letters. Perhaps the translation "finally" would capture the meaning of *pro pantōn* better. In this way James turns attention to a major theme that has run throughout the letter, namely the misuse of speech. The phrase, then, draws attention to the end of the letter (Francis 125; Laws [1980] 220). Once again the address *adelphoi mou* ("my brothers [and sisters]") is a further marker that a new section is being introduced.

do not take oaths, either by heaven, or by earth, or any other oath: the verb *omnyein* is a form of *omnynai* that is common in Hellenistic Greek. BDAG defines its meaning as: "to affirm the veracity of one's statement by invoking a transcendent entity, frequently with implied invitation of punishment if one is untruthful, swear, take an oath with the accusative of person or thing by which one swears" (705). This command not to take oaths must be read against the background of the Jewish understanding of the practice. On the one hand the Hebrew tradition readily upheld the taking of oaths. For example, Deut 6:13 instructs the people to swear by the name of God: "The LORD your God you shall fear; him you shall serve, and by his name alone you shall swear." See also Ps 63:11: "But the king shall rejoice in God; all who swear by him shall exult"; Isa 65:16: "Then whoever invokes a blessing in the land shall bless by the God of faithfulness, and whoever takes an oath in the land shall swear by the God of faithfulness"; Jer 12:16: "And then, if they will diligently learn the ways of my people, to swear by my name, 'As the LORD lives'. . . ." The practice of the prophets is to swear by God to the truth of what they say: "Now Elijah the Tishbite, of Tishbe in Gilead, said to Ahab, '*As the* LORD *the God of Israel lives,* before whom I stand, there shall be neither dew nor rain these years, except by my word" (1 Kgs 17:1). "But Micaiah said, '*As the* LORD *lives,* whatever the LORD says to me, that I will speak'" (1 Kgs 22:14). Even God is seen to take an oath by God's own self: "*By myself I have sworn,* says the LORD: Because you have done this, and have not withheld your son, your only son" (Gen 22:16). The letter to the Hebrews continues this tradition: "Human beings, of course, swear by someone greater than themselves, and an oath given as confirmation puts an end to all disputes. In the same way, when God desired to show even more clearly to the heirs of the promise the unchangeable character of his purpose, *he guaranteed it by an oath*" (Heb 6:16-17; see also 7:21). On the other hand, there is a tradition that shows a certain hesitancy toward the taking of oaths in the Jewish tradition and an increasing decline in the practice (see *TDNT* 5:461): e.g., "Listen, my children, to instruction concerning the mouth. . . . Do not accustom your mouth to oaths, nor habitually utter the name of the Holy One . . . so also the person who always swears and utters the Name will never be cleansed from sin. The one who swears many oaths is full of iniquity and the scourge will not leave his house. If he swears in error, his sin remains on him, and if he disregards it, he sins doubly; if he swears a false oath, he will not be justified, for his house will be filled with calamities" (Sir 23:7-11). Blaspheming God was understood to be the cursing of God or the blaming of God for one's tragedies: "Anyone who curses God shall bear the sin. One who blasphemes the name of the LORD shall be put to death; the whole congregation shall stone the blasphemer" (Lev 24:15-16). Concern for misusing the name of God in this way led to a variety of ways of taking an oath that avoided the use of God's name: e.g., Philo says: "However, if a man must swear and is so inclined, let him add, if he pleases, not indeed the highest name of all, and the most important cause of all things, but the earth, the sun, the stars, the heaven, the universal world . . ." (*Spec.* 2:5; see also 2:2-38). See also Philo in *Decal.*: "Next to not swearing at all, the second best thing is to keep one's oath; for by the mere fact of swearing at all, the swearer shows that there is some suspicion of his not being trustworthy. Let a man, therefore, be dilatory, and slow if there is any chance that by delay he may be able to avoid the necessity of taking an oath at all; but if necessity compels him to swear, then, he must consider with no superficial attention, everyone of the subjects, or parts of the subject, before him. . . . For an oath is the calling of God to give his testimony concerning the matters which are in doubt; and it is a most impious thing to invoke God to be witness to a lie" (*Decal.* 84-86). With regard to the Essenes and the community of Qumran the evidence is mixed. Josephus states that the Essenes forbade the taking of oaths: "Any word of theirs has more force than an oath; swearing they avoid, regarding it as worse than perjury, for they say that one who is not believed without an appeal to God stands condemned already" (*B.J.* 2:135 [Thackeray, LCL]; see also *A.J.* 15:370-72). However, he does acknowledge that they took oaths at their initiation into the community: "But, before he may touch the common food, he is made to swear tremendous oaths. . . . He swears, moreover, to transmit their rules exactly as he himself received them . . ." (*B.J.* 2:139-142 [Thackeray, LCL]). This is supported by the evidence from the Rule of the Community: "Whoever enters the council of the Community enters the covenant of God in the presence of all who freely volunteer. He shall swear with a binding oath to revert to the Law of Moses with all that it decrees, with whole heart and whole soul . . ." (1QS 5:7-8; see also CD 9:8-10). In the Greek world a developing hesitation regarding the taking of oaths is also observable, especially among Greek moralists. Diogenes Laertius notes that Pythagoras taught his disciples "not to call the gods to witness, man's duty being rather to strive to make his own word carry conviction" (*Lives of the Philosophers* 8:22 [Hicks, LCL]). Epictetus also taught: "Refuse, if you can, to take an oath at all, but if that is impossible, refuse as far as circumstances allow" (*Ench.* 33:5 [Oldfather, LCL]).

But let your "Yes" be yes, and your "No" be no, so that you may not fall under judgment: Jesus' teaching shows a sharp criticism of the misuse of oaths (Matt 23:16-22; Mark 7:9-13). Without doubt the closest parallel to James's unqualified statement on prohibiting the taking of oaths is the Jesus saying in the Sermon on the Mount (Matt 5:33-37). The closest contact between James and a

Jesus saying is found here in this verse. A comparison of the two accounts is instructive:

Matt 5:34-37 (NRSV)	James 5:12
But I say to you,	Finally, my brothers (and sisters),
Do not swear at all,	*do not take oaths,*
either by heaven, for it is the throne of God,	*either by heaven,*
or by the earth, for it is his footstool,	*or by earth,*
or by Jerusalem, for it is the city of the great King.	or any other oath.
And do not swear by your head, for you cannot make one hair white or black.	
Let your word be "Yes, Yes"	But *let your "Yes" be yes,*
or "No, No";	*and your "No" be no,*
anything more than this comes from the evil one.	so that you may not fall under judgment.

Matthew presents the command not to take oaths as a saying of Jesus within the context of the Sermon on the Mount. James, however, does not identify it as a Jesus saying. This conforms to James's way of expression. While nowhere in the letter does he ever directly quote a saying of Jesus, our examination has demonstrated that his instruction surely uses Jesus' sayings in his own way. The most obvious difference between the two is that Matthew's account contains more examples that are developed in detail than the account in the letter of James. This would point to James's account being the more ancient form. A principle of the development of traditions always looks to the shorter version as being the more primitive. Another difference between the two is that the verbal forms in Matthew's version (5:34, 36) are in the aorist, while in James's version they are in the present. This could perhaps point to different situations within the communities of Matthew and James. Matthew could be warning his hearers/readers against beginning the practice of taking oaths, while James could be warning against a practice that had already started in his communities. Turner explains the difference succinctly: "Somewhat preemptory and categorical, they (aorist imperatives) tend to be ingressive, giving either a command to commence some action or a prohibition against commencing it. On the other hand, present imperatives give a command to do something constantly, to continue to do it; or else a prohibition against its continuance, and interruption of an action already begun" (Moulton et al., 3:74–75). Moreover, the grammar in both versions is significantly different: James's is more classical (he uses the accusative after *omnyein* ["to swear; to take an oath"]) while Matthew has *en* plus the dative, which conforms to the style of the Hellenistic Greek of the New Testament (see also Matt 23:16-22). Matthew attributes the taking of oaths to the influence of the evil one while James says that the taking of oaths leads to condemnation. In effect the meaning of both versions is the same: the taking of oaths is evil and will bring condemnation. The double repetition in both Matthew and James of "Yes, yes and No, no" essentially establishes a connection between thought and speech: Let what you think "yes" be stated as "yes" and what you think "no" be stated as "no" (Mussner [1981] 215–16).

What the differences between Matthew and James indicate is that this saying condemning the taking of oaths circulated in the early church in two forms: Matthew had a longer form while James's short form was expressed in more classical Greek. It is not easy to establish which one is the more original. It is possible that we are dealing with two independent versions of a Jesus saying that was handed on in different forms. Laws ([1980] 223) notes that, given the wide differences in the two forms in Matthew and James, it is feasible that we are dealing with two independent transmissions of this saying. However, these are the only two categorical rejections of the taking of oaths in the entire New Testament. Given the other numerous similarities between James and the Sermon on the Mount, this becomes a further argument for seeing these traditions as dependent in some form on each other rather than as developing totally in isolation (see Hartin [1991] 188–91). An interesting development of this tradition on avoiding the taking of oaths is found in Justin Martyr (*1 Apol.* 16:5) and Clement of Alexandria (*Strom.* 5:99, 1; 7:67, 5) who quote this saying in a form that appears closer to the text of James, although neither of them seems to demonstrate a knowledge of the actual letter of James.

INTERPRETATION

As we indicated above in discussing 5:7-11, this verse (5:12) is the second part of the concluding section, where James takes up themes he has developed throughout the course of his letter. Here James threads the final knot in the golden thread he has woven throughout, namely the theme of the correct use of speech. The use of the phrase *pro pantōn* ("finally") shows that the letter is drawing to a conclusion. At the same time the passage continues the thought of the previous section (5:7-11), where James had called his hearers/readers to patient endurance as they awaited the coming of the Lord and the judge who is standing at the doors (5:8-9). James concludes 5:12 with a reminder: "so that you may not fall under judgment." Simplicity in speech, according to James, is one of the ways to practice endurance in this final time and not fall under God's judgment.

James's teaching on avoiding the taking of oaths falls into the context of his developing theme relating to the misuse of speech. He introduced this theme in 1:19 when he said: "Let every person be quick to hear, slow to speak, slow to anger." In the call to be a doer of the word and not just a hearer (1:22) James drew attention to another concern, namely the avoidance of duplicity: the truthfulness of one's faith must demonstrate itself through actions that conform to that faith. James goes further to connect the misuse of speech with his understanding of religion: "If any think they are religious, and do not bridle their tongues, but deceive their hearts, their religion is worthless" (1:26). Again James is pointing to the duplicity that exists between the tongue and the heart: what one says does not conform to what one thinks or believes. Without doubt the categorical statement James makes in 5:12, "But let your 'Yes' be yes and your 'No' be no," is a reinforcement of what he has said about ensuring that heart and tongue are in harmony.

In 3:1-12 James reflected on the misuse of the tongue, and again its duplicity was illustrated: "With it we bless the Lord and Father, and with it we curse human beings made in God's likeness" (3:9). Finally, James drew attention to speaking evil against another (4:11-12). Such speech betrayed an arrogance whereby one set oneself above both the law and the one lawgiver, God. The consequences of evil speech are horrendous, as they make claims for the individual that deny his or her relationship with God.

Given the importance James has assigned to this theme of the misuse of the tongue throughout this letter, it is appropriate that he draws attention to it once more at the conclusion. As the Notes have indicated, the Jewish tradition to which James is heir shows a twofold concern. In the first place there is the desire to uphold the practice of the taking of oaths as an essential feature of their religion. By the oath the divine is asked to guarantee the truthfulness of human speech. At the same time, thanks to the vicissitudes of human nature, there is always the danger that such formal declarations will become trivialized. It is this second aspect with which James is concerned. He does not reject the taking of oaths in general. I would say he upholds it as part of his Jewish heritage. However, it is the trivialization of the oath to which he gives attention: "Do not take oaths by heaven, or by earth, or any other oath" (5:12). For James simplicity of speech is the goal for which every believer should strive. "Let your 'Yes' be yes, and your 'No' be no" demands that one's thought and speech are in harmony. Truthfulness should be the hallmark of every believer and of every community that claims to follow Jesus. Consequently, there should be no need to invoke divine support for what one says, even in small matters. The presumption should also be that one's thought and speech are in unison. As Mitton says: "The meaning of James, when translated into *our* social customs, is that our mere word should be as utterly trustworthy as a signed document, legally correct and complete" (193). Simplicity of speech and truthfulness are James's ultimate concern. A community can only be built up when one is able to presume the honesty and truthfulness of its members, for trust can only exist when one can rely upon the word of another.

This prohibition against taking oaths is directed toward everyday speech rather than the taking of public official oaths. "Let your 'Yes' be yes" indicates the call to see that what one says conforms to what one thinks. In the context of the community it should not be necessary for the believer to take an oath since his/her yes or no should conform automatically to what he/she thought or what was true. His or her honesty could be presumed, and thus the taking of any oaths would be unnecessary. Just as the developing Jewish tradition forbade the taking of oaths in unimportant matters, so too this saying in James and Matthew stresses the need for total honesty in daily speech and the avoidance of the punctuation of speech with a call to an oath in order to establish one's truthfulness.

Simplicity of speech opposes any form of duplicity whereby one either professes an oath and then does not carry it out, or on the other hand manipulates the divine in order to achieve one's own ends. Peppering speech with a constant appeal to divine support (however veiled it might be) is undoubtedly an attempt to use the divine to buttress what one says. This is even more serious if one has no intention of carrying out the promise one makes under divine sanction. It is invoking divine judgment on the most insignificant of affairs.

Within the confines of any community or society there needs to be the requirement that its members tell the truth. "Honesty in speech affects both the integrity of the individual as well as the integrity of the community" (Hartin [1999] 106). Simplicity and honesty in speech is a value James invokes for his community. It is one of those social markers that gives an identity to the community and distinguishes its members from the wider society. This is who we are, says James. We are a people whose speech conforms to our intentions. There is no need to call for any other witness to our honesty or truthfulness, for our identity is rooted in our truthfulness. By invoking a simple approach to speech individuals express the values of the community to which they belong and strengthen the bonds that unite them to the community. It is an important feature of the socialization process within James's community. These final verses of James strive to strengthen and build up the community and its individual members as they wait for the imminent coming of the Lord (see Wall [1997] 260). Those will endure who know what is right and wrong and act accordingly: their "Yes" is yes and their "No" is no!

An oath is serious because it invokes God's guarantee for what is being said. Consequently, one is placing oneself under God's judgment for the truthfulness of the statement or the carrying out of the promise ("so that you may not fall under judgment"). As Davids says: "Since God holds one to this standard, oaths are dangerous, for they make some speech more honest than other speech" ([1982] 190). Ultimately, for a follower of Jesus, his or her word should be the bond. "It is expected of the Christian, however, that his word will be unconditionally rivetted to the truth" (*TDNT* 5:182). The virtue of sincerity is at the core of all human relationships and is pleasing to God. As the Jesus of the Gospel of John says in reference to Nathanael: "Here is truly an Israelite in whom there is no deceit!" (John 1:47).

FOR REFERENCE AND FURTHER STUDY

Baker, William R. "'Above All Else:' Contexts of the Call for Verbal Integrity in James 5:12," *JSNT* 54 (1994) 57–71.

Dautzenberg, Gerhard. "Ist das Schwurverbot Mt 5,33-37; Jak 5,12 ein Beispiel für die Torakritik Jesu?" *BZ* 25 (1981) 47–66.

Exler, Francis Xavier J. *The Form of the Ancient Greek Letter: A Study in Greek Epistolography.* Washington, D.C.: Catholic University of America, 1923.

Hiebert, D. Edmond. "The Worldliness of Self-Serving Oaths," *Direction* 6, 4 (1977) 39–43.

Kutsch, Ernst. "Eure Rede aber sei ja ja, nein nein," *EvT* 20 (1960) 206–17.

Marconi, Gilberto. "La Debolezza in Forma di Attesta: Appunti Per Un' Esegesi di Gc 5,7-12," *RivistB* 37 (1989) 173–83.

Minear, Paul S. "Yes or No: The Demand for Honesty in the Early Church," *NovT* 13 (1971) 1–13.

Moulton, James H., Wilbert F. Howard, and Nigel Turner. *A Grammar of New Testament Greek.* Vols. 1–3. Edinburgh: T & T Clark, 1963.

Schneider, Johannes. "*omnyō*," *TDNT* 5:176–85.

_____. "*horkos*," *TDNT* 5:457–62.

White, John L. *Light from Ancient Letters.* Philadelphia: Fortress, 1986.

12. *Prayer* (5:13-18)

13. Are any of you suffering misfortune? Let them pray. Are any cheerful? Let them sing praises (to God). 14. Are any of you sick? Let them call on the elders of the assembly and let them pray over them, anointing them with oil in the name of the Lord. 15. And the prayer of faith will save the sick, and the Lord will raise them up. And if they have committed sins, they will be forgiven. 16. Therefore, confess your sins to one another and pray for one another so that you may be healed. The righteous person's prayer is powerful in its effect. 17. Elijah was a man with the same

nature as ours, and he prayed earnestly that it might not rain. And it did
not rain on the earth for three years and six months. 18. And he prayed
again, and the heaven gave rain, and the earth produced its fruit.

NOTES

13. *Are any of you suffering misfortune? Let them pray:* In this context the enclitic *tis*
is an indefinite pronoun ("anyone"), not an interrogative pronoun ("who"). A
threefold series of brief questions and answers follows, with each containing
the pronoun *tis*. This style of brief question and answer conforms to that of the
diatribe (Ropes 303). The rhetorical force of these questions is the same as if
they were constructed as conditionals. Some translations do in fact translate
them in this way: "If any one of you is in trouble, he should pray . . ." (see *JB*,
and Mussner's explanation [1981] 217). While the Greek text has the singular
throughout this paragraph, James clearly intends this as a universal example
and instruction. For this reason, while the nouns and verbs are literally in the
singular I have translated them in the plural to achieve consistency and to preserve the universal applicability James intends. "*Are you* suffering . . . let *them*
pray." The verb *kakopathein* reminds the reader of the noun *kakopathias* ("suffering") in 5:10. As with the noun, the verb reflects the aspect of passive suffering and endurance of hardships (see Philo, *Somn.* 2:181; see also Xenophon,
Mem. 1:4, 11; 2:1, 17). This verb occurs in the New Testament only here and in
2 Timothy: "Share in suffering *(synkakopathēson)* like a good soldier of Christ
Jesus" (2:3); "for which I suffer hardship *(kakopathō)* . . ." (2:9); "As for you, always be sober, endure suffering *(kakopathēson)* . . ." (4:5). The suffering to
which James refers is not physical illness, but rather hardships and misfor-
tunes of life (see BDAG 500). The verb *proseuchesthō* ("let him pray") occurs for
the first time here in this verse but is repeated frequently in what follows (5:14,
16, 17, 18). The aspect of prayer intended is that of supplication (see BDAG
879; Johnson [1995] 329), which is evident throughout the LXX and the New
Testament (e.g., "She was deeply distressed and prayed *[proseuxato]* to the
LORD, and wept bitterly" [1 Sam 1:10] and "Love your enemies and pray
[proseuchesthe] for those who persecute you" [Matt 5:44]). The prayer James
advocates is not a prayer to remove the hardships, but rather to endure them.
As Michaelis observes: "In 5:13 . . . *kakopatheō* suggests, not so much the dis-
tressing situation as such, but the spiritual burden which it brings with it, and
which drives us to prayer. Hence the prayer is more for the giving of strength
than the removal of the situation" (*TDNT* 5:937).

Are any cheerful? Then let them sing praises (to God): The second of the indefinite
pronouns is introduced as a question that functions in the manner of a conditional. The verb *euthymein* is classical Greek. It does not occur in the LXX, or in
the rest of the New Testament. It only appears in Acts 27:22, 25 with the meaning "to keep up your courage." In James's context it expresses the meaning "to
be cheerful" (BDAG 406). The cheerfulness to which the hearers/readers are
called is not dependent on external circumstances. It is a joy and peace of the
heart, an inner contentment (Moo 175). The response *psalletō* is a call "to sing

praises to God." Not only does prayer petition God, as in the previous phrase; prayer is also offered as praise to God. This verb means "to sing songs of praise, with or without instrumental accompaniment" (BDAG 1096). It is used frequently in the LXX (some fifty-six times), especially with the meaning "sing to the music of a harp" (Ropes 303) (e.g., "Praise the LORD with the lyre, make melody [*psalate*] to him with the harp of ten strings" [Ps 33:2 {32:2 LXX}]). As time went on the connection with a musical instrument diminished and the word was used to designate the human voice or human heart that sings praise to God without any accompaniment (e.g., "I will pray with the spirit, but I will pray with the mind also; I will sing praise [*psalō*] with the spirit, but I will sing praise [*psalō*] with the mind also" [1 Cor 14:15] and "as you sing psalms and hymns and spiritual songs, among yourselves, singing and making melody [*psallontes*] to the Lord in your hearts" [Eph 5:19]). James shows that one should turn to God in prayer in every situation, whether in sadness or cheerfulness.

14. *Are any of you sick?* This is the third situation that calls for a response of prayer. The verb *asthenein* can have the more general sense of "to experience some personal incapacity or limitation, be weak" (BDAG 142) as, e.g., "He did not weaken in faith *(asthenēsas)* . . ." (Rom 4:19; see also 1 Cor 8:11-12; 2 Cor 12:10; *2 Clem.* 17:2). In this context it means especially "to suffer a debilitating illness, be sick" (BDAG 142) as it is used in Matt 25:39; John 4:46; 11:1-3; Phil 2:26-27; 2 Tim 4:20.

Let them call on the elders of the assembly and let them pray over them, anointing them with oil in the name of the Lord: The verb *proskalein* is used here in the sense of issuing a call "in order to secure someone's presence" (BDAG 881) (see also Matt 10:1; 15:10; Mark 3:13; 15:44; Luke 7:18; 15:26; Acts 6:2; 23:17). The elders *(presbyteroi)* to whom James refers are those who exercise leadership roles within the community. Functionaries such as elders or *presbyteroi* were a reality that can be traced throughout the Hebrew, Jewish, and Hellenistic worlds. Elders exercised roles as community leaders within the different organizational groupings of the social world of Judaism. They were leaders within villages, towns, and synagogues (e.g., Ezra 5:5; Sir 7:14; 1 Macc 1:26; Josephus, *A.J.* 11:105). Without doubt the synagogue structure owed much of its origin to the "elders of Israel" or the "elders of the people," going back to the earliest times of Israel's existence (see Exod 19:7; 24:1; see also McKenzie 522–40). As Bornkamm argues: "It is generally assumed that their origin lies in the most ancient patriarchal period when Israel was made up of tribes long before the settlement and national hegemony. As head and representatives of the great families and clans the elders were leaders in the large units which were then in process of formation" (*TDNT* 6:655). Not just in the Jewish world but throughout the Hellenistic world elders were also the heads of households who "exercised an authority that is informal, representative and collective" (Campbell 65). This authority emerged traditionally because of their position as heads of families. It is natural to presume that since the development of early Christianity revolved around the household, the leadership of the family would carry over into the world of early Christianity. This leadership dimension of elders flowed by nature or by tradition from the very fabric of Jewish and Hellenistic society. While the gospels offer no indication of the existence of such groups of leaders, elders clearly exercised an important role within developing Christian communities. This is evident in most New Testament communities apart from those of Paul: e.g., in the Acts of the Apostles (11:30; 14:23; 15:2; 16:4; 20:17; 21:18), in writings such as 1 Tim 5:17-19 and Titus 1:5-6 that reflect a close connection between elders and house churches, and in other New Testament letters where an elder addresses members of a household: "The elder to the elect lady and her children, whom I love in the truth . . . the children of your elect sister send you their greetings" (2 John 1, 13; see also 3 John 1; 1 Pet 5:1). The references in Acts are particularly noteworthy, as they indicate a group within the communities who are exercising a leadership role. Acts 21:18 makes reference to a group assembled around James in Jerusalem: "The next day Paul went with us to visit James; and all the elders were present." John H. Elliott ([2000] 813–16) has made an insightful study of the role of elders in the early Christian communities in his commentary on 1 Peter and sums up their origin within the Christian movement in this way:

> Within the developing messianic movement, it was neither the elders' endowment with the Spirit nor their accomplishments that earned them status and roles of leadership but their age and the prestige of the households of which they were heads . . . it is also probable that, when leaders of house churches were designated "elders," the term "elder" was extended beyond seniority in age to include those who were "seniors" in the faith ([2000] 815).

Essentially, then, an elder *(presbyteros)* was not an office bearer, but a functionary who exercised within the community traditional leadership roles that were derived from the heads of households. James uses the Greek word *ekklēsia* ("the assembly") consciously to refer to the group of people as distinct from the *synagōgē* (2:2) or place where the group gathered. This use of the word *ekklēsia* conforms to the usage within the LXX, which uses it in reference to the people of Israel as they gathered together to worship or to hear the word of the Lord proclaimed (Deut 4:10; 9:10; 18:16; 31:30). The further description of the actions of the elders reflects their role. They are to "pray over" *(proseuxasthōsan ep'auton)* the sick person. The use of the preposition *epi* is revealing. It indicates either the prayer that is directed toward the sick person, or perhaps the custom of laying hands on the sick person (Davids [1982] 193). The elders also anoint the sick person with oil *(aleipsantes [auton] elaiō)*. While the use of the aorist participle *(aleipsantes)* may indicate that the anointing preceded the prayer, this is not necessarily the case. The aorist can also show that the action of anointing is occurring contemporaneously or simultaneously with the action of praying (see Ropes 305; Zerwick 533; Mussner [1981] 219–20; Martin 207).

Anointing of the sick was a customary practice in both the Hellenistic and Jewish worlds. The use of oil for healing purposes is referred to in the writings of Hippocrates: "Exercises in dust differ from those in oil thus. Dust is cold, oil is warm. In winter oil promotes growth more, because it prevents the cold from being carried from the body. In summer, oil, producing excess of heat, melts the flesh, when the latter is heated by the season, by the oil and by the exercise" (*Vict. salubr.* 2:65 [Jones, LCL]; see also Menander, *Georg.* 55-61; Pliny the Elder, *Nat.* 23:47-49). In the Hebrew and Jewish world there are many references to the medicinal usages of oil (e.g., Josephus: "And when his physicians decided to warm his body there and had seated him in a tub of (warm) oil . . ." [*A.J.* 17:172 {Marcus, LCL}]; see also *B.J.* 1:657; Isa 1:6; Jer 8:22; *Apoc. Mos.* 9:3; Philo, *Somn.* 2:58). In the New Testament the healing power of oil is also presumed (see Mark 6:13; Luke 10:34). The anointing is performed "in the name of the Lord." This is the third action in this ritual of healing: prayer, anointing, and the invoking of the name of the Lord. James's thought and language correspond to the practice to which other traditions within early Christianity bear witness: e.g., in the Acts of the Apostles people are baptized "in the name of Jesus Christ" (2:38; 8:16; 10:48) and the sick are healed "in the name of Jesus" (3:6; 4:10). The reference to the Lord here, as in 2:7 ("the excellent name that was invoked over you"), refers undoubtedly to Jesus (see Dibelius 253). By calling on the name of Jesus the elders were invoking the power of Jesus for the action of healing. As Bietenhard says: "This kind of healing does not take place through the use of magic formulae . . . nor does it stand in the power or at the whim of the healer. It is Jesus Himself who heals" (*TDNT* 5:277).

15. *And the prayer of faith will save the sick, and the Lord will raise them up:* One of the meanings of the noun *euchē* is "a solemn promise with the understanding that one is subject to penalty for failure to discharge the obligation, *vow*" (BDAG 416) (e.g., "At Cenchreae he [Paul] had his hair cut, for he was under a vow [*euchēn*]" [Acts 18:18]). Ropes (308) notes that in Hellenistic Greek it is actually difficult to distinguish between a vow and prayer, as both have the same meaning: e.g., Xenophon: "So, this mother of yours is kindly disposed towards you . . . she prays (*euchomenēn*) the gods to bless you abundantly and pays vows (*euchas*) on your behalf" (*Mem.* 2:2, 10 [Marchant, LCL]). In the LXX this word generally has the meaning of a vow (e.g., "Then Jacob made a vow (*euchēn*) saying . . ." [Gen 28:20]). This cannot be the meaning here, given James's strong teaching against the taking of an oath (5:12) (Johnson [1995] 332). Instead, it has the meaning of "speech or petition directed to God, *prayer*" (BDAG 416) as is also found in Hellenistic Greek (see, e.g., Xenophon: "on the contrary, our prayer (*euchē*) that the goddess will bestow her grace on our words and deeds is manifestly answered" (*Symposium* 8:15 [Todd, LCL]; and Josephus, *B.J.* 7:155). In James this word continues the theme of prayer that dominates this section. The prayer of faith (*tēs pisteōs*) is based on the faith of the elders who make the prayer. The power of prayer "will save (*sōsei*)" the sick. While the concept of salvation relates first of all to healing or the restoring to fullness of health in this present life, there is also the further implication of eschatological salvation, as occurs elsewhere in 1:21; 2:14; 4:12. The further promise *kai egerei auton ho kyrios* ("and the Lord will raise them up") also demonstrates this twofold meaning. On the one level it echoes the language of the gospels and Acts, where this phrase occurs frequently in the miracles of

Jesus: Jesus "raises up" *(egerei)* the sick and grants both physical and spiritual healing (see Matt 9:5-7; Mark 1:31; 2:9-12; 9:27; Acts 3:7; and cf. Josephus: "God raises up *[egeirein]* what has fallen down" [*A.J.* 19:294]). On the deeper level this phrase also refers to the future, when the Lord Jesus raises the person to fullness of life in the future resurrection (5:20). The word *kamnonta* is the present participle of the verb *kamnein* in the sense of "to be ill or sick." While this verb can have the meaning "to be hopelessly sick, to waste away . . . or even die" (BDAG 506), it is not necessary to restrict it to the seriously ill. We may see it as referring to the sick in general, as it is used frequently in Hellenistic Greek (e.g., Herodotus: ". . . having no use for physicians, they carry the sick *(kamnontas)* into the market-place" [*Hist.* 1:197 {Godley, LCL}]; Plato, *Resp.* 407C). This verb is found neither in the LXX nor in the rest of the New Testament. The form of the verb is singular, but undoubtedly it is intended to have a general, all-inclusive reference. I translate it here, as I have done consistently in this section, in a plural sense to capture the universal applicability of this example.

And if they have committed sins, they will be forgiven: James uses a periphrastic construction here: the present subjunctive of the verb *eimi* ("to be") plus the perfect participle of the verb *poieō* ("to do"). Literally the translation would be: "If he is the one who has done (committed) sins." The use of the perfect tense is significant, for it indicates an influence on the present. If someone has done something wrong in the past, it continues to affect him or her now. The past sin continues to influence that person in his or her relationship with God until she or he attains forgiveness. There is a tradition in the Hebrew Scriptures that connects illness with sin. The clearest illustration of this is found in Deut 28:58-62: "If you do not diligently observe all the words of this law that are written in this book, fearing this glorious and awesome name, the LORD your God, then the LORD will overwhelm both you and your offspring with severe and lasting afflictions and grievous and lasting maladies." This traditional understanding was challenged by the wisdom literature, especially the book of Job (9:13-21). This perspective on the connection between sin and illness also makes its way into the thought patterns of the New Testament world (e.g., "Later Jesus found him in the temple and said to him, 'See, you have been made well! Do not sin any more, so that nothing worse happens to you'" [John 5:14]; see also Mark 2:5). In this context James does not directly say that sin causes illness. He uses a conditional: "And if *(kan)* he has committed sins," which gives the indication that he is going on to discuss another aspect. In fact, James is referring in this verse to healing, both physical (sickness of the body—*kamnonta*) and spiritual (sickness of the soul—[sin] *hamartia*). The expression *aphethēsetai autō* contains an impersonal passive (Ropes 309) that translates literally: "and it will be forgiven to him."

16. *Therefore, confess your sins . . . so that you may be healed:* The particle *oun* ("therefore") makes a direct connection to the previous verses. The members of James's community are urged: *exomologeisthe oun allēlois tas hamartias* ("confess your sins to one another"). This concept of confession of sins is found frequently within the Hebrew Scriptures, embracing both individual and

community confession. Individual confession of sins is seen in Ps 32:5: "Then I acknowledged my sin to you, and did not hide my iniquity; I said, 'I will confess my transgressions to the LORD, and you forgave the guilt of my sin'" (see also Lev 5:5; Num 5:7; Ps 51:3-5; Job 33:27-28). The confession of the sins of the community is also stressed: e.g., "Then Aaron shall lay both his hands on the head of the live goat, and confess over it all the iniquities of the people of Israel, and all their transgressions, all their sins, putting them on the head of the goat, and sending it away into the wilderness by means of someone designated for the task" (Lev 16:21; see also Dan 9:4-10; Bar 1:14–2:10; Tob 3:1-6). This tradition of the confession of sins continues to be reflected in the writings of the Qumran community: e.g., "And the levites shall recite the sins of the children of Israel, all their blameworthy transgressions and their sins during the dominion of Belial. [And all] those who enter the covenant shall confess after them and they shall say: 'We have acted sinfully, [we have transgressed, we have si]nned, we have acted irreverently, we and our fathers before us . . .'" (1QS 1:23–2:1; see also CD 20:28-29). In the same vein the New Testament shows an awareness of the confession of sins (Matt 3:6; Mark 1:5; Acts 19:18, where the verb *exomologein* is used [as here] for the confession of sins, while 1 John 1:9 uses the simple form of the verb, *homologein*). The early Christian church shows how it continued this tradition of the confession of sins (e.g., "for it is better for man to confess *(exomologeisthai)* his transgressions than to harden his heart . . ." [1 *Clem.* 51:3]; see also 1 *Clem.* 52:1; *Did.* 4:14; 14:1; *Barn.* 19:12; Herm. *Vis.* 1:1, 3; 3:1, 5-6; *Sim.* 9:23, 4). The letter of James continues this tradition of the community setting of the confession of sins. He goes further and stresses that the individuals within the community are called to confess their sins "to one another" *(allēlois)*. Openness and reciprocity are characteristics of this confession of sins. The consequence of the confession of sins is *hopōs iathēte* ("so that you may be healed"). The healing envisaged here is both physical and spiritual (forgiveness). In this instance the Greek text uses the plural form of the second person, *iathēte* ("you may be healed"), showing the application of healing to the entire community. Sirach 38:9 appears to be very close to this instruction of James: "My child, when you are ill, do not delay, but pray to the Lord, and he will heal you."

The righteous person's prayer is powerful in its effect: The reference to the righteous person *(dikaios)* is a reminder of the righteous one in 5:6 who is put to death. In the Hebrew tradition the righteous person is the one who follows the way of the Lord (Ps 1:6). The expression *poly ischyei* means literally "it has much power or ability" (see BDAG 484). Hence the translation "the righteous person's prayer is powerful." The participle *energoumenē* is difficult to translate. Some commentators take it as an adjective qualifying prayer. For example, Dibelius (256) sees it in analogy to its usage in Wis 15:11 as "active prayer." Laws ([1980] 234) interprets it in the same way and BDAG translates it as "effective prayer" (335). Others see it as modifying the main verb *ischyein*, "to be able, to be strong" (e.g., Ropes translates it: "when it is exercised" [309]; see also Mussner [{1981} 228). The direction of Ropes and Mussner is to be followed, since what is stressed is not the powerful nature of the prayer itself, but rather the response of God to the prayer. Prayer is effective in that God responds to it. Hence my translation: "powerful in its effect."

17. *Elijah was a man with the same nature as ours:* James brings his argument to a close by citing a biblical example, as is his custom. The other Old Testament examples he refers to are Abraham, Rahab, and Job. James makes many statements about Elijah. The first says that he is *anthrōpos ēn homoiopathēs hēmin* ("a man with the same nature as ours"). The adjective *homoiopathēs* means "suffering the like with us" (Ropes 311) or "pertaining to experiencing similarity in feelings or circumstances, *with the same nature . . . as someone* Ac 14:15; Jas 5:17" (BDAG 706). It creates a bond between Elijah and James's hearers/readers in that they all share the same humanity. This is evident from the only other usage of this term in the rest of the New Testament, where Paul and Barnabas appeal to the people of Lystra not to treat them as gods but as human beings like themselves: "Friends, why are you doing this? We are mortals just like you *(homoiopatheis) . . .*" (Acts 14:15). The identification between Elijah and James's hearers/readers achieves three things: (1) The stress on the same humanity that bonds Elijah and James's community together establishes Elijah not as some remote or heavenly figure beyond their reach, but as someone exactly like them. (2) Elijah is presented as a person of prayer, implying that James's community can be people of prayer in like manner. (3) Included in the Greek word "with the same nature" is the aspect of suffering *(pathos):* the bond of common struggle and suffering lies between them.

The biblical basis for the traditions that later arose around Elijah is the series of accounts in 1 Kgs 17:1–2 Kgs 2:12 that records how the prophet preserved the religion of Israel from the inroads made by the worship of Baal during the ninth century B.C.E. Thereafter the tradition regarding the figure of Elijah developed greatly. In the biblical tradition itself there are references to Elijah in 2 Chr 21:12-19; Mal 4:5; Sir 48:1-12; 1 Macc 2:58. But it is his return at the end of time that becomes central, since he is God's messenger preparing the way for the coming of the heavenly King (Mal 3:1-4; 4:5). Sirach 48:10 further reflects on Elijah's task at the end-time when it sees the prophet placating the wrath of God and reconciling parents and children to one another. What is significant from the perspective of the letter of James is his task "to restore the tribes of Jacob" (Sir 48:10). Is it by chance that James refers to Elijah at the conclusion of his letter? Elijah's role in the restoration of the tribes of Israel is a reminder of James's opening address to the twelve tribes in the Dispersion (1:1). In this intertestamental period the picture of Elijah continued to grow enormously in the traditions and popular imagination (see *TDNT* 2:928–41). The focus in the speculations on Elijah was largely on his heavenly role, stemming from his ascent to heaven before his death and anticipating his return at the end-time.

and he prayed earnestly that it might not rain. And it did not rain on the earth for three years and six months: James's expression *proseuchē proseuxato* (literally "in prayer he prayed") reflects a Semitic idiom and expresses the earnestness of Elijah's prayer (BDAG 879). The biblical tradition portrayed Elijah as a man of prayer only indirectly. 1 Kings 17:1 presents Elijah in the role of prophesying, while the picture of prayer is probably derived by way of inference from the statement: "As the LORD God of Israel lives, before whom I stand," which may be understood as calling on the power of God, as well as from the following miracle, when Elijah prays to God before he raises the child back to life (17:20). The final example occurs before Elijah's triumph over the prophets of Baal, where he prays earnestly to God (18:36-37). This probably gave rise to the tradition that the miracles of Elijah were the result of his effective prayer: e.g., Sirach 48:3 interprets the drought that came upon Israel as a result of the power of Elijah's word. Revelation 11:6 shows how this tradition continued to develop: "They have authority to shut the sky, so that no rain may fall during the days of their prophesying. . . ." The period of time for the drought, "three years and six months," is not mentioned in the narrative of 1 Kings 17. Neither Sir 48:3 nor 4 Ezra 7:39 mentions a length of time when referring to this miracle of Elijah. However, the same tradition of time is noted in Luke 4:25: "There were many widows in Israel in the time of Elijah, when the heaven was shut up three years and six months, and there was a severe famine over all the land." While many explanations have been given to account for this number, the clearest is to see it emanating from the apocalyptic tradition where the numbers "three and a half" represent half the perfect number ("seven") and become symbolic for a period of limited judgment, misfortune, or evil (see Dan 7:25; 12:7; Rev 11:2; 12:14, where the tradition has varied: three and a half years, or forty-two months, or twelve hundred sixty days).

18. *And he prayed again, and the heaven gave rain, and the earth produced its fruit:* James fills in the gaps in the narrative of Elijah's miracle in 1 Kgs 18:42: "Elijah went up to the top of Carmel: there he bowed himself down upon the earth and put his face between his knees. . . ." This description of Elijah's posture is clearly that of someone at prayer. Following this prayer action, the drought was broken with the coming of the rains. "The heaven gave rain" is James's graphic way of illustrating a major theme of his letter, namely that God is the giver of all good gifts (1:5; 1:17; 3:15-17; 4:6). "And the earth produced its fruit" is the consequence of God's gift of rain. While the narrative in 1 Kings does not describe the consequences of the gift of rain, James deliberately draws it out because it illustrates a number of his themes. The gift of rain brings with it fruitfulness *(karpos)*. James is also making a literary connection back to 5:7, where the farmer waits patiently for the early and the late rain for his crop *(karpos)*. The reference to *karpos* would also call to mind 3:18 where the promise was made that "the fruit *(karpos)* that is righteousness is sown in peace by those who make peace." The implication for James's community is clear: just as Elijah's prayer was effective in bringing new life, so too the prayer of the righteous person could be effective in bringing the fruit of healing.

INTERPRETATION

In this third section of the conclusion James establishes a literary *inclusio* with the opening of the letter. The themes of suffering and testing (1:2-3) and of prayer (1:5) open the letter. The same two themes are the pulsating heart of this section. At the same time James gives us an insight into the spiritual and religious thought world and practices of one community within earliest Christianity. What is distinctive and impressive about James's teaching is how closely these thoughts reflect those of the Jesus of the gospels. Among the themes addressed are the following:

Prayer: James considers that prayer is to be addressed to God at every phase of the believer's life journey. He admonishes his hearers/readers to pray at three important moments of their lives: when they experience misfortune, when they are joyful, and when they fall ill (5:13-14). James demonstrates a confidence in the power of prayer that knows no limits. This reflects Jesus' approach to prayer in the gospels. What is striking about Jesus' teaching on prayer in the gospels is that every tradition (whether it be Q, Mark, or John) agrees in presenting the picture of Jesus encouraging his followers to pray earnestly, with unlimited confidence and without bounds: "Ask, and it will be given you; search, and you will find; knock, and the door will be opened for you" (Matt 7:7; see also Luke 11:9; Mark 11:22-24; John 16:23-24).

James has struggled throughout the letter with the apparent question of how God responds to prayer. He upholds the unconditional nature of God's response in the opening of the letter: "But if any of you is lacking in wisdom, let him ask God who gives to everyone without hesitation and without reproach, and it will be given him" (1:5). However, James realizes that not every prayer is answered in the manner in which it is requested. He offers a number of reasons to explain why not all prayers are answered. In the opening chapter he goes on to say: "But let him ask in faith, never doubting, for the one who doubts is like a wave of the sea, driven and blown about by the wind. Let not that type of person imagine that he will receive anything from the Lord" (1:6-7). A little later he gives a further explanation as to why prayers fail: "You ask and you do not receive because you ask wickedly in order to spend it on your desires" (4:3). For James, true prayer needs to be made in faith with full confidence and trust in God. In effect, the focus must be on God, not on the individual. When prayer is made solely with the intention of furthering human desire, it is bound to fail. Once again prayer is situated within the struggle between friendship with the world and friendship with God. True prayer is centered upon faith in God and is open to the furthering of a relationship with God. Even the gospels present an understanding that God's response to prayer is limited by what God sees as good for the human person. Making use of the beautiful analogy of the human parent who gives what is good for the well being of the child, Jesus shows how God acts in like manner: "Is there any one among you who, if your child asks for a fish, will give a snake instead of a fish?" (Luke 11:11-13; Matt 7:9-11). The example of Jesus is also presented in the gospels to show that one of the basic features of all prayer is that it must be made in openness to God's will. In the Garden of Gethsemane Jesus prays to the Father: "Father, if you are willing, remove this cup from me; yet, not my will but yours be done" (Luke 22:42; Matt 26:42; Mark 14:36). Other New Testament traditions also give attention to this question of unanswered prayers. Paul shows this in his own life: "Three times I appealed to the Lord about this, that it would leave me, but he said to me, 'My grace is sufficient for you, for power is made perfect in weakness'" (2 Cor 12:8-9). The Johannine tradition places this queston in the context of keeping the commandments: "Beloved . . . we receive from him whatever we ask, because we obey his commandments and do what pleases him. And this is his commandment, that we should believe in the name of his Son Jesus Christ and love one another, just as he has commanded us" (1 John 3:21-23).

For James prayer is not simply an individual experience; it also characteristically defines the community since there is an essential community dimension to all prayer. In this context of prayer James introduces the term *ekklēsia* ("assembly, church") to identify the followers of Jesus. This term is what Laws describes as "the chosen self-designation of the Christian community" ([1980] 225). James shows his awareness and usage of the vocabulary, thought, and self-identification of early Christianity. Paul's characteristic way of opening his letters is to identify the community to whom he writes as an *ekklēsia* (e.g., 1 Cor 1:2; 2 Cor 1:1; Gal 1:2). While this term *ekklēsia* can refer either to the Christian community as a whole (Matt 16:18; Col 1:18), or to a specific group of believers located in a particular place, James's reference clearly points to the localized community to whom he is writing. James gives attention to the role community prayer plays in the context of sickness (5:14-15). The elders, as the representatives of the community, are called upon to pray for the sick while anointing them with oil. For James, one of the essential roles of the leaders of the community is to pray on behalf of the sick. In the presence of these elders the assembly or community reaches out to its weakest members (the sick) and through prayer strives to reintegrate them into the community. The role of elders is for both the spiritual and the bodily welfare of the community (Tamez 71). James also does not limit the community dimension of prayer to the elders, but shows a concern that everyone should pray for one another: "Therefore, confess your sins to one another and pray for one another so that you may be healed" (5:16). Once again James reflects his Jewish heritage. The reference to a community confession of sins reflects the traditional Jewish custom of the community acknowledging its sins to the Lord. It is well illustrated in the custom on the Day of Atonement (see Lev 16:21 and the Notes on Jas 5:16; see also Lev 26:40; Dan 9:4-19). The acknowledgment of guilt occurs both in the heart of the individual and of the community as a whole. The grace of forgiveness is experienced in the context of the communal prayer for forgiveness where the sick person is restored to both spiritual and physical health. "The community that accepts this challenge will enter into the deep process of integrity to which it is invited" (Tamez 72).

This section provides some further characteristics of prayer. Using the example of Elijah (5:17-18), James illustrates the powerful nature of prayer. The prayer of the community should take the person of Elijah as its model and example. Elijah certainly is a "righteous person . . . with the same nature as ours" (5:17) who shows that all prayer should be marked by earnestness and constancy. Fervent prayer is powerful in its effects (5:16). Above all the prayer offered in faith (5:15) defines the community as people who share the same faith, the same relationship of friendship with God, together with concern for one another. The community dimension of prayer is most significant, as it helps to bring both spiritual and physical healing. Finally, prayer enables the community to discover its own identity: who we are in relationship to one another and to God. It is another social marker central to James's letter that helps the members of the community define their identity by distinguishing them from the wider society.

Sickness and sin: James's letter concludes also with the theme of healing from sickness. A characteristic feature of many Hellenistic letters was the inclusion of some form of health wishes at the end (Davids [1982] 191). The experience of sickness confronts the community with a question: What should be the response of a follower of Jesus? A number of possible approaches could have been adopted. There was the perspective of the Stoics, who advocated the acceptance of suffering with resignation. In contrast, the Jewish tradition called upon the believer to pray to God. Many of the psalms capture this dimension of crying out to God in time of distress (e.g., Psalm 91).

The role of elders with regard to those who are ill is threefold: they are to pray for them; they are to anoint them with oil; they are to call on the name of the Lord. Without doubt James reflects a ritual that must be operative within his own community. The reference to anointing with oil is reminiscent of the Jesus tradition, where the disciples anoint the sick and cast out demons: "They cast out many demons, and anointed with oil many who were sick and cured them" (Mark 6:13). The healing powers of oil are also seen in the well-known parable of the Good Samaritan (Luke 10:25-37): "(The Samaritan) went to him (the victim) and bandaged his wounds, having poured oil and wine on them . . ." (10:34). Anointing with oil is not to be viewed as some magical ritual. Rather, it demonstrates an expression of faith in the power of God to intervene and heal. The traditions of the early church, as seen in Mark, Luke, and James, witness to a widespread belief that in the customary practices of the time (where oil was judged to have curative properties) God was also working to bring about healing to the sick. By connecting anointing with oil and calling on the Lord's name the community shows its belief that healing is accomplished only through God's power working through the ritual of anointing with oil. The sick belong to a community that in its turn belongs to the Lord. The elders' role in the anointing shows they are leaders working on behalf of the community *(ekklēsia)* and exercising a role in the name of the community.

In anointing the sick, the elders call on "the name of the Lord." This has a twofold significance. In the first place, they demonstrate their relationship as a community that belongs to the Lord. In the dualism between friendship with God and friendship with the world they show that as a community they are God's friends. As such they call upon their patron, God, to help the sick through the power of the risen Lord Jesus. Second, calling on the name of the Lord indicates that this healing ministry continues that of Jesus. One of the clearest illustrations of the apostles continuing this healing ministry occurs in the Acts of the Apostles, where Peter heals the crippled beggar (Acts 3:1-10). At the Temple gate Peter says to the cripple: "I have no silver or gold, but what I have I give you: in the name of Jesus Christ of Nazareth, stand up and walk" (Acts 3:6). Peter shows that the healing occurs through the power of the risen Lord Jesus as he explains: "and you killed the Author of life, whom God raised from the dead. To this we are witnesses. And by faith in his name, his name itself has made this man strong, whom you see and know; and the faith that is through Jesus has given him this perfect health in the presence of all of you" (Acts 3:15-16). This same thought permeates healing in the letter of James. Not only is it performed in the name of the Lord (Jesus); it is also connected essentially with Jesus' resurrection. The use of the verbs "to save" and "to raise up" *(sōsei . . . egerei)* situates the healing in the context of Jesus' resurrection. To experience healing is to share in the resurrection power of God that has been communicated to the community. As Wall expresses it: "The subsequent use of the 'resurrection' verbs 'heal' *(sōsō)* and 'raise up' *(egerō)* underscores healing as an experience of God's resurrection power, given now to the community in anticipation of the restoration of the entire created order at the Lord's *parousia*" ([1997] 266). In addressing the letter to the twelve tribes in the Dispersion (1:1) James sees the community to whom he writes as the reconstitution of God's new kingdom. They are the "first fruits of his (God's) creatures" (1:18). James's community experiences the working of God's resurrection power in the new creation as the beginning of the new created order. Once again the boundaries between those who belong to God and those who belong to the world are redefined. Those in friendship with God define their relationship with God by calling on God for healing (see Wall [1997] 266–67).

How does James see the connection between sickness and sin? In the cultural and symbolic world of Judaism, sin and sickness were inextricably intertwined. This is well presented in the warnings against disobedience in the book of Deuteronomy: "But if you will not obey the LORD your God by diligently observing all his commandments and decrees, which I am commanding you today, then all these curses shall come upon you and overtake you. . . . The LORD will afflict you with consumption, fever, inflammation, with fiery heat and drought . . ." (28:15-22). Psalm 38 offers a penitent's plea for healing and shows again the connection between sin and sickness: "There is no soundness in my flesh because of your indignation; there is no health in my bones because of my sin" (38:3). The book of Sirach gives advice to the reader that presumes, as in the case of James, the connection between sin and illness: "Before falling ill, humble yourself; and when you have sinned, repent" (18:21). This same connection between sin and illness is presumed in some gospel traditions, e.g., John 5:14 (see the Notes above at Jas 5:15). However, later in the Fourth Gospel Jesus rejects the connection: "'Rabbi, who sinned, this man or his parents, that he was born blind?' Jesus answered, 'Neither this man nor his parents sinned; he was born blind so that God's works might be revealed in him'" (John 9:2-3).

Set against this cultural world, James's views are nevertheless distinctive. James does not uphold a direct causal connection between sin and sickness. When speaking about the two he says: "And if they have committed sins, they will be forgiven. Therefore, confess your sins to one another and pray for one another so that you may be healed" (5:15-16). James deliberately uses the conditional construction here (*kan* ["and if"] plus the subjunctive) in order to avoid establishing a causal connection between the two. Further, while many perspectives in the Hebrew Scriptures do present God as the cause and origin of sin (e.g., Job 5:18), James does not. He could not attribute evil or suffering to God. He is careful to stress that no temptation comes from God (1:13); but he also stresses that God is the origin of all good gifts (1:17). James's understanding of God cannot embrace a concept in which suffering is sent by God as a consequence of sin.

In an excellent article entitled "'Are Any Among You Sick?' The Health Care System in the Letter of James," Martin Albl discusses the etiology of illness. He draws a distinction between naturalistic and personalistic causation, which he defines in this way: "A naturalistic etiology looks for the cause of disease within the framework of the 'natural' system of the body, while a personalistic etiology identifies personal forces, such as spirits or deities, as the causes of diseases" (133). This distinction is important for understanding the worldview of James, and I acknowledge my dependence here on Albl's insights. While James does not directly discuss or attribute any specific cause to illness or suffering, one could deduce that he believes demonic forces are responsible for sin and sickness, as other traditions hold. In James's worldview there is a dualism between friendship with God and friendship with the world (4:4), and all people are called to make a choice for or against each one. If all good gifts come from God, the presumption is that the evil that is sickness is necessarily the result of the forces of evil, the demonic.

James provides two strategies for overcoming illness and obtaining healing (see Albl 136). Taken together, these strategies demonstrate both a naturalistic and a personalistic approach to healing. When James instructs the elders to anoint the sick with oil, he is demonstrating a naturalistic perspective. The anointing shows James's dependence on and acceptance of the medicinal qualities the world of his time attributed to oil (see the Notes on Jas 5:14).

For James, however, the naturalistic approach was not sufficient. The actions needed to be accompanied by prayer in which the elders called upon the name of the Lord. This embraces the personalistic approach whereby true healing can only occur through the power of God or of the Lord Jesus. As I have indicated above, this healing power of God is connected to God's resurrection power, whereby God reconstitutes the created universe. Healing is a consequence of God's resurrection power, which restores both the individual and the community to wholeness. Some Hellenistic Jewish writings show a perspective similar to that of James, where anointing with oil is connected with the gift of the eschatological age. For example, in the Greek text of the work known as the *Apocalypse of Moses* (see *OTP* 2:259–95) healing is reserved for the future eschatological age, as the angel Michael tells Seth: "Seth, man of God, do not labor, praying with this supplication about the tree from which the oil flows, to anoint your father Adam; it shall not come to be yours now but at the end of times. Then all flesh from Adam up to that great day shall be raised . . ." (*Apoc. Mos.* 13:2-3 [*OTP* 2:275]; see Albl [138] for further examples).

Too sharp a distinction should not be drawn between the naturalistic and personalistic approaches. In the worldview of the first-century Mediterranean the natural and supernatural are not two separate worlds, but one; humans inhabit the same world as the divine (see Laws ([1980] 227). In James's description, anointing with oil together with prayer and invocation of the name of the Lord are in effect different aspects of one action. The oil is the means by which the divine healing power is communicated to the sick. Davids expresses this understanding very well: "But the function of the oil in James is not medicinal except insofar as it partakes of the eschatological oils . . . it is either the outward sign of the inward power of prayer or, more likely, a sacramental vehicle of divine power . . ." ([1982] 193).

As with the discussion about the relationship between James and Paul, this text has received a disproportionate amount of attention. Roman Catholics have shown a natural concern to regard it as a basis for the Sacrament of the Sick (or Extreme Unction, as it was formerly called). From the side of Protestant scholars the concern has been to bring this connection into question. While the foundation for the sacrament is rooted in this passage of James (see Council of Trent, Session XIV, November 25, 1551, *De Sacramento Extremae Unctionis* [Denzinger 1695-1700; 1716-19]), one must be careful not to make the text say things that were not its intent or to read back into the text later developments and understandings. For example, Chapter 1 of *De Sacramento Extremae Unctionis* reads:

> This holy anointing of the sick was instituted as a true and proper sacrament of the New Testament by Christ our Lord. While implied in the Gospel of Mark (cf. 6:13), it was commended and promulgated to the faithful by James, the Apostle and brother of the Lord (canon 1) . . . (Jas 5:14f) (Denzinger 1695).

As can be seen from this definition, the Council of Trent is speaking in language and thought processes that were a common way of expression and understanding in the sixteenth century. When proclaiming the anointing of the sick to be a sacrament it was in no way stating that James and the Christians of the first century C.E. understood it by this terminology. However, James certainly saw this action as a sacred rite whereby God confers God's eschatological salvation and healing to the one who is sick through the actions of anointing and prayer. Later centuries would develop terminology such as "sacrament" to give expression to James's understanding (see Brown [1997] 736–39 for a further discussion of this issue).

Community confession of sins: As the Notes have indicated, the community confession of sins or the public acknowledgment of sins was important in the context of the Jewish religious tradition (see, e.g., Lev 16:21). James shows again his debt to his Jewish heritage in this particular verse. The action envisaged here by 5:16 is a new one, distinct from 5:15 yet complementing it. Besides the anointing and the prayer of the community leaders, there is also the confession of sins to one another and the prayer of the community at large. James points again to a custom or ritual that is community based: the members acknowledge their sins to one another and pray for one another. The *Didache* gives a further tradition that illustrates this same custom within the early Christian community: "In the assembly you will confess your sins, and you will not occupy yourself with prayer with an evil conscience" (*Did.* 4:14). James had already drawn attention to the presence of sin within the community in 3:2: "For we all fail often." The response to sin is to acknowledge its presence both individually and communally. In this way one humbly acknowledges one's fault and receives the necessary support and strength from the community. Further, if the community is meant to consist of those who exist in friendship with God, it is important for the members of the community to acknowledge their fault in order to redefine their adherence to God. This is a way of redefining the community's boundaries. The individual and the community obtain spiritual healing and restoration to friendship with God through the forgiveness of sins. Those who belong to the community are those who have experienced God's forgiveness. While the prayers include requests for forgiveness of sins, they must also contain (given the context of this passage) prayers for the physical healing of the sick. The righteous person to whom James refers is the ordinary believer, the member of the community who in humility and honesty confesses his or her sins and abides by the values and standards of the community. The righteous person is "the ordinary member" (Davids [1982] 196) of the community who is in a true relationship of friendship with God.

The community dimension of these admonitions: As with the rest of the letter of James, the admonitions are addressed on two levels: first to the individual and then through the individual to the community. The identity of the individual believer is as a member of the "twelve tribes" who are the "first fruits of his (God's) creatures" (1:18). When sin besets the individual it also disrupts the integrity of the community. The same is true of illness. When people are ill they present a challenge to the wider community. How is the community going to respond to them? They could respond in the manner of the wider society by relegating them to the margins. One can see this in the world of Israel, where the sick were excluded from society, where people such as lepers and those with discharges of blood were judged to be impure and all contact was to be avoided. James adopts another approach. His concern is to ensure that these sufferers are embraced by the whole Christian society. By calling on the elders of the community one is asking those who represent the community to come and minister to the sick. The aim is to attempt to reintegrate the sick back into the body of the community (see Albl 131). For James the healing of the community both spiritually and bodily is a restoration to integrity, to the perfection to which appeal has been made throughout the letter.

Ritual practices within early Christianity: This section opens a window onto the religious world of early Christianity in a way that few passages in the rest of the letter, or even other letters of the New Testament, do. While many questions still remain concerning the nature of many of these references, we do gain an insight into one particular community or tradition within early Christianity that is distinct from other branches such as the Pauline churches. The term *ekklēsia* is a self-definition found in many other traditions of those early followers of Jesus. It characterizes their gathering together as an assembly to pray and to worship the Lord. While the structures of the community are not defined, the roles of its leaders emerge more clearly. Through the functions of the elders the community supports the sick in their need and extends healing to them. The rituals of anointing the sick and confession of sins to one another are characteristic features of this community. Such actions gave an identity to James's community by separating it from those outside. In these actions and in James's teaching, what is noteworthy is how closely James has remained to the foundational ministry of Jesus. What was characteristic about Jesus' ministry, particularly in the way it is described in the synoptic gospels, is how he extended both forgiveness and healing to those he encountered. For Jesus the breaking in of God's kingdom among humanity was demonstrated through the twofold gifts of healing and forgiveness. Through these gifts Jesus touched the whole human person, spiritually and bodily. Jesus' actions were designed to restore the human person to integrity, to wholeness and perfection in the sense of conformity to the image of the human person that God had at the beginning of creation. James is concerned with exactly the same healing of body and spirit. Like Jesus, he intends to restore integrity to the individual as well as to the community bearing the likeness of God. As a community they are "the first fruits of his (God's) creatures" (1:18) living in friendship with God (4:4).

One of the essential features of this assembly is that it involves a community of prayer. In using the example of Elijah from the Hebrew Scriptures, James shows that prayer is not a prerogative of the leadership, but is an identity marker for all members of the community. The power of the constant prayers of the ordinary believers is effective, for Elijah "was a man with the same nature as ours." The effectiveness of prayer extends to every righteous person, for every member of the community is called to embrace the habit of constant prayer. "Prayer will comfort them in their oppression, will exalt them in their hope, and will help them to achieve integrity in the practice of justice, as Christians faithful to God" (Tamez 72).

For Reference and Further Study

Albl, Martin C. "'Are Any Among You Sick?' The Health Care System in the Letter of James," *JBL* 121 (2002) 123–43.

Avalos, Hector. *Health Care and the Rise of Christianity*. Peabody, Mass.: Hendrickson, 1999.

Bietenhard, Hans. *"onoma," TDNT* 5:242–83.

Bornkamm, Günther. *"presbyteros," TDNT* 6:651–80.

Campbell, R. Alistair. *The Elders: Seniority within Earliest Christianity*. Studies of the New Testament and its World. Edinburgh: T & T Clark, 1994.

Coppens, Joseph. "Jacques V, 13-15 et l'Onction des Malades," *ETL* 53 (1977) 201–207.

Dudley, Martin, and Geoffrey Rowell, eds. *The Oil of Gladness: Anointing in the Christian Tradition.* London: SPCK; Collegeville: The Liturgical Press, 1993.

Elliott, John H. *1 Peter: A New Translation with Introduction and Commentary.* AB 37B. New York: Doubleday, 2000.

Hayden, Daniel R. "Calling the Elders to Pray," *BSac* 138 (1981) 258–66.

Jeremias, Joachim. *"Hēl(e)ias,"* TDNT 2:928–41.

Kelsey, Morton T. *Healing and Christianity.* New York: Harper & Row, 1973.

McKenzie, John L. "The Elders in the Old Testament," *Bib* 40 (1959) 522–40.

Michaelis, Wilhelm. *"kakopatheō,"* TDNT 5:936–39.

Pilch, John J. *Healing in the New Testament: Insights from Medical and Mediterranean Anthropology.* Minneapolis: Fortress, 2000.

Reicke, Bo Ivar. "L'onction des malades d'après Saint Jacques," *La Maison Dieu* 113 (1973) 50–56.

Thomas, John Christopher. *The Devil, Disease and Deliverance: Origins of Illness in New Testament Thought.* Journal of Pentecostal Theology Supplement Series 13. Sheffield: Sheffield Academic Press, 1998.

Unger, Merrill F. "Divine Healing," *BSac* 128 (1971) 234–44.

Wilkinson, John. "Healing in the Epistle of James," *SJT* 24 (1971) 326–45.

_____. *The Bible and Healing: A Medical and Theological Commentary.* Grand Rapids: Eerdmans, 1998.

13. *The Great Commission* (5:19-20)

19. My brothers (and sisters), if anyone of you wanders from the truth, and is turned back by another, 20. know that whoever turns back a sinner from the way of error will save that soul from death and will cover a multitude of sins.

NOTES

19. *My brothers (and sisters), if anyone of you wanders from the truth:* The address *adelphoi mou* ("My brothers [and sisters]") indicates, as it has done throughout the letter, that this is a separate section. This does not mean it is unconnected to what has preceded it, but it may be James's way of indicating that he is concluding the letter (see, e.g., 1 John, which ends similarly: "Little children, keep yourselves from idols" [5:21]). The use of *en hymin* (literally "among you") indicates that James is referring to those within the community who have strayed, rather than those outside. The verb *planan* has a variety of nuances of meaning (BDAG 821–22). The verb can also be used in the sense of "to proceed

without a sense of proper direction, *go astray, be misled, wander about aimlessly*" (BDAG 821). James adopts this meaning in a figurative way. See e.g., 1:16, where *mē planasthe* was used in the sense of "do not be deceived" (BDAG 822). In 5:19 James uses the verb in the sense of turning or "wandering away from the truth" (BDAG 822). In the LXX this term is used for apostasy (e.g., "So it was we who strayed from the way of truth *[ara eplanēthēmen apo hodou alētheias]*, and the light of righteousness did not shine on us, and the sun did not rise upon us" [Wis 5:6]). While Wis 5:6 has the phrase *apo hodou alētheias* ("from the way of truth"), James has simply *apo tēs alētheias* ("from the truth"). However, some manuscripts do insert the phrase "from the way of truth" into James's text or simply add "from the way" (see 𝔓⁷⁴ and Codex Sinaiticus; see also Aland [1997] 100). While this is clearly James's meaning, the best manuscripts do not include the word "way" *(hodos)*. It does occur later at 5:20. See also "For they went far astray on the paths of error *(kai gar tōn planēs hodōn makroteron eplanēthēsan)* . . ." (Wis 12:24). James used the noun *alētheia* ("truth") on a number of previous occasions. In 1:18 he spoke about being reborn through "the word of truth." In this context he was referring to truth in the sense of "the gospel of salvation" that gives rebirth as God's new creation (see the Notes on 1:18). This gospel of salvation maps out the way of life the community is to lead: it provides the boundaries that identify its members as Jesus' followers. It occurs in this sense in 3:14: "do not boast and lie against the truth." There (see the Notes on 3:14) it captures the manner of life they are leading, which must not be seen to betray or deny the message of salvation they have received. The same meaning is indicated here in 5:19; the truth James is concerned about is not *orthodoxy* so much as what is termed *orthopraxis* (see Martin 219). James's teaching centers on faith being put into action (2:14-26). He captures this here by referring to "wandering from the truth." One's way of life shows that one is putting faith into practice. The Jewish Scriptures also capture this understanding of truth as a way of life that expresses one's faith. "Lead me in your truth, and teach me . . ." (Ps 25:5 [24:5 LXX: *hodēgēson me epi tēn alētheian sou* . . .]); see also Ps 26:3 [25:3 LXX]).

and is turned back by another: The task of bringing back someone who wanders is not confined to the elders, but is a responsibility for the whole community. This echoes the Jesus saying in Matt 18:15-20 about correcting an erring member of the community. While the masculine singular pronoun is used *(auton,* "him"), it certainly has the force of being all-inclusive. To capture this inclusiveness I have translated the phrase *kai epistrepsē tis auton* (literally "one [of you] turns him back") by the passive "is turned back by another." The verb *epistrephein* can be used literally in the sense of "to return to a point where one has been, *turn around, go back*" (BDAG 382), or it can be used figuratively and metaphorically in the sense of "to cause a person to change belief or course of conduct with focus on the thing to which one turns, *turn*" (BDAG 382). It is used here in James in this figurative sense, corresponding to the figurative usage of the previous verb, *planan.* James refers not to the initial conversion of the sinner, but rather the reconversion of one who had embraced the Christian message but later turned away. A dominant theme throughout the Hebrew

Scriptures, particularly the prophets, was the call to Israelites to turn back from their evil ways (e.g., "True instruction *[nomos alētheias]* was in his mouth, and no wrong was found on his lips. He walked with me in integrity and uprightness, and he turned many *[epestrepsen]* from iniquity" [Mal 2:6; see also 3:7; Isa 6:10; Jer 3:12; Ezek 18:30]). The same thought continues in those New Testament traditions that express a "turning back" to the God from whom some have wandered (e.g., "but I have prayed for you that your own faith may not fail; and you, when once you have turned back *[epistrepsas]*, strengthen your brothers" [Luke 22:32; see also Mark 4:12]).

20. *know that whoever turns back a sinner from the way of error:* The form of the opening imperative here is disputed. In place of the reading *ginōsketō hoti* ("let him know that" [third person singular present imperative]) found in Codices Sinaiticus and Alexandrinus, some manuscripts (e.g., Codex Vaticanus) have *ginōskete hoti* ("know that" [second person plural present imperative]). Probably the latter reading was introduced to bring consistency with the opening address ("my brothers [and sisters]") "in order to avoid the ambiguity of who is to be regarded (the converter or the converted) as the subject of the verb" (Metzger [1975] 686). While I accept the reading of the text as *ginōsketō hoti* ("let him know that"), I translate it as "know that" in order to maintain the inclusiveness intended by the text. The verb *ginōskein* ("to know") occurred in 1:3, and so this phrase appears as a "bookend" to the letter, embracing it in the opening and the conclusion. James intended to bring understanding to his hearers/readers concerning their relationship of friendship with God, and this verb is a reminder to his hearers/readers of this. This phrase *ginōsketē hoti* ("let him know that") is the apodosis of the conditional sentence introduced in 5:19 "If anyone of you. . . ." James repeats the focus of the sentence again in a slightly different form: "whoever turns back a sinner from the way of error" (literally: "from the error of his way"). He does this for effect and for emphasis. Mayor suggests that the repetition occurs because it forms part of a quotation and that the author also wishes "to avoid ambiguity" (182).

    will save that soul from death and will cover a multitude of sins: Again there is dispute regarding the reading and interpretation of the text. This translation follows the text of the *Greek New Testament* of the fourth revised edition of the UBS and the twenty-seventh revised edition of *Nestle-Aland,* which read *psychēn autou ek thanatou* ("his soul from death"), based on the strong witnesses of Codices Sinaiticus and Alexandrinus. I have translated the pronoun *autou* ("his") as "that" in order to preserve the inclusiveness of the translation. One of the problems in interpretation here is exactly whose soul is being referred to. Is it the soul of the converted sinner or the soul of the one who converts the sinner? Metzger ([1975] 686) suggests that this confusion led the scribes to make changes in the text in this way: "(a) transferred *autou* to follow *ek thanatou* ("from death itself" 𝔓⁷⁴ B 614 1108 1611 1852 2138 itᶠᶠ) or (b) omitted it entirely (K L Ψ 049 056 0142 most minuscules)." The "soul" *(psychē)* is the eternal soul of the human person that has been saved from eternal death (Martin 219). The death to which James refers is more than just physical death. It is also the eschatological death that lasts forever. Here, as in 1:15, James presents death as the consequence of sin. The reference "will cover a multitude of sins" *(kalypsei plēthos hamartiōn)* is parallel to "will save that soul from death." First Peter 4:8 has a similar phrase: "for love covers a multitude of sins *(hoti agapē kalyptei plēthos hamartiōn)*." The difference between Peter and James is that for Peter it is love that covers one's sins in the present, while for James it is the action of bringing the brother back that will cover the sins. This phrase appears to be reminiscent of Prov 10:12: "Hatred stirs up strife, but love covers *(kalyptei)* all those who hate strife." At first glance Prov 10:12 seems to be closer to Peter's version. However, there are two noteworthy differences: the word Peter uses for love is *agapē,* while in the LXX text the word is *philia.* Second, both Peter and James have a brief object ("love covers sins" [Peter]; "will cover a multitude of sins" [James]), while Prov 10:12 has a much more expansive object: "all those who hate strife." These differences show that neither Peter nor James can be said to be quoting Prov 10:12 directly. *First Clement* 49:5 and *Second Clement* 16:4 also show the usage of this phrase that occurs in 1 Pet 4:8. Perhaps the best solution to the relationship among these texts is to see James and Peter as using a saying that derives from the Scriptures but has become part of oral culture in a popular way. James adapted it to suit his context and argument, while Peter probably preserved the saying more faithfully, as does Clement (Laws [1980] 241). The phrase "to cover sins" is a biblical one expressing the concept of the forgiveness of sins. "Happy are those whose transgression is forgiven, whose sin is covered *(kai hōn epekalyphthēsan hai hamartiai)*" (Ps 32:1 [Ps 31:1 LXX]). The parallelism of the two phrases shows that forgiveness is what is intended by the notion of "to cover" (e.g., "You forgave the iniquity of your people, you covered all their sins" [Ps 85:2 {Ps 84:3 LXX}]). After the final word *hamartiōn* ("of sins") a few manuscripts add the word *amēn,* while three manuscripts add an entire phrase: *hoti autǭ hē doxa eis tous aiōnas. amēn* ("for to him be glory for ever. Amen") (see Metzger [1975] 686; Aland [1997] 101).

INTERPRETATION

As noted throughout this commentary, the letter of James ends abruptly without the usual final greetings so characteristic of Paul's letters. Instead, James concludes with a call to assume responsibility for one's brothers and sisters and to help them turn from sin. Such a conclusion bears similarities to the endings of two other New Testament writings, 1 John and Jude. First John 5:14-21 calls on the community to pray that those who sin will change their ways: e.g., "If you see your brother or sister committing what is not a mortal sin, you will ask, and God will give life to such a one—to those whose sin is not mortal" (1 John 5:16). Jude 17-25 also challenges readers to act on behalf of the erring brother or sister: e.g., "And have mercy on some who are wavering; save others by snatching them out of the fire; and have mercy on still others with fear, hating even the tunic defiled by their bodies" (Jude 22-23). Consequently James, 1 John, and Jude show evidence of the existence of other traditional ways of concluding letters.

The final appeal to *adelphoi mou* ("my brothers [and sisters]") is undoubtedly James's marker that shows he is bringing the letter to a conclusion. It is similar to 1 John's final verse: "Little children, keep yourselves from idols," where "little children" *(teknia)* is 1 John's marker. For James "my brothers (and sisters)" is a reminder to the hearers/readers of their relationship with one another, a relationship based on mutual equality and respect rather than on hierarchical positions of authority and subordination. James concludes his letter with a final commission to accept responsibility for the members of one's own community, particularly those "brothers (and sisters)" who err. It shows a close connection to the previous section (5:13-18), where James had focused on the importance of prayer, the confession of sins, and the desire for salvation and healing. At the same time this section ends with a challenge to the hearers/readers to put faith into action by assuming responsibility for one's brother and sister.

One of the many disputed issues in this short section is the question: "Whose soul is saved from death?" or "Whose sins are covered?" The problem arises from the ambiguity of the pronoun *autou* that is used in defining "soul" *(psychē):* "His soul" can refer to either the soul of the repentant sinner or the soul of the one who converted the sinner. Vouga (146) argues that it is impossible to make a decision because of the ambiguity. However, an argument can clearly be made to interpret this verse as a reference to the soul of the "converter" who accepts responsibility for bringing the brother/sister back to leading life in conformity with the community. The "converter" will save his/her own soul and obtain his/her own forgiveness as well as forgiveness for the one who has repented (see Cantinat 262). There is some biblical support for such a perspective (see, e.g., Ezek 3:18-21, especially v. 21: "If, however, you warn the righteous not to sin, and they do not sin, they shall surely live, because they took warning; and you will have saved your life"). However, many commentators interpret the references in a twofold way: they see the phrase "saving of that soul from death" as referring to the soul of the repentant sinner, while the "covering of sins" refers to the sins of the one who converted the sinner (see Ropes 315–16; Dibelius 258–60; Laws [1980] 240–41; Mussner [1981] 233). This solution, to my mind, is confusing and does not give any reason to explain why James would suddenly jump in the course of this brief verse from one referent to another. The logic of the sentence requires a consistency that conforms to James's usual stylistic way of expression, which regularly features parallelism (see the frequent use of it in 4:7-9). The most logical way of interpreting this text is to see the reference as to one person. In 5:19 James uses the pronoun *auton* ("him") to refer to the repentant sinner. It makes sense, then, to see the same pronoun, *autou,* in 5:20 as referring to the same person, the repentant sinner. Consistency would demand that the final phrase "cover a multitude of sins" would refer to the same person. Consequently, James's line of thought speaks about a sinner who turns from the error of his or her way, and as a result that person's soul is saved and his or her sins are forgiven (see Davids [1982] 200–201; Martin 220; Johnson [1995] 339). Johnson adds an interesting insight to this concept of "covering a multitude of sins." He interprets the word "cover" *(kalypsei)* as meaning "suppress or prevent" ([1995] 339). If we understand the passage in this light James is not simply looking to the past and the forgiveness of past sins, but also to the future where sins are prevented simply because "the converted person is now no longer going to commit" them (Johnson [1995] 339). The correction of the sinner that leads to repentance and forgiveness has implications both for the individual and for the community. The social consequences of sin are no longer felt within the community and its wholeness is restored. As Reicke says: "The reference is to the erring persons and their community, so that the salvation of those who err prevents the perpetration of numerous sins in society" (63).

The perspective that has woven like a golden thread throughout this letter has been the search for wholeness and integrity ("perfection" as James has indicated it), both for the individual and for the community. Integrity demands that faith give direction to a specific way of life, of action. Faith in action is what is distinctive about the theological perspective of this letter. As Martin indicated: "The stress, as throughout the letter, is on practical faith, on orthopraxis more than orthodoxy, as 3:13-18 illustrate" (218). James 5:19-20 is concerned with those who wander from the truth. The truth, as James has indicated elsewhere in 1:18 and 3:14, is the gospel of salvation that gives direction to one's whole way of life. An impressive feature of this way of life is concern for others. This has been demonstrated throughout the letter with concern for the widow and orphan in their distress (1:27), for the poor (2:1-7), for loving one's neighbor as oneself (2:8), for responding to the physical needs of the fellow members of the community (2:14-19), and for accepting responsibility as a teacher for one's speech (3:1-12). In fact, the entire letter bears this ethos. The culmination of the letter with a call to show concern for a brother or sister who wanders from the truth is a reflection of another major theme, namely, the relationship of friendship with God. When such friendship is broken or lost, members of the community must reach out and enable the lost brother or sister to turn and reestablish that relationship.

The ending of this writing makes perfect sense in light of James's intention. As it now stands, the ending has a significant rhetorical function. In a sense this ending is similar to the synoptic gospels, which culminate with a commission by the risen Jesus to his followers to go out and bring the message of salvation to others (see Matt 28:19-20; Mark 16:7, 19-20; Luke 24:44-53). James differs from the commission of the synoptic gospels in that his commission is not intended to be missionary in the sense of making new disciples from nations or peoples who had never heard of Jesus. James holds his focus squarely on his own community and those who had come in recent times to accept the significance of Jesus as the Christ for their faith journey. While the focus of the synoptic gospels was to extend the message beyond the confines of the community and to strive to attract new adherents, James's concern rests within the boundaries of his community. His intent is to ensure that those who are Jesus' followers remain true to their commitment. James works within the horizon of a faith community for whom Jesus is the Christ. His final concern reaches out to those who have failed the test. The letter opened with a consideration of the testing of the faith of the members of the community (1:2-3). The opening presumed that the hearers/readers of this letter had remained true to their calling and had successfully overcome the testing of their faith. However, the ending of the letter turns attention to that other group of those who had not been faithful and whose faith had wavered and been lost. Instead of condemning them or ostracizing them or even excommunicating them, James shows how clearly he had embraced the message of Jesus. He challenges his hearers/readers to reach out to those who were lost and to reclaim them for the community. All the members of the community are commissioned to see that this is a central dimension of their faith. It is an application of Jesus' parable of the lost sheep, in which the shepherd leaves the ninety-nine safe sheep to go in search of one that had been lost (Matt 18:10-14; Luke 15:1-7).

James gives expression to a vision of community in which all members take responsibility for each other, particularly those who are not living according to the values and standards of the community. James shows a realistic understanding of human nature and of the Christian faith. He shows that sin is always a possibility within the community. Despite the ever-present possibility of sinning, Christians support one another and are there for one another, especially when tempted to wander from the boundaries defined by the community. Not only is James realistic; he is also optimistic. He does not consider failure, and speaks with a tone of confidence that the errant brother/sister will be reclaimed by and for the community. This is noticeably different from the struggle Matt 18:17 envisages for the errant brother/sister or the way Heb 6:4-6 paints the hopeless fate of those who have fallen away (for the epistle to the Hebrews there is no possibility of reclaiming the errant brother/sister).

In these final verses, as in the letter as a whole, James's focus rests within the boundaries of his own community. He has been intent on defining their identity as those for whom friendship with God is the ulti-mate test and criterion. The letter ends with a vision of true pastoral care for those who through their humanity have lost the fire and the direction that used to be such an important dimension of their lives. While the boundaries of the community have been defined, the community is not one that is shut off from the world in the manner of the Qumran commu-nity. James acknowledges openness within his community to extend a welcome to strangers, but he warns his hearers/readers to be careful about how this welcome could lead to the betrayal of their basic values, in that a preference for the rich could lead to the denigration of the poor within their community (2:1-7). Nowhere does James show a desire to extend the message beyond the confines of his community or to evange-lize the world as the synoptic gospels do. Without doubt the ending of this letter reflects the tone of a leader who is vitally concerned about the members of his own community and is encouraging all to imbibe a simi-lar feeling of concern and responsibility.

FOR REFERENCE AND FURTHER STUDY

Bonnard, Pierre. "Matthieu Éducateur du Peuple Chrétien," in Albert Descamps and André de Halleux, eds., *Mélanges Bibliques en Hommage au R. P. Béda Rigaux*. Gembloux: Duculot, 1970, 1–7.

Thyen, Hartwig. *Studien zur Sündenvergebung im Neuen Testament und seinen alttes-tamentlichen und jüdischen Voraussetzungen*. FRLANT 96. Göttingen: Vanden-hoeck & Ruprecht, 1970.

INDEXES

SCRIPTURAL INDEX

INDEX OF ANCIENT WRITINGS

2. Greco-Roman Authors

3. Christian Writings

AUTHOR INDEX

Abegg, M. G., 40
Adamson, J. B., 39, 40, 62, 125
Aland, B. A., 6, 45, 149, 153, 154, 174,
    176, 181, 193, 224, 242, 250, 283, 285
Aland, K., 6, 41, 93, 149, 153, 154, 174,
    176, 181, 193, 224, 242, 250, 283, 285
Albl, M. C., 277, 278, 280, 281
Allison, D. C., 41
Alonso-Schökel, L., 41, 240
Alter, R., 82, 88
Amphoux, C-B., 92, 110
Avalos, H., 281

Baasland, E., 74, 75, 80
Backmann, E. T., 9
Bacon, B. W., 162
Baird, W., 162
Baker, W. R., 222, 264
Balz, H. R., 40
Barclay, W., 39
Barkman, P. F., 75
Bauckham R. J., 11, 28, 41, 75, 79, 80
Beardslee, W. A., 80
Berger, K., 14, 71
Berger, P. L., 13
Bertram, G., 216
Betz, H. D., 203
Bietenhard, H., 268, 281
Black, M., 110
Blackman, E. C., 39
Blevins, W. L., 240
Bonnard, P., 289
Bornkamm, G., 266, 281
Boyle, M. O'R., 138
Bradley, D. G., 203, 216
Bratcher, R. G., 190
Braumann, G., 71

Brooks, P. J., 54, 82
Brooks, S. H., 55, 82
Brown, R. E., 24, 41, 279
Bruce, F. F., 41
Buchanan, G. W., 41, 73
Bultmann, R., 125, 138, 153, 171, 190, 191
Burchard, C., 41

Calvin, J., 39
Campbell, R. A., 266, 281
Cantinat, J., 39, 62, 91, 256, 286
Caplan, H., 126
Cargal, T. B., 41, 80
Casciaro, J. M., 39, 104
Chaine, J., 39, 117
Charles, R. H., 46
Charlesworth, J. H., 46
Charue, A. M., 41
Chester, A., 41
Chilton, B. D., 11, 41, 75
Chow, J. K., 148
Collins, J. J., 254, 257
Cooper, R. M., 71
Coppens, J., 282
Cosgrove, C. H., 171
Countryman, L. W., 139
Cranfield, C.E.B., 41
Crouzel, H., 41

Dautzenberg, G., 264
Davids, P. H., xi, 15, 35, 39, 41, 58, 61,
    62, 63, 82, 83, 91, 92, 95, 104, 110,
    117, 119, 123, 125, 135, 176, 191, 192,
    195, 199, 219, 228, 232, 233, 242, 243,
    247, 250, 264, 267, 275, 278, 280, 287
Davies, W. D., 41, 59, 82
Deissmann, A., 14

SUPPLEMENTARY BIBLIOGRAPHY

Commentaries

Brosend, William F. *James and Jude*. Cambridge, UK; New York: Cambridge University Press, 2004.

Burchard, Christoph. *Der Jakobusbrief*. Tübingen: Mohr Siebeck, 2000.

Fabris, Rinaldo. *Lettera di Giacomo: Introduzione, Versione, Commento*. Bologna: EDB, 2004.

Isaacs, Marie E. *Reading Hebrews and James: A Literary and Theological Commentary*. Macon, Ga.: Smyth & Helwys, 2002.

Maier, Gerhard. *Der Brief des Jakobus*. Wuppertal: Brockhaus; Giessen: Brunnen, 2004.

McKnight, Edgar V., and Christopher Church. *Hebrews–James*. Macon, Ga.: Smyth & Helwys, 2004.

Popkes, Wiard. *Der Brief des Jakobus*. Leipzig: Evangelische Verlagsanstalt, 2001.

Witherington, Ben, III. *Letters and Homilies for Jewish Christians: A Socio-Rhetorical Commentary on Hebrews, James and Jude*. Downers Grove, Ill.: InterVarsity Press Academic, 2007.

Studies

Allison, Dale C. "The Fiction of James and Its Sitz im Leben," *Revue biblique* 108 (2001) 529–70.

Avemarie, F. "Die Werke des Gesetzes im Spiegel des Jakobusbriefs: A Very Old Perspective on Paul," *Zeitschrift für Theologie und Kirche* 98 (2001) 282–309.

Baker, William R. "Christology in the Epistle of James," *Evangelical Quarterly* 74 (2002) 47–57.

Baker, William R., and Thomas D. Ellsworth. *Preaching James*. Preaching Classic Texts. St. Louis, Mo.: Chalice Press, 2004.

Batten, Alicia. "God in the Letter of James: Patron or Benefactor?" *New Testament Studies* 50 (2004) 257–72.

Bauckham, Richard J. "James and Jesus," in Bruce Chilton and Jacob Neusner, eds., *The Brother of Jesus: James the Just and His Mission*. Louisville: Westminster John Knox, 2001, 100–37.

Cheung, Luke L. *The Genre, Composition and Hermeneutics of James*. Paternoster Biblical and Theological Monographs. Carlisle: Paternoster Press, 2003.

Chilton, Bruce, and Jacob Neusner, eds. *The Brother of Jesus: James the Just and His Mission*. Louisville: Westminster John Knox, 2001.

Clabeaux, J. "Faith and Works in James and Paul," *The Bible Today* 44 (2006) 279–85.

Davids, Peter H. "James's Message: The Literary Record," in Bruce Chilton and Jacob Neusner, eds., *The Brother of Jesus: James the Just and His Mission*. Louisville: Westminster John Knox, 2001, 66–87.

Draper, Jonathan. "Apostles, Teachers, and Evangelists: Stability and Movement of Functionaries in Matthew, James, and the Didache," in Huub van de Sandt and Jürgen K. Zangenberg, eds., *Matthew, James, and Didache: Three Related Documents in Their Jewish and Christian Settings*. SBL Symposium Series 45. Atlanta: Society of Biblical Literature, 2008, 139–76.

Evans, Craig A. "Comparing Judaisms: Qumranic, Rabbinic, and Jacobean Judaisms Compared," in Bruce Chilton and Jacob Neusner, eds., *The Brother of Jesus: James the Just and His Mission*. Louisville: Westminster John Knox, 2001, 161–83.

Hartin, Patrick J. " 'Who Is Wise and Understanding among You?' (James 3:13): An Analysis of Wisdom, Eschatology, and Apocalypticism in the Letter of James," in Benjamin G. Wright III and Lawrence M. Wills, eds., *Conflicted Boundaries in Wisdom and Apocalypticism*. SBL Symposium Series 35. Atlanta: Society of Biblical Literature, 2005, 149–68.

———. "The Letter of James: Its Vision, Ethics and Ethos," in Jan G. van der Watt and François S. Malan, eds., *Identity, Ethics, and Ethos in the New Testament*. Beihefte zur Zeitschrift für die neutestamentliche Wissenschaft und die Kunde der älteren Kirche 141. Berlin: Walter de Gruyter, 2006, 445–71.

———. "The Religious Content of the Letter of James," in Matt Jackson-McCabe, ed., *Jewish Christianity Reconsidered: Rethinking Ancient Groups and Texts*. Minneapolis: Fortress, 2007, 203–31.

———. "Ethics in the Letter of James, the Gospel of Matthew, and the Didache: Their Place in Early Christian Literature," in Huub van de Sandt and Jürgen K. Zangenberg, eds., *Matthew, James, and Didache: Three Related Documents in Their Jewish and Christian Settings*. SBL Symposium Series 45. Atlanta: Society of Biblical Literature, 2008, 289–314.

Jackson-McCabe, Matt. "The Messiah Jesus in the Mythic World of James," *Journal of Biblical Literature* 122 (2003) 701–30.

Jenkins, C. Ryan. "Faith and Works in Paul and James," *Bibliotheca sacra* 159 (2002) 62–78.

Johnson, Luke Timothy. "Reading Wisdom Wisely," *Louvain Studies* 28 (2003) 99–112.

———. *Brother of Jesus, Friend of God: Studies in the Letter of James*. Grand Rapids: Eerdmans, 2004.

Kloppenborg, John S. "The Reception of the Jesus Tradition in James," in J. Schlosser, ed., *The Catholic Epistles and the Tradition*. Bibliotheca ephemeridum theologicarum lovaniensium 176. Leuven: Peeters, 2004, 93–141.

———. "*Didache* 1.1–6.1, James, Matthew, and the Torah" in Andrew Gregory and Christopher Tuckett, eds., *Trajectories through the New Testament and the Apostolic Fathers*. Oxford: Oxford University Press, 2005, 193–221.

———. "Emulation of the Jesus Tradition in James," in Robert L. Webb and John S. Kloppenborg, eds., *Reading James with New Eyes*. Library of New Testament Studies 342. London: T & T Clark, 2007, 121–50.

———. "Q, *Thomas*, and James," in idem, *Q, the Earliest Gospel. An Introduction to the Original Stories and Sayings of Jesus*. Louisville: Westminster John Knox, 2008a, 98–121.

———. "Poverty and Piety in Matthew, James, and the Didache," in Huub van de Sandt and Jürgen K. Zangenberg, eds., *Matthew, James, and Didache: Three Related Documents in Their Jewish and Christian Settings*. SBL Symposium Series 45. Atlanta: Society of Biblical Literature, 2008b, 201–32.

Konradt, Matthias. *Christliche Existenz nach dem Jakobusbrief. Eine Studie zu seiner soteriologischen und ethischen Konzeption*. Studien zur Umwelt des Neuen Testaments 22. Gottingen: Vandenhoeck & Ruprecht, 1998.

———. "Der Jakobusbrief als Brief des Jakobus: Erwägungen zum historischen Kontext des Jakobusbriefes im Licht der traditionsgeschichtlichen Beziehungen zum 1. Petrusbrief and zum Hintergrund der Autorfiktion," in Petra von Gemünden, Matthias Konradt and Gerd Thiessen, eds., *Der Jakobusbrief: Beiträge zur Rehabilitierung der "strohernen Epistel."* Beiträge zum Verstehen der Bibel 3. Münster: Lit, 2003, 16–53.

———. "Der Jakobusbrief im frühchristlichen Kontext: Überlegegungen zum traditionsgeschichtlichen Verhältnis des Jakobusbriefes zur Jesusüberlieferung, zur paulinischen Tradition und zum 1. Petrusbrief," in J. Schlosser, ed., *The Catholic Epistles and the Tradition*. Bibliotheca ephemeridum theologicarum lovaniensium 176. Leuven: Peeters, 2004, 171–212.

———. "The Love Command in Matthew, James, and the Didache," in Huub van de Sandt and Jürgen K. Zangenberg, eds., *Matthew, James, and Didache: Three Related Documents in Their Jewish and Christian Settings*. SBL Symposium Series 45. Atlanta: Society of Biblical Literature, 2008, 271–88.

Kot, Tomasz. *Le Fede, Via della Vita: Composizione e Interpretazione della Lettera di Giacomo*. Bologna: Dehoniane, 2002.

Levine, Amy-Jill, and Maria Mayo Robbins, eds. *A Feminist Companion to the Catholic Epistles and Hebrews*. London: T & T Clark, 2004.

Neusner, Jacob. "Sin, Repentance, Atonement and Resurrection: The Perspective of Rabbinic Theology on the Views of James 1–2 and Paul in Romans 3–4," *Annali di Storia dell' Esegesi* 18 (2001) 409–31.

Ng, Esther Yue L. "Father-God Language and Old Testament Allusions in James," *Tyndale Bulletin* 54 (2003) 41–54.

Niebuhr, Karl-Wilhelm. "A New Perspective on James? Neuere Forschungen zum Jakobusbrief," *Theologische Literaturzeitung* 129 (2004) 1019–44.

Overman, J. Andrew. "Problems with Pluralism in the Second Temple Judaism: Matthew, James, and the Didache in Their Jewish-Roman Milieu," in Huub van de Sandt and Jürgen K. Zangenberg, eds., *Matthew, James, and Didache: Three Related Documents in Their Jewish and Christian Settings*. SBL Symposium Series 45. Atlanta: Society of Biblical Literature, 2008, 259–70.

Popkes, Wiard. "James and Scripture: An Exercise in Intertextuality," *New Testament Studies* 45 (1999) 213–29.

———. "Tradition und Traditionsbrüche im Jakobusbrief," in J. Schlosser, ed., *The Catholic Epistles and the Tradition*. Bibliotheca ephemeridum theologicarum lovaniensium 176. Leuven: Peeters, 2004, 143–70.

———. "Two Interpretations of 'Justification' in the New Testament: Reflections on Galatians 2:15-21 and James 2:21-25," *Studia theologica* 59 (2005) 129–46.

Porter, Virgil V. "The Sermon on the Mount in the Book of James: Part 1," *Bibliotheca sacra* 162 (2005) 344–60.

Repschinski, Boris. "Purity in Matthew, James, and the Didache," in Huub van de Sandt and Jürgen K. Zangenberg, eds., *Matthew, James, and Didache: Three Related Documents in Their Jewish and Christian Settings*. SBL Symposium Series 45. Atlanta: Society of Biblical Literature, 2008, 379–95.

Sandt, Huub van de. "James 4,1-4 in Light of the Jewish Two Ways Tradition 3,1-6," *Biblica* 88 (2007) 38–63.

———. "Law and Ethics in Matthew's Antitheses and James's Letter: A Reorientation of Halakah in Line with the Jewish Two Ways 3:1-6," in idem and Jürgen K. Zangenberg, eds., *Matthew, James, and Didache: Three Related Documents in Their Jewish and Christian Settings*. SBL Symposium Series 45. Atlanta: Society of Biblical Literature, 2008, 315–38.

Sandt, Huub van de, and Jürgen K. Zangenberg, eds. *Matthew, James, and Didache: Three Related Documents in Their Jewish and Christian Settings*. SBL Symposium Series 45. Atlanta: Society of Biblical Literature, 2008.

Schlosser, J., ed. *The Catholic Epistles and the Tradition*. Bibliotheca ephemeridum theologicarum lovaniensium 176. Leuven: Leuven University Press, 2004.

Schröter, Jens. "Jesus Tradition in Matthew, James, and the Didache: Searching for Characteristic Emphases," in Huub van de Sandt and Jürgen K. Zangenberg, eds., *Matthew, James, and Didache: Three Related Documents in Their Jewish and Christian Settings*. SBL Symposium Series 45. Atlanta: Society of Biblical Literature, 2008, 233–55.

Taylor, Mark E. "Recent Scholarship on the Structure of James," *Currents in Biblical Research* 3 (2004) 86–115.

———. *A Text-Linguistic Investigation into the Discourse Structure of James*. London: T & T Clark, 2006a.

Taylor, Mark E., and George H. Guthrie. "The Structure of James," *Catholic Biblical Quarterly* 68 (2006b) 681–705.

Tomson, Peter. "Transformations of Post-70 Judaism: Scholarly Reconstructions and Their Implications for our Perception of Matthew, Didache, and James," in Huub van de Sandt and Jürgen K. Zangenberg, eds., *Matthew, James, and Didache: Three Related Documents in Their Jewish and Christian Settings*. SBL Symposium Series 45. Atlanta: Society of Biblical Literature, 2008, 91–121.

Vahrenhorst, Martin. "The Presence and Absence of a Prohibition of Oath in James, Matthew, and the Didache and its Significance for Contextualization," in Huub van de Sandt and Jürgen K. Zangenberg, eds., *Matthew, James, and Didache: Three Related Documents in Their Jewish and Christian Settings*. SBL Symposium Series 45. Atlanta: Society of Biblical Literature, 2008, 361–77.

Verheyden, Joseph. "Jewish Christianity, A State of Affairs: Affinities and Differences with Respect to Matthew, James, and the Didache," in Huub van de Sandt and Jürgen K. Zangenberg, eds., *Matthew, James, and Didache: Three Related Documents in Their Jewish and Christian Settings*. SBL Symposium Series 45. Atlanta: Society of Biblical Literature, 2008, 123–35.

Viviano, Benedict T. "La Loi Parfaite de Liberté. Jacques 1,25 et la Loi," in J. Schlosser, ed., *The Catholic Epistles and the Tradition*. Bibliotheca ephemeridum theologicarum lovaniensium 176. Leuven: Peeters, 2004, 213–26.

Webb, Robert L., and John S. Kloppenborg. *Reading James with New Eyes*. Library of New Testament Studies 342. London and New York: T & T Clark, 2007.

Weren, Wim J. C. "The Ideal Community according to Matthew, James, and the Didache," in Huub van de Sandt and Jürgen K. Zangenberg, eds., *Matthew, James, and Didache: Three Related Documents in Their Jewish and Christian Settings*. SBL Symposium Series 45. Atlanta: Society of Biblical Literature, 2008, 177–200.

Whitters, Mark F. "The Letter of James and the Season of Advent: Common Themes," *Word & World* 26 (2006) 429–35.

Wilson, Walter T. "Sin as Sex and Sex with Sin: The Anthropology of James 1.12-15," *Harvard Theological Review* 95 (2002) 147–68.

Wischmeyer, Oda. "Beobachtungen zu Kommunikation und Gliederung des Jakobusbriefes," in Dieter Sänger and Matthias Konradt, eds., *Das Gesetz im frühen Judentum und im Neuen Testament*. Novum Testamentum et Orbis Antiquus 57. Göttingen: Vandenhoeck & Ruprecht, 2006, 319–27.

―――. "Reconstructing the Social and Religious Milieu of James: Methods, Sources, and Possible Results," in Huub van de Sandt and Jürgen K. Zangenberg, eds., *Matthew, James, and Didache: Three Related Documents in Their Jewish and Christian Settings*. SBL Symposium Series 45. Atlanta: Society of Biblical Literature, 2008, 33–41.

Wright, Benjamin G., III, and Lawrence M. Wills, eds. *Conflicted Boundaries in Wisdom and Apocalypticism*. SBL Symposium Series 35. Atlanta: Society of Biblical Literature, 2005.

Zangenberg, Jürgen. "Matthew and James," in David C. Sim and Boris Repschinski, eds., *Matthew and His Christian Contemporaries*. London: Continuum, 2008, 104–22.

Zetterholm, Magnus. "The Didache, Matthew, James – and Paul: Reconstructing Historical Developments in Antioch," in Huub van de Sandt and Jürgen K. Zangenberg, eds., *Matthew, James, and Didache: Three Related Documents in Their Jewish and Christian Settings*. SBL Symposium Series 45. Atlanta: Society of Biblical Literature, 2008, 73–90.